The Breaking of the American Social Compact

Frances Fox Piven and Richard A. Cloward

The New Press

New York

Library of Congress Catalog Card Number 97-68412
ISBN 1-56584-476-9

Published in the United States by The New Press, New York
Distributed by W. W. Norton & Company, Inc., New York

The New Press was established in 1990 as a not-for-profit alternative to the large,
commercial publishing houses currently dominating the book publishing industry.

The New Press operates in the public interest rather than for private gain, and is
committed to publishing, in innovative ways, works of educational, cultural, and
community value that might not normally be commercially viable.

The New Press's editorial offices are located at the City University of New York.

Printed in the United States of America

9 8 7 6 5 4 3 2 1

The Breaking of the American Social Compact

Also by the authors

Regulating the Poor
Poor People's Movements
The New Class War
Why Americans Don't Vote

Contents

Acknowledgments

The editors are grateful to reprint the following copyrighted material. Articles not cited here were written for this collection.

"The Decline of Labor Parties" originally appeared in *Labor Parties and Postindustrial Societies,* edited by Frances Fox Piven (New York: Oxford University Press, 1992). Reprinted with permission of Oxford University Press.

"Globalizing Capitalism and the Rise of Identity Politics" originally appeared in *The Socialist Register*, 1995. Reprinted with permission of *The Socialist Register*.

Portions of "Welfare and the Transformation of Electoral Politics" were first published in *The New Left Review*, No. 213, September/October 1995; in *The Progressive*, February 1995; and in *Dissent*, fall 1996. A longer version was published in *Clinton and the Conservative Agenda,* edited by Clarence Y.H. Lo and Michael Schwartz (New York: Blackwell, 1997).

"The Case Against Urban Desegregation" originally appeared in *Social Work*, 1967.

"The Urban Fiscal Crisis: Who Got What, and Why?" originally appeared in *1984 Revisited: Prospects for American Politics*, edited by Robert Paul Wolff (New York: Alfred A. Knopf, 1973).

"The Historical Sources of the Contemporary Relief Debate" originally appeared in *The Mean Season*, edited by Fred L. Block, Barbara Ehrenreich, Richard A. Cloward, and Frances Fox Piven (New York: Pantheon, 1987).

"Women and the State" originally appeared in *Gender and the Life Course*, edited by Alice Rossi (Aldine, 1985).

"Low-Income People and the Political Process" was originally prepared in 1963 for a training program sponsored by the community organization staff of Mobilization for Youth. It was first published in *The Politics of Turmoil: Essays on Poverty, Race, and the Urban Crisis* (New York: Pantheon, 1974).

An earlier version of "Movements and Dissensus Politics" originally appeared in *the New Republic*, April 20, 1968, under the title "Dissensus Politics: A Strategy for Winning Economics Rights." It was reprinted *in The Politics of Turmoil: Essays on Poverty, Race, and the Urban Crisis* (New York: Pantheon, 1974).

"Organizing the Poor: An Argument with Frances Fox Piven and Richard A. Cloward's *Poor People's Movements*," by William A. Gamson and Emilie Schmeidler" originally appeared in *Theory and Society*, 1984.

"Disruption and Organization: A Reply to Gamson and Schmeidler" originally appeared in *Theory and Society*, 1984.

"Normalizing Collective Protest" originally appeared in *Frontiers of Social Movement Theory,* edited by Alden Morris and Carol Mueller (New Haven, Conn.: Yale University Press, 1984). Reprinted here with permission of Yale University Press.

"Federal Policy and Urban Fiscal Strain" originally appeared in the *Yale Law and Policy Review,* 1984.

"Structural Constraints and Political Development: The Case of the American Democratic Party" originally appeared in *Labor Parties and Postindustrial Societies*, edited by Frances Fox Piven (New York: Oxford University Press, 1992). Reprinted with permission of Oxford University Press.

The Breaking of the American Social Compact

Introduction

Breaking the Social Compact:
The Globalization Hoax

In the 1960s, the United States was at the peak of industrial development, signified by flourishing mass production industries in steel, autos, rubber, and electrical products, by high rates of growth in productivity and profits, and by unrivaled dominance of the world economy. As elsewhere, a vigorous industrial economy yielded a measure of power to the industrial union movement. The economic leverage of the strike, together with mass unionism which the strike power made possible, resulted in a tacit compact between labor and capital.

The post–World War II social compact brought unprecedented prosperity to many workers. Big industry negotiated with big labor, with the result that unionized workers won regular improvements in their wage and benefit packages, making them partners not only as production workers but as consumers of the new homes, refrigerators, cars and television sets spilling off the assembly lines. And the dominant Democratic party coalition included the main parties to the social compact. So did our modest New Deal welfare state programs, mainly in the form of old age pensions and unemployment insurance which, together with the workplace health and pension benefits that strong unions were able to win from their employers, guaranteed many workers a modicum of economic security. Meanwhile, Keynesian doctrines guided the government policies of macroeconomic adjustment and social welfare spending that sustained these arrangements, and also provided an intellectual framework that gave Americans confidence the golden age would last forever.

Many people were excluded from the compact, including workers in sectors of the economy where unionism had made little headway, and in regions such as the right-to-work south or the backwaters of Appalachia. The growing number, of migrants from Puerto Rico and Mexico were also excluded, as were the disabled and the elderly who were of little use in the labor market and who were dealt with harshly by the American welfare state. Most important for the politics of the period, the overwhelming majority of African Americans who in the 1940s were only beginning the great trek from indentured agricultural labor in the south to the urban centers, were excluded. The eruption of black protests in the 1960s set in motion an expansion of the social compact that overcame some of those exclusions, with the passage of new voting rights legislation and the inauguration of Great Society measures which created new social programs and liberalized existing ones. By the end of the 1960s, the social compact had broadened.

Now in the late 1990s, the compact is under attack: the unions are on the ropes, their membership decimated; welfare state programs are being rolled back; and income and wealth inequalities have widened to historic extremes. There are parallels elsewhere. Unions, the bedrock of working-class power, are on the defensive in Western Europe and Japan, and have begun to lose members (Western 1995), although nowhere is there the bloodletting that is occurring in the United States. Left parties are in disarray in most Western countries. Welfare state protections are under assault in campaigns to make the labor market more 'flexible,' with the consequence that coverage is being narrowed, and expenditures are falling, particularly for the crucial programs that reach the active labor force (Hicks, Misra, and Nah Ng 1995). And economic inequalities are growing. In the United States, where the wages of the less skilled have fallen steadily for two decades, and real poverty has increased, the richest 1 percent of households owns more than 40 percent of wealth (Wolff 1995, Pascale 1995).

These dismal trends help account for another important development. In all the countries of advanced capitalism, the left is profoundly discouraged, not only about the declining economic prospects of the working class, but about the possibility of working-class power, now or in the foreseeable future. After more than a century of gradual if uneven expansion of unions, of Left parties, and of social democratic policies, after a century dominated for the Left by a heady belief in labor as the agency of progressive change, the working class seems not to have any future at all. Instead we hope that somehow workers can muster the political muscle just to resist incursions on past gains by a capitalist class on the move. Even the Left parliamentary opposition in Western social welfare states is reduced to arguing not that it holds the key to a better future, but that it can offer a more intelligent, more efficient, perhaps gentler, administration of the new and inevitable austerities.

Globalization

The usual explanation for the assault on the working class is a commonplace, quick to spring to the lips of intellectuals and workers alike. The key fact of our historical moment is said to be economic globalization, together with the domestic restructuring of the "Fordist" industrial era regime of mass production and mass consumption. These transformations are said to entail shattering consequences for the economic wellbeing of the working class, and especially for the power of the working class and, indeed, the power of democratic publics more generally.

We don't think this explanation is entirely wrong but it is deployed so sweepingly as to be misleading. The implication is that the global economy is in command; in effect, markets no longer permit politics, at least not a politics which sustains the industrial era social compact. And right or wrong, the explanation itself has become a political force, helping to create the institutional realities it purportedly merely describes. In fact, globalization is as much political strategy as economic imperative.

There are important variations in how economic globalization is characterized. When the argument emerged some two decades ago, the emphasis was on the decentralization of production from older industrial hubs to low-wage countries on the periphery of advanced capitalism. Somewhat later the emphasis shifted from actual plant relocation to the expansion of trade, and the enlarging share of national markets commanded by imports and exports, a development facilitated by new communication and transportation technologies. Either way, the consequences were to pit the organized and better-paid workers of the developed north against vulnerable workers everywhere. Enlarging circuits of migration that tapped a bottomless reservoir of workers from the South and then from Eastern Europe for labor markets in the metropole had similar consequences (Gallin 1994). And finally, in its most recent variant, economic globalism is defined as the vastly accelerated movement of financial capital, pinioning not only workers but entire economies to the wall, and rendering national governments helpless to intervene as, in the words of a *Barron's* columnist, "capital market vigilantes [roam] the globe in search of high returns at relatively low risk."

Whatever the emphasis, belief in economic globalization leads to a chilling conclusion about the prospects for worker power, and even the prospects for democratic influence. The exercise of labor power throughout the history of capitalist markets has always depended on the limited ability of capital to exit or threaten to exit from ongoing economic relationships. Labor power depends, after all, on the fundamental interdependence of capital and labor. That is what gives the strike or the slowdown its punch. But economic globalization, together with domestic restructuring and downsizing made possible by technological change, seem to be opening unlimited options for capital exit, whether through the relocation of production, or accelerated trade, or through worker replacement, or through capital mobility. And it is simply in the nature of the human condition that workers, tied as they are to place and kin, constrained by their human fear of change, are unlikely to match these options, ever. More than anything else, it is this understanding that something entirely new has developed in the economic relations between capital and labor that underlies the widespread sense of hopelessness about worker power and democratic possibility.

If this understanding of globalization strips workers of power in their relations with capital, so does it strip voters of influence in their relationship with national governments. The reasoning is similar. Democratic governments depend on capital for the investment which leads to prosperity and contented voters, as well as for the tax revenues that fund government activities. So, of course, has capital also depended on the nation state for a range of policies which promote economic growth. But with globalization, capital can threaten to exit this relationship, while the nation state is by definition tied to the territory over which it is sovereign. Consequently the balance of power shifts, both between the nation state and capital, and between democratic publics and the investor groups that contend for influence over the nation state.

However, we think this analysis is entirely too simple. It treats globalization as a set of economic changes which have necessary and inevitable consequences for politics and the terms of the social compact. This economic determinism ignores the dimensions of globalization which are in fact political and strategic. Expanded global markets for goods, labor, and capital may make exit or the threat of exit *possible*, at least in some industries and in some capitalist regimes. Even this is only a possibility, its realization usually contingent on government policies which facilitate exit. Less obvious but very important, exit threats are political strategies constructed by power-seeking agents who draw variously on the actual reality of exit, on exit as an ideological ruse, and who also may invoke state authority to expedite the threat of exit or to suppress countervailing threats.

A mere glance at earlier episodes of power struggles between capital and labor reveals ample evidence of political stratagems undertaken by capital precisely to exercise power by changing exit options. Capital has often mobilized politically to change government laws and policies in order to enlarge employer exit options or narrow worker exit options. As early as the fourteenth century, at a time when agricultural workers were only beginning to take to the road in search of new opportunities and better earnings made possible by labor scarcity, English landlords tried to limit their exit options with the Law of Vagrancy (Chambliss). The strategy was elaborated over the succeeding centuries with laws of settlement, maximum wage laws, the curtailment of outdoor relief, and, in the United States, "yellow-dog" employment contracts. Or, at the beginning of the nineteenth century, as the factory system was replacing the putting-out system in England, manufacturers shunned the displaced male handloom weavers in favor of more pliant children and women who were often supplied by the parish poorhouses. Or the free immigration policies promoted by American industrialists produced a labor reservoir that enabled employers to exit or threaten exit from ongoing relations with workers, especially during the industrial takeoff at the turn of the century. And then there were government troops which regularly helped employers to break strikes. These political strategies to block worker exit enlarge employer exit or were often deployed on a vast scale relative to the scale of the markets in which they were undertaken. And each had devastating consequences on the ability of workers to exercise power in production relations. The important point is simply that exit or the threat of exit has often been a power strategy, designed by human agents locked in struggle with other human agents, and accomplished by drawing on state authority.

The United States nicely illustrates our point. The U.S. is the undisputed world leader in dismantling the industrial-era social compact, and is regularly held up as the model by European neo-liberal reformers who want to move further and faster in the American direction. But the United States is less integrated into the global economy than most other advanced capitalist nations. Nevertheless, the rollback of social rights is greater here than elsewhere, which is altogether inconsistent with the globalization thesis.

Consider first the evidence of the shattering of the compact. American unions have been decimated in just two decades, their membership falling from about thirty-five million to fifteen million. The Democratic party is fragmented and disorganized, and has veered sharply rightward in its policies and appeals. After more than a decade in which the regulatory and social protection programs of the American welfare state were whittled back, a new round of huge rollbacks in the social programs is underway. By any measure, the United States is now the most economically stratified industrial country in the world, whether measured by income distribution or wealth. Politics, which was once shaped in part by class, is now taking form in dangerous scapegoating, drawing on race hatred, xenophobia, and the peculiar sexual obsessions that American culture provides as fuel for reaction.

Consider now that the United States is far less exposed to international economic currents than Western Europe, and than most less-developed nations. The ratio of imports and exports to GDP stands at 21 percent, unchanged since 1980. Foreign investment in U.S. stocks and bonds has risen, but in 1993 it still accounted for only 6 percent of US stocks, and 14 percent of corporate bonds. And fully 95 percent of investment by Americans is in domestic stocks or bonds (Samuelson 1995; Henwood 1996).

Or, we can make the point in a more commonsensical way. If indeed capital, goods, and labor are circulating the globe with increasing velocity, how can German workers continue to earn—if social benefits are included—twice what workers earn in the United States, or eleven times what workers earn in Thailand? And yet the German economy has absorbed the huge costs associated with unification. How, if international markets are in command, can there even be much of a German economy. Business Week's Bonn bureau chief answers the question by asserting that Germany is "sleepwalking." But that is merely to elevate conviction about the imperatives of global competition over the evidence. And, we might ask more generally, if international markets are in command, why does there continue to be such large variation among national economies, both in the rewards to labor and in profit margins?

Perhaps the advance of global integration of the American economy is only a matter of time. Nevertheless, and even then, a good deal of light can be cast on the globalization phenomenon if we focus on politics. Post-industrial economic changes, including internationalism, are facilitating much more aggressive capitalist political efforts to dismantle the industrial era social compact. The campaign first unfolded in the workplace, where employers mobilized to get rid of unions and to roll back wages and benefits, and worker rights, using the threat of plant closings to intimidate workers. And now business is in full campaign mode in the public sphere, with an agenda of business tax cuts, deregulation, and cuts in social provision.

Put another way, business is using its formidable propaganda resources to persuade workers and democratic publics about the inevitable primacy of markets over politics, and of capital over labor, in a global world. The argument succeeds, at least for the time, because it resonates with primal American laissez-faire convictions, as well as with the palpable evidence of globalization—of Japanese VCRs and Taiwanese slippers—in consumer markets.

Moreover, the ideology of globalization is being deployed politically to mold institutions which confirm the ideology by encouraging capital mobility and trade penetration. In part this is evident in the creation of a host of new institutional arrangements, from supranational organizations like the International Monetary Fund (IMF) to favorable tax policies that reward offshore investment and trade pacts that smooth the way for increased international exchange (Korpi and Palme). In part it is evident in systematic efforts in the United States to cripple the capacity of the federal government by reducing its regulatory authority and its revenues and devolving authority to the states.

The attack on the federal government is especially significant because most of the actual capital mobility in the United States is not in fact international, but within our borders, and therefore susceptible to regulation by a strong national government. On the one hand, this capital mobility adds credibility to arguments about globalization. People see the plants closing in their community; where they reopen is far less vivid. But important interregional shifts in industrial production actually began a century ago, with the movement of the textile industry from New England to the low-wage South. And up to now, most plants have relocated from the old industrial centers of the northeast and midwest to the sunbelt and the new cities. Productive capital has largely remained within national borders. The importance of this point cannot be overstated. It means that, in principle, the national government retains the capacity to regulate the economy.

Why has the business political mobilization against the social compact been so much more successful here than in Europe? Why have threats of capital exit been more potent, even though there is in fact less of it? The answer has as much to do with the weakness of the resistance as the strength of the assailants. Elsewhere—in Italy, France, Germany, and Canada, for example—far more modest efforts to chip away at the welfare state provoked massive strikes and demonstrations by workers and their unions, and the demonstrations met with strong public approval.

This scenario is so far virtually unimaginable in the United States, where politicians of both parties actually try to win elections by calling for social program cutbacks, even as they ignore the erosion of wages, benefits, and rights in the workplace.

The weak defense of the industrial era social compact reflects the fragmentation and disorientation of working-class politics at the end of the 20th century. In Western Europe, the compact was sustained and expanded in the post World War II period by labor or socialist parties and their union allies. In the United States, the compact originated and expanded largely in response to the mass protests launched by the industrial workers' movement of the 1930s and the black movement of the 1960s. The political party that depended on the organized working class was the Democratic party. But from its renaissance during the New Deal as something like a labor party, the party was hopelessly compromised as a labor party by the influence of its near-feudal southern wing. The rise of the Democrats in the 1930s was the result of large-scale voter shifts in the metropole, particularly among the urban working class. But the ascendance of the party was also the ascendance of the southern section, which came to draw a line in the sand against national programs that would dismantle the South's caste-based labor system. In effect, the possibility of the Democratic party as a labor party was forfeited to its southern wing.

The long term implications for party growth were devastating. The South consistently blocked legislation to shore up unions, and, indeed, secured a "right to work" exemption from unionism for the southern states which meant that unions would be weakest in the Sunbelt where industrial growth rates were highest. And southern legislators insisted on local control of welfare state programs that threatened to undermine the South's low wage labor system, and later simply blocked expansion of welfare state programs altogether. Workers got less, and this took its toll: eroding working-class party loyalties were evident as early as the 1950s. Meanwhile, the unions on which the party relied for infrastructure in the industrial north ceased to grow.

Compromises over welfare state programs deserve special note in any explanation of weak popular resistance to attacks on the social compact in the United States. Walter Korpi and his associates have long argued that the institutional structures of the welfare state help to shape the way people define their interests. The American welfare state is significant in this regard not only, as commentators often stress, because its emphasis on targeted or means-tested programs separates the poor from the middle-class, but even more importantly because the American programs were stingy or non-existent. Blocked from achieving health care or adequate old age security by politics, organized workers turned to employers for these protections, with the result that the stakes of unionized workers in the public programs atrophied. Under these conditions, the targeted nature of the public programs, and their growing identification with the minority poor, did indeed sap public support for these parts of the social compact.

The race conflicts of the 1960s that are often blamed for the troubles of the Democrats emerged in this context. As newly urbanized blacks rose up and made demands for racial equity, an already fragile party coalition was sundered: the white South turned Republican, first in presidential elections and then in congressional elections, and many white working-class voters in the North responded to third party or Republican racial demagoguery by deserting the Democrats.

The Democrats were compromised as the party of the working class from the start. These new sources of disarray at the base have combined with rising business influence to make its leaders into weaklings. They neither explain the globalization hoax, nor encourage resistance to it.

The essays that follow explore these issues. We begin with essays that deal with "The Breaking of the Social Compact" in the postindustrial era which witnessed the decline of labor parties, the increasing salience of identity politics, and the attacks on social welfare programs. In the United States, especially, these developments were coupled with the rise of a kind of moral fundamentalism which flamboyantly singled out minorities and women as the source of America's problems.

We then turn in the section on "Race Politics" to the rise of the black movement and its role in our current debacle, with essays that deal with race and the troubles of the Democratic party, the longstanding and troubling issue of integration, and the bearing of race conflict on the fiscal troubles of the older industrial cities.

The essays in "The Assault on Contemporary Poor Relief" try to explain the centrality of the program called "welfare" in contemporary political campaigns against the social compact. We first explore what we think are illuminating parallels between the current conjuncture and earlier attacks on income-maintenance programs; then we turn to an exploration of the prominence of women in contemporary political conflicts over social welfare programs; and finally we examine the troubling role of the social scientists who are the policy experts in the debacle called welfare reform.

The next section—"Disruptive Movements and Their Electoral Impact"—looks backward in time to examine the dynamics of the protest movements that helped shape the industrial era social compact. We begin with an essay explaining why the poor are unlikely to have much influence if they confine themselves to regular politics, and then go on to examine the dynamics of the disruptive protest movements that emerged in the 1930s and 1960s and their bearing on electoral politics. Finally we take up a number of troubling issues in the way that the literature on social movements deals with disruptive protest.

The final section on "Power and Political Institutions" considers the changes or "reforms" of governmental structures during the decades in which the social compact was expanded and then rolled back. We examine the successive innovations in intergovernmental relations known as "The Great Society" and "The New Federalism," the first initiated by Democratic leaders, the second by their Republican successors, as strategies which reflected the political troubles and opportunities confronted by regime leaders. And finally, we try to show how all of these influences combined to bring the Democratic party to its current state of disorganization and disrepute.

A closing word. The political moment is grim. The measures won by working-class and poor people over the course of the last century, measures which humanized western capitalism, are at risk. But they are not at risk because the structural imperatives of this new stage of capitalist development has made the social rights won in the past economically dysfunctional. Rather, they have been put at risk by the political mobilization of some human actors against other human actors. Capitalism and capitalists are on the move, inspired by the missionary sense bred by their own ideology. Markets, international markets, will shape our destiny, and capitalists are the class of progress.

But capitalism has been on the move before, and with very similar ideas. It has also been halted before, and forced to concede the public spaces and social protections that make human life tolerable.

1997

References

CHAMBLISS, WILLIAM J. "On the Law of Vagrancy." *Social Problems*, vol. 12, no. 1, 1964.

GALLIN, DAN. "Inside the New World Order: Drawing the Battle Lines." *New Politics*, vol. 5, no. 1, 1994.

HICKS, ALEXANDER, JOYA MISRA AND TANG NAH NG. "The Programmatic Emergence of the Social Security State." *American Sociological Review*, vol. 60, no. 3, June 1995.

KORPI, WALTER AND JOAKIM PALME. oContested Citizenship: Introduction." Draft chapter for "Contested Citizenship: A Century of Social Policy," presented at Conference on The Welfare State at the Crossroads, Sigtuna, Sweden, January 9–12, 1997.

PASCALE, CELINE-MARIE. "Normalizing Poverty." *Z Magazine*, June 1995.

SAMUELSON, ROBERT J. "Global Mythmaking." *Newsweek*, May 29, 1995.

WESTERN, BRUCE. "Union Decline in Eighteen Advanced Capitalist Countries." *American Sociological Review*, vol. 60, no. 2, April 1995.

WOLFF, EDWARD N. "How the Pie Is Sliced: America's Growing Concentration of Wealth." *American Prospect*, summer 1995.

Part I

Breaking the Social Compact

I

The Decline of Labor Parties

The sweeping changes in industrial societies signaled by events of the last decade are making familiar political guideposts unclear. Not least, the prospects of the labor-based political parties that emerged in most industrial countries a century ago, and then grew to become major contenders for governmental power, have faded.

Of course, there is no single storyline. Each party confronts different national economic and political contexts, and each party is weighted with different internal organizational and ideological legacies. As a result, labor parties have fared quite differently; the British Labour Party, for example, suffered a steep and precipitous loss of support after 1979, while the Swedish Social Democrats more or less held their own, and returned to power in 1982, as the French Socialists did in 1988. Nevertheless, the emerging postindustrial economic order has generated problems for Left parties everywhere.

Industrialization and Labor-Based Parties

The life-course of Western labor parties began more or less a century ago, in the aftermath of the emergence of manufacturing economies in the West. As the story is usually told, the growth of factory production and of cities meant that increasing numbers of men and women were no longer dispersed and fragmented by the localisms of traditional village life, but instead came to be concentrated in factories and towns where their common circumstances bound them together in new solidarities, nourished a distinctive political consciousness embedded in what Hobsbawm calls the "common style" of proletarian life,[1] and also led to characteristic forms of workplace struggle and organization, most importantly the trade union and the strike.

The new working class also entered electoral politics. In most industrial countries, the franchise was extended to male workers at the turn of the twentieth century, often as a result of the struggles of workers themselves. The creation of a reservoir of working class votes, in turn, spurred the growth of fledgling socialist or labor parties. As Adam Przeworski and John Sprague report, in Germany the Social Democrats actually won the largest share of the vote immediately after the antisocialist laws which had disenfranchised many workers were allowed to lapse in 1890. The Austrian Social Democrats won 21 percent of the vote in the first election after the universal male franchise was granted in 1907; and the Finnish Social Democrats won 37 percent, also after the universal male franchise was established in 1907. And as manufacturing advanced, and the industrial working class grew, so did the new political parties. By 1912, the German Social Democrats won 34.8 percent of the vote, twice the share of the next largest party; the Austrian Social Democrats claimed a plurality of 40.8 percent of the vote by 1919; the total Belgian Workers' Party vote rose from 13.2 percent immediately after the introduction of the franchise in 1894 to a plurality of 39.4 percent in 1925.[2]

Of course the pace of these political developments varied among countries, partly because the pace of industrialization varied, and partly because the impact of industrialization on class politics was complexly modulated by the strategies of dominant political coalitions in each country, and also by the pre-existing traditions and organization of the popular classes.[3] Nevertheless, a common pattern can be discerned: for more than half a century—less in some countries, longer in others—the industrial working class, trade union membership, and the vote totals of labor-based political parties grew in tandem. To be sure, except in coalition or at moments of crisis, the left parties did not usually control governments. Nevertheless, they became major electoral contenders, and were in most places able to win legal and political protections for their union allies. The growth of unions, in turn, provided the parties with an infrastructure to mobilize the working class vote. Generations of working people came of age in a political world organized to express class interests and class cleavages.[4]

Industrialization generated a working-class politics in the United States as well, although the articulation of class politics in electoral arenas was blunted, a fact that has inspired a huge literature exploring the intricacies of "American exceptionalism." Most of this literature fastens on the stubbornly individualistic American political culture which inhibited the development of class identities and solidarities. In turn, individualism is often traced to a variety of distinctive features of the American experience: the absence of a feudal past, the open frontier, rapid economic mobility, regional diversity in a vast country, racial, ethnic and religious divisions, and so on. We are inclined to think that, taken as a whole, these arguments exaggerate American distinctiveness. Specific political institutions worked to prevent the emergence of a labor party, and the lack of a party vehicle in turn inhibited the subsequent articulation and development of working class politics.[5] Nevertheless, the industrial working class figured in American electoral politics, and for some years after the realignment of the 1930s the Democratic Party was its vehicle. And, at least for a time, the Democrats acted like labor parties elsewhere, supporting new policies which extended legal protections to unions and actually facilitating membership growth, with the result that at the close of the Second World War union density levels in the United States were about as high as in Western Europe. Moreover, as elsewhere, the unions in turn served as an organizing infrastructure for Democratic vote mobilization, so that in these respects, at least, the United States also witnessed the development of something like a labor party.

The rise of new political formations also spurred new theories of how the society that people knew was organized, and how it could be changed. The growth of the industrial working class and its characteristic union and party formations encouraged interpretations of political life which stressed the centrality of the new classes and conflicts created by industrial capitalism. This Marxist intellectual tradition was inaugurated even as industrialization began, in the mid-nineteenth century. In an important sense, it was the Marxist tradition that created the proletariat, and also created its antagonist, the bourgeoisie. And Marxism also posited that, as industrial capitalism advanced, the potential and transforming power of the proletariat would also grow, even as its misery increased. This was a theory about power so compelling that it created power, both by pointing to the institutional levers of worker power in industrial relations, and by ennobling the particular struggles of workers with the mission of historical agency.

By the end of the century, with the winning of the franchise and the growth of labor-based political parties, these ideas about a class power that inhered in the institutions of industrial capitalism were being reformulated—not only by Eduard Bernstein but by Engels himself—as ideas about electoral power that inhered in the institutions of the national state and representative democracy. In this context, the growing power of the proletariat rested on its numbers. As industrial capitalism advanced, not only would the power of workers as a force of production increase, but so would its numbers grow, as all of society would be absorbed into the two great classes, the bourgeoisie and the proletariat. Growing numbers, and especially numerical majorities, opened another and different route to power for the working class in the influence it could exert on the national state. True, many of the leaders of the Second International furiously disagreed with the notion of an electoral path to proletarian power. However, among the leaders of the trade union and party formations generated by industrial capitalism, the view that labor-based political parties were vehicles for the rise of the proletariat and the transformation of society clearly prevailed.

These twin power analyses, the one focusing on the power that workers could exert because they had leverage in the mass production industries, the other focusing on the power that worker citizens could exert because their votes could be organized to control the state and because the nation state itself was the very nexus of power, were at the ideological heart of labor politics, along with the conviction that the politics of workers was inevitably politics in the general interest.[6] For almost a century, these ideas lent energy and confidence to labor efforts because they showed how workers could exert power on the institutions that dominated social life, and they also lent elan to labor struggles because they asserted that these were struggles on behalf of all humankind.

The main political project of labor parties became the use of state power to develop the welfare state, by which we mean both the range of income and health programs that shield workers from biographical or market exigencies, and the macroeconomic policies intended to regulate and stabilize growth. There were, of course, other more revolutionary currents in labor politics, and there were moments when these currents seemed ascendant. But for most of their histories, labor parties have responded to the constraints and opportunities of both industrial capitalism and electoral politics by promoting programs to moderate the effects of capitalist markets rather than to transform them. We need to take some care here, since welfare state programs were often initiated and supported by diverse elite alliances. As usual, however, the issue is complicated, since labor disturbances, and the effort to curb the electoral growth of labor parties, no doubt helped spur elite initiatives. It is also true that welfare state programs were influenced by distinctive national traditions, particularly by religious traditions.[7] Different national configurations of welfare state policy show the strong markings of these diverse origins.[8] But whatever the origins, labor party strength in government appears to have ensured the enlargement of the programs, particularly in the 1960s, when the great expansion of the welfare state occurred in most Western countries.[9] And labor parties also used their governmental power to promote the range of post–Second World War economic stabilization policies which, together with income protections, came to be known as Keynesianism: As Przeworski says, Keynesianism was important. It not only provided guidelines for administering capitalist economies, but justified policies that favored the working class in terms that, like Marxism, "granted universalistic status to the interests of workers."[10]

For a long time, the political landscape created by these developments was taken for granted, as were the predictions that the industrial working class would steadily enlarge, along with its distinctive political formations and its twin sources of power in industrial capitalism and political democracy. It was in a way a momentous development. As Hobsbawm says in retrospect about the British Labour Party, "A class party of labor...became the mass party of the British working class...by giving unity to the class consciousness of this class as a whole, and offering, in addition to the defence of material or other special interests, confidence, self-respect and hope of a different and better society."[11] To be sure, after the first decades of the twentieth century, the proportional size of the working class did not actually grow very much, and in some countries it even began to decline.[12] Nevertheless, labor-based parties held their own, sustained on the one hand by the trade union and welfare state infrastructures they had helped to create, and on the other hand by the economic stability and growth yielded by Keynesian policies. Moreover, successful macroeconomic management and the ideological moderation that success encouraged, along with the expansion of welfare state employment, created new sources of support for labor parties in the middle class salariat. The vote totals of labor-based parties remained at least stable through the 1960s, lending credibility to a program of labor reformism through electoral politics.

Deindustrialization and Labor Parties

The story of the decline of labor politics is the mirror image of the story of its rise. If industrial capitalism and the democratic nation state nurtured labor politics, then the economic transformation of industrial societies, together with the declining importance of the nation state in an international economy, spelled trouble. And, indeed, both the political formations and intellectual outlooks associated with industrial era politics are in upheaval. Support for labor-based political parties and the welfare state institutions they helped sustain and expand is eroding everywhere in the West, including in the fabled social democracies of the Scandinavian countries, as an aspect of what appears to be a general process of partisan decomposition and fractionalization associated with post-industrial trends.[13] Figure 1 illustrates the trend.

Figure 1

The trend in class voting in four western democracies, 1948–83.
Alford index of class voting.

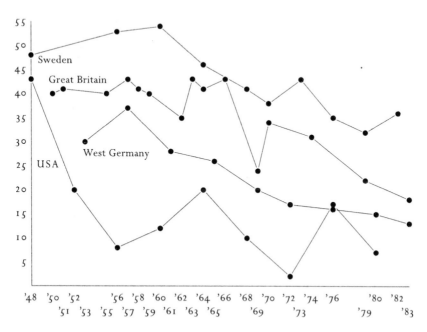

SOURCE: R. Inglehart, "The persistence of materialist and postmaterialist value orientations," *European Journal of Political Research*, 11 (1983), pp. 81–2.

The scope of this development is evidence that large-scale influences are at work. The industrial order within which these parties emerged and grew is giving way to a new international economic order, variously characterized as postfordist and postindustrial. This means that in Western Europe and North America, the old working class based in mining and heavy industry is shrinking, and its unions are contracting. True, other sorts of employment are expanding in at least some of these countries, and especially in the United States where low-wage service jobs have proliferated. Still, the mass production industries were at the very core of the class politics generated by industrialism, and their contraction inevitably has a telling effect on labor-based political parties.

The shift from large-scale industrial establishments to more decen-

tralized production locations, and from industrial to service employment, has also altered the possibilities of workplace solidarity and organization. The mass production factory brought together vast numbers of
workers under one roof in work routines that dominated their waking
lives, and joined them together in battles against a common antagonist.
By comparison, the characteristic work settings of much "postindustrial"
employment are small and dispersed, work schedules are more irregular, and work routines themselves do not build the solidarities that were
fostered by assembly-line production.[14] Moreover, the expansion of the
service sector has spurred the influx of women and racial or ethnic
minorities into the workforce. All of this means not only the reduction
of the numbers of the old industrial working class, but the erosion of old
class identities and issues, and the rise of new and fragmenting identities
and issues.

Changes in the location of production, as well as changing patterns of
settlement and consumption, are also transforming the communities
and the culture even of those who remain industrial workers.[15] The old
segregated working-class towns and enclaves are giving way to more
dispersed patterns of settlement; television and a life organized around
patterns of mass consumption replace the working class pub and insular
working class traditions; and locally based party organizations give way
to national media campaigns. And new generations come of age in a
world where class and class conflict no longer seem salient.[16] Inevitably
as a result of all these developments, the cultural glue of the working
class is dissolved and the old working class organizational bastions in the
trade unions, local parties, and government agencies are enfeebled,
even as they are also hobbled by the problems of maintaining schlerotic
organizations in a period of decline.[17]

Perhaps most important, the confidence and elan which labor politics
gained from the twin power analyses which guided and inspired it are
fading, because the analyses do not seem to fit the contemporary world.
The once-stirring idea that the working class could organize to wield
power over industrial capitalism has lost its force as industrial capitalism
has reorganized domestically and dispersed globally, disorganizing the
working class and escaping its leverage. And so has the idea that workers could transform their societies by the power they exercised as citi-

zens in the democratic nation state lost credibility, because the nation state seems only one player in a world dominated by international market organizations. After all, labor party constituencies everywhere watched as the French Socialists gained state power in alliance with the Communists in the early 1980s, rapidly began to implement a Left Keynesian "common program," only to be forced to their knees by the combined response of French and international capital. When the Socialists reemerged later in the decade, they had learned the lesson taught by international markets well.

Does Politics Matter?

Still, this market-driven account is not the whole story. We said earlier that historical explanations of the rise of labor politics which focus mainly on the determining influence exerted by economic structures miss important variations in national experience. We think it indisputable that labor parties as a group have been badly jostled by the impact of shifts in the world economy on the constituencies, infrastructures, and intellectual moorings of labor parties. Nevertheless, the differences between labor parties is large in ways that are turning out to matter both for the future of labor politics, and for the pattern of postindustrial restructuring in different countries.

One obvious difference is in the extent of labor party losses, which vary in ways not predicted by the impact of postindustrial trends, as the table shows. As Ivor Crewe demonstrates, labour party support in Britain slipped much faster than economic change or its correlates would predict.[18] In Sweden it slipped less. In turn, labor parties that have continued to wield government power have been able to buffer the impact of deindustrialization on party constituencies and party infrastructure. Sweden under the Social Democrats, for example, boasted very low unemployment levels even in the 1980s, partly because of its system for creating jobs and retraining workers, and also because it maintained and even expanded its large welfare state programs. More recently, however, the Swedish political tides have also shifted toward greater public austerity.

There is also growing evidence that labor governments are more suc-

Table 1. The Left's vote in economically developed democracies, 1944–1978 to 1979–1988

COUNTRY	TOTAL LEFT VOTE			SOCIAL DEMOCRAT/LABOR VOTE			COMMUNIST VOTE		
	1944–78 (%)	1979–88* (%)	Change (%)	1944–78 (%)	1979–88* (%)	Change (%)	1944–78 (%)	1979–88* (%)	Change (%)
(Greece)	n.a.	(51.9)ᵃ	n.a.	n.a.	(39.8)	n.a.	n.a.	(12.1)	n.a.
Sweden	51.2	49.9	−1.3	46.0	44.3	−0.7	5.2	5.6	+0.4
France	43.3	49.5	+6.2	18.3	30.6	+12.3	23.4	12.4	−11.0
(Spain)	n.a.	(48.9)	n.a.	n.a.	(40.4)	n.a.	n.a	(6.4)	n.a.
Austria	47.9	48.0	+0.1	44.9	47.2	+2.3	3.0	0.8	−2.2
Denmark	45.4	47.8	+2.4	37.1	32.4	−4.7	3.8	1.1	−2.7
Australia	46.3	47.0	+0.7	45.7	47.0	+1.3	0.6	0.1	−0.5
Norway	50.5	45.9	−0.6	44.0	40.2	−3.8	3.9	0.3	−3.6
Italy	42.7	44.6	+1.9	13.6	11.8	−1.8	25.4	30.0	+4.6
New Zealand	44.9	43.2	−1.7	44.9	43.2	−1.7	0.1	0.0	−0.1
(Portugal)	n.a.	(44.7)	n.a.	n.a.	(27.7)	n.a.	n.a.	(16.7)	n.a.
Israel	48.6	41.3	−7.3	44.6	34.7	−9.9	3.0	3.5	+0.5
Finland	46.5	40.2	−6.3	25.9	24.9	−1.0	20.6	13.9	−6.7
Germany	39.1	40.4	+1.3	37.0	39.4	+2.4	2.1	1.0	−0.9
Luxembourg	46.4	36.8ᵇ	−9.6	34.0	29.0	−5.0	11.2	7.1	−4.1

Japan	34.3	34.8	+0.5	27.7	25.5	−2.2	5.1	9.3	+4.2
Netherlands	36.1	34.4	−1.7	28.3	30.8	+2.5	4.8	1.5	−3.3
Iceland	33.3	34.0	+0.7	14.5	14.8	+0.3	17.1	16.8	−0.3
United Kingdom	44.7	31.8	−12.9	44.5	31.8	−12.7	0.2	0.0	−0.2
Belgium	35.6	29.9	−5.7	31.1	28.0	−3.1	4.5	1.4	−3.1
Switzerland	28.3	24.3[d]	−4.0	25.4	21.9	−3.5	2.9	1.3	−1.6
Canada	14.5	19.3	+4.8	14.1	19.4	+5.3	0.4	0.1	−0.3
Ireland	12.2	8.3	−3.9	12.2	8.3	−3.9	0.0	0.0	0.0
All (mean)e	39.6	37.6	−2.0	31.7	30.3	−1.4	6.9	5.3	−1.6

n.a., not applicable. "Total Left" includes extreme Left, regional socialist, left radical and "Socialist Peoples" parties and can therefore add up to more than the combined social democrat/labor and communist vote; Green parties are excluded. Right-wing or Centerist breakaways from social democratic/labor parties are excluded (e.g. British SDP; Australian Democratic Labour Party).

* Or most recent three elections, if fewer than three held since 1978. [a] Includes 1977 election.

[b] Includes 1974 election. [d] Includes 1977 election.

[e] Excludes "interrupted" democracies (Greece, Spain, Portugal). SOURCE: I. Crewe, "The decline of labour and the decline of Labour," *Essex Papers in Politics and Government*, 65 (September 1989)

cessful not only in mitigating the costs of postindustrial transformation, but in orchestrating adaptations to an international economy in ways that sustain growth levels and market shares over time.[19] All in all, the evidence suggests that the complex of policies associated with labor party governments, including government economic planning capacities, centralized unions, and strong welfare state programs, work not only to humanize economic transition, but to rationalize it. Both productivity and market shares seem to be holding up better where labor parties are strong than under the neo-laissez-faire regimes in Great Britain and the United States.[20] And, of course, successful economic management by labor governments shores up the electoral support that makes this kind of postindustrial Keynesianism possible in the first place.

The political conditions specific to different countries have mattered a great deal in accounting for the variable fate of labor parties (see table 1) and their policies. One condition has to do with a complex heritage of national political institutions, and of labor party infrastructure and ideologies, which together constitute a kind of historically accumulated topography of obstructions to new political adaptations to new conditions. Thus what emerges as the strong argument explaining differences in the fate of labor parties is the great and constraining weight of the politics of the past. A historical politics creates institutional structures, policies, party organizations, and ideologies that have to be treated as largely given by particular actors at particular times and places. Political actors are constrained not only by aspects of the economy that are beyond their reach. They are also constrained by the accumulated consequences of a history of strategic politics. The politics of the past thus comes to constitute the objective conditions which confront new generations of political actors, and also helps construct the collectivities we call political actors.[21]

But politics is not only a legacy of constraints. Strategic political actors continually try to reshape or overcome old constraints and to create new ones. The political topography constantly shifts, as calculating political actors work to alter features of political institutions, party organization, or the character of symbolic appeals (and also try to use politics to alter economic constraints). We turn to some of these points.

Electoral institutions and alliances

Labor parties competing in elections have always needed electoral support beyond the working class, in part because the working class never actually became a majority, and in any case the working class was never unanimous in its support for labor parties. As Przeworski proclaims, "The crucial choice was whether to participate."[22] Once the decision was made to compete in elections, the electoral representative system itself and the principle of majority rule on which it rests, forced labor parties to try to build alliances. But alliances with whom? The impact of economic change on the labor party vote has depended in part on the kinds of alliances which these parties constructed at key turning points in their history. The weakness of labor politics in the United States owes a good deal to the fragility of the alliance on which it rested between the northern working class and a backward and racist rural oligarchy in the South. In contrast, social democratic parties in Scandinavia forged alliances with small farmer parties which posed less restrictive conditions on labor party strategy and were also more durable. Indeed, Göran Therborn attributes the durability of the Swedish Social Democrats at least partly to the distinctive politics of the contemporary successor to the farmers' party which, while it is only a sometimes ally, nevertheless prevented the development of a solidified bourgeois opposition.[23]

The electoral coalitions on which labor party success depends, however, are not fixed, but the object of strategic maneuvering, especially at a time when exogenous economic and social change makes electoral allegiances unstable. Numerous examples can make the point. The American Republican party worked actively to whip up the racial fears that were undermining the Democratic party, and that in fact destroyed its southern base. For their part, labor parties are not oblivious to the problem and have actively pursued new constituency support, particularly among women, environmentalists, and the middle class salariat, to compensate for a contracting industrial working class. Therborn credits the Swedish Social Democrats for their flexible and opportunistic use of environmental concerns and gender appeals to recruit voters. George Ross depicts the French Socialists as supremely adaptive, easily shedding the baggage of their common front with the Communists in favor of neo-liberal growth-oriented policies and a technocratic cadre and style which could win support from the middle class.[24]

State centralization and decentralization

The organization of the state itself also constitutes both inherited topography and an arena of strategic maneuvering. Neil Bradford and Jane Jenson, for example, emphasize the difficulties posed for the Canadian New Democratic Party and its union supporters by state decentralization.[25] The challenge to this minority third party was to develop an electoral strategy responsive to the problems posed by foreign economic penetration and domestic economic restructuring. But the challenge was made far more difficult by constitutional decentralization which forced the party to contend not only with the economic reality of regional diversity, but with the fragmenting political reality of strong provincial governments. Similarly, our account of the travails of the American Democratic party also emphasizes the importance of constitutional arrangements in accounting for the failure of the party to develop along the lines of labor parties elsewhere. A constitutionally fragmented and decentralized government structure not only gave privileged access to sectional and interest group forces, but also had the effect of disorganizing the party, making coherent strategy and organization unlikely if not impossible.[26]

State structures are also the objects of partisan contention. The Thatcher regime was persistent in its efforts to strip local governments of money and authority in an effort to stymie those local governments which remained Labour Party bastions.[27] The Reagan administration also was persistent in its efforts to shift power in the federal system by promoting changes in federal grant-in-aid programs—some already pioneered by the earlier Republican administration of Richard Nixon—that reduced the funds and authority of the big city bastions of the Democratic Party. The federal contribution to municipal budgets plummeted, from 26 percent in 1978 to 8 percent in 1987.[28]

The welfare state

Labor party policies also contributed to the creation of new structures which then came to be part of the topography of postindustrial politics. Where welfare state institutions were extensive, and not so closely market conditioned, these institutions have worked to shield party constituencies from market exigencies, and simultaneously to limit the strategies of opposition parties and investor interest groups striving to adapt to a new international division of labor. The characteristic elements of strong welfare states include policies which sustain high levels of employment, provide income protections for those who are pushed out of the labor market, and create a large public service sector. Together with strong unions, these policies delimit national adaptations to international competition. Gøsta Esping-Andersen's comparison of postindustrial labor market patterns in Sweden, Germany, and the United States provides evidence of the bearing of different welfare state systems on labor markets.[29] More generally, where income protections (and strong unions) shield workers from the pressures on jobs and wages which might otherwise be generated by international labor markets (and by national capitalists taking advantage not only of the reality but of the spectre of international wage competition to shore up profits by cutting wages and taxes), the adaptation to postindustrialism is less likely to take the form of expanded low wage employment and public sector cutbacks, and more likely to take the form of capital intensive investment and expanded public employment.[30]

Moreover, a large public sector also means large public employee unions, whose membership is largely female and supportive of the welfare state. The support of these unions has partly compensated for the vote loss that the Social Democrats in Sweden suffered from postindustrial economic change, a pattern that is replicated in other Scandinavian countries. Indeed, the development of a partisan gender gap in a number of Western countries suggests that women voters generally are turning out to be an important potential constituency for labor-based parties, and survey evidence suggests that this is related to their strong support for welfare state policies. Strong welfare states may thus generate important new coalition partners for labor parties in a postindustrial era.

It hardly needs to be pointed out that welfare state programs have been the focus of political battle, particularly in the United States and Great Britain where ascendant conservative parties have succeeded in forcing significant cutbacks in expenditures and coverage. Moreover, welfare state institutions cannot be described on only one dimension, as merely strong or weak, as many studies that measure "welfare state effort" by expenditures imply. There are also important variations among welfare states having to do with the specific structure of programs and the political interests created by these structures. Claus Offe writes about the West German welfare state, which is a relatively big spender and has not so far been subjected to the relatively large cutbacks that have occurred in the United States. But Offe is not optimistic. He argues that economic shifts are combining with the restructuring of the German programs to marginalize increasing numbers of people, thus undermining popular confidence in the programs and fracturing support, in ways that ultimately pave the way for cutbacks in response to postindustrial pressures. [31]

Party infrastructure

Political parties depend on an infrastructure to create and sustain constituency support. Labor parties have mainly relied on unions, and in some places on branches of the state apparatus that they came to control, particularly local governments. Where this apparatus remains vigorous, it has helped to buffer the impact of postindustrialism. But infrastructures also develop an organizational dynamic of their own which can have perverse effects on the party, as internal oligarchies hobble adaptations to new political conditions. Thus programs and agencies originally created to organize constituency support may ultimately become political liabilities. For example, Alan DiGaetano shows that urban development policies in the United States, begun in the New Deal period in part to shore up the big city partners of the national Democrats, were by the 1950s implemented by local "progrowth" regimes in ways that had perverse consequences for the fortunes of the national party. [32]

Asher Arian and Ilan Talmud provide a particularly dramatic example of the costs to the Israeli Labor Party of its party infrastructure.[33] In this instance, the vast apparatus of the Histadrut labor federation and the jobs and benefits it generated for European Israelis helped to foster the deep animosities among newer immigrants that eventually fueled the rise of the opposition Likud coalition. And once the Likud gained power, a Labor Party saddled with the imperative of maintaining the state-dependent Histadrut was forced to participate in a Likud-dominated government for fear of jeopardizing the funds and programs on which its infrastructure depended.

Labor Party infrastructures have naturally become the object of attack by conservative parties, and have often proved vulnerable, in part because the rigidity of the infrastructure organizations themselves has weakened popular support for them. The Thatcher program for the privatization of council housing, for example, was a direct assault on what had been a Labour Party effort not only to provide desperately needed housing to its working class constituency, but to consolidate working class voters and a working class culture in bright socialist communities. But council housing became something quite different, and privatization initiatives proved popular in part because of widespread dissatisfaction with grim and poorly administered council houses. Similarly, the extraordinarily aggressive campaign against American unions by employer groups and the Reagan administration was as successful as it was because the charge that the unions were merely a "special interest" was not entirely farfetched.

Ideology

The substance of popular politics depends on interpretations which tell people what is within the realm of the politically possible, and what is naturalized as beyond the reach of politics. Interpretations also organize the realm of the political, helping to shape collectivities and cleavages, and to identify issues of contention. The construction of this political culture is in large measure the achievement of political parties who mobilize people around a common set of programs and symbols.[34] Parties in power are especially effective in constructing political interpretations since they have at their disposal the enormous resources of the state to communicate definitions and, indeed, to create realities consistent with those interpretations. But a party culture developed in the context of industrial politics is likely to stress identities and interests that can hobble the mobilization of new constituencies under new circumstances by stressing identities, symbols, and arguments that seem old and tired.[35] Thus still another problem of the British Labour Party, as Joel Krieger argues, is that it failed to adapt appeals to take account of the identities and interests of the minorities and women who are its potential constituencies, just as it failed to adapt its productivist political arguments to the more fluid collective problems of a postindustrial era.[36] Overcoming the dead weight of inherited labor party iconography can be wrenching, as illustrated by the extended conflict generated by leadership efforts to rename the Italian Communist party, or by the inability of the French Communist party to adapt its party symbols and arguments.

We think, in fact, that the great battle of postindustrial politics is being fought on the terrain of ideology, and it may be here that the future prospects of labor parties are decided. So far, it is the bourgeoisie that has taken the strategic initiative, with an analysis of the power of capital in a global economy, and its transforming mission, that parallels and supersedes the ideology of labor power. Postindustrial economic developments have both inspired and justified new and winning arguments by conservative parties and their business allies about the imperatives of international markets, and the inevitable need to align domestic wages and public policies with the terms of those markets. In this ideological effort, not only is the power of capital and labor reversed, but so is their moral standing, for it is capital and not labor that is the agency of progress. The historic political mobilization of the right in the United States that began in the 1970s is an example. The Republican Party and its corporate interest group allies mobilized party and class resources to promulgate arguments to the effect that, whatever else their merits, trade union demands and welfare state programs constituted a drag on the competitive position of the United States. And there is enough evidence in the simultaneous contraction of the old domestic industries and the proliferation of goods produced in Japan or Korea to make that argument seem very plausible. Indeed, so forceful has this ideological assault proved that labor parties in most countries are deserting the field, acknowledging the necessity of adapting to international markets and of the austerity policies capital has demanded, arguing mainly their own superior technical capacity to develop and administer the neo-liberal policies that will match market imperatives.

Future Prospects

This seems the worst of all possible moments to hazard predictions. As we write these words in the fall of 1990, the electoral fortunes of both labor and conservative parties are in flux. On the one hand, even such stalwarts of labor politics as the Norwegian and Swedish parties are clearly faltering as popular support slips and the parties reconnoiter. The Swedish Social Democrats alternately promise further expansion of the welfare state and tax cuts, labor unrest is growing and centralized wage bargaining seems to be unraveling, and Sweden's share of the world market in manufactured goods is falling as the government searches for ways to translate the profits of international Swedish corporations into domestic productivity growth.[29] Meanwhile, the rush of events in Eastern Europe has also weakened social democracy symbolically, by generating a powerful iconography fusing the ideas of the free market and democracy, as if the one necessarily entailed the other. But so are the "hypercapitalist" conservative parties of England and the United States showing evidence of increasing internal disarray.

Still, even conservative disarray does not lead us to think a revival of labor politics as we once knew it is likely. Labor parties may win some elections, relying on the repertoire of strategies to cope with postindustrial decline described in these essays, including appeals to environmental concerns and to women, and the perfecting of classless appeals oriented to a generalized public opinion. But the specific economic and social arrangements which nourished the labor politics of the past have changed too much to expect the revival of class politics in familiar forms. Most telling to us, the twin power analyses which fueled the rise of labor politics by revealing the possibilities of worker power over a national capitalist class on the one hand, and over the sovereign nation state on the other, have lost their force because they do not match the institutional realities of the new world order of international capitalism. It is not that class inequities and conflicts of interest have faded. If anything, postindustrial trends have made class divisions sharper and harsher. But the strong articulation of these interests awaits the "construction of a new 'social imaginary,' capable of carrying a whole population forward."[38] Central to that social imaginary will be a new argument about the possibilities of popular power in postindustrial societies which, we firmly believe, the continuing experience of political conflict will begin to delineate.

Originally published in 1992.

Notes

1. E. J. Hobsbawm et al., *The Forward March of Labour Halted?* (London: Verso, in association with *Marxism Today* and New Left Books, 1981), p. 8.

2. A. Przeworski and J. Sprague, *Paper Stones: A History of Electoral Socialism* (Chicago, IL: University of Chicago Press, 1986), pp. 27–8.

3. The sources of national variations in class politics have been the focus of an enormous literature. For a review, see S. M. Lipset, "Political cleavages in 'developed' and 'emerging' polities," in *Mass Politics: Studies in Political Sociology*, ed. E. Allardt and S. Rokkan (New York: Free Press, 1970), pp. 26–32.

4. On the importance of class cleavages in structuring and freezing contemporary political alignments, see S. M. Lipset and S. Rokkan, "Cleavage structures, party systems and voter alignments: an introduction," in *Party Systems and Voter Alignments*, ed. S. M. Lipset and S. Rokkan (New York: Free Press, 1967), pp. 1–64

5. On the critical role of political mobilization in shaping or failing to shape "class sentiments" in the United States, see R. Oestreicher, "Urban working-class political behavior and theories of American electoral politics, 1870–1940," *Journal of American History*, 74, 4 (March 1988), pp. 1268–9.

6. On the argument that the melding of particularistic claims to the general interest was the "unique and extraordinary" feature of the workers' movement, see Raymond Williams, in Hobsbawm, *The Forward March of Labour Halted?*, p. 144.

7. On this point, and for a more general discussion of the importance of altruistic cultural traditions in shaping welfare state programs, see M. Paci, "The welfare state as a problem of hegemony," *Planning Theory Newsletter* (Summer 1989), pp. 3–22.

8. On the politics of the origins of welfare state programs, see for example H. Heclo, *Modern Social Politics in Britain and Sweden* (New Haven, CT: Yale University Press, 1974); P. Flora and J. Alber, "Modernization, democratization and the development of welfare states in Western Europe," in *The Development of Welfare States in Europe and America*, ed. P. Flora and A. Heidenheimer (New Brunswick, NJ: Transaction Books, 1981), pp. 37–80. Gøsta Esping-Andersen develops a typology of conservative, liberal, and socialist welfare state regimes, reflecting the constellations of power under which national welfare states were constructed in *The Three Worlds of Welfare Capitalism* (Princeton, NJ: Princeton University Press, 1990). And Hans Keman develops another typology, emphasizing differences in social democratic (or labor) parties in different countries, in "Social democracy and welfare," *Netherlands Journal of Social Sciences*, 26, 1 (April 1990), pp. 17–34.

9. For a review of efforts to measure the impact of labor party power on welfare state growth see M. Shalev, "The social democratic model and beyond: two generations of comparative social research on the welfare state," *Comparative Social Research*, 6 (1983), pp. 315–52. See also G. Esping-Andersen, "Power and distributional regimes," *Politics and Society*, 14, 2 (1985), especially p. 249, table 2, which shows the remarkable increase in labor influence on social security expenditures over time. See also W. Korpi, "Power, politics, and state autonomy in the development of social citizenship," *American Sociological Review*, 54, 3 (June 1989), pp. 309–28. We should also point out that the 1960s expansion may also have owed a good deal of its impetus to the historic escalation of labor unrest in that decade, to which neither labor parties nor their trade union allies contributed. On the 1960s surge of worker protest see G. Arrighi, "Marxism and its history," *New Left Review*, 179, especially p. 49.

10. A. Przeworski, *Capitalism and Social Democracy* (Cambridge: Cambridge University Press, 1985).

11. Hobsbawm, *The Forward March of Labour Halted?*, p. 71.

12. See Przeworski and Sprague, *Paper Stones*, p. 30, table 2.2.

13. For a discussion of the secular decline in social class voting see R. J. Dalton, S. C. Flanagan, and P. A. Beck, *Electoral Change in Advanced Industrial Democracies: Realignment or Dealignment?* (Princeton, NJ: Princeton University Press, 1984), especially pp. 29–30, 352–3, and 453–5.

14. For a discussion of the variable impact of industrial restructuring on union strength see D. Kettler and V. Meja, "Social progress after the age of progressivism: the end of trade unionism in the West?," Working Paper 17, The Jerome Levy Economics Institute of Bard College, Annandale-On-Hudson, NY, 1989. On restructuring and unionism in Italy, see R. M. Locke, "The resurgence of local unions: industrial restructuring and industrial relations in Italy," *Politics and Society*, 18, 3 (September 1990), pp. 347–79.

15. On this dimension of postindustrial change, see S. Lash and J. Urry, *The End of Organized Capitalism* (Cambridge: Polity Press, 1987).

16. On this point, see Dalton et al., *Electoral Change in Advanced Industrial Democracies*, p. 353.

17. On the erosion of class attachments among workers, including attachments to unions, see W. Korpi, *The Working Class in Welfare Capitalism* (London: Routledge and Kegan Paul, 1978).

18. Ivor Crewe, "Labor Force Changes, Working Class Decline, and the Labour Vote: Social and Electoral Trends in Postwar Britain" in *Labor Parties in Postindustrial Societies*, ed. Frances Fox Piven (New York: Oxford University Press, 1992).

19. See A. Hicks, "Social democratic corporatism and economic growth," Journal of Politics, 50 (1988), pp. 677–704; P. Lange and G. Garrett, "Performance in a hostile world: economic growth in capitalist democracies," *World Politics*, 38 (1986), pp. 517–45; R. Friedland and J. Sanders, "The public economy and economic growth in Western market economies," *American Sociological Review*, 50 (1985), pp. 421–37.

20. For a recent discussion, see B. Jessop, K. Bonnett, and S. Bromley, "The Thatcher balance-sheet," *New Left Review*, 179 (January–February 1990), pp. 81–102.

21. Peter Hall discusses some of these same factors under the rubric of "organization." Organization, he says, not only facilitates the expression of interests, but helps shape interests, and also affects the nature of the policies produced in reflection of interests, and their implementation. See *Governing the Economy* (Cambridge: Polity Press, 1986), especially pp. 232–3.

22. Przeworski, *Capitalism and Social Democracy*, p. 7.

23. See Göran Therborn, "Swedish Social Democracy and the Transition from Industrial to Postindustrial Politics," in *Labor Parties in Postindustrial Societies*, ed., Frances Fox Piven (New York: Oxford University Press, 1992). The bourgeois parties in Norway have also been plagued by divisions, helping to account for the strength of labor parties there as well. See J. Fagerberg, A. Cappelen, L. Mjoset, and R. Skarstein, "The decline of social democratic state capitalism in Norway," *New Left Review*, 181 (1990), pp. 60–94. Esping-Andersen makes the point that, while Austrian and Swedish labor have comparable resources, the bourgeois block in Austria is unified. See Esping-Andersen, "Power and distributional regimes." p. 226.

24. See George Ross, "The Changing Face of Popular Power in France," in *Labor Parties in Postindustrial Societies*, ed., Frances Fox Piven (New York: Oxford University Press, 1992).

25. See Neil Bradford and Jane Jenson, "Facing Economic Restructuring and Constitutional Renewal: Social Democracy Adrift in Canada," in *Labor Parties in Postindustrial Societies*, ed., Frances Fox Piven (New York: Oxford University Press, 1992).

26. See chapter 16 in this volume.

27. For examples of this kind of Thatcher strategy, see Hall, *Governing the Economy*, especially pp. 127–9.

28. D. Kirschten, "More problems, less clout," *National Journal* (August 12, 1989), p. 2030.

29. See Gøsta Esping Andersen, *Three Worlds of Welfare Capitalism* (NJ: Princeton, University Press, 1990).

30. For comparative data showing the relationship between the institutional and political position of labor and the rate of growth in public employment, see M. F. Masters and J. D. Robertson, "Class compromises in industrial democracies," *American Political Science Review*, 82, 4 (December 1988), pp. 1183–202.

31. See Claus Offe, "Smooth Consolidation in the West German Welfare State: Structural Change, Fiscal Policies, and Populist Politics," in *Labor Parties in Postindustrial Societies*, ed., Frances Fox Piven (New York: Oxford University Press, 1992). Offe's emphasis on status divisions encouraged by contemporary welfare state programs is at least reminiscent of Lipset's much earlier characterization of the importance of status groupings in German politics. See Lipset, "Political cleavages in developed and emerging polities," especially pp. 26–8.

32. Alan DiGaetano, "The Democratic Party and City Politics in the Postindustrial Era," in *Labor Parties in Postindustrial Societies*, ed., Frances Fox Piven (New York: Oxford University Press, 1992).

33. Asher Arian and Ilan Talmud, "Electoral Politics and Economic Control in Israel," in *Labor Parties in Postindustrial Societies*, ed., Frances Fox Piven (New York: Oxford University Press, 1992).

34. See Lipset and Rokkan, "Cleavage structures, party systems and voter alignments." On the role of parties in class formation in particular, see A. Przeworski, "Proletariat into a class: the process of class formation from Karl Kautsky's 'The Class Struggle' to recent controversies," *Politics and Society*, 7, 4 (1977), pp. 343–402.

35. On this point, see Z. Bauman, "Britain's exit from politics," *New Statesman and Society* (July 29, 1988), pp. 34–48.

36. Joel Krieger, "Class, Consumption, and Collectivism: Perspectives on the Labour Party and Electoral Competition in Britain," in *Labor Parties in Postindustrial Societies*, ed., Frances Fox Piven (New York: Oxford University Press, 1992).

37. See J. Pontusson, "Austerity, government crisis, and political realignment in Sweden 1989–90," Paper presented at the Annual Meeting of the American Political Science Association, San Francisco, CA, September 1990.

38. C. Leys, "Still a question of hegemony," *New Left Review*, 181 (May–June 1990), p. 128.

2

Globalizing Capitalism and
the Rise of Identity Politics

For more than a century, the Left has been guided by the conviction that industrial capitalism would inevitably homogenize social life, and thus lay the basis for a universalizing politics. Capitalism meant the expansion of a bourgeoisie whose search for profit would steadily penetrate the social life of traditional societies, and eventually reach across the globe, in the process wiping out "all fixed relations and their train of ancient and venerable prejudices and opinions." Meanwhile, industrial capitalism would also nourish an ever-larger working class based in the mass production industries that would bind diverse people together in class-based solidarity. And this class would reap the harvest of capitalist destruction and possibility, for it would become the carrier of an emancipatory creed uniting all humankind. Capitalism itself, by obliterating ancient differences and polarizing humanity into two great classes, would pave the way for the universalizing mission of the proletariat.

This model now seems shattered. Capitalism has indeed penetrated societies and spanned the globe. In this sense, it is homogenizing social life. But instead of universalizing popular politics, capitalist expansion is weakening and conceivably destroying working class politics. The advance of international markets and technological change are eviscerating the mass production industries, at least in the mother countries, diminishing the working class numbers and organizations which once gave life to the idea of the proletariat as the hope of humankind. And the new mobility of capitalist investment is also reducing the autonomy of the nation state, with a crushing impact on existing forms of working class organization and influence.

Moreover, instead of wiping out all ancient prejudices, a globalizing capital is prompting a rising tide of fractious racial, ethnic, religious, and gender conflict. It is contributing to an identity politics which expresses not only the ancient and venerable prejudices and opinions which were presumably to be swept aside, but the apparently inexhaustible human capacity to create new prejudices and opinions, albeit often in the name of an imagined ancient past. We can see this most awesomely in the conflicts between Hindus and Muslims, Sikhs and Hindus, Hindus and Kashmiris in India; between Xhosa and Zulu, Christians, animists, and Muslims in Africa; or between Germans and Turks, French and Algerians, Serbs and Muslims and Croats in Europe; or among Chechens, Ossetians, Abhkazians, and Russians; or between Jews and Blacks, Gays and fundamentalists in the United States. Even the Cossacks are on the move again, demanding recognition, in the words of their supreme leader, 'as a distinct people' with 'our territory, property and traditions all restored.'¹ Two decades ago, even a decade ago, such proclamations from the past would have seemed exotic. Now they seem unremarkable. No people, no place, is immune from the tide of identity politics.

As always, intellectual fashion refracts these real world developments, and perhaps contributes to them as well. After all, the old idea that industrial capitalism nourished universalizing classes was itself an intellectual construction, with large consequences in energizing and guiding the development of working class politics. Left intellectuals took for granted the idea that class mattered in politics, that the social structure of modern societies generated broad collectivities, bound together for political action by common interests, a common experience, and perhaps common visions of emancipation. Now, however, those premises seem hopelessly out-of-date, overshadowed by a stream of theorizing which emphasizes the fractured and evanescent nature of political identities constructed and reconstructed by actors more influenced by cultural orientations than by the constraints of socially structured class divisions.[2] In a way, this sort of perspective with its emphasis on the fluidity of culture seems a poor fit with the apparent rootedness and hardness of the inherited ethnic and religious identities which underly many contemporary conflicts.[3] Nevertheless, the new intellectual fashion challenges the old confidence in class in favor of an emphasis on culture as a force in its own right. So does Samuel Huntington's view that the grand axes of conflict in the world are no longer between princes or nation states or ideologies, but rather between religious cultures.[4]

A good deal of the recent discussion of identity politics takes the form of arguments about whether to be for it, or against it.[5] The dispute is in one sense pointless. Identity politics is almost surely inevitable, because it is a way of thinking that reflects something very elemental about human experience. Identity politics seems to be rooted quite simply in attachments to the group, attachments that are common to humankind, and that probably reflect primordial needs that are satisfied by the group, for material survival in a predatory world, as well as for recognition, community, security, and perhaps also a yearning for immortality. Hence people construct the 'collective identities' which define the common traits and common interests of the group, and inherit and invent shared traditions and rituals which bind them together. The mirror image of this collective identity is the invention of the Other, whoever that may be, and however many they may be. And as is often pointed out, it is partly through the construction of the Other, the naming of its traits, the demarcation of its locality, and the construction of a myth-like history of struggle between the group and the Other, that the group recognizes itself.[6] All of this seems natural enough.

If identification with the group is ubiquitous, it is also typically the case that groupness and Otherness are understood as the result of biological nature. Perhaps this is simply because nature provides the most obvious explanation of "groupness" that is available to people. Even when groups are demarcated by their religion or culture, these mentalities are often regarded as traits so deeply rooted as to be virtually biological, inevitably passed on to future generations. Moreover, the pernicious traits attributed to the Other can easily be woven into explanations of the travails that people experience, into theories of why the rains don't come, or why children sicken and die, or why jobs are scarce

43

and wages fall. This sort of racial theorizing makes the world as people experience it more comprehensible. Even labour politics, ideas about a universalistic proletarian class notwithstanding, was riddled with identity politics. Thus Hobsbawm makes the sensible point that the very fact that 20th century political movements proferred religious, nationalist, socialist, and confessional credos suggests that their potential followers were responsive to all these appeals.[7] Politicized workers were bonded together not only and perhaps not mainly by common class position, but by the particularisms of maleness, of whiteness, and of diverse European ethnic and religious identities. In short, features of the human condition seem to drive people to identity politics and, if it is not an inevitable way of thinking, it is surely widespread.

But if identity politics is ubiquitous because of what it offers people in protection, comfort, and pride, it has also been a bane upon humankind, the source of unending tragedy. The fatal flaw in identity politics is easily recognized. Class politics, at least in principle, promotes vertical cleavages, mobilizing people around axes which broadly correspond to hierarchies of power, and which promote challenges to these hierarchies. By contrast, identity politics fosters lateral cleavages which are unlikely to reflect fundamental conflicts over societal power and resources and, indeed, may seal popular allegiance to the ruling classes that exploit them. This fatal flaw at the very heart of a popular politics based on identity is in turn regularly exploited by elites. We can see it dramatically, for example, in the unfolding of the genocidal tribal massacres in Rwanda, fomented by a Hutu governing class which found itself losing a war with Tutsi rebels. And of course the vulnerability to manipulation resulting from identity politics is as characteristic of modern societies as tribal societies.

Thus identity politics makes people susceptible to the appeals of modern nationalism, to the bloody idea of loyalty to state and flag, which is surely one of the more murderous ideas to beset humankind. State builders cultivate a sort of race pride to build allegiance to an abstract state, drawing on the ordinary and human attachments that people form to their group and their locality,[8] and drawing also on the animosity to the Other that is typically the complement of these attachments. The actual group that people experience, the local territory that they actually know, comes to be joined with the remote state and its flag, just as the external enemy of the state comes to be seen as the menacing Other, now depicted as a threat not only to the group and its locale, but as a threat to the nation state. We hardly need add that this melding of identity politics with state patriotism can stir people to extraordinary acts of destruction and self-destruction in the name of mystical abstractions, and the identity politics that energizes them. Napoleon was able to waste his own men easily in his murderous march across Europe because they were quickly replaced with waves of recruits drawn from a French population enthused by their new attachment to the French nation. And World War I showed that modern states could extract even more extraordinary contributions of life and material well-being from their citizenry, as Europeans seized by nationalist passions joined in a frenzy of destruction and death in the name of state patriotism.[9]

In the United States, popular politics has usually been primarily about race, ethnicity, and religion. Perhaps a population of slaves and immigrants of diverse origins, captive and free, provided some objective basis for the cultivation of identity politics, constructed by ordinary people themselves, and of course by political and economic elites who have never been slow to see that division ensured domination.[10] From the colonial era, public policy engraved distinctions among whites, blacks ,and native Americans by enshrining elaborate racial hierarchies in law, by prohibiting sexual liaisons across racial lines, and by punishing with particular ferocity the insurrections in which humble people of different races joined together.

The institutions of the American South, especially the post-Reconstruction South, are illustrative, for they can be understood as a vast complex of social arrangements which, by strictly segregating African Americans, and specifying their obligations of deference, made factitious racial differences real. Similar practices by industrialists had similar if less total consequences in inscribing difference. Employers deliberately drew from diverse ethnic groups for their workforce, and then artfully arranged job assignments, wage scales, and residential quarters in company towns so as to maintain and underline those differences. Or note the strident emphasis on ethnic, religious, and later racial identities in the organizations, the mobilizing strategies and the policy outcomes of big city politics. The labor movement was riddled by these influences and, if it was sometimes strengthened by the gender, racial and ethnic solidarities that flourished within it, particularistic identities also blinded workers to their commonalities, making them vulnerable to employers who pitted one group against another, and leading them also to engage in terrible episodes of labor fratricide. Needless perhaps to add, this history still marks American politics today.

All this notwithstanding, identity politics can also be a potentially liberating and even equalizing development, especially among subordinate groups, and the more so in a political culture already dominated by identity politics. This possibility has sometimes been difficult for liberals honed on ideals of universalism to appreciate. Certainly it has been difficult for a Left preoccupied with class to appreciate.

Contemporary complaints about identity politics would be more understandable if they were aimed at elites who help foment and manipulate divisions. Instead, however, they are often directed at the subordinate groups who assert fractious identities. It may well be, however, that identity politics is especially necessary to lower status peoples, to those who are more insecure, and who are more likely to be deprived of recognition and respect by wider currents of culture and social interaction. Subordinate groups try to construct distinctive and sometimes defiant group identities, perhaps to defend themselves against dominant definitions, at least when they are allowed the cultural space to do so. Moreover, the construction of distinctive identities may be a necessary prelude to self-organization and political assertion, and particularly so in a political culture organized by identity politics. Indeed, in the cauldron of an American politics based on difference, immigrants who had previously recognized only a village or a locale as their homeland invented new national identities the better to survive and do battle in contests among nationalities. For them, the construction of new identities was a vehicle of at least psychic emancipation, and sometimes of political empowerment as well.

The black movement of the post–World War II era, which is often (unreasonably) blamed for heightened identity politics, is a good example of the emancipatory construction and assertion of group identity.

The celebration of Blackness was in the first instance reactive to the racism of American society: to the experience of racial subordination and terror in the South, to the extreme subordination imposed by the North whose cultural imagery at its most benign featured minstrels in blackface, Sambos, and so on. Blacks reconstructed their identity in the face of these imposed identities, and this was almost surely essential to the rise of a movement demanding racial liberation—and to the substantial achievements of that movement in dismantling the caste arrangements which had engraved racial identity politics.

However, these achievements set in motion a train of repercussions that were not simple. The new assertions of black pride and the political demands that pride fuelled provoked alarmed and angry reactions from other groups whose own identities depended on the subordination of blacks. And of course political elites, especially but not only Republican party operatives, who stood to benefit from the politics of backlash, worked to sharpen these reactions, making such code words of race hatred as "quotas," or "law and order," or "welfare dependency," focal to their popular appeals. Still, the very emergence of far-reaching race conflict reflected the fact that subordination had come to be contested. Blacks were no longer allowing others to define their identity, repress their interests, and stamp out their aspirations. That was an achievement.

The rise of gender politics followed a similar course. While women do not have what is recognized as a distinctive language or turf, the understanding of gender has in other ways been prototypical of the understanding of group identity. Gender identities are closely similar to racial identities, because the traits which were thought to be feminine or masculine, and the social roles to which women and men were consigned, were always understood as the natural consequence of biological difference. Necessarily, therefore, the emergence of a liberatory movement among women was preceded and accompanied by an effort to cast off this inherited identity and construct new identities that disavowed biological fatalism or, in some variants, celebrated biological difference. Indeed, Zaretsky writes of "the profundity and the intensity of the identity impulse among women that emerged in the early seventies."[1] The most salient issues of the women's movement—the struggle for the Equal Rights Amendment, for reproductive rights, and the campaigns against rape and sexual harassment—are closely reflective of this effort to reconstruct the meaning of gender by challenging the biological underpinnings of traditional meanings. The mounting of such a challenge to the most ancient of subordinations, and a subordination rooted in understandings of nature itself, is surely a stunning accomplishment.

As with blacks, the consequences were not simple. Liberatory reconstructions of gender struck at deeply imprinted understandings, threatening and arousing people still embedded in more traditional relationships, including many women embedded in traditional relationships. And as had been the case with conflict over racial identities, the contest over understandings of gender became the focus of elite manipulations in electoral politics. By 1980, the Republicans had taken notice, and in an effort to turn the widening anxieties provoked by gender conflict to electoral advantage, struck support for ERA from their platform, and initiated a campaign that culminated in the odd spectacle of American Presidents—leaders of the richest and most technologically advanced nation in the world—casting themselves as leaders of a holy-war against abortion.

While identity politics may always be with us, the contemporary world appears to be engulfed by particularistic conflicts of rising intensity and destructiveness, in a pattern reminiscent of the rising tide of nationalist furies of the late 19th century. The main reasons for this, then and now, can be traced to the transformation of world capitalism. First, in the contemporary period, capitalist expansion is at least partly responsible for the weakening or collapse of nation states, with horrific consequences for ethnic and religious conflict. Second, economic restructuring is enfeebling existing forms of working class political organization which in the past sometimes restrained particularistic conflicts in the interests of class solidarity. Finally, even while the restraining capacities of governments and working class organizations are diminishing, capitalist restructuring is aggravating group conflict, by accelerating the migration of peoples, by intensifying competition for scarce resources, and by creating the widespread economic and social insecurity which always accompanies large-scale change, and particularly so when the changes for many people are for the worse.

Of course, not every instance of the weakening or collapse of central governments that had previously restrained group conflict can be traced to the current global capitalist transformation. Ancient animosities can erupt whenever central governments no longer hold them in check. The withdrawal of the British Raj unleashed bloody conflicts in India which persist to this day, and the withdrawal of the colonial powers from Africa also spurred tribal conflicts. But other instances of central government collapse cannot easily be disentangled from the changes wrought by world capitalism. Waves of anarchic warfare in the developing world are at least partly the result of saddling third world governments with debt through the imposition of neo-liberal credit policies.[12] The fall of the Yugoslavian government, and the ethnic wars that resulted, was similarly at least partly the result of the shock therapy administered by the IMF. And other Eastern European governments were undermined by the spread of a consumer culture which fuelled popular discontent with state provision. (The Eastern European revolutions, says Benjamin R. Barber, were less over the right to vote than the right to shop.[13])

Other consequences of capitalist tranformation for the intensification of identity politics are more direct. In a sense, the old prediction has proved true; the bourgeoisie is on the move with a series of universalizing projects which promise utterly to transform the world, penetrating and homogenizing social life across the globe. But instead of nourishing a growing proletariat, a missionary capitalism is destroying the working class formations of the older industrial order, at least in the rich countries of the West.

We do not want to overstate the unifying influence of the labour movement at its peak. We have already pointed out that worker mobilizations were riven by the particularistic divisions of race and ethnicity, and sometimes gender. Nevertheless, the promise of the labour movement was that class solidarity would override particularisms, and even that proletarian internationalism would override state patriotism. And in instance after instance, where the successful use of the strike power demanded it, labor did indeed override the divisions of identity politics, even in the United States. Now that moderating influence has weakened.

The basic lines of capitalist restructuring and the impact on organized labor are familiar. First, the expansion of global trade, itself promoted by the internationalizing of markets in finance and production, as well as by improvements in transportation and communications, has lead to the intensified exploitation of labor and resources across the globe. From Indonesia to China to Haiti, previously peripheral peoples and places are being incorporated into capitalist markets, with the consequence that organized workers in the mother countries find themselves competing with products made by low-wage workers across the globe, including workers made docile by coercive authoritarian governments.

Second, the power constellations patterning the policies of national governments have shifted. Organized labor has lost ground dramatically to new supra-national institutions created by capital. It is true, as Panitch says, that the nation states are major authors of these institutions, and also continue to serve important functions for internationalizing capital.[14] Nevertheless, once in existence, international organizations and networks, including multinational corporations and international banking organizations, together with their domestic corporate and financial allies who freely use the threat of disinvestment as leverage in their dealings with governments, become major constraints on the policy options of the state. Constraints on the state are also constraints on the ability of democratic publics, including the organized working class, to exert influence through electoral-representative arrangements. The trade unions and political parties constructed by organized workers in the mother countries gained what influence they had through their leverage on governments, since strike power, trade union organization, and working-class voting numbers made them a force with which to be reckoned. If capitalist internationalism circumscribes what national governments can do, it inevitably also circumscribes working class political power.

Third, as a consequence of both internationalism and the shifting power constellations within nations, the economies and polities of the mother-countries of industrial capitalism are being restructured, with dire consequences for the old working class. This process is most advanced in England and the United States where unions are weaker and welfare state protections less adequate. The old mass production industries which created the industrial working class are being dismantled or reorganized and decentralized, with the consequence that the numbers of blue collar workers are shrinking. And as communities disperse and the mass media supplants the local pub, the old working class culture also crumbles. Those who remain have become excruciatingly vulnerable to the threat power of a mobile capital, unable to resist shrinking wages and benefits, and the worsening terms of work, including speedup, and forced overtime for some, and involuntary part-time or temporary work for others, all of which undermines union organization. At the same time, capitalists have launched a specifically political project to dismantle the institutional supports created by working-class politics, by attacking unions, and slashing welfare state income and service protections which shielded workers from the market, and by discrediting Keynesian macro-economic political regulation. [15]

Finally, a capitalist class on the move has launched an ideological campaign to justify and promote its expansionary mission. International markets exist, but they have also been cast as a superordinate order, operating according to a kind of natural law, penetrating national economies more deeply than they actually do, and beyond the reach of politics. In fact, this neo-laissez faire doctrine cloaks the capitalist class with the mantle once claimed by the proletariat. Capital is forging the way to the future, it is the great force for progress, the hope of humankind. And as with 19th century laissez faire notions to which this doctrine owes its main tenets, the ideology is touched with fanaticism, with a zealous utopianism that ignores the actual needs of the human subjects of any world order. Of course, this ideological campaign is as persuasive as it is because international markets are also real, and the palpable evidence of capital and goods mobility lends the sweeping doctrine of neo-laissez faire a certain material reality.

In all of these ways a universalizing capitalism has weakened the old industrial working class as a political force. No wonder unions and labor parties that were the instrument of this class have also lost their ideological footing. The imagery which gave working-class politics its élan, the idea that the future belonged to the workers, and that workers acted for all humankind, has collapsed. That universalizing myth now belongs to a capitalist class on the move.

The surge of identity politics is not just the result of a collapsing central governments or a receding class politics. It is also the result of the massive dislocations of people set in motion by capitalist restructuring. More and more people are being drawn into the orbit of capitalism. Considered abstractly, that process is universalizing. In the actual experience of people, it has had the effect of heightening particularistic identities and conflicts. Gellner, writing of an earlier phase of capitalist transformation and the nationalist furies it helped to set loose, showed how an "explosive blend of early industrialism (dislocation, mobility, acute inequality not hallowed by time and custom) seeks out, as it were, all the available nooks and crannies of cultural differentiation, wherever they be."[16] The pattern is being repeated in the contemporary era. In other words, instead of wiping out the "train of ancient and venerable prejudices," the advance of global capitalism is whipping ancient prejudices to fever pitch.

Identity politics is pervasive, and probably inevitable. But group conflict is likely to rise under some conditions, and subside under others. One important source of disturbance has to do with the large-scale migration of people spurred by capitalist penetration of subsistence agricultural economies, with the consequence that conflicts over land escalate, and people no longer able to survive in agriculture migrate to urban centers.[17] At the same time, the spread of consumer culture also attracts people from the periphery, while the development of globe-spanning circuits of communication and transportation facilitates the recruitment of cheap labor to the metropole.[18] "Every migration," says Enzensberger, "no matter what triggered it, what motive underlies it, whether it is voluntary or involuntary, and what scale it assumes, leads to conflicts."[19] Or as Jean Daniel, editor of *Le Nouvel Observateur*, warns about population movements and the "unprecedented" mingling of peoples, we should remember that "Babel...was a curse."[20]

If unfamiliar proximity is likely to intensify group consciousness and fractionalism, this is especially so when outsider groups are seen as competitors for limited jobs, neighborhood space, honor and influence. In his last book, Ralph Miliband wrote that intra-class conflicts among wage-earners involving race or gender or ethnicity or religion can reasonably be understood as the effort to find scapegoats to explain insecurity and alienation.[21] If he was not entirely right, he was surely at least

52

significantly right. Group conflict is far more likely when people feel growing uncertainty about their own future and, as is true in many instances, are experiencing real declines in living standards. When times get harder, and competition for scarce resources intensifies, theories about the Other, and how the Other is to blame for these turns in events, being ubiquitous, are readily available. And, of course, such interpretations are more likely to be seized upon when alternative and perhaps more systemic explanations of the troubles people face are not available, or when such explanations yield no practicable line of action. No wonder there has been a spread of an identity politics, often a hate-filled identity politics, in the metropole. As Vaclav Havel says, "The world of our experiences seems chaotic, confusing.... And the fewer answers the era of rational knowledge provides...the more deeply it would seem that people, behind its back as it were, cling to the ancient certainties of their tribe."[22]

Finally, as so many times before, the group divisions of identity politics are being worsened by political elites who seize the opportunity for gaining advantage from popular division. In particular, politicians on the Right—Le Pen's Front National in France, the Christian Right in the United States, the Freedom Party in Austria, the Falangists in Spain, the Lombardy League in Italy, or the Republicans in Germany where half a million immigrants arrived in 1992 alone—work to stoke the anger against outsiders. They draw popular attention away from the economic transformations underway, and try to hold or win anxious voters by directing resentment against outsiders. Or, as a retired Russian officer commented to a *New York Times* reporter about the conflict between the Tatars and ethnic Russians, "Half the population is building mosques, the other half is building churches. And the bosses are building big brick houses for themselves."

Once again, the United States is at the forefront. In October, 1994 *BusinessWeek* editorialized about the "unprecedented widening of the income gap between winners and losers in the workplace." *BusinessWeek* worried that the losers might ignore its advice that "Growth is the single most important salve for the high-risk, high gain society" and seek scapegoats, such as "elitist big business."

There are of course reasons for *BusinessWeek*'s concerns about the resurgence of class politics. Big business is politically mobilized as never before, having developed over the past two decades a range of vehicles to do ideological and policy warfare, from big think tanks, to revived trade associations, to new associations of peak corporations. Reflecting both these developments and the changed international economic context in which they have unfolded, enormous changes have taken place in the American class structure, as the rich have gotten much richer, the poor much poorer, and most people have gotten poorer as well. National wealth increased, but the vast majority of wage earners lost ground, with the consequence that more people are working, working longer, and harder. The U. S. Census reported that between 1973 and 1989, the real income of male high school graduates dropped by a third; the income of those who didn't make it through high school dropped by 40 percent. And the palpable evidence of economic trauma also grew, in the form of visible poverty and pathology, of beggars and spreading homeless encampments in all of the major cities.

Still, *BusinessWeek* needn't worry, at least not so far. Americans are being led by their political leaders to other scapegoats, and certain conditions prepare the way. For one thing, organized labor is on its back, its membership at 11 percent of the private sector labor force, down from 30 percent only two decades ago. For another, economic changes are not the only shocks to the American psyche. Cultural changes which undermine the established bases of identity are contributing to widespread unease. Contested racial boundaries and, not less important, changing sexual and family mores are eroding a world in which whites were in command, men were men, women were women, and the rules for mating and family life were clear. Needless to say, in a society in which the culture of group identity figures so largely, changes of this sort generate a distinctive terror. In this sense, the numerous commentators who blame the black movement and the women's movement for the rightward shift of the past two decades are not entirely wrong. In a world of identity politics, mobilization by the Other is always a provocation.

Thus economic and cultural change are combining to generate popular anxiety and anger. But the economic transformation, its impact on hard-hit groups, the measures that might moderate the transformation or its impact, do not figure much in American political discussion, except sometimes in the speculations of pundits trying to account for electoral discontent. Instead, public anger has easily been routed into the familiar channels of identity politics, as issues like immigration, crime, and welfare, all code terms for African American and Latino minorities, (with welfare a code evoking wanton women besides) dominate the political discussion. Republican and Democratic leaders alike are following the precedents of American history. Hemmed in by a politically mobilized and aggressive capitalist class, party leaders promulgate arguments which account for the felt problems of ordinary people by singling out the Other. Political discourse is dominated by a narrative in which immigrants, or criminals, or welfare recipients, are variously pointed to as the source of America's problems.

The focus on welfare is a good illustration. As these thing go, welfare (or AFDC) is a small program. Yet to listen to all of the talk, including talk about "reforms" that would slash millions of children and their mothers from the rolls, one would think that this small and benighted program is a main reason for high taxes, spreading poverty, out-of-wedlock births, and just about everything else that people find upsetting. The argument works as well as it does because it meshes with American racism and chauvinism, (and also because people are prepared for it by a history of welfare practices which denigrate recipients by keeping them so miserably poor that they are inevitably outsiders, and by stripping them of any procedural rights).

Interestingly, the old intellectual justification for identity politics is also having a modest renaissance. As economic hardship spreads, theories about the genetic roots of economic success and failure are once more respectable, as signalled by the reception given *The Bell Curve*, the racist tome by Charles Murray and Richard Herrnstein. Their argument is a justification for the most extreme sort of identity politics, proposing as it does that an innate and biologically determined intelligence influences economic and social circumstances, making it more likely that some people end up poor (and deviant), and others end up rich. In other words, the argument goes, class itself, and especially the widening class polarization of the contemporary period, is rooted in biology.

But identity politics is not only a weapon of the ruling class in a strategy of division and domination. It can also become the sinews of resistance, including working class resistance. Indeed, identity politics has often strengthened labor mobilizations in American history by lending these efforts the sense of commonality borne both of common traditions and the shared experience of exclusion. One possibility is that women generally will become a more important force. Another is that class will re-emerge, especially if the labor movement succeeds in more fully organizing the service sector, where legions of women and minorities will bring the politics of identity into the heart of a class mobilization.

We will see.

Originally published in 1995.

Notes

1. Quoted in Fred Weir, "Riders on the Storm," *In These Times*, May 16, 1994.

2. For similar observations, see Ellen Meiksins Wood. 'Identity Crisis,' *In These Times*, June 13, 1994.

3. Of course, inherited identities may serve merely as the raw material from which contemporary identities are constructed, a point made by Zygmunt Bauman, among others. See "Europe of Nations, Europe of Tribes," *Sociologisk Rapportserie*, no. 2, 1993, Department of Sociology, University of Copenhagen.

4. See Samuel Huntington, "The Clash of Civilizations?" *Foreign Affairs*, summer, 1993, and Samuel Huntington, "If Not Civilizations, What?" in *Foreign Affairs*, November/December 1993.

5. See for example Todd Gitlin who faults proponents of identity politics for fracturing the commitment of the Left to universalism, leading to 'paranoid, jargon-clotted, post-modernist groupthink, cult celebrations of victimization and stylized marginality.' 'From Universality to Difference: Notes on the Fragmentation of the Idea of the Left,' *Contention*, Vol. 2, no. 2, Winter 1993, p. 21.

6. Weber discussed racial groups as subjective constructions, resulting from common political actions, or common experiences in antagonism to members of an obviously different group. See *Economy and Society*, Berkeley, University of California Press, 1922, vol. 1, p. 387. See also Stuart Hall, "Ethnicity: Identity and Difference," *Radical America*, Vol. 23, no. 4, October 1991.

7. On the overlap and tension between the appeals of national identity and class in working class political mobilization, see Eric Hobsbawm, *Nations and Nationalism since 1789*, Cambridge University Press, 1990.

8. On the relationship between the development of the nation state and nationalism as ideology, see John Breuilly, *Nationalism and the State*, University of Chicago Press, 1982.

9. Hobsbawm defines nationalism as a principle which holds that the duty of the citizen to the nation overrides all other obligations. See *Nations and Nationalism*, p. 9.

10. Wacquant points out that "the symbolic work necessary to establish race or class as salient subjective principles...can be successful only to the extent that it corresponds to the material differences inscribed in objectivity." See Loïc J. D. Wacquant, "The Puzzle of Race and Class in American Society and Social Science," *Scholarship and Excellence*, Benjamin E. Mays Monograph Series, Vol. 2, no. 1.

11. Eli Zaretsky, "Responses," *Socialist Review*, Vol 23, no. 3, 1994.

12. See Manfred Bienefeld, "Capitalism and the Nation State in the Dog Days of the Twentieth Century," *The Socialist Register*, London: Merlin Press, 1994. Hobsbawm and Bauman both argue that, in general, the assumption by supra-national agencies of functions once performed by nation states may so eviscerate the idea of nationhood as to encourage the proliferation of claims by upstart "nations."

13. "Jihad Vs. McWorld," *Atlantic Monthly*, March, 1992.

14. See Leo Panitch, "Globalization and the State," *The Socialist Register* 1994.

15. These developments are clearest in the United States. However, see the Organizations for Economic Cooperation and Development, *The OECD Jobs Study*, Paris, 1994, which recommends broadly the same directions for Europe.

16. Gellner, *Nations and Nationalism*, p. 112.

17. The *New York Times* reported that the number of intrastate and interstate refugees in the world had reached 49 million. See August 8, 1994.

18. On the push and pull factors in migration, see Amartya Sen, "Population: Delusion and Reality," *New York Review of Books*, September 22, 1994.

19. Hans Enzensberger, *Civil Wars from L.A. to Bosnia*, The New Press, 1994.

20. See Jean Daniel, "God Is Not a Head of State," *New Perspective Quarterly*, Vol. 11, no. 2, spring, 1994.

21. Ralph Miliband, *Socialism for a Sceptical Age*, Cambridge: Polity Press, 1994, p. 22, 192–3.

22. "The New Measure of Man," *New York Times*, July 8, 1994.

3

Welfare and the Transformation
of Electoral Politics

At the end of July 1996, as the election campaign heated up, President Clinton announced he would sign a bill then making its way through the Congress that terminated the sixty-year-old Aid to Families with Dependent Children program. This was another move in the several-years-long contest among Democrats and Republicans, national and state politicians, all trying to position themselves as the frontrunners in the campaign against welfare.

Not that this was an entirely new development. For nearly two decades, Republican campaigners for the presidency regularly homed in on welfare as if the burgeoning rolls were a main problem confronting the country. And defensive Democrats have tried to ward off the challenge by reciting their belief in "work-not-welfare," and proposing a variety of schemes which would presumably put recipients to work. Meanwhile, state-level anti-tax campaigns, beginning with the Proposition 13 crusade to slash property taxes in California, also helped make the issue focal by advertising out-of-control welfare costs as a main reason to cut taxes and thus brake state spending.

But it was the 1992 presidential campaign that brought welfare to center stage. As had become customary, George Bush bashed welfare in his January 1992 State of the Union message. And then, during the campaign, Bill Clinton tried to take the initiative and steal the issue for the Democrats by ratcheting up the rhetoric and promising to "end welfare as we know it" with reforms that would mean "two years and off to work."[2]

With that, the race was on. At first the Clinton administration talked of new programs in job training and job creation, health care and day care, all of which would presumably make it possible for mothers to work. However, such programs cost big money, much more than the current AFDC program. As the dollar estimates mounted, the services and job promotion side of the plan shrank. In the end, the most important feature of the Clinton proposal was a two-year lifetime limit on cash assistance.

After the 1994 congressional election, it was inevitable that the victorious Republicans would try to go the President one better. Almost immediately, they proposed to eliminate federal responsibility for cash assistance to poor mothers and children in favor of block grants, which would give the states less federal money over time, but broader latitude in deciding how that money should be spent, or whether it should be spent at all. And should a state be inclined toward generosity, other provisions would impose rigid work requirements on mothers, as well as strict time limits on the receipt of aid over a lifetime, but without funding for the child care, job training, or job creation that would be needed. Similar restructuring was proposed for the Medicaid program—big funding cuts combined with the devolution of responsibility to the states—and sharp cuts were also proposed for food stamp and other nutritional programs, for low income housing, child protection, and so on. The President vetoed two early versions of the bill, which the Republican congressional leadership thought gave them an advantage as the election approached, but the final bill was not significantly different. In some ways it was worse. It barred the use of federal funds for aid to legal immigrants, and to large numbers of disabled children, and it also restricted food stamp aid to low-wage workers and some of the unemployed.

Meanwhile, state politicians pioneered their own battery of welfare reforms. Indeed, not only did a number of state politicians play a large role in bringing the issue to a boil by campaigning on the promise to slash welfare and then forging ahead with grant cuts and time limits,[3] but they invented some of the symbolically potent features of congressional welfare reform proposals. Douglas Besharov and Karen Gardiner (1996) from the American Enterprise Institute reported (approvingly) that two-thirds of the states have adopted "behavior-related" welfare rules. The formula for these rules is simple: family benefits are cut if a woman or her children misbehave, if the child is truant from school, for example, or if the mother gives birth while on welfare. As a result of these various state level initiatives, many of which had to be approved by the Clinton administration before they were implemented, AFDC caseloads were already dropping rapidly, even before the new federal cutbacks were legislated. In July 1995, national caseloads were down 6.4% from the 1994 average, and some states had dropped much more. Indiana was down 18.4%, Massachusetts 15.8%, Michigan 14.3%, and this at a time when child poverty was increasing (Center for Law and Social Policy 1995). And then in early 1996, the nation's governors announced a bipartisan compromise on welfare reform that would allow huge cuts in welfare and the food stamp programs, impose time limits on the receipt of benefits, and rip away federal support for additional spending when need increases.

Why did this happen? Why the trumpeting of welfare as somehow a major and growing problem of American society when Aid to Families of Dependent Children was in fact a not a large program, however it is measured? Fewer than five million adults were on the rolls, and except for the recent recession, the number had not risen since the early 1970s. Measured as a proportion of the poor, or as a proportion of single parent households, the numbers on the rolls had in fact shrunk. And program costs were modest, to say the least, amounting to about 1 percent of the federal budget.

So, why the uproar? The question is highlighted when we also consider that the incessant talk about welfare by politicians simply doesn't fit the dominant view of how elections are won or lost in the United States. For more than half a century, both political scientists and pundits have taken for granted that voters were moved by "pocket book" issues. There were debates, of course, about whether voters responded to general economic conditions or to their personal economic condition, about whether they voted in response to past economic troubles or simply voted their current economic standing. But whatever the specific variants, it was assumed that economic conditions dominated modern elections, indeed that electoral outcomes could virtually be read off the economic indicators. Consistent with this view, incumbents campaigned by trying to deliver economic improvements as the election approached, and candidates campaigned with promises to do the same or better if the voters put them in office.

The preoccupation with welfare contradicts this model of electoral economism. While AFDC is a small program, the "reforms" proffered by all contenders, along with proposed cuts in other means-tested programs including Medicaid and social services, will inevitably mean not only benefit cuts for the poor, but massive public sector job losses, and downward pressure on wages among a huge number of less skilled workers in the private sector who will find themselves competing with the increasingly desperate people who lose their public jobs or benefits. In effect, instead of competing with promises of economic improvement, politicians are competing with proposals to worsen economic conditions for wide swaths of the voting public.

In this essay we will try to explain these developments. Our main argument is that the rise of welfare politics is symptomatic of the weakening of the electoral economism, or political Keynesianism, that has described American politics reasonably well since the New Deal. This development is often shrugged off as an inevitable reflection of the inability of government to deliver economic concessions as a result of the globalization of the economy. We think this argument about globalization is altogether too broad, and in any case, less applicable to the United States than to other advanced industrial nations. American politicians, especially Democratic politicians, are less inclined to campaign with economic appeals not because the measures that would be required are beyond the reach of government, but because they are pinioned by activated and politicized business interests. But either way, whether the causes lie in the penetration of global markets or in the politics of the capitalist class, the mode of electoral mobilization by means of economic appeals characteristic of the industrial era has weakened. And for the moment at least, a very American kind of fundamentalist irrationalism is taking its place, which the obsession with welfare signifies. In other words, the rise of welfare politics in the late 20th century U.S. reveals aspects of the twisted dynamics of the transition from industrial to postindustrial electoral politics in America.

The Usual Explanations

But before we turn to this broader argument, we need to deal with more familiar explanations, some of which do indeed have some bearing on the rise of welfare politics. One is that the drive for tax cuts is forcing welfare spending cuts. Another is that politicians are merely responding to the fact that Americans detest welfare.

First, tax cuts and spending cuts. The assault on the means-tested programs can be viewed simply as an expression of the greed of organized and mobilized business interests and the politicians they fund. This part of the story goes back at least to 1981. One of Reagan's first initiatives was a round of tax cuts, skewed toward business and the affluent. The cuts were huge, reducing federal revenues by about $750 billion in the first Reagan term. And the tax cuts were coupled with rapid increases in military spending. Of course, the deficit widened which, as we later learned from David Stockman, was not exactly unintentional (Stockman, 1986; Wills, 1996). The expectation was that the growing deficit would generate powerful pressures for reductions in spending on social programs. In the 1980s, however, the congress resisted these attempted cuts (and in 1983 went along with a social security tax increase that fell on working people instead).

After the election of 1994, the new Republican majority in the congress proposed another round of huge tax cuts, again tilted to benefit the most affluent, who stood to realize a windfall through cuts in capital gains and estate taxes. This time the plan to make up for the forfeited tax revenues with cuts in programs for the poor and the elderly was on the table. The earned income tax credit, which benefits low-income working families, would be slashed, and big cuts were proposed in all of the means-tested programs, and in student loans and Medicare as well.[4] But the program singled out for the biggest cuts was AFDC, which would lose an estimated 57% of its federal funding over the seven year projected budget (compared to Congressional Budget Office forecasts in 1995 of projected spending if there were no changes in the program). The reason for this tilt against programs for the poor seems transparent. The well-off want more big tax cuts. The easiest way to get them is to take them from the poor, who generally have neither lobbyists or beholden politicians to defend them. Indeed, one suspects that if there were more money in the budget for means-tested programs, the Congress would shy away from attempting cuts in better defended programs like Medicare altogether.

Still, greed could not be the whole of it. After all, the politicians leading this campaign are elected. They need voter support. And the polls do show popular support, both for the attack on government in general, and for the attack on programs for the poor. Why these animosities?

An obvious answer is that Americans, bred to a market culture that celebrates individual self-reliance·and material success, just don't like welfare or the poor who rely on it. Longstanding and widely shared convictions about the virtue of self-reliance and material success, and antipathy toward the poor, might thus also be part of the explanation for the meanness of current welfare policy initiatives. This possibility gains weight when we add that welfare policies and practices have always worked to reenforce such antipathies. Think, for example, of the meanings communicated by ancient practices for dealing with the supplicant poor, including the lash, the brand, and other rituals of public humiliation. Or think of the 19th century poor law system, with its elaborate arrangements for consigning the supplicant poor to hellholes called "houses of industry."

It is easy to recognize these practices as Durkheimian rituals for defining the poor as the marginal Other. They are not, however, only features of poor relief. They are also embedded in contemporary American relief practices. Thus the intricately different programs divide people into intricately differentiated categories—the able-bodied unemployed, impoverished adults without children, poor single parent families, the aged or disabled poor, the "insured" aged or disabled—helping to construct different identities, and different interests. And then, each of these program-constructed categories of people is dealt with differently: each program confers different rights on prospective beneficiaries, subjects them to different procedures for determining and maintaining eligibility, and each program provides beneficiaries with different levels of economic support.

By segregating the poor into different programs, American welfare policy reinforces the separation of the poor from working- and middle-class Americans, and also creates sharp divisions among the poor. And once categorized by the programs, the poor are then denigrated by the treatment accorded them. Benefits in the poor-serving programs are less likely to be a matter of right and more likely to be discretionary, subject to the successful hurdling of bureaucratic inquisitions and runabouts, and continuing bureaucratic surveillance, all of which shapes the understandings both of the people who endure this treatment, and the people who in a sense are the public audience for these rituals. Finally, and very important, recipients receive benefits which keep them very poor, ensuring their marginalization in an affluent and materialistic society.

So, there is something to the argument that attributes welfare cutbacks to the voters' antipathy to the program.[5] However, by definition, American cultural antipathies toward welfare and the poor are long-standing, and the policies and practices which reinforce them are long-standing as well.[6] But the zeal and stridency of the contemporary campaign for welfare reform is relatively new. While there are deep currents of dislike for the poor and the "dependent" in American culture, we still have to understand why they have welled up now. This is, we think, the big question. And a thoughtful answer will consider the broad developments that have contributed to the feebleness of electoral economism in contemporary American politics.

The Decline of Electoral Economism

Conditions would seem to be ripe for economic appeals to the electorate. The enormous changes sweeping through the American economy are clearly generating discontent and anxiety, perhaps even terror. Wages are falling, for most people, despite the fact that worktime is lengthening.[7] And as the old mass production industries shrink, new and onerous forms of work are spreading, in chicken processing or garbage recycling plants, for example, where the pace is hard and the work filthy, or in speeded-up service sector businesses where computers monitor strokes or bathroom breaks. Sweatshops again cluster in the older cities.

Meanwhile, inequalities are widening at a dizzying pace, as income and wealth shifts from workers to owners and managers of capital, and their corps of experts.[8] One measure captures the change: in the mid-1970s, chief executives earned 41 times the average wage; now the multiplier has increased to 225.[9] Meanwhile, the concentration of wealth in the United States has reached historic levels, with the top 1 percent claiming ownership of 42 percent of total assets, up from 33.7 percent in 1983, and up from 19 percent in 1976 (Wolff 1995 and 1996).

Naturally, there is discontent. But why does it take such perverse form? Why is popular ire now directed not to demands for economic reform, but instead against programs which provide at least some minimum security for the most vulnerable? And why, in the 1994 election, were there heavy Democratic losses to the Republicans—who promised such program cuts—among less-educated whites, who are among the big losers from labor market change, and are themselves at risk when income support programs are cut (Texiera and Rogers 1994)?[10]

The first thing to notice is the failure of political leaders, Democrats and Republicans alike, to articulate rational solutions to the economic hardships and insecurities that pervade the popular mood. FDR, JFK to an extent, and LBJ all talked to voters about broad economic and social conditions, promised public action, and in that context were even able to talk about the marginalized poor, and to build voter support for public action to ameliorate poverty. Clinton did the reverse. True, he campaigned in 1992 with "it's the economy, stupid" although he coupled that with welfare bashing and a good deal of rhetoric about family values and individual responsibility. More important, he did not deliver on his economic promises. He allowed a weak economic stimulus package to fail, never pushed hard for a restoration of the buying power of the minimum wage,[11] nor promoted legislation to stem the losses of the bleeding unions, and instead joined with the Republicans to become a champion of free trade and promoted the deregulation of international markets under NAFTA and GATT. Of course, there were economic promises: once international markets were unfettered, a a golden era of economic growth would ensue, a laissez faire utopia.[12] In fact, a Democratic president presided over an economic upturn in which productivity and profits moved up briskly, but wages stagnated, part-time and temporary work expanded, and earnings for the less educated continued to fall. And as the 1996 campaign began, Clinton was artfully echoing the Republican budget balancing, tax cut, and spending cut proposals. [13]

The key fact about our era which is said to explain these developments is the rise of global economic competition, fatally weakening the ability of nation states to control their economies. Government has suddenly been made helpless before markets, as Clinton seems to be helpless before the financial markets. To be sure, the penetration of goods, labor, and capital from abroad is a real factor in the economy, and especially in some industries. But the argument is deployed so broadly as to be misleading, although it is nevertheless a powerful factor in American politics.

This point made, we should also say that there is a good deal of capital mobility in the United States, which may lend a public credibility to arguments about globalization. But much of this mobility is within our own borders. In fact, important inter-regional shifts of industrial production began more than a century ago with the movement of the textile industry from New England to the South. Still, today most plant relocations have been from the old industrial centers of the Northeast and Midwest to the Sunbelt and the new cities. In other words, so far at least, most productive capital has remained within national borders. So far as markets are concerned, the national government retains the capacity to regulate the economy.

In fact, new production methods which facilitate outsourcing and reliance on less-skilled workers may have more to do with the alarming contemporary trend of increasing productivity and stagnant or declining wages than internation competition. [14] But this argument has none of the politically emasculating implications of the globalization argument. For one thing, technological changes in production methods are hardly unprecedented. From the replacement of the putting-out system with the factory, to the introduction of the assembly line, to the current explosion of computer-based tecnologies, the history of industrial capitalism has been the history of wrenching transformations. For another, and this is the point of our argument, the consequences of such innovations are entirely susceptible to government regulation, and therefore as much a question of political determination as market determination.

In short, while American political leaders have turned away from voter moblization through economic appeals, it is not because the American government is helpless to regulate the economy. Most other industrial nations are far more exposed to international trade and capital movements than the United States. Yet no other rich democratic nation has been so hard hit by the traumas which are widely attributed to globalization, including the evisceration of unions, wage cuts, the slashing of the public sector, and the widening extremes of poverty and wealth. Something is missing in the argument.

We think it is illuminating to shift attention from markets and market determinisms to the politics associated with globalization. A series of economic changes associated with postindustrialism, including not only increasing international circulation, but the introduction of "lean production" methods made possible by the new information technology, have paved the way for a much more aggressive capitalist class politics. Capital is pyramiding the leverage it gains from the increased mobility of goods and capital—or perhaps from the spectre of increased mobility— as well as from the insecurities generated by downsizing, in a series of vigorous political campaigns to achieve its preferred public policies.

To understand the paralyzing impact of fears internationalism in the United States, we have to attend not only or mainly to the economic data, which are ambiguous, but to politics, and particularly to business politics during the past two decades. Beginning in the 1970s, large employers became much more belligerent toward unions, stridently resisting new organizing efforts, and working to roll back earlier union gains. At the same time, business organized to change public policies. Of course, particular firms and industries have industries had always worked to promote their interests in politics. But in the past twenty years, business political ambitions have expanded, and so have business strategies. Near dormant business trade groups were revived, and new peak business coalitions were created and honed for political action. Business representatives and business money moved into the Republican party and electoral politics, developing sophisticated campaign techniques and the tight organization that money makes possible. And big business developed and perfected a political agenda, funding new national think tanks to do the work that, after the 1960s, universities could not be relied upon to do.

With organization and agenda in formation, business groups mounted a formidable ideological campaign (Herman 1996); they launched an argument about the natural and inevitable primacy of markets over politics and the state (no matter that organized business was itself using politics and the state to secure enormous new advantages, and not least to create some of the conditions for international penetration which were then described as natural and inevitable). The argument was, of course, in essence a revival of 19th century laissez faire, of the theory that market processes reflected the unfolding of the law of supply and demand. If there were social costs as a consequence of the unfettered operation of this species of natural law, if there were suffering, it was because people or places failed to meet the implacable tests of the market. Political interference with natural law only risked calamity. The new end-of-twentieth century twist on 19th century doctrine was that market law now operated on an international scale. Capital and goods now circled the globe in search of local markets where costs were lowest and profits highest, and these processes were beyond the reach of nation states whose authority was limited to their sovereign territories.

Americans have always been more susceptible to laissez faire doctrine than Europeans. For reasons much discussed in the literature on American exceptionalism, features of American culture, especially the emphasis on individualism, reinforced by racism and sectionalism, worked against class consciousness.[15] Moreover, this culture coexisted with and in some ways nourished institutional arrangements which inhibited class politics, including a fragmented and decentralized state structure and widespread disenfranchisement. When worker power did become important in the 1930s, the welfare state programs that emerged were themselves fragmented and decentralized, and heavily marked by racism, with the consequence that welfare state programs continued to nourish the ideological biases which had blunted working class influence in the first place.

Still, this large argument about the distinctiveness of American political culture notwithstanding, interpretations of the relationship of state and market in the contemporary United States seem remarkably fluid. After all, the experience of the Great Depression and the tutelage of Franklin Delano Roosevelt—who talked of "strong central government as a haven of refuge to the individual"—weakened if it did not shatter laissez-faire convictions.[16] And until very recently, belief in the responsibility of government for popular economic well-being continued to hold sway, even in the United States. Popular opinion remains volatile, and susceptible to counter arguments, whether mounted by oppositional political leaders, or by social movements that have yet to emerge.

But ideology does not merely reflect experience. It can also be a powerful force in the politics which shapes the institutions which in turn mold experience. A process like this helps to account for the institutional changes—the dismantling of Bretton Woods, the creation of the IMF—which facilitated international capital mobility, and the new institutions such as GATT and NAFTA which are now encouraging the expansion of trade. In these instances, a hegemonic ideology about the necessity and inevitability of the free movement of capital and goods helped to create the institutional conditions which then contributed to making the free movement of capital and goods a reality.[17]

This may well explain why the Republican juggernaut in Washington, tutored no doubt by business-backed think tanks, is moving to weaken the national government, and thus make the neo-laissez faire ideology of globalism "true," in the sense that people will come to experience the world in a way that confirms the ideology. The Republican Contract With America calls for new constraints on the national government that if enacted will indeed make government helpless to regulate markets.

Of course, the Contract is many things. It is, for example, propaganda, as suggested by the baldly rhetorical titles of its legislative planks: the American Dream Restoration Act; The Personal Responsibility Act; The Legal Accountability Act. Even the use of the language of contract can be seen as an argument, a symbolic importation of a market idea into political relations between the state and its citizenry. And behind the fog created by this sort of rhetoric, the Contract is also a set of tax and spending measures which accelerate the redistribution of income and wealth from the poor to the rich.

But we want to direct attention to another and important feature of this legislative program. Taken as a whole, it would strip the national government of the capacity to do what contemporary governments do (or did) to reduce the extremes of inequality, regulate economic instabilities, and curb business excesses. One large way to limit government is to limit its ability to spend. The proposal for a balanced budget amendment to the Constitution was intended to put a brake not only on spending by the national government, but on its ability to raise taxes as well, by requiring super majorities for the passage of tax increases in the congress. The route of constitutional amendment is extremely cumbersome, and the amendment for the time being has been shelved, although the simplistic balanced budget rhetoric invoking images of thrift and good housekeeping has clearly not receded. In the absence of a constitutional amendment, a new House rule requires 60% majorities on measures to raise taxes. Another severe limit on spending restricts the imposition by the federal government of unfunded mandates on state or local governments. Other bills would impede the federal government's ability to regulate business by requiring obstructive review procedures, or extravagant compensation to private owners for losses due to regulation. And still other measures are designed to discourage citizens from turning to the courts to resolve grievances against corporations. Finally, there are the proposals to radically slash and restructure federal means-tested programs.

Viewed together, these proposals suggest a pattern: the decentralized structure of the America state is being reinforced. As the national government is less and less able to do what governments do, responsibilities will devolve to the states, and in some program areas, federal funds will be transferred to the states as well.

The banner hoisted to explain these changes is that state governments are "closer to the people."[18] The slogan resonates with the convictions of the late 18th century anti-federalists who fought the original Constitution because they feared a remote central government would become the instrument of elites. But in the twentieth century, it is the state governments that are more sensitive to business political pressures, simply because state (and localities) are far more vulnerable to the threat of disinvestment.[19] This has been true for a long time. Early in this century, for example, efforts to pass state worker compensation laws were stymied by business threats to move to other states—until, that is, manufacturers themselves, prodded by multiplying damage suits in the courts, decided to back model and modest legislation.[20]

But if state governments have always been more susceptible to the bribe and threat of business investment and disinvestment, they are far more susceptible now, when capital is increasingly mobile, and when even a single corporate relocation can devastate a community (Chernick and Reschovsky 1995).[21] This, together with the fact that most movement of American business still takes place within our national borders, as plants move from Massachusetts to South Carolina, from Michigan to Tennessee, makes the fiscal and regulatory powers of the federal government more important than ever. And this may well be why congressional Republicans are working to cripple those powers.

In sum, a mobilized business class allied with a resurgent Republican party is both invoking the threat of capital mobility that appears to weaken state power, and taking large steps to make that threat real. Whether this agenda will actually be realized remains to be seen, of course. If it is, the ideology of neo-laissez faire will have contributed to the construction of institutional arrangements which do indeed make the state nearly helpless before markets.

The Rise of Fundamentalism

Everywhere in the world, when people are blocked from dealing with the problems of livelihood, community, respect, and security through politics, they become more susceptible to fundamentalist appeals. When institutional reforms seem impossible, frustrated publics are more likely to respond to calls for a politics of individual moral rejuvenation, typically coupled with calls to mobilize against some vulnerable group. This group becomes the Other, embodying a kind of moral pollution that is somehow to blame for the problems people experience in daily life.

Something like this seems to be underway in the United States. Politicians' appeals are directing popular political attention away from the issues of wages and jobs, for example, which had been taken for granted as the dominant preoccupations of electoral politics since the New Deal, to a politics of individual responsibility and "values." At the same time, and relatedly, political leaders are pointing to minorities and the poor, and especially poor women, as the miscreants, the polluters, whose transgressions of core values are responsible for contemporary troubles.

To be sure, these manipulative appeals draw on real anxieties generated by a culture in flux. Not least important, sexual and family mores are changing, eroding a world in which men are men, women are women, and the rules for mating and family life are clear. Changes of this sort can generate a distinctive terror, perhaps because the meanings they challenge are so deeply imprinted in early childhood. These cultural insecurities clearly helped to fuel the rise of the Christian Right and its entry into Republican politics. But fundamentalist appeals are not restricted to the Christian Right. They have become central to the electioneering of both Democrats and Republicans, as suggested by the "family values" theme of the Clinton 1996 State of the Union message.

The campaign against welfare plays a central part in this electioneering. Indeed, the relentless public charges leveled by politicians and conservative think tank experts are as much an argument about what is wrong with America as an argument about welfare policy. And the heart of the argument is the idea that big American problems—deepening poverty, the breakdown of family and community, a kind of demoralization overtaking our society—are centered on poor and minority women. These women are said to contradict all of the old Protestant virtues of industry and self-reliance, of chastity and self-restraint. And their moral turpitude is perversely encouraged by government welfare programs.

The availability of welfare, the argument goes, allows young women to quit school or work and have out-of-wedlock babies. And once on the dole, these women become trapped and dependent, unable to summon the initiative to get a job, indeed unable even to raise their children properly. As a consequence, children raised on welfare turn into school dropout, and delinquents, and then into welfare users themselves. Welfare, in short, is encouraging the spread of a moral rot in American society. The solution is not hard to see: eliminate the perverse incentives. This "tough love" will deter young women from having babies in the first place, and those who already have will be forced to go to work to support their child or children. There may be some hardship along the way, but this is the only way to make poor women moral and self-reliant.

This litany is by now so familiar that it has worn ruts in our minds. But familiar or not, the argument does not stand up to scrutiny. What sense does it make to force women into the labor market if there are not jobs out there for unskilled women with childrearing responsibilities that pay enough to support a family? Even during this economic upturn, the labor market is saturated, with 8 million officially unemployed, and some 25 million part-time and temporary workers, many of whom would prefer regular full-time work if they could get it.[22] Real wages for the unskilled and the young continue to fall, and fewer of these jobs pay health or pension benefits. Simply slashing welfare will not create jobs or raise wages. In fact, it will make the working conditions of those who have jobs worse, for welfare cutoffs will crowd the low wage labor market with millions of desperate women, ready to work at any wage and under any conditions.[23]

The documented results of actual efforts to end welfare by sending these women "off to work" also argue their absurdity as policy, if not as political talk. We have in fact been "solving" the welfare problem for twenty five years with a series of much-heralded welfare-to-work programs, all premised on the idea that what welfare mothers need is a little training and a big shove to make it in the job market. And for 25 years we have been evaluating the results of these reforms, called WIP or WIN or GAIN or JOBS or whatever. The results are trivial, or non-existent. The programs increase the job success of women by tiny percentages, when they increase job placement at all, and they have a similarly negligible effect on earnings. Even tiny percentages produce a few smiling and successful women for the TV talk shows. But no TV host invites the women who couldn't make it in the jobs they got and had to return to welfare. And no one invites the mothers who suffer the harassment of being hustled from one foolish work preparedness scheme to another, and who are then perhaps sanctioned with slashed benefits if they do not cooperate. Nor, needless to say, is there research to measure this harassment, because researchers study the questions that government or foundation funders want answered.

74

The political talk about welfare causing a tide of "illegitimacy" is, needless to say, even more potent than the talk about work and dependency. The polemics get very excited, as when Charles Murray announced in the Wall Street Journal in 1993 that illegitimacy was "the most important social problem of our time," driving poverty, crime, drugs, illiteracy, homelessness, and so on. But while out-of-wedlock births are indeed increasing, they are increasing in all strata of the society and not only among welfare recipients or potential recipients. Indeed, they are increasing in all western countries. Both divorce rates and single parenthood have skyrocketed throughout the west in the past two decades. This is almost certainly the result of epochal changes in sexual and family mores, and not the result of the American AFDC program.

To be sure, the United States does have more single-parent families than other western countries. But this very fact suggests that welfare is not significantly related to single-parent family formation, since most other rich countries provide far more generous assistance to single mothers.[24] Other facts also argue against this familiar "welfare causes illegitimacy" argument. Most obviously, welfare benefits have declined sharply over the past two decades, but out-of-wedlock births have not.[25] Nor is there a discernible relationship between the level of state welfare benefits and out-of-wedlock birthrates.

Moreover, the all-too-familiar view that welfare is the cause of illegitimacy among black women does not stand up. The nonmarital birth rates of black women have in fact not changed in two decades. What has changed is that marital birth rates have declined, for the reason that there are fewer men in black communities who have the income or stability to be reasonable husbands. In any case, the percentage of single mothers collecting welfare has actually declined over time, which would not be the case if women were having babies to get welfare.

So much for the facts. But this sort of argument is not won or lost with facts, and certainly not with facts alone. Opinions are too inflamed. They evoke preoccupations deeply etched in American culture, including our age-old dislike of the poor, especially the supplicant poor, our racial antipathies, and our strange American obsession with sexual transgression memorialized in the figure of Hester Prynne. And they draw

finally on the awful vulnerabilities that people experience as their familiar worlds collapse, for the "the dynamic force of otherness...[is] the
projection of the internal other as a defense against one's own vulnerability" (Crawford 1994).

Will the invocation of these ancient American devils continue to distract majorities of American voters? Or, rather, will it distract them
enough to allow governing elites to continue to ignore economic issues,
especially declining wages and spiraling inequalities? The evidence so far
is not definitive. A sitting Democratic president continues to talk mainly
about family values, and his Republican challengers try to ease economic
discontents with incantations about balanced budgets and tax cuts. And
both sides compete to rouse support with calls for welfare reform that
tell a story of American decline and demoralization that singles out welfare mothers as the main culprit.

So, what are likely to be the political consequences of the draconian
cutbacks in means-tested programs, coupled with continued rhetorical
assaults on the poor? The palpable evidence of desperate poverty will
accumulate, in child beggars on the streets, women and babies huddled
over grates, already devastated urban slums turned into medieval waste-
lands. But these cruelties by no means guaranteee a reversal of course.
To the contrary, the visible and deepening impoverishment of poor
women and children may well only confirm the corruption imputed to
the Other in the story of welfare reform.

We can spin the scenario out. Economic insecurity continues and
worsens, and so does the degradation of the worst off, feeding fundamentalist calls for individual moral rejuvenation and the purging of the
Other. This sort of politics is not, after all, entirely alien to the American experience. It recalls episodes of murderous hate politics that have
swept through the country before, as when Chinese immigrants were
stoned, their homes torched; or black newcomers to the cities mur-
dered by enraged white crowds; or impoverished whites in the South
who expressed their rage in the lynch mob and in a system of terror that
sustained the southern caste order for more than a century. All such
episodes drew on economic grievances. Yet all channeled economic discontent into a crazed politics of scapegoating.

Pat Buchanan with his appeals that stir economic anger but suggest no program beyond a fierce hostility to a government that gives hard-earned tax dollars to welfare moms; the rise of the paranoid militias and their doctrine of national and racial purity; the Christian Right and their preoccupation with sexual morality, all of these recent developments argue that fundamentalism is flourishing in American politics.

But other parts of our history suggest that hate politics will not work forever, and maybe not for long. For one thing, the actual program cutbacks planned under the banner of "welfare reform" will have very wide reverberations. It will not only be poor women and their babies who will huddle over the grates. The huge take-backs contemplated are not mainly in welfare spending, but in Medicaid, housing, and social service programs. These cuts will mean enormous job losses in the public and voluntary sector, with potentially devastating effects on working class urban neighborhoods, and on the landlords and small businesses that depend on poor and working class consumers. And, of course, as the consequences of "welfare reform" spread, dragging down broader swaths of the population, the raw and simple politics of victim-blaming becomes less persuasive.

Earlier periods of aggressive and reckless business mobilization, in the 1890s and 1920s, helped precipitate the popular mobilizations and electoral convulsions that made possible the great political reforms of the twentieth century. First in the Progressive era, then again during the New Deal, social movements combined with electoral instability to force the forging of new government initiatives which tempered business excesses and reduced the extremes of inequality.

No one has ever successfully predicted the moments when ordinary people find their footing, discover new capacities for solidarity and power, and new visions of the possible. Still, American democracy depends on the perennial emergence of popular revolt, now as always.

Originally published in 1995.

Notes

1. Portions of this article were first published in *The New Left Review*, no. 213, September/October 1995, in *The Progressive*, February 1995, and in Dissent, fall 1996. A longer version was published in Clarence Y.H. Lo and Michael Schwartz, eds., *Clinton and the Conservative Agenda*, Blackwell 1997.

2. Many Democratic pundits applauded Clinton's welfare initiatives, arguing that it would bring defecting middle class Democrats back to the party. See for example the "Afterword" on the 1992 election in Edsall and Edsall (1992).

3. Some 22 states have imposed some type of time limit on benefits, according to the Health and Human Services Department, as reported in the *Washington Post*, February 3, 1996.

4. The Center on Budget and Policy Priorities (1995) reports that entitlement programs for the poor, which account for one-quarter of entitlement spending, were slated by the Congress to absorb 50 percent of entitlement cuts. Non-entitlement programs for the poor, which account for 12 percent of federal spending for non-entitlement programs, were targeted for 62 percent of funding cuts.

5. David Ellwood (1988), who later became a Clinton advisor and the architect of the Clinton welfare proposals, thought strict time limits on the receipt of cash benefits would appease public hostility and make other worthwhile reforms possible.

6. In fact, while Americans don't like welfare, they express little hostility toward the poor children who constitute two-thirds of the welfare roles. A *New York Times*/CBS poll in December 1994 found that only 9 percent favored cuts in spending for poor children, while 47 percent favored an increase. See Herman 1996.

7. On this point, there are of course numerous sources. See for example Mishel and Bernstein (1996) and Danziger and Gottschalk (1995).

8. Income gaps are at their widest point since the Census Bureau began collecting these data in 1967.

9. The estimate, by executive compensation expert Graef Crystal, is cited in *U.S. News and World Report*, January 22, 1996. Crystal elsewhere estimates that CEO's at the biggest U.S. companies earn on average 6 times what their Japanese counterparts earn, and 4 times what their German counterparts earn. See the *New York Times*, March 9, 1996.

10. Duane Swank (1995) identifies a suggestively parallel pattern in Western Europe where marginal workers and postindustrial economic change contribute to the fortunes of radical right parties.

11. Clinton proposed a modest 90 cent an hour increase in the minimum wage at the end of 1994, (and reiterated his support for an increase in his 1996 State of

the Union message). But while his proposal would prevent the minimum from dipping to its lowest level in 40 years, it would by no means restore it to the levels of twenty five years ago.

12. Polanyi (1957) characterized 19th century convictions about the unregulated free market as a utopian and disasterous ideology.

13. The polls clearly reflected these political maneuvers. In 1992, a whopping 51 percent of those surveyed said the economy and jobs were the country's most pressing problems. By 1996, the polls showed overwhelming dissatisfaction with "the way things are going," and intense personal economic insecurity. But reducing the deficit had replaced jobs as the most important political issue. See *The New York Times*, January 23 and February 1, 1996.

14. For a discussion, see Head (1996). Jason De Parle (1994) reports an informal poll at a meeting of 18 prominent economists at the end of 1994 at the Federal Reserve Bank in New York. They attributed, on average, only 10 percent of increased wage inequality to international trade. A far larger factor, they thought, was technological change.

15. For one of the more recent excursions into this huge literature, see Lipset (1996).

16. The quote is from a speech to the Commonwealth Club in 1932. See Singer (1976) cited in Schurin (1996). Schurin argues that this definition of the role of government was a strong and consistent theme in FDR's public addresses.

17. On this point, see Domhoff 1996.

18. *The New York Times*, in an article entitled "The States Won't Be Cruel" on February 9, 1996 quotes Governor William Weld of Massachusetts: "We're closer and more directly answerable to our citizens than the cloud-dwellers in Washington are."

19. This generalization should be tempered by another: business interests play the federal system, using multiple and overlapping sources of authority opportunistically, or even parlaying them against each other. Thus Goldberg (1996) points out that business interests are turning to national government to override state product liability and environmental standards, rhetorical assaults on big government notwithstanding. For a general discussion of the political uses of centralization and decentralization, see Piven and Friedland (1984).

20. FDR seemed to understand the problem well in 1936 when, in a Chicago speech, he likened corporate financiers to "kidnappers and bank robbers [who] could in high-powered cars speed across state lines" and for that reason had to be controlled by federal law (Zevin 1946, pp. 63-64.).

22. Lester Thurow (1996) estimates the number of job seekers by including contingent workers and those who drop out of the normal economy. He concludes that real unemployment is about one-third of the workforce.

23. Mishel and Schmitt (1996) estimate the impact of welfare recipients pushed into the low-wage labor market could be nearly 12 percent nationally, and much higher in states with large welfare populations.

24. According to K. McFate, R. L. Lawson, and W. J. Wilson (1991) the U.S. lifts fewer single-parent families out of poverty through income transfers than any of seven Western industrial nations studied. In the Netherlands, Sweden, and the United Kingdom, at least 75 percent of all single-parent families in poverty were lifted out of poverty; in France about half; in West Germany a third; in Canada a fifth; in the U.S. 4.6 percent.

25. For recent reviews of the evidence on out-of-wedlock births, see McLanahan (1994) and Hoynes (1996). For a more general review of data on welfare utilization, Twentieth Century Fund (1995).

References

BESHAROV, DOUGLAS J. AND KAREN N. GARDINER. 1996. "Paternalism and Welfare Reform," *The Public Interest*, No. 122, Winter.

BURTLESS, GARY 1995. "Widening U.S. Income Inequality and the Growth in World Trade." Paper prepared for the September 1995 meeting of the Tokyo Club in Dresden, Germany.

CENTER FOR LAW AND SOCIAL POLICY. 1995. "AFDC Caseload Declines: Implications for Block Grant Planning," Washington D.C.

CENTER ON BUDGET AND POLICY PRIORITIES, "Only High-Income Households Have Recovered Fully From the Recession," Washington D.C., October 24, 1995.

CHERNICK, HOWARD AND ANDREW RESCHOVSKY, "Devolution in Federalism: Prospects and Policy Responses," paper prepared for Economic Policy Institute Conference on Devolution in Federalism, Washington D.C., November 27, 1995.

CONGRESSIONAL BUDGET OFFICE, *The Economic and Budget Outlook: An Update*, August 1995.

ROB CRAWFORD, "Reflections on Health, Culture, and AIDS," *Social Science Medicine*, vol. 39, no. 10, Elsevier Science Limited, 1994.

Danziger and Gottschalk 1995

DEPARLE, JASON. 1994. See "Class is No Longer a Four-Letter Word," *New York Times Magazine*, March 17.

DOMHOFF, G. WILLIAM. *State Autonomy or Class Dominance? Case Studies on Policy Making in America*, New York, Aldine de Gruyter, 1996.

EDSALL, THOMAS BYRNE WITH MARY D. EDSALL. 1992. *Chain Reaction*, New York, Norton.

ELLWOOD, DAVID. *Poor Support*, New York, Basic Books, 1988.

HEAD, SIMON. 1996. "The New, Ruthless Economy," *The New York Review*, February

HERMAN, EDWARD. 1996. "The Balanced Budget Ploy." *XUZ Magazine*. February.

———. 1996. "The Market Attack on Dissent," *Z Magazine*, March.

HOYNES, HILARY WILLIAMSON. 1996. "Does Welfare Play Any Role in Female Headship Decisions?" Institue for Research on Poverty Discusssion Paper No. 1078-95, Madison, Wisconsin.

GOLDBERG, LENNY. 1996. See "Come the Devolution," *The American Prospect*, Winter.

GORDON, DAVID. "The Global Economy: New Edifice or Crumbling Foundations?" *New Left Review*, no. 168, March/April 1988.

LIPSET, SEYMOUR MARTIN. 1996. *American Exceptionalism: A Double Edged Sword*. New York, W. W. Norton.

MCFATE, K., R.L.LAWSON, AND W. J. WILSON. 1991. "Poverty, Inequality and the Crisis of Social Policy: Summary of Findings," Joint Center for Political and Economic Studies, Washington D.C., September.

MCLANAHAN, SARA S. 1994. "The Consequences of Single Motherhood," *The American Prospect*, Summer.

MISHEL L. AND J. BERNSTEIN, "America's Continuing Wages Problems: Deteriorating Real Wages for Most and Growing Inequality," in L. Mishel and J. Schmitt, eds., *Beware of the U.S. Model: Jobs and Wages in a Deregulating Economy*. Economic Policy Institute, 1996

PIVEN, FRANCES FOX AND ROGER FRIEDLAND. 1984. "Public Choice and Private Power," in Andrew Kirby, Paul Knox, and Steve Pinch, eds., *Public Service Provision and Urban Development*, New York St. Martins Press.

POLANYI, KARL. 1957. *The Great Transformation*, Boston, Beacon Press.

STOCKMAN, DAVID. 1986. *The Triumph of Politics: Why the Reagan Revolution Failed*, New York: Harper and Row, 1986.

MISHEL, LAWRENCE AND JOHN SCHMITT. 1996. "Cutting Wages by Cutting Welfare: The Impact of Reform on the Low-Wage Labor Market," Briefing Paper, Economic Policy Institute, Washington D.C..

ROBERT J. SAMUELSON, "Global Mythmaking," *Newsweek* May 29, 1995.

RONALD SCHURIN, "A Party Form of Government," Ph.D. dissertation completed at the Graduate School and University Center of the City University of New York, 1996.

AARON SINGER, ED., *Campaign Speeches of American Presidential Candidates*, New York, Unger, 1976,

SWANK, DUANE. "Right-Wing Populism in Western Europe," paper prepared for delivery at the 1995 Annual Meetings of the American Political Science Association, August 31-September 3, Chicago, Illinois.

TEXIERA, RUY AND JOEL ROGERS, "Who Deserted the Democrats in 1994?" *The American Propect*, 1994.

THUROW, LESTER. 1996. "The Crusade That's Killing Prosperity," *The American Prospect*, March-April.

TWENTIETH CENTURY FUND. 1995. *Welfare Reform: A Twentieth Century Fund Guide to the Issues*, New York, Twentieth Century Fund Press.

WESTERN, BRUCE. 1995. "Union Decline in Eighteen Advanced Capitalist Countries," *American Sociological Review*, vol. 60, no. 2, April.

WILLS, GARY. 1996. "It's His Party." *New York Times Magazine*, August 11.

WOLFF, EDWARD N. "How the Pie Is Sliced: America's Growing Concentration of Wealth," *The American Prospect* summer 1995.

————— "Time for a Wealth Tax," *Boston Review*, February/March 1996.

ZEVIN, B. D. 1946. *The Selected Addresses of Franklin Delano Roosevelt*, Boston: Houghton Mifflin.

Part II

Race Politics

4

Introduction

The party of the New Deal is wrecked, having lost much of its base in the South and in the big cities. Most white southerners are Republicans; many northern working class whites have also switched. There will never again be a national Democratic party system predicated on the one-party oligarchy that governed the feudal political economy of the South. Nor will there ever again be a Democratic party predicated on the industrial political economy of the North.

Blacks and their liberal/left allies are being blamed for the demise of the party because they called for policies which alienated southern whites and blue-collar workers. One analyst after another claims that the demands blacks made—such as affirmative action and busing—"debilitated the Democratic party"[1] by setting "the white and black working classes at each other's throats"[2] and thus destroyed class-based politics in the United States. We take up this claim in the first paper in this section, "Race, Class, and the Travails of the Democratic Party," which was written expressly for the present volume. We show that it was the white racist South, not black demands, that destroyed the possibility for working class politics.

The plain fact is that any demands by blacks would and did cause trouble for the Democratic Party. When blacks demanded jobs, housing, schools, and political power, that caused an uproar among big city Democrats, and accelerated defections. When they demanded the right to vote and an end to Jim Crow, that caused an uproar among southern Democrats, which is why the northern wing acquiesced in the southern caste system for so long.

So, the Democratic Party that rose to national power in the 1930s colluded in the subjugation of blacks, exempting the South from labor legislation to fit the needs of planters, and resisting civil rights legislation. If the party had continued to be stable and dominant, the South would continue to enjoy its inordinate power to block civil rights legislation in the Congress, and the struggle for greater racial equality would have been stymied. Gains for blacks and party breakup went together. That's the way it was.

Southern white Republication voters have since become a major constituency supporting the attack on labor and civil rights, and income-maintenance entitlements. This is the political legacy of the Democratic Party's southern bourbons. They not only prevented a labor party from developing earlier in the century, but they created a political culture that now undergirds the attack on the social compact.

For most of this century, black hopes for liberation from racial subjugation oscillated between strategies of either integration or separatism. During the early and heady days of the civil rights movement, the ideal of integration prevailed, especially in the wake of the 1954 U.S. Supreme Court opinion striking down segregated education in the South (a ruling that was itself the culmination of years of civil rights litigation). At first, the northern black movement adopted the integrationist goal of the southern movement. However, by the mid-1960s, some blacks began to define white resistance to integrating the sacred precincts of school and neighborhood as intractable. As anger and street protests flared on both sides, many in the black movement turned away from the historic goal of integration and called instead for black power and "community control." This shift in the movement distressed many black leaders and especially their liberal sympathizers who viewed the turn away from integration as the betrayal of moral principle.

For our part, we were also deeply skeptical of the integrationist strategy as a way to improve the conditions of the black poor. As we saw it, years-long efforts by liberals to promote integrated housing and schools had done nothing to dent residential racial concentration. The few victories that were won were quickly undone by the segregationist strategies of the real estate industry. By the late 1960s the pattern of segregation was already so massive that the scale of population redistribution required by any serious integration effort boggled the mind. Hundreds of thousands of whites would have had to move from the suburbs to the ghettos, and equal numbers from the ghettos relocated to the suburbs. The idea was preposterous.

Not only was integration failing, but the effort was defeating other parts of the black and liberal agenda. Persistent efforts to saddle government programs for the inner city poor with the requirement for integration had undermined white political support for these programs, so that urban blacks lost both the ephemeral goal of integration and the very practical benefits of improved schools, or housing, or public facilities. We also argued that it was not even clear that housing integration, the kingpin of other integration efforts, was desirable. The main problem urban blacks confronted was, after all, a problem of power, and the main chance we saw for them to gain political power was residential concentration.

There was nothing especially novel in observing that minorities could gain influence in a geographically based electoral-representative system only if they were geographically concentrated. This was certainly how earlier ethnic minorities had gained a measure of influence, first in city politics, and then with the rise of the New Deal, in national politics. After all, today's Congressional Black Caucus has been made possible by residential segregation. There was, then, the prospect that blacks might follow the path of European ethnic groups, although we also saw a grim difference. Blacks would rise to ascendance in the big industrial cities at the very moment when those cities were losing influence in national politics to the suburbs and to the new cities of the sunbelt.

In 1966, we published an article, included here, called "The Case Against Urban Segregation," in which we predicted both that housing integration would fail and that the quality of housing in the ghetto would deteriorate. The article was eagerly seized upon by some black leaders as justification for the turn toward separatism and "black power." However, many civil rights and liberal leaders were outraged. Whitney M. Young, Jr., director of the National Urban League, published a response called "The Case for Urban Desegregation: An Answer to Piven and Cloward"[3] in which he deplored the turn toward separatism and claimed that it came, "strangely enough, at a time when there is almost unprecedented intellectual ferment, a time when new ideas and new solutions for the enormous problems afflicting the black poor abound."

It's now 30 years later. What of those "new ideas and new solutions"? The fact is that the quality of ghetto housing in many older cities is worse, and the ghettos are as segregated as ever, much as we predicted. Douglas D. Massey and Nancy Denton in their recent book, *American Apartheid: Segregation and the Making of the Underclass*,[4] conclude that the "level of segregation is well above the highest ever recorded for European ethnic groups," and that the cities have become "hypersegregated."

Nevertheless, Massey and Denton, like others before them, insist that nothing short of massive desegregation can solve the ills of the ghetto, from school failure to crime. "If segregation is permitted to continue," they claim, "poverty will inevitably deepen and become more persistent, crime and drugs will become more firmly rooted, and social institutions will fragment further under the weight of deteriorating conditions (p. 236)."

But why would integration efforts succeed now? Hundreds of thousands of whites are no more likely to trade places with ghetto residents than they were earlier, and in any case the subsidies that would be required to provide housing in the suburbs for poorer people have been slashed. Urban desegregation is not going to happen. The problem with the Massey and Denton "solution," in short, is that it won't work politically. And if it won't work, why write a book advocating it? By focusing on this unworkable solution, the housing of the black poor will continue to be neglected because there will be fewer funds for construction and rehabilitation.

In the final article in this section, "The Urban Fiscal Crisis," written in the 1970s, we explain the intense conflicts then welling up between largely white municipal employees and black newcomers. Blacks were, we said, competing for a share of the municipal jobs, services and honors that earlier arrivals to the cities had won. Organized municipal employees not only defended their turf against black wage and benefit demands, but they took advantage of the political instabilities associated with racial transition to escalate their demands. These conflicts were the more bitter, we thought, because they were fought out within the limits of strained municipal budgets.

The old battles over desegregation and municipal patronage are now overshadowed by the relentless assault on the basic terms of the social compact. But the battles are part of the story of the assault because they both exposed and deepened the searing race conflicts that divide the American working class, and thus help explain why the attack on the popular victories of the 1930s and 1960s has been so successful.

1997

Notes

1. Thomas Byrne Edsall, with Mary Edsall, *Chain Reaction*, W.W. Norton, 1991, p. 292.

2. Michael Tomasky, *Left for Dead*, NY The Free Press, 1996, p. 26. See also Jim Sleeper, *The Closest of Strangers: Liberalism and the Politics of Race in New York*. New York, W.W. Norton, 1990.

3. "The Case for Urban Integration: An Answer to Piven and Cloward," *Social Work*, Volume 12, No. 3 (July 1967).

4. Cambridge, Harvard University Press, 1993.

5

Race, Class, and the Travails
of the Democratic Party

That the Democratic party has been foundering for the past quarter of century is indisputable. Its once overwhelming majority in party identification has been whittled away, and except in the aftermath of Watergate, the party has been unable to win the Presidency—the pinnacle of the American party system—since 1964. The usual reason offered for the party's decline is race conflict. As blacks urbanized and became more important among Democratic constituencies, their presence and their demands drove many whites who had been the stalwarts of the party into Republican columns, especially in Presidential contests.

While this racial explanation ignores too much, especially the impact of gender and of broad "postindustrial" changes in the American economy and society on Democratic loyalties, it also contains a good deal of truth. The conflicts generated by the post-World War II black movement did weaken the Democrats, driving southern whites out of the party, and a good many northern whites as well. There are powerful reasons this is so. Race has been the most searing cleavage in American political life, and the feelings it aroused have been the very stuff of Democratic party appeals since the Civil War. The "identity politics" of white supremacy in the South, and of white ethnic parochialism in the northern cities, was the glue of Democratic constituency building.[1] That a movement to press black interests would wreak havoc within a party built on racism was virtually inevitable.

Little of this is acknowledged in recent discussions of race and the decline of the Democratic party. Instead of beginning at what is a reasonable beginning and probing into the long history of white racism and the Democratic party, the new wisdom dates the party's troubles from the emergence of the contemporary black movement. The trouble is not racism and its deep roots in American society, in party organization, and indeed in governmental structure. Rather, the problem begins with the the divisive demands of blacks and their liberal allies for civil and political rights, and for race-specific remedies, to overcome the effects of discrimination, such as affirmative action or school integration, or—most egregious of all—"welfare rights."[2] These demands were perverse in their effects. By highlighting race, they exacerbated racial divisions among Democratic constituencies, and fragmented the party. And if it was foolish to raise these demands, it was nothing short of madness to advance them with the flamboyant and disruptive tactics that characterized the black movement. The ultimate effect was to antagonize white working class voters, driving them into the arms of the Republican party.

Undergirding this argument is the premise that by weakening the party of the New Deal, the black movement weakened America's labor party, whatever its faults. Black demands drove whites from the party, ending Democratic chances of winning the presidency, and with that, the possibility of advancing progressive causes generally. If only blacks had been less demanding, the Democratic party would have remained intact, and its progressive agenda triumphant. And a dominant New Deal labor party would have benefitted blacks far more than the divisive and contorted politics of the 1960s.

This analysis turns history on its head. Race-specific demands by blacks did not destroy a labor party because there was no such party to destroy, and a main reason had to do with the the racist accommodations and appeals on which the New Deal party was built. These arrangements not only doomed black aspirations for political rights and economic progress. They also prevented the Democratic party from developing into a labor party during the brief period in American history when that seemed possible. Ultimately, the black movement contributed to the fracturing of the racist arrangements that undergirded the Democrats. This should be viewed as an achievement. To be sure, the conditions which had once made a labor party seem possible in the United States have passed, at least if we think of a labor party as based on workers in the mass production industries. But labor party or no, some progress was finally made in realizing black aspirations for political and economic rights. That of itself was a historic change. Moreover, by removing some of the obstacles which doomed earlier labor party hopes, it may make more feasible the emergence of a party formation that enlists the new and diverse working class of a postindustrial society.

The currently popular charge that black-inspired race conflict fractured the American version of a labor party is of course nourished by nostalgia for the New Deal. And there was a brief moment at the depth of the depression when the transformation of the Democrats into a labor party seemed possible. In the election of 1932, widespread panic and rising protests in the urban north prodded Franklin Delano Roosevelt to inject the language of class into national political rhetoric. Within a few years, continuing depression and a militant working class goaded a reluctant FDR into finally supporting a number of labor-oriented policies, including the Social Security Act, the National Labor Relations Act, and Fair Labor Standards Act. With these developments, the AF of L disavowed its traditional policy of abstaining from electoral politics, and the newly organized CIO mobilized to work hard for the party, and even became something like a local party apparatus in some industrial centers.[3] By the 1940s, working class support for the party reached peak levels.[4] However, the moment did not last. By the 1950s, labor support for the party was ebbing rapidly, and the era when the Democratic party looked something like a labor party was over.[5] Democratic accommodation of the racist South was a major reason.

Over the only slightly longer run it became clear that the Democratic leadership was responsive less to a galvanized labor movement, than to elements in the party that predated the convulsions of the New Deal. The Democratic party as it developed in the post–Civil War years was a peculiar sectional coalition between state bosses from the one-party south and big city Democratic bosses in the industrial North. Underpinning this political coalition were the economic ties between big city bankers and merchants and the cotton economy of the south. But whether in the urban north or the south, ethnic and racial hatreds were the stuff out of which popular party loyalty was often built. These arrangements predated the New Deal, and blocked the emergence of a labor-oriented party when that seemed possible. Moreover, there was no way that blacks could make substantial gains from Democratic leaders, and especially from Democratic presidents, so long as this coalition and its racially-based organizing strategies remained dominant.

In particular, the national party was hostage to its southern wing. The South had in fact been the bedrock of Democratic strength since the Civil War, and especially after the Democratic debacle in the election of 1896. However, for much of that time, Republicans controlled the national government, and southern Democrats were a minority influence. Ironically, the ascendance of the Democrats to unchallenged national power in the 1930s, an ascendance made possible by the shift of urban workers and western farmers, gave the southern wing a virtual hammerlock on federal policy.

The grip of the South was rooted in part in constitutionally defined features of American government, which both decentralized governmental power to the states, and fragmented national authority so as to give state power blocs a veto over national policy.[6] These arrangements were not accidental, but reflected the post-revolutionary compromise struck with the slave states that made the union possible. From the outset, the decentralization of governmental authority permitted the southern oligarchy to construct a political system that shored up the caste-based plantation economy without interference from the national government. Under the banner of "states rights," southern elites forged a virtually autonomous regional power structure, using the authority granted the states under the Tenth Amendment to create the laws and practices which undergirded the plantation economy and the caste labor system on which it rested. Not least important, decentralization allowed the southern oligarchy to eliminate electoral insurgency during the late 19th century by passing state laws that disenfranchised most of the population, blacks and poorer whites alike. Even as late as the 1930s, southern turnout in presidential elections averaged only 25 percent of the age-eligible electorate.

Constitutional arrangements also helped account for the grip of the South on national policy. Southern power in the Congress was ensured by the representation of states, not persons, in the Senate, and then shored up again by the filibuster. A constitutional system of divided powers meant that Democratic presidents had to bargain with southern powerbrokers to get their legislative agenda passed. Moreover, the disproportionate weight of the South in the electoral college made Presidents bend toward the South to ensure their own electoral prospects.

Other procedural protections were grafted onto these constitutional safeguards of sectional power, including the creation of standing legislative committees and a powerful rules committee whose chairmen were selected according to a seniority system which privileged representatives from uncontested one-party districts. And until 1936, the Democratic party rule that the presidential nominee had to be approved by two-thirds of the convention delegates gave the south virtual veto power over the selection process.[7]

For a time, the alliance with the South shored up the national Democratic party. Roosevelt consistently won the overwhelming majority of southern whites who had the vote. But the South extracted a high price for its fealty, effectively blocking the possibility of building a more labor-oriented Democratic party. Not least, the South opposed strong unions which, in other countries, made up the social base and mobilizing infrastructure of labor parties. Strong unions would have wreaked havoc with the southern system, and especially with its low-wage and caste-bound labor system. Accordingly, once the desperate years of the early Depression passed, southern members of the congress exerted themselves to limit New Deal reforms, and especially to limit their impact on the South.[8] By the late 1930s, southern congressmen joined with Republicans to protect state right-to-work laws and promote anti-labor legislation generally, to defeat social welfare programs, and to ensure that states retained authority over those social welfare programs that would undermine the low wage policies of the South.

These developments foreclosed the possibility that the Democratic party would be reborn as a labor party, or even that it would give great weight to its union constituency. Legal protection for unionism had been won in 1935, when a mass strike movement forced Roosevelt to support the National Labor Relations Act. For a brief period, the resulting union-party formation did not look very different from those in Western Europe. But Democratic support for unionism did not last. Within a few years, the once prolabor National Labor Relations Board was reconstituted to reflect the influence of southern Democrats and their business-oriented Republican allies in the Congress, and the legislative protections of unions were gradually whittled away. The Taft-Hartley Act, for example, passed by the alliance of Southern Democrats and Republicans in 1947, granted employers "free speech" rights to weaken labor organizing efforts, and introduced new curbs on the strike power. Classic labor solidary tactics like sympathy strikes, secondary boycotts, and mass picketing were prohibited. Most pernicious over the longer run, the Act explicitly legalized the right-to-work laws which had been spreading, especially in the southern states.[9]

These measures were a direct assault on the unions, weakening them in the short run, and crushing them as a force in American politics in the longer run, as the changing geography of American industrial investment shifted jobs to the sunbelt where unions were weak and right to work laws prevailed.[10] And if mass unionism was doomed, so were the prospects of a Democratic reconstruction as a labor party.

But the leaders of the actual Democratic party, still dominated by a sectional coalition in which the South had critical leverage, and in which labor influence in the North was offset by the continuing power of the big city bosses and their ethnic machines,[11] did not much resist. To be sure, facing a third party challenge from the Left in the 1948 election, Truman vetoed Taft-Hartley. But when Southern Democrats provided the margin of votes permitting the Congress to override his veto, Truman went on to use the powers the Act granted him repeatedly. Not until the late 1970s did a Democratic president take the initiative in trying to staunch the bleeding of the unions by restoring some of the protections won in the 1930s. But even Carter's feeble effort was defeated, again by an alliance of southern Democrats and business-oriented Republicans in the congress.

The southern wing of the Democratic party was nothing less than triumphant in shaping national social welfare policy, and that too helped spell the decline of the party. In western Europe, labor parties promote government regulatory and social welfare programs which provide a measure of economic security to their working class constituencies. But while the southern oligarchy had supported emergency relief during the desperate years of the early New Deal, its support for more lasting social welfare measures was at best grudging and conditional. By the late 1930s, southern congressmen were regularly joining with Republicans to defeat more liberal social welfare measures. As a result, the income security policies promoted by labor parties in Europe—income protections for the unemployed, the old and the poor, minimum wages, and so on—remained niggardly. Nor did the Democratic party champion the national health care or social housing policies that were so central to Western Europe welfare states. Moreover, in contrast to Western Europe, Democratic macroeconomic strategies favored employers by keeping unemployment levels high and inflation low, rather than favoring workers by keeping unemployment low and labor markets tight.[12]

The strangulation of welfare state development may well have foreclosed the prospect of a working-class-based Democratic party, quite apart from the betrayal of unionism. Contemporary critics who focus on race, when they discuss welfare state policies at all, usually point to the fragmented character of American welfare state programs, which resulted in the isolation of blacks in particular programs. We will turn to this issue in a moment. For now we want to stress the devastating consequences of another and probably more important feature of the American welfare state. It was simply too meager to cement working class loyalty to the Democratic party.

The failure to develop public programs explains the eventual large weight of employment-based health and pension provisions in the American welfare state. Facing resistance to the expansion of the public-sector initiatives of the 1930s, organized labor turned to the private-sector workplace for a measure of economic security. And in the immediate post–World War II period, when unions remained strong, they won significant pension and health benefits as part of the wage contract. As a consequence, employment-based social benefits became more important than public benefits, at least to organized workers. This pattern helped explain a deep cleavage within the working class that often took racial form. As better organized workers won private sector benefits, they were more likely to resent paying taxes to finance benefits for others who were forced to rely on public sector welfare programs. But long before this cleavage developed, the failure to expand welfare state programs contributed to flagging worker allegiance to the Democrats. Having won less economic security through the state, American workers showed less robust support than Europeans for both their governments and their parties. Small wonder that working class support for the Democratic party peaked in the 1940s and began to slip in the 1950s, long before race emerged as a central issue in electoral politics.

If the power of the southern Democrats crippled the prospects of labor party development, it surely blocked the aspirations of blacks. From early on, Roosevelt tried to keep southern Democrats loyal by conceding on race issues. He refused to support anti-lynching legislation, for example, arguing much as contemporary critics do that the best course for blacks was not to raise civil rights and other race-specific demands but to support the New Deal's overall program which would presumably benefit blacks as a byproduct of its broad reforms.

In fact, Roosevelt's (and especially Eleanor Roosevelt's) symbolic conciliation of blacks notwithstanding, the New Deal dealt harshly with blacks. The support that southern congressmen in control of key committees had ceded to such New Deal reform measures as the National Labor Relations Act, the Social Security Act, and the Fair Labor Standards Act had been conditional on the exemption of agricultural and domestic workers. This meant that low wage workers in the South were denied the protection of federal labor law and the main social welfare legislation, as well as the protection of wages and hours regulation. Needless to add, in the 1930s, the overwhelming majority of blacks were in the agricultural and domestic labor force of the south.

Meanwhile, depression conditions together with New Deal agricultural support programs which paid plantation owners to take land out of production, forced millions of black (and white) tenants and sharecroppers off the land. What remained as a recourse for these displaced people were the categorical or "welfare" programs. Southern congressmen had attended closely to the crafting of these "relief" programs for mothers and children, and the old, fearing that the availability of relief would give tenants a measure of independence from planters, and drive agricultural wages up generally, if and when commodity markets and the need for labor recovered.[13] The solution embedded in the Social Security Act was to give states and localities virtually total control of eligibility criteria and benefit levels in these programs. The predictable result was that the programs remained small, and benefit levels remained low, especially in the South. Thus, while it is true that their extreme poverty combined with their exclusion from other programs meant that blacks were from the start overrepresented on the relief rolls, the fact of overrepresentation can be misleading. Until the mid-1960s, the total number of beneficiaries of the programs remained small.[14] Particularly in the rural south, where most blacks were concentrated, local officials made it difficult for blacks to get relief, especially when they were wanted in the fields. And as southern agriculture mechanized, and black labor was no longer needed, the denial of relief by local officials became a way to drive blacks out of the south.[15]

So long as Democratic party leaders were held captive by the southern section, party policies toward blacks were not likely to change very much. To be sure, there were some efforts to overcome the constraints of the peculiar sectional coalition, at least in the 1930s. In 1936, the party eliminated the South's veto power over presidential nominations by removing the two-thirds majority rule. In the election of 1938, Roosevelt and his CIO allies made a serious but unsuccessful effort to defeat a number of the southern congressional powerbrokers. And in the early 1940s, in the culmination of a legal strategy reflecting the cooperation of the Justice Department, the NAACP won a Supreme Court ruling declaring the white primary unconstitutional.[16] Still, these efforts were shortlived and the reforms achieved were small, given the weight of formal arrangements which privileged the South. The grip of the South on the national Democratic party did not much loosen, and the peculiar sectional coalition remained intact.

But a party coalition that embraced the feudal South and the urban working class North was not likely to last. Indeed, New Deal policies helped to undermine it, by favoring the South with policies to promote economic modernization. Industrialization and urbanization in turn promoted the growth of a new middle class with Republican preferences, as became evident in the presidential elections of 1952 and 1956, when Eisenhower won a number of southern states, despite the efforts of the Democratic contender to appease the South on racial issues.[17]

The modernization of the South had another politically troublesome effect on the Democrats. It meant the migration of blacks out of the plantation economy and to the cities, where they gained the vote and became a factor in Democratic electoral calculations as early as 1948. The eruption of the civil rights movement in the late 1950s galvanized this new electoral force, pushing racial issues to the fore of national politics, at a time when Democratic leaders were anxiously trying to conciliate weakening southern allegiance. For three decades, party leaders were forced to choose and lose. They could defer to the white South, where outrage at even rhetorical inroads on the caste system was escalating, especially in the Deep South, and this at a time when Republican voting was increasing elsewhere in the region as a result of economic change. But if they conciliated the south on civil rights, they risked losing black support in the north, as became evident in the elections of 1956 and 1960, and this at a time when northern working class allegiance to the party was slipping, making defections by blacks dangerous. Or they could defer to newly insistent black demands, and risk more severe defections in the white South.

There was, in short, no way to hold together the sectional coalition that economic change and the politicization of blacks was rending asunder. By the mid-1960s, as the civil rights movement escalated, Democratic presidents finally threw their support behind the landmark civil rights legislation that would abolish the legal underpinnings of the southern caste system. Newly enfranchised southern blacks became loyal Democrats, but the white South, the mainstay of the Democratic party for more than a century, was lost.

Meanwhile, black protests escalated in the urban centers of the north as well, contributing to the erosion of white working class support which had begun in the late 1940s. This long term trend was obscured by the election of 1964, when the right wing takeover of the Republican party by the Goldwater faction combined with national grieving over the Kennedy assasination to attract many voters back to Democratic columns. But the deeper reasons for the fraying of Democratic working class support were not reversed. Unions were losing ground as a proportion of the workforce. and there were few social welfare reforms to buttress working class loyalties to the Democrats. Meanwhile, the nasty politics of racial resentment was stoked by George Wallace, especially in the presidential campaign of 1968.[18] Under these conditions, urban black protests over segregated housing, schools, and employment, along with black demands for political representation and influence in local government, easily drove even more white working class voters away from the Democratic party.[19]

But that was not the whole of it. The Democratic debacle was not just the inevitable working out of a deep conflict buried in the peculiar coalition which economic modernization exposed, both by changing the class structure of the South, and by bringing blacks into electoral politics. Historical anomalies may create new possibilities, but it is people who act to realize them, whether by resisting change and forcing the preservation of otherwise anomalous arrangements or by spurring the creation of new accomodations. For decades, even as the plantation system was giving way to the new South, southern politicians exerted themselves to preserve the caste arrangements in the south that had been forged in the post–Civil War years because they shored up their political organizations and their power. Similarly, as blacks were freed from the overwhelming power of the planter class by their migration to the cities, they also emerged as political actors in the effort to realize the new possibilities they sensed historical change had made ready. But southern powerbrokers and black protestors were not the only political actors in these tumultuous developments.

The leaching of Democratic support could hardly have gone unnoticed by Republican strategists. Democratic troubles in the South had been signalled as early as 1948, when Truman, worried about a third party challenge from the Left, had tried to conciliate emerging black demands, and precipitated a Dixiecrat revolt. The Democrats backed off, the Dixiecrats returned, but the troubles in the South nevertheless became clearer in the 1950s as Eisenhower piled up record tallies in the popular vote. By the early 1960s, the Republican National Committee was clearly taking the opportunity offered by the fragmenting of the "solid South" seriously, and investing substantial resources in building a Republican infrastructure in the region.[20] By the late 1960s, Republican pundits were trumpeting a new Republican majority that would begin with the realignment of white southerners.[21] True, during the 1960s, Republicans supported civil rights legislation, but they surely knew southern whites would blame northern Democrats. And as racial conflict flared in the North, Nixon promoted affirmative action in the construction trades with his "Philadelphia Plan," and with his subsequent 1974 Executive Order instituting compliance reviews.[22] At the same time, the Nixon Justice Department pressed the courts for school integration by means of busing in the cities which were now the main Democratic base. That these were Republican initiatives was not much noticed, either at the time or by contemporary commentators. It was within the Democratic party that the anxiety and anger they provoked unfolded. As the 1970s wore on, and the economy began to falter, declining working class earnings and economic uncertainty also helped to fuel racial antagonism.[23] By the 1980s, the Republican race strategy had taken yet another turn as Justice Department officials invoked the Voting Rights Act to force court-ordered creation of majority black districts. The pious justification was increased black representation, but the side benefits were obvious and probably not coincidental, as white Democratic incumbents lost the benefit of black support, and racial divisions were more deeply engraved in patterns of political representation.

Consistency was never the bane of Republican strategies to aggravate the Democrats' racial weakness. Early in the 1970s, with as many as 70% of southern whites voting Republican, and the northern white working class defecting in droves, Republicans adroitly shifted position by playing on white discontent over the affirmative action and integration measures they had themselves promoted. Meanwhile, Republicans campaigners from Richard Nixon to George Bush trumpeted the issues of law and order, neighborhood schools, quotas, and malingering welfare cheats, which became the coded language for fanning the anger toward blacks which was spurring Democratic defections. And in the 1990s, when the new majority black districts drawn in response to Justice Department suits had spurred an increase in black voter participation, local Republican officials developed tactics reminiscent of the post–Reconstruction south to keep blacks away from the polls, including the initiation of voter fraud suits against black electoral organizers.[24]

In these several more complicated ways, race is indeed—as the critics charge—a major reason that the Democrats have been unable to win the presidency in a quarter of a century, the post-Watergate election aside. Oddly, though, the critics have little to say about the racist accommodations at the very heart of the old Democratic coalition, or about the fateful consequences of those accommodations for labor, for blacks, and for the longer-term future of the party. Nor do they have much to say about the southern power brokers who took advantage of the structural and procedural advantages produced by earlier sectional compromises to cripple the Democratic party's capacity to build a firm working class base and a truly national party. And finally they ignore the Republican strategists who for a quarter of a century maneuvered to worsen racial divisions to reap partisan advantage.

Instead, it is blacks and liberals who are castigated for the racial conflicts that weakened the Democrats. Somehow, they should have devised a strategy that would advance black aspirations while avoiding the shoals of racial conflict. If this charge were to make sense, it would have to be made in two parts. First, since the most devastating Democratic loss was the loss of the South, blacks should have found a way to topple the caste system without jeopardizing the Democratic sectional partnership. But this was clearly impossible and, given the distorting influence of the South on the party, and especially on its relations to the working class, hardly even desirable. Second, blacks and their liberal allies should have found a way to avoid antagonizing whites in the north, presumably by avoiding race-specific demands in favor of a broader class-oriented agenda, crafted around universal demands. Presumably, this approach would have made possible a bi-racial class-based alliance that would overcome a history of working class racism, and also overcome divisive contemporary Republican stratagems.

As a matter of historical fact, as far back as the 1930s, major black organizations supported and promoted class-based solutions to the problems of blacks, throwing their support behind the New Deal, although to little avail.[25] When the contemporary black movement emerged, the policies it demanded were precisely the universalistic rights which had heretofore been denied blacks, which is why the movement provoked such anger. In the 1950s and 1960s, blacks rallied and marched and went to jail for integration in education, in housing, and in employment, as well as for the extension to blacks of the political rights which are presumably universal in our society. And in response to these demands for a more universalistic society, white southerners rose up in outrage, joined Citizens Councils, and defected from the Democratic Party. The notion, often taken as axiomatic by political analysts, that universalistic demands avoid conflict is simply wrong.

Moreover, even as blacks made universalistic demands, what they often got in response were particularistic programs, even race-specific programs, designed by national Democratic politicians in an effort to avert the conflict with the white working class that universal solutions were sure to aggravate. Many of the Great Society programs, often taken to exemplify wrong-headed race-specific programs[26] because they funneled services and jobs directly to black neighborhoods, were fashioned as they were to avert rising white resentment over black challenges to white (and ethnic) control of municipal services and jobs.[27] That this strategy to avoid race conflict was not entirely successful speaks as much to the depth of the problem as to the wisdom of the strategy. As black rage mounted in the ghettos, it overwhelmed the dikes which the Great Society programs had attempted to construct by localizing and particularizing concessions to blacks. Inevitably, some of the community action programs even became launching pads for protest, litigation, and political mobilization against white domination in the big cities. The critics who now blame blacks and liberals for the resulting working class rage and defections define the "social engineering" of the Great Society as a disasterous policy error. But this simplistic conclusion, which ignores the deep roots of racial conflict and the real stakes in municipal government that were at issue, assumes that racial conflict would somehow have been averted in the absence of these programs. More likely, without these programs, it would have been worse.

Nothing so incenses these critics of the 1960s as the successful drives to gain more income for blacks through welfare. Blacks, they say, should instead have demanded full employment or universal income programs, such as children's allowances. But this criticism also ignores history.

More precisely, it ignores the crippling policies inherited from the 1930s. American workers—struggling against both the business-dominated Republican party and the Southern oligarchy—ended up with a fragmented system of employment-based private programs, and work-conditioned and means-tested public programs, as well as with a system of macroeconomic regulation that favored high unemployment and low inflation. And as we noted earlier, agricultural workers were simply excluded from a number of the broader insurance programs. Consequently, when agricultural modernization in the South produced millions of unemployed after World War II, displaced rural blacks were certainly not eligible for employment-based benefits, and they were not eligible for the main insurance programs either. In practical terms, most were not even eligible for welfare, which fended them off with state residence laws, employable mothers rules, suitable home regulations, man-in-the-house provisions, and bureaucratic rebuffs and runarounds. In 1960, in the wake of the massive displacement from agriculture of some twenty million people in two decades, white and black, less than three-quarters of a million families were receiving AFDC in the entire country. This did not change until women, mainly black women, broke out in "welfare rights" protests in the mid-1960s.

We thought at the time that obtaining welfare benefits would be a gain for the growing numbers of impoverished families in the big cities (and we haven't changed our minds). Moreover, we thought rising welfare rolls, by producing fiscal strain and worsening racial tension, would prompt the national Democratic party to federalize welfare in order to moderate at least this source of urban and state fiscal stress, and also to moderate internal conflict in its big-city base. We were as it happens slightly off in this prediction: Congress instead reduced fiscal pressure on state and local governments by incorporating the old age and disability categorical assistance programs (other forms of "welfare") in a new Supplemental Security Income program. Still, S.S.I. was one of the most significant reforms of the means-tested programs since they were created by the Social Security Act of 1935. It benefitted the aged and disabled poor of all races, but it was indisputably an achievement of the black movement.

In any case, the critics who argue that blacks and liberals were strategically inept seem to think that these impoverished women shouldn't have demanded welfare because the white working class would be offended. Instead, they should have waited for the opportunity to link arms with white workers in a fight for full employment programs, or for more universal income support programs. But it would have been a long wait. There was about as much chance of that happening as of southern whites linking arms with blacks in the struggle for desegregation and voting rights. The political truth is that blacks got what they got precisely because their disruptive protests, by exacerbating divisions in the peculiar sectional coalition, and in the big cities as well, forced the Democratic party to make voting-rights concessions in the effort to rebuild its base in the South, and social welfare concessions in the effort to moderate conflict in the cities.

The nostalgic reconstruction of the old New Deal Democratic Party as a labor party is close cousin to the more general view that political parties in the United States were once organs for popular influence, but have been overtaken and weakened by the rise of the mass media, and the growing role of big money in electoral campaigns. In the past the parties were ostensibly both better organized, and organized in terms of the calculus of winning voters (and recruiting grassroots activists) rather than the financial and advertising calculus of today. Or, to put the same point another way, the parties have become "capital intensive" where once they were "labor intensive".[28]

It is of course true that money and the mass media play an enormous role in electoral politics. Nevertheless, the contrast with the past is overstated. The major parties have always been important arenas for the machinations of a power elite, and big money has been important in national elections at least since the end of the 19th century, and for longer in many state and local elections.[29]

While money and machination is a big part of electoral politics, it is not the whole of it, or not always the whole of it.[30] Contenders for state power do have to win elections, and that requires they appeal to popular opinion, at least when outright fraud is kept in check. Electoral representative arrangements mean that, at least some of the time, and at least on keenly felt issues, popular interests can matter. But just which popular interests are articulated and recognized depends very much on the shape of dominant coalitions, and the political culture promoted by the parties to build and cement those coalitions.

The Democratic coalition rooted in the 19th century and modified in the Great Depression suppressed the emergence of class identities and interests in favor of racial, ethnic and sectional identities, thus destroying the possibility of a working class electoral politics, and also shutting the door on racial liberalism. That coalition was wrecked by the conflicts of the 1960s, probably never to be restored, and that may turn out to have not been such a bad thing. True, the changes in economy and social life signalled by postindustrialism mean that the time has past for a labor party built on mass production workers and their unions. But while the ranks of the working class are no longer mainly male or mainly white, there is nevertheless still a working class, made up of the tens of millions of women and men in the new industries and in the service sector. Their grievances are growing, and they need political representation. The destruction of the old Democratic party may have been a necessary first step.

1997

Notes

1. On ethnicity and party building, see for example Mink (1986), and Piven and Cloward (1988). See also Wilentz (1984). On race and the urban Democrats, see for example Katznelson (1973).

2. For variations of this argument, see Edsall and Edsall (1991); Sleeper (1991); Reider (1985 and 1989); Morris (1980). For closely similar arguments that focus specifically on race and social welfare, see Skocpol (1988).

3. Greenstone (1969).

4. Labor support for the Democrats peaked in 1948, when 79 percent of white union members, and 76 percent of white working class voters, voted Democratic. See Abramson, et. al. (1983, figures 5-2, 5-3 and 5-4).

5. In the election of 1952, the Democratic margin among white union members had fallen to 53 percent, and in 1956 it fell to 50 percent (*ibid*).

6. On constitutional fragmentation, see Schattschneider (1942).

7. See Potter (1972) and Domhoff (1990).

8. Tindall (1972,31) sums up the problem posed to the traditional southern elite, which "rested on the control of property, labor, credit, and local government.

Relief projects reduced dependency [on employers]; labor standards raised wages; farm programs upset traditional landlord-tenant relationships; government credit bypassed bankers; new federal programs skirted county commissioners and sometimes even state agencies."

9. Taft-Hartley also laid down the requirement that union leaders had to sign non-communist affidavits in order to enjoy the protections of the National Labor Relations Board, a development which encouraged the union-wide purge of many of the most activist unionists. Later, in 1959, the passage of the Lanrum-Griffin Act further weakened the union strike power.

10. On the migration of industrial capital to the sunbelt and overseas, see Bluestone and Harrison (1982).

11. Domhoff (1990, 242) points out that while machine Democrats usually voted for social welfare and labor legislation on the floor, they also steadfastly voted with the South on the crucial questions of committee leadership, and it was in the committees that many of the key legislative decisions were made.

12. See Hibbs (1977).

13. See Johnson, Embree, and Alexander (1935); Piven and Cloward (1971, chapters 4 and 5); Alston and Ferrie (1985); Brown (1992). For a general discussion of the opposition to income-maintenance programs by southern planters because they would weaken their control over the labor market, see Piven and Cloward (1971, Chs. 7 and 8). Quadagno (1988) points out that southern plantation owners had also vigorously opposed state level old age pension proposals because they might weaken the dependence of tenants and laborers on the planters. The same concerns about national programs undermining local labor markets led southerners to line up with small business to oppose a national system of unemployment insurance.

14. For a discussion of the disproportionate numbers of blacks on relief and the conditions which accounted for it, see Brown (1992).

15. See Piven and Cloward (1971, chapter 7).

16. For an account of the role played by the Justice Department's newly established Civil Liberties Unit, see Valelly (1992).

17. On Republican recruitment of a younger and more professional middle class, see Klinkner (1992).

18. Strong unions might have tempered the surge of racist resentment among the white working class in the North. For example, the UAW led a massive campaign against George Wallace in Michigan in the 1968 presidential race. See Thomas J. Sugrue, "The Origins of White Backlash in the Urban North." Paper presented at the 1992 Annual Meeting of the American Political Science Association.

19. On urban race conflict, especially over housing integration, see Sugrue, *ibid.*

20. On the development of this Republican "Operation Dixie" campaign, see Klinkner, op. cit.

21. See Phillips (1969).

22. See Quadagno (1992).

23. The impact of economic stagnation combined with rising taxes on white working class political allegiances and racial attitudes is emphasized by Thomas and Mary Edsall (1991, 69).

24. See for example Ronald Smothers, "Blacks Say G.O.P. Ballot Challenges are Tactic to Harass Minority Voters," *New York Times*, Sunday, October 25, 1992, p.20.

25. See Brown (1992).

26. See Skocpol, et. al. (1988).

27. On competition for municipal jobs and services, see Piven (1974).

28. Ginsberg (1984)

29. See for example, Larry McGerr on the invention of the first mass advertising national election campaign in 1896.

30. Ferguson's (1983) depiction of American electoral history as a series of investor realignments is illuminating, but incomplete. The very fact of investor electoral mobilizations suggests the existence or at least the potential for popular electoral opposition to investor interests which he ignores. See also Ferguson and Rogers (1986).

References

ABRAMSON, PAUL R., JOHN W. ALDRICH, AND DAVID W. RHODE. 1983. *Change and Continuity in the 1980 Elections*. Washington, D.C.: Congressional Quarterly Press.

ALSTON, LEE J., AND JOSEPH P. FERRIE. 1985. "Labor Costs, Paternalism, and Loyalty in Southern Agriculture: A Constraint on the Growth of the Welfare State." *Journal of Economic History* XIV, 1.

BLUESTONE, BARRY, AND BENNETT HARRISON. 1982. *The Deindustrialization of America*. New York: Basic Books.

BROWN, PETER. 1991. *Minority Party: Why the Democrats Face Defeat in 1992 and Beyond*. Wasington, D.C.: Regnery Gateway.

DOMHOFF, G. WILLIAM. 1990. *The Power Elite and The State: How Policy is Made in America*. New York: Aldine de Gruyter.

EDSALL, THOMAS BYRNE, AND MARY D. EDSALL. 1991. *Chain Reaction: The Impact of the Race, Rights, and Taxes on American Politics*. New York: Norton.

FERGUSON, THOMAS. 1983. "Party Realignment and American Industrial Structure: The Investment Theory of Political Parties in Historical Perspective." *Research in Political Economy*, Volume 6, JAI Press.

FERGUSON, THOMAS, AND JOEL ROGERS. 1986. *Right Turn*. New York: Hill and Wang.

FIORINA, MORRIS. 1981. *Retrospective Voting in American Presidential Elections*. New Haven: Yale University Press.

GINSBERG, BENJAMIN. 1984. "Money and Power: The New Political Economy in American Elections," In Thomas Ferguson and Joel Rogers, eds., *The Political Economy*. Armonk, N.Y., M. E. Sharpe.

GREENSTONE, J. DAVID. 1969. *Labor in American Politics*. New York: Vintage Books.

HIBBS, DOUGLAS A. 1977. "Political Parties and Macroeconomic Policy." *American Political Science Review* 71, 4 (December).

KATZNELSON, IRA. 1973. *White Men, Black Cites*. New York, Oxford University Press.

KLINKER, PHILIP A. 1992. "Race and the Republican Party: The Rise of the Southern Strategy in the Republican National Committee, 1960–1964." Paper delivered at the 1992 Annual Meeting of the American Political Sicnece Association, September 3–6, 1992.

McGERR, MICHAEL E. 1986. *The Decline of Popular Politics: The American North. 1865–1928*. New York, Oxford University Press.

MINK, GWENDOLYN. 1986. *Old Labor and New Immigrants in American Political Development*. 1986. Ithaca, Cornell Univerity Press.

MORRIS, CHARLES. 1980. *The Cost of Good Intentions: New York City and the Liberal Experiment, 1960–1975*. New York McGraw Hill.

PHILLIPS, KEVIN P. 1969. *The Emerging Republican Majority*. New Rochelle, N.Y.: Arlington House.

PIVEN, FRANCES FOX. 1974. "The Urban Crisis: Who Got What, and Why?" In Richard A. Cloward and Frances Fox Piven, *The Politics of Turmoil: Essays on Poverty, Race, and the Urban Crisis*. New York: Pantheon Books.

PIVEN, FRANCES FOX, AND RICHARD A. CLOWARD. 1971. *Regulating the Poor*, New York: Pantheon Books.

———. 1988. *Why Americans Don't Vote*. New York, Pantheon Books.

QUADAGNO, JILL. 1988. *The Transformation of Old Age Security: Class and Politics in the American Welfare State*. Chicago, University of Chicago Press.

———. 1992. "Social Movements and State Transformation: Labor Unions and Political Conflict in the War on Poverty." *American Sociological Review*, 57, 5, October.

REIDER, JONATHAN. 1985. *Canarsie: The Jews and Italians of Brooklyn Against Liberalism.* Cambridge: Harvard University Press.

————. 1989. "The Rise of the Silent Majority," In Steve Fraser and Gary Gerstle, eds., *The Rise and Fall of the New Deal Order.* Princeton: Princeton University Press.

SCHATTSCHNEIDER, E. E. 1942. *Party Government.* Westport, Ct., Greenwood Press. New York: Holt, Rinehart and Winston.

SKOCPOL, THEDA. 1988. "The Limits of the New Deal System and the Roots of Contemporary Welfare Dilemmas." In Margaret Weir, Ann Shola Orloff, and Theda Skocpol, Ed., *The Politics of Social Policy in the United States.* Princeton, Princeton University Press.

SLEEPER, JIM. 1991. *The Closest of Strangers: The Politics of Liberalism in New York City.* New York: Simon and Schuster.

SUGRUE, THOMAS J. 1992. "The Origins of White Backlash in the Urban North." Paper presented at the 1992 Political Science Association Annual Meeting.

TINDALL, GEORGE BROWN. 1972. *The Disruption of the Solid South.* Athens: University of Georgia Press.

VALELLY, RICHARD M. 1992. "Making the Rules Count: American Exceptionalism and Black Voting Rights Struggle, 1867–1965." Unpublished.

WILENTZ, SEAN. 1984. *Chants Democratic: New York City and the Rise of the Working Class, 1977–1850.* New York, Oxford University Press.

6

The Case Against Urban Desegregation

For years the chief efforts of a broad coalition of liberals and reformers, in dealing with the problems of the African American, have been directed against segregation. Some significant gains have been made, particularly in the laws governing African American rights in certain institutional spheres, such as voting and the use of public accommodations. But in some areas the thrust for integration seems to have worked against African American interests. This is especially true with regard to housing and education of the black poor in large cities.

There are two main reasons for this: (1) Efforts to ameliorate basic social inequities, such as deteriorated ghetto housing and inferior educational facilities, have been closely linked to the goal of integration, and, since integration measures arouse fierce resistance, proposals to redress these social inequities have usually failed. It is for this reason that after several decades of civil-rights struggle the lot of the black urban poor has actually worsened in some respects. (2) If the African American is to develop the power to enter the mainstream of American life, it is separatism—not integration—that will be essential to achieve results in certain institutional arenas. Both of these points have implications for both public policy and political action.

Desegregating Housing

Reformers oriented to the urban ghetto have generally sought two objectives that they have seen as closely linked—to promote desegregation and to obtain better housing and education for the poor. Efforts to desegregate housing, however, have been roundly defeated by massive white opposition. Indeed, residential segregation is increasing rapidly.[1] Moreover, because provision of decent housing for the poor has been tied to desegregation, this end also has been defeated. Despite the huge congressional majorities enjoyed by President Johnson in the 89th Congress, not much was done for the slums of our cities. Some promising legislation was enacted: the Housing Act of 1965, the rent-supplement bill, the demonstration-cities bill. But in each case the issue of racial integration endangered the passage of bills, then emasculated them by the meagerness of appropriations. And now, with the 90th Congress, we have probably lost the small margins by which most of the housing legislation survived, and we may forfeit the small gains already made. It is time, therefore, to reexamine the relation, if any, between racial dispersion and decent housing for the slum poor.

Restricted housing is regarded by reformers as the key factor in creating and maintaining racial barriers, and in turn racial barriers are said to force African Americans into the deteriorated slum; therefore, it is felt that desegregation should be a central objective of housing-and-redevelopment programs for the poor. But since there is, at best, little public support for low-income-housing programs, and this tenuous support has been overwhelmed by fierce opposition to residential integration, the struggle for residential integration has cost the poor, especially the black poor, dearly. In effect, the desperate need for better housing and facilities in the ghetto has been and continues to be sacrificed to the goal of residential integration—a goal which, given the political realities of racial conflict in urban areas, can only be said to be receding from view. And as this goal recedes, so too does decent low-income housing.

In fact, segregation has increased! Nor is there any reason to believe that this trend will abate. For one thing, differential birthrates reinforce existing patterns of segregation, concentrating larger and larger numbers of blacks wherever they live. Between 1950 and 1960, for example, the nonwhite population of the nation increased by 26.7 percent and the white population by only 17.5 percent. For this reason, as well as because of the relatively higher rate of movement of nonwhites toward central cities, the black population in urban areas is growing more rapidly than the white. During the decade which ended in 1960, the nonwhite population in American cities increased by half, urban whites by one-fourth.

As the urban black population rises, segregation is intensified. The most dramatic separation by color within the urban area has taken place between the central city and suburban ring. Between 1950 and 1960 the nonwhite population in the central cities swelled by sixty-three percent, while the number of whites continued to decline.[2] Central cities now contain less than half the urban white population, but eighty percent of urban nonwhites. One-third of urban blacks are in the nation's ten largest central cities. Within a decade or two, blacks will probably constitute a majority in a dozen or more of our largest cities. (The nation's capital is already sixty-three percent black.)

What Would Integration Require?

In view of these trends, the task of maintaining racial balance in the city seems insuperable; to offset them, huge numbers of families would have to be shuffled about by desegregation programs. This point was spelled out in 1966 by George Schermer at a "national housing workshop" sponsored by the National Committee Against Discrimination in Housing. Schermer estimated the numbers of people who would have to be moved each year in order to insure a fifty-fifty population balance in Washington, D.C., in the year 2000. Assuming that migration trends and birthrates remain constant, 12,000 nonwhite families would have to be dispersed to suburban areas and 4000 white families induced to return to the District every year until 2000.[3]

Even if whites could be induced back to the city and blacks accommodated in the suburbs, residential integration would not result. For within the central city itself, residential concentration by color is on the upswing. In 1910, for example, sixty percent of New York City's blacks lived in assembly districts which were less than five percent black; by 1960, sixty-two percent were in districts over half black. In southern cities, which traditionally have tended toward more dispersed patterns of settlement (with black servants and artisans living near those they serve), ghettos are being formed by the concentration of growing black populations.

Again, assuming that present trends persist, Schermer estimates that to achieve integration neighborhood-by-neighborhood in Philadelphia by the end of the century, 6000 African American families would have to go to the suburbs and 3000 whites settle exclusively in ghetto areas each year. The numbers, of course, would be infinitely greater in cities like New York and Chicago, which have much larger aggregations of African Americans. Little wonder that the staff of the New York City Department of City Planning concluded in an unpublished report last year that even if all current housing and planning programs were directed to the goal of desegregation, the city could at best only halt the spread of ghettoization, not reverse it.

Our experience with a variety of approaches to desegregating housing has not been in the least encouraging. The most popular approach is legal reforms, coupled with information and education programs. Legislation is sought which prohibits prejudicial treatment of blacks, whether by deed restrictions, by discriminatory actions of private realtors or landlords, or by governmental policies themselves (such as the FHA mortgage-underwriting policy, rescinded in 1945, which prescribed racially homogeneous housing). These reforms reflect an essentially libertarian ideal: a legal structure which ensures the individual rights of minority-group members. But it is by now self-evident that such reforms have little actual impact on urban segregation in housing (or in education or employment).

Substantial legal gains in the housing field were made years ago, long before the recent "activist" phase of the civil-rights movement. Indeed, the very proliferation of legal-reform measures may account for the prevalence of the view among liberals that there has been progress in desegregating housing. Racial zoning ordinances, for example, were struck down by the courts in 1917; race-restrictive deeds (covenants), which were developed to serve the same function as racial zoning, were declared unconstitutional in 1948; and in 1958 New York City developed the nation's first statute outlawing discrimination in housing financed wholly with private funds. Legal reforms proliferate, but patterns of segregation widen.

Part of the reason that legal reforms have had little effect is the weakness of the laws themselves. Many of the discriminatory acts which produce segregation in private housing involve the sacred precincts of property and domicile. Efforts to protect by law the rights of minorities shade into infringements of the rights of others and may even be contrary to other laws which protect rights of property and privacy.

Legal reforms are further weakened by the reluctance to provide for effective enforcement. New York has both a State Commission on Human Rights and a parallel City Commission. The procedures for securing redress, however, ordinarily require knowledge and patience on the part of the plaintiff which cannot in fairness be expected of someone merely looking for a decent place to live. Moreover, although one apartment may be "opened" after torturous procedures, there is no deterrence to further violations, no carryover effect. Each negotiated enforcement of the law remains an isolated event, and so members of a minority have little confidence in the efficacy of registering complaints. Recently, New York's two agencies proudly announced a "great increase" in complaints received, but the total amounted to a mere 528 complaints during the first half of 1966.[4] Philadelphia's counterpart agency, the Commission on Human Relations, has received only 466 complaints in the entire three years since a fair-housing ordinance was adopted.

Broad educational efforts are intended to change discriminatory attitudes in the white community. "Fair-housing committees" in receiving communities are intended to overcome hostility toward entering blacks. Information and broker services are designed to remedy communication gaps, such as lack of information about housing opportunities outside the ghetto and difficulties in gaining access for inspection. The Urban League's "Operation Open City" combines all these strategies to help African American families find housing.

Housing opportunities are still, however, overwhelmingly controlled by the regular institutions of the private real-estate market, and the mores of the market have been only incidentally affected by legal advances and desegregation programs. Private real-estate agents reflect the inclinations of the vast majority of housing consumers, and so they distribute information concerning available housing and provide access for inspection in ways that accord with existing class and racial neighborhood patterns. Fair-housing committees have at best opened just a few housing opportunities beyond the ghetto. Furthermore, these efforts reach predominantly middle-class African Americans: Housing in outlying communities generally requires at least a lower-middle income. The ghetto poor are resisted by white neighborhoods generally, but the most furious opposition comes from white working-class neighborhoods—the very ones with housing many blacks might be able to afford.

If Blacks Had More Money

Eliminating the poverty of the ghetto masses is the basis of a second general approach to residential integration. Proceeding from our belief in individual opportunity and the "open" society, the argument is that African Americans will be able to bid competitively for housing outside the ghetto once they have better jobs and incomes. There are a number of fallacies here.

First, programs intended to advance blacks economically—by education and job training—currently reach a mere one in ten of America's poor, white as well as African American. Even if the scope of these programs were vastly expanded, millions of the poor would still not be helped. Of the 35 million people below the federal poverty line (e.g., $3100 per annum for an urban family of four in 1965), several million are aged and are permanently unemployable. One-third of the poor are in families headed by females, and it does not seem reasonable to expect this group to raise itself from poverty by entering the labor force. Many of the remaining poor are ill; others are permanently noncompetitive for a host of additional reasons, not the least being the debilitating effects of years of chronic unemployment and underemployment.

More than half of the poor are under eighteen. Presumably, the optimists who advocate skills-enhancement as a solution to poverty have the potential of this group in mind. But in the past the upward journey to

the middle class has taken low-income groups as much as three generations. African Americans are handicapped at the outset by chronic deprivation; they confront persisting barriers of economic and social
discrimination; they must surmount new barriers posed by automation
and the professionalization of occupations. Under the circumstances
they can hardly be expected to lift themselves, one by one, more rapidly
than members of groups before them which had much greater economic
opportunity. For most poor of the present generation, and perhaps for
many in the next, a strategy of individual mobility is irrelevant.

Even if large numbers of African Americans are lifted either to or
somewhat above the poverty line, their chance of getting decent housing will not greatly improve. In urban areas adequate housing is hard to
come by for families with annual incomes of less than $7000; in 1960,
only 3.4 percent of African Americans had such incomes. Indeed,
middle-class whites have obtained huge governmental subsidies to bring
decent housing within their reach (e.g., urban-renewal land write-
downs, low-cost government-insured mortgages, special federal tax
advantages for builders and realtors, as well as local tax abatements).

Furthermore, because of discriminatory patterns, blacks in effect pay
more for housing than whites. Although in most metropolitan areas
African Americans pay slightly lower rentals than whites in each income
group, they get vastly inferior housing. Income gains will continue to be
partly dissipated in excessive rentals.[5]

We must also stress that resistance in the receiving community per-
sists, whatever the incomes of potential black invaders. Karl and Alma
Taeuber conclude after extensive analysis of census data that "residential
segregation prevails regardless of the relative economic status of the
white and African American resident."[6]

Consequences of Our Good Intentions

The myth that integrationist measures are bringing better housing to the
negro poor comforts liberals; it placates (and victimizes) the African
American masses; and it antagonizes and arouses the bulk of white
Americans. The "backlash" is part of its legacy. While turmoil rages over
integration, housing conditions worsen. They worsen partly because the

solution continues to be defined in terms of desegregation, so that the energies and attention of reformers are diverted from attempts to ameliorate housing in the ghetto itself.

By being linked to the goal of integration, traditional programs for low-income housing (e.g., public housing) have become so controversial that appropriations are kept low and in many places are not even used. Although the 1949 Housing Act alone authorized 810,000 units of low-rent housing, a mere 600,000 units have been constructed since the first National Housing Act in 1937. During the past few years we have constructed only about 26,000 units annually or about half of what could have been built under existing legislation. The ghetto poor have paid in this way for the struggle over whether black and white shall mingle, neighborhood by neighborhood.

Public housing was intended, by at least some of its proponents, to facilitate integration as a by-product of rehousing the poor. And it has always been plagued by that secondary goal. Integrated projects have been thwarted because, as African Americans move in, low-income whites leave or are reluctant to apply. (The Federal Public Housing Agency classifies only twenty-seven percent of its projects as integrated and these include an unspecified number which have only one or two African American families.) The resulting high-rise brick ghettos offend liberals, and they attack. But when housing officials attempt to bring about integration by such devices as quota systems, other critics are offended on the ground that such procedures are discriminatory. The New York City Housing Authority has been alternately forced to "reform" by making commitments to foster integrated projects, only to be asked to "reform" again by abolishing its color-conscious procedures.

Efforts to further integration by locating housing projects in white neighborhoods have provoked far more serious opposition than efforts to integrate the projects themselves. Only when white tenants predominate is there any degree of tolerance for public housing in these communities. Thus, the New York City Housing Authority has long accommodated to the wishes of borough presidents in site selections (and is much criticized for it), and has also used its full share of public-housing subsidies. But in many localities disputes over the location of public housing projects have evoked furious controversy, often leading to the reduction of the program and surely making its political future shaky. In a study of public-housing decisions in Chicago, Martin Meyerson and Edward Banfield showed how volatile the site-selection issue is. By proposing locations which raised the integration issue, the public-housing authority provoked a two-and-a-half-year struggle which not only defeated the site proposal but consolidated opposition to public housing, itself. A similar struggle is now going on in New York City; the Lindsay administration has insisted that public housing be located on vacant land in outlying areas, and so the current sites have still not been approved.

The new rent-supplement law bears the same political onus as public housing. The appropriation of $20 million will permit only a few show-piece displays. If experience with public housing is any predictor, the opposition which rent supplements provoked in Congress and which almost defeated it will be repeated in each local community as efforts are made to implement the plan. White majorities will veto any project they feel will threaten their neighborhood and will eventually ban the program that raises the threat. Public subsidies, in short, have failed to reverse the trend toward segregation in urban areas and have not produced new or rehabilitated housing for the poor.

While the poor are left with token programs and token funds ("demonstration" projects for rehousing the poor have become a favorite device), huge new subsidies have been finding their way into the hands of middle- and upper-class interests in the central city. These programs, put forward as attempts to serve "the city as a whole" by clearing slums, improving the tax base, or retrieving the middle class from the suburbs, have had the effect of intensifying ghetto deterioration. We have spent some $3 billion on urban-renewal programs, and in the process whole low-income communities have been destroyed, including some 328,000 units of housing (most of them low rental). Only some 13,000 units of low-rent public housing have been constructed on the area sites. Luxury apartment houses, stadiums, coliseums, auditoriums, and office buildings now stand where the poor once lived.[7] (Highway development has had equally devastating effects.) Curiously, these measures are sometimes justified by the goal of integration, for it is hoped they will lure middle-class whites back from the suburbs.

Nor has much been done to mitigate the cruel cost to ghetto residents of clearance and redevelopment. Procedures for interim management on sites scheduled for clearance place owners and tenants in a prolonged state of uncertainty, making them either the agents or the victims of quick exploitation. The effects on those eventually dislocated, about seventy percent of whom are nonwhite, are only partially tempered by relocation provisions.[8] The stalemate we now see in some urban-renewal programs (e.g., as a result of Saul Alinsky's activities in Chicago and Rochester) represents an achievement for the poor: They have finally been spurred by the accumulated abuses of years of dislocation to protest against the further destruction of their homes and communities.[9]

In the housing act of 1949, Congress asserted a national responsibility to provide a decent dwelling for every family. The nation, however, has not progressed very far. In New York City, for example, Mayor Lindsay's housing task force reported that there were half a million unsound units currently occupied (roughly the same number reported through years of new public assaults on the slums) and that the number was on the increase even though the number of low-rental units has decreased more than thirty percent between 1960 and 1965.[10] In Boston, the last family-size public-housing unit was built in 1954; the city's nationally acclaimed urban-renewal effort diminished by twelve percent the supply of low-rental housing (less than $50 a month) between 1960 and 1965.[11] The federal public-housing program has produced only 600,000 low-income dwelling units in the three decades since it was initiated. The federal urban-renewal program and the federal highway program have together demolished close to 700,000 units, most of which were low rental, in less than half that time. Meanwhile, private builders, spurred on by federal tax incentives and mortgage programs designed to encourage construction, have made still further inroads on the supply of low-income housing by reclaiming land to erect middle- and upper-income units. The cheap accommodations that remain in large cities are in buildings that have been permitted to run down without maintenance and repairs or in which rents are pushed to the limit the captive slum market can afford. High-minded public policies notwithstanding, the dimensions of housing needs among the nonwhites in big cities have, in fact, enlarged.

Desegregating Education

To emphasize the importance of upgrading ghetto housing is also to accept racially homogeneous elementary schools in large cities, at least for the foreseeable future. Integrated education has been one of the central goals of reformers, and few seem prepared to relinquish this objective. However, the demographic and political realities in large cities cast grave doubts on the feasibility of achieving anything resembling integrated education at the early grade levels.

As a result of the housing patterns described earlier, blacks are rapidly becoming the largest group (in some cases, the majority) in the central areas of many large cities. Furthermore, they represent an even greater proportion of the school-age population because African American families are usually younger, larger and without the resources to place their children in private schools.[12] The white youngsters with whom black children presumably are to be integrated are slowly vanishing from inner-city areas, and there is every reason to expect that these demographic trends will continue.

The issue of integrated education is also complicated by socioeconomic factors, particularly in the cities. Recent evidence suggests that diverse economic backgrounds of pupils may be more important than racial diversity in the education of the African American student. One study of American education, for example, shows that mixing middle-class students (either black or white) with lower-class students (either black or white) usually has a decidedly beneficial effect on the achievement of the lower-class student and does not usually diminish the middle-class student's achievement.[13] By contrast, the integration of poor whites and poor blacks does not seem to yield improved achievement in either group.[14]

But the number of middle-class whites available to be mixed educationally with lower-class African Americans is rapidly declining, and of the whites left in the city with children who attend public schools, an increasing proportion is poor. (As for middle-class African Americans, their numbers are very small to begin with, and many send their children to private schools.) If mixing along class lines is to be achieved, therefore, educational arrangements in which suburban and ghetto children are brought together will be required. Such arrangements are improbable. The defense of the neighborhood school is ardent; it reflects both racial and class cleavages in American society. Efforts to bring about racial mixing, especially when coupled with the more meaningful demand for economic-class mixing, run head-on into some of the most firmly rooted and passionately defended attitudes of white families.

Busing versus "educational parks." Two schemes have been advocated for achieving racial integration while minimizing political resistance. One involves reshuffling children to achieve a racial balance by busing them to distant schools. Aside from the logistical problems this poses, busing usually has met violent opposition from all sides.[15] The second scheme is the development of massive "educational parks," which would centralize upper-grade facilities for children from a wide area. The superiority of these new plants, it is argued, will help to overcome the opposition of white parents to integration. However, even in such plants segregation is likely to persist on the classroom level as a result of the "tracking system," particularly because educational parks are intended only for older children, whose academic levels already reflect wide inequalities in home environment and early schooling. Equally important is the fact that the cost of such educational parks would be enormous. It is improbable that many such parks would be built, and the merits of such an investment must be weighed against alternative uses of funds for the direct improvement of program and staff in ghetto schools.

Improving ghetto schools. The lower-class school, particularly in the large-city ghetto, has always been an inferior institution. Recently the physical facilities in many ghetto schools have improved because of new building programs, but the lower-class black school still reflects significant inequalities when it is compared to its white middle-class counterpart. For example, the quality of the teachers has been shown to have a critical influence on the child's learning—lower-class schools, however (especially ghetto schools in large cities), have inferior teachers and are generally characterized by higher staff turnover. To overcome historic inequalities of this kind would be no small achievement.[16]

We conclude, in short, that although schools that are racially and economically heterogeneous are probably superior, removing class inequities in the quality of teachers and programs is also an important goal—and a far more realistic one. Such educational improvements in the ghetto will require public action and expenditure, and these are likely to be achieved only if massive political opposition to demands for class and racial mixing is avoided. As in the case of housing, the coupling of measures for integration of education with measures to improve existing conditions in large-city ghettos must lead to the defeat of both. The choice is between total defeat and partial victory; to many it may appear a difficult choice—but at least it is a choice.

Need for Separatist Organizations

Even if huge rebuilding programs were to be undertaken in the next several decades, does it follow that desegregation will result? Even the most cursory examination of urban political trends dictates precisely the opposite conclusion. The white suburbs now contain more people than the cities, and reapportionment has given them electoral power commensurate with their numbers. These suburban majorities, in alliance with inner-city whites, will dominate the shaping of future governmental programs for the urban community. Nor is it difficult to imagine what the priorities will be—such as long-term, government-insured mortgage programs to proliferate single-family suburban dwellings. In the suburban-dominated constituencies that will shape future governmental policies, the African American will simply be shunted aside if he insists on integrated housing and education.

On the other hand, by consolidating his power within the central city the African American might have some impact on the environment of the ghetto itself. To exact even these concessions from the white urban coalition, however, the African American must organize as a bloc—that is, he must organize separately. And the route to effective separatist power does not begin with proclamations that the ghetto must be dispersed.

Class power in the United States is intimately connected with the strength of ethnic institutions. Powerlessness and poverty are disproportionately concentrated among minority groups—Puerto Ricans,

Mexicans and so forth. The success of traditional ethnic and religious social agencies in resisting the emergence of African American institutions is a reflection of class power differentials. But it also reveals that class power is produced and maintained in part by racial and ethnic power differentials.

Liberals, however, are inclined to take a "melting pot" view of American communities and to stress the enriching qualities of heterogeneous living. The history of ethnic groups in American society belies this view. There have always been ethnic institutions, and these, as has been widely observed, have served important functions in the advancement of different groups. An important precondition for the establishment of such separatist institutions—particularly when the members of the ethnic group are poor—has been the existence of substantial aggregations of people in residential proximity. The current emphasis on integrating people physically in schools and neighborhoods thus deflects attention from a fundamental problem confronting blacks—the lack of organizational vehicles to enable them to compete with whites for control of major institutions that shape the destiny of the ghetto (housing and educational systems, governmental bureaucracies, corporate economic complexes, political parties, and so forth). Without separatist organizations the African American is not likely to come to share control in these spheres, and the powerlessness of the ghetto's population will persist.

The value of separatist institutions is revealed clearly in the field of social welfare. There is, of course, considerable precedent for ethnically based social-welfare institutions, which symbolize for many the highest values of self-help. Networks of agencies have been formed by Jews and white Catholics; even Protestants—under the impact of a pluralism that has made them act like a minority as well—have formed essentially white ethnic welfare institutions to advance their interests. Throughout the country these voluntary agencies raise a huge amount of money, which is directed to the less fortunate in their respective ethnic and religious communities (and sometimes to those in other communities as well).

A new system of voluntary social-welfare agencies in the ghetto can hardly be expected to produce the collective force to overcome the deep inequalities in our society. Ethnic identity, solidarity and power must be forged through a series of organized communal experiences in a variety of institutional areas. In housing, for example, energy should be directed not only toward improving ghetto conditions but also toward creating within the ghetto the organizational vehicles for renovating buildings and, more important, for managing them.[17] Similarly, educational reforms should mean not only improvements in facilities and staff but also arrangements under which the local community can participate in and influence the administration of the schools.[18]

What blacks need, in short, are the means to organize separately and a heightened awareness of the distinctive goals to which their organizations must be directed. The black poor in our society do have interests distinct from and, more often than not, in conflict with those of other groups. Unless they organize along separatist lines, it is unlikely that they will have much success in advancing these interests. Judging from the history of those ethnic groups that have succeeded in gaining a foothold in our pluralistic society, it seems clear that ethnic separatism is a precondition for eventual achievement of full economic integration. Minority groups will win acceptance from the majority by developing their own bases of power, not by submerging their unorganized and leaderless numbers in coalitions dominated by other and more groups. Once they have formed separatist organizations, participation in coalitions (whether councils of social agencies or political parties) can then be a meaningful tactic in bargaining for a share of power over crucial institutional processes in the broader society.

In these terms, then, physical desegregation is not only irrelevant to the ghetto but can actually prevent the eventual integration of blacks in the institutional life of this society. For integration must be understood not as the mingling of bodies in school and neighborhood but as participation in and shared control over the major institutional spheres of American life. And that is a question of developing communal associations that can be bases for power—not of dispersing a community that is powerless.

One final point. A distinguished body of intellectual and integrationist leaders have engulfed us with reports and studies purporting to show that the negro community is a tangle of pathology, that the African American family has deteriorated beyond precedent and that the African American personality is deformed by profound feelings of inferiority.

And what is the solution to these problems? Integration. Not reallocation of governmental subsidies and other community wealth to make the African American ghetto as suitable a place to live as the many white ethnic communities, not the building of black power to give the African American some measure of control over his destiny, but submergence of the negro in the white majority.

What is it that we whites are implying about the African American and the African American about himself by this integrationist strategy? To say that African American children are not learning for lack of pride and motivation is one thing; to insist that they cannot find pride and motivation unless surrounded by whites in the classroom is quite another. For this precisely has been the tragedy of the African American: that he has seen himself through our eyes and has made his own feeling of personal and collective worth dependent on our feelings toward him. Thus, the African American has waited helplessly for us to proffer brotherhood. And he has waited in vain. One day an interpretation of American racism will be written, and it will say that White supremacy ultimately succeeded because the African American was led to believe that he could have no reality, no identity, except as a reflection of whites.

There is another solution to the African American's predicament, and some African Americans are struggling toward it. That solution seeks to protect the African American from the devastating effects of American racism by building black pride, black solidarity, and black power. If any lesson is to be drawn from the experience of other minorities in America, it is that the strength to resist majority prejudices, to advance in spite of them and ultimately to overcome them must be found within a countervailing ethnic community.

Originally published in 1966.

Notes

1. The proportion of nonwhites living in segregated census tracts in New York City rose from forty-nine to fifty-three percent between 1940 and 1950. In 1910 sixty percent of the African Americans in that city lived in assembly districts that were less than five percent African American. By 1960 sixty-two percent were in districts that were over fifty percent African American. "The Program for an Open City: Summary Report" (New York: Department of City Planning,

May 1965). (Mimeographed.) See also Davis McEntire, *Residence and Race: Final and Comprehensive Report to the Commission on Race and Housing* (Berkeley: University of California Press, 1960), p. 41.

2. See *Our Nonwhite Population and Its Housing* (Washington, D.C.: Housing and Home Finance Agency, 1963), pp. 1–3. The nonwhite population in central cities reached 10.3 million in 1960 and may exceed 16 million by 1975, according to McEntire, op. cit., pp. 4–5, 21–24.

3. George Schermer, "Desegregating the Metropolitan Area." Paper presented at the National Housing Workshop, National Committee Against Discrimination in Housing, West Point, N.Y., April 1966.

4. "More Negro Families Are Utilizing Fair Housing Law Here and in Suburbs," *New York Times*, October 23, 1966, p. 117.

5. McEntire, op. cit., pp. 135–147. In New York City, for example, there are three times as many substandard units occupied by nonwhites as whites at each income level.

6. *Negroes in Cities: Residential Segregation and Neighborhood Change* (Chicago: Aldine Publishing Co., 1965).

7. Criticism of urban renewal has been launched from both the right and the left. See Martin Anderson, *The Federal Bulldozer* (Cambridge, Mass.: MIT Press, 1965); Herbert J. Gans, "The Failure of Urban Renewal," *Commentary*, Vol. 39, No. 4 (April 1965), pp. 29–37; and the replies to Gans by George M. Raymond and Malcolm D. Rivkin, "Urban Renewal," *Commentary*, Vol. 40, No. 1 (July 1965), pp. 72–80.

8. For a review of experience with relocation see Chester Hartman, "The Housing of Relocated Families," *Journal of the American Institute of Planners*, Vol. 30, No. 4 (November 1964), pp. 266–268.

9. James Q. Wilson analyzes the political dilemmas created by renewal programs in "Planning and Politics: Citizen Participation in Urban Renewal," *Journal of the American Institute of Planners*, Vol. 29, No. 4 (November 1963), pp. 242–249.

10. "An Analysis of Current City-Wide Housing Needs" (New York: Department of City Planning, Community Renewal Program, December 1965), p. 67. (Mimeographed.)

11. Michael D. Appleby, "Logue's Record in Boston: An Analysis of His Renewal and Planning Activities" (New York: Council for New York Housing and Planning Policy, May 1966), p. 43. (Mimeographed.)

12. Blacks already comprise over fifty percent of the school-age populations in Chicago, Philadelphia, and Washington, D.C. (where they comprise more than eighty percent). In other cities they are rapidly approaching the majority— Detroit, for example, has well over a forty percent population of school-age African Americans.

13. James R. Coleman et al., *Equality of Educational Opportunity*, (Washington, D.C.: U.S. Government Printing Office, 1966).

14. Several studies show that by no means do African Americans do uniformly better in integrated schools. They either do better or worse than in segregated schools. One intervening variable appears to be the degree of bigotry exhibited by whites: The greater the bigotry, the more likely that African Americans will achieve less than in segregated schools. Poor and working-class whites have traditionally held the most prejudiced attitudes: integrating them with poor African Americans may actually hurt African Americans. *Ibid.*, especially pp. 330–333. See also Irwin Katz, "Review of Evidence Relating to Effects of Desegregation in the Intellectual Performance of Negroes," *American Psychologist*, Vol. 19 (June 1964), pp. 381–399.

15. There seems to be a somewhat easier acceptance when numbers of black children are assigned to white schools than when white children are assigned to ghetto schools. This has not been tried on a sufficient scale to put white tolerance to a genuine test, however. It is also true that African American parents do not want their children to travel far, either.

16. There have been many studies—including the work of Allison Davis and subsequent studies by August B. Hollingshead—on class biases in the intelligence test and the differential response of the school system to children of different socio-economic backgrounds. Many other studies document the sharp differences between the low-income school and its middle-class counterpart. For a recent study of inequalities by class in a large northern urban school system see Patricia Cayo Sexton, *Education and Income: Inequalities in Our Public Schools* (New York: Viking Press, 1961).

17. In a tentative way, this possibility is now being explored by some groups (e.g., churches), which are receiving loans to rehabilitate ghetto buildings under the federal low-cost mortgage program. These groups form local corporations to rehabilitate and later to manage houses.

18. Parent groups in East Harlem recently boycotted a new school (P. S. 201); they abandoned earlier demands for school integration to insist that the Board of Education cede a large measure of control to the local community. The ensuing controversy brought to the fore certain issues in professional and community control. As of this writing, a final resolution has not been reached. Without some administrative arrangement to insure greater involvement by the ghetto community, the schools will continue to be responsive to other, better-organized religious, ethnic, and class groupings that traditionally have been powerful enough to assert the superiority of their claims for educational services and resources over that of the ghetto. There is some indication that such arrangements may also bring educational benefits. A recent study showed a high correlation between the achievement of African American children and their feeling that they can control their own destinies. See Coleman et al., op. cit.

7

The Urban Fiscal Crisis:
Who Got What, and Why?

For quite a while, complaints about the urban fiscal crisis have been droning on, becoming as familiar as complaints about big government, or big bureaucracy, or high taxes—and almost as boring as well. Now suddenly the crisis seems indeed to be upon us: School closings are threatened, library services are curtailed, subway trains go unrepaired, welfare grants are cut, all because big-city costs have escalated to the point where local governments can no longer foot the bill. Yet for all the talk, and all the complaints, there has been no convincing explanation of just how it happened that, quite suddenly in the 1960s, the whole municipal housekeeping system seemed to become virtually unmanageable. This is especially odd because, not long ago, the study of city politics and city services was a favorite among American political scientists, and one subject they had gone far to illuminate. Now, with everything knocked askew, they seem to have very little to say that could stand as political analysis.

To be sure, there is a widely accepted explanation. The big cities are said to be in trouble because of the "needs" of blacks for services—a view given authority by the professionals who man the service agencies and echoed by the politicians who depend upon these agencies. Service "needs," the argument goes, have been increasing at a much faster rate than local revenues. The alleged reason is demographic: The large number of impoverished black southern migrants to the cities presumably requires far greater investments in services, including more elaborate educational programs, more frequent garbage collection, more intensive policing, if the city is to be maintained at accustomed levels of civil decency and order. Thus, city agencies have been forced to expand and elaborate their activities. However, the necessary expansion is presumably constricted for lack of local revenues, particularly since the better-off taxpaying residents and businesses have been leaving the city (hastened on their way by the black migration).[1] To this standard explanation of the crisis, there is also a standard remedy: namely, to increase municipal revenues, whether by enlarging federal and state aid to the cities or by redrawing jurisdictional boundaries to recapture suburban taxpayers.[2]

It is true, of course, that black children who receive little in the way of skills or motivation at home may require more effort from the schools; that densely packed slums require more garbage collection; that disorganized neighborhoods require more policing. For instance, the New York City Fire Department reports a 300 percent increase in fires in the last twenty years [between 1950–70]. But fires and similar calamities that threaten a wide public are one thing; welfare, education and health services, which "account" for by far the largest portion of big-city budgets, quite another. And while by any objective measure the new residents of the city have greater needs for such services, there are several reasons to doubt that the urban crisis is the simple result of rising needs and declining revenues.

For one thing, the trend in service budgets suggests otherwise. Blacks began to pour into the cities in very large numbers after World War II, but costs did not rise precipitously until the mid-1960s.[3] In other words, the needs of the black poor were not recognized for two decades. For another, any scrutiny of agency budgets shows that, except for public welfare, the expansion of services to the poor, as such, does not account for a very large proportion of increased expenditures. It was other groups, mainly organized provider groups, who reaped the lion's share of the swollen budgets. The notion that services are being strained to respond to the needs of the new urban poor, in short, takes little account either of when the strains occurred or of the groups who actually benefited from increased expenditures.

These two facts should lead us to look beyond the "rising needs-declining revenues" theory for an explanation of urban troubles. And once we do, perhaps some political common sense can emerge. School administrators and sanitation commissioners may describe their agencies as ruled by professional standards and as shaped by disinterested commitments to the public good, and thus define rising costs as a direct and proper response to the needs of people. But schools and sanitation departments are, after all, agencies of local government, substructures of the local political apparatus, and are managed in response to local political forces. The mere fact that people are poor or that the poor need special services has never led government to respond. Service agencies are political agencies, administered to deal with political problems, not service problems.

Now this view is not especially novel. Indeed, if there is any aspect of the American political system that was persuasively analyzed in the past, it was the political uses of municipal services in promoting allegiance and muting conflict. Public jobs, contracts, and services were dispensed by city bosses to maintain loyal cadres and loyal followers among the heterogeneous groups of the city. Somehow political analysts have forgotten this in their accounts of the contemporary urban crisis, testimony perhaps to the extent to which the doublethink of professional bureaucrats has befogged the common sense of us all. That is, we are confused by changes in the style of urban-service politics, failing to see that although the style has changed, the function has not. In the era of the big-city machine, municipal authorities managed to maintain a degree of consensus and allegiance among diverse groups by distributing public goods in the form of private favors. Today public goods are distributed through the service bureaucracies. With that change, the process of dispensing public goods has become more formalized, the struggles between groups more public, and the language of city politics more professional. As we will try to explain a little later, these changes were in some ways crucial in the development of what we call the urban crisis. Our main point for now, however, is that while we may refer to the schools or the sanitation department as if they are politically neutral, these agencies yield up a whole variety of benefits, and it is by distributing, redistributing and adapting these payoffs of the city agencies that urban political leaders manage to keep peace and build allegiances among the diverse groups in the city. In other words, the jobs, contracts, perquisites, as well as the actual services of the municipal housekeeping agencies, are just as much the substance of urban politics as they ever were.

All of which is to say that when there is a severe disturbance in the administration and financing of municipal services, the underlying cause is likely to be a fundamental disturbance in political relations. To account for the service "crisis" we should look at the changing relationship between political forces—at rising group conflict and weakening allegiances—and the way in which these disturbances set off an avalanche of new demands. To cope with these strains, political leaders expanded and proliferated the benefits of the city agencies. What we shall argue, in sum, is that the urban crisis is not a crisis of rising needs but a crisis of rising demands.

Any number of circumstances may disturb existing political relationships, with the result that political leaders are less capable of restraining the demands of various groups. Severe economic dislocations may activate groups that previously asked little of government, as in the 1930s. Or groups may rise in the economic structure, acquiring political force and pressing new demands as a result. Or large-scale migrations may alter the balance between groups. Any of these situations may generate sharp antagonism among groups, and as some new groups acquire a measure of influence, they may undermine established political relationships. In the period of uncertainty that ensues, discontent is likely to spread, political alignments may shift, and allegiances to a political leadership may become insecure. In the context of this general unrest, political leaders, unsure of their footing, are far more likely to respond to the specific demands of specific groups for enlarged benefits or new "rights." Periods of political instability, in other words, nurture new claims and claimants. This is what happened in the cities in the 1960s, and it happened at a time when the urban political system was uniquely ill-equipped to curb the spiral of rising demands that resulted.

The Political Disturbances That Led to Rising Demands

If the service needs of the black poor do not account for the troubles in the cities, the political impact of the black migration probably does. Massive shifts of population are almost always disturbing to a political system, for new relations have to be formed between a political leadership and constituent groups. The migration of large numbers of blacks from the rural South to a few core cities during and after World War II, leading many middle-class white constituents to leave for the suburbs, posed just this challenge to the existing political organization of the cities. But for a long time local governments resisted responding to the newcomers with the services, symbols and benefits that might have won the allegiance of these newcomers, just as the allegiance of other groups had previously been won.

The task of political integration was made difficult by at least four circumstances. One was the very magnitude of the influx. Between 1940 and 1960, nearly 4 million blacks left the land and, for the most part, settled in big northern cities. Consequently, by 1960 at least one in five residents of our fifty largest cities was black, and in the biggest cities the proportions were much greater. It is no exaggeration to say that the cities were inundated by sheer numbers.

Second, these large numbers were mainly lower-class blacks, whose presence aroused ferocious race and class hatreds, especially among the white ethnics who lived in neighborhoods bordering the ghettos and who felt their homes and schools endangered. As ghetto numbers enlarged, race and class polarities worsened, and political leaders, still firmly tied to the traditional inhabitants of the cities, were in no position to give concessions to the black poor.

Not only was race pitted against race, class against class, but the changing style of urban politics made concessions to conflicting groups a very treacherous matter. Just because the jobs, services and contracts that fueled the urban political organization were no longer dispensed covertly, in the form of private favors, but rather as matters of public policy, each concession was destined to become a subject of open political conflict. As a result, mayors found it very difficult to finesse their traditional constituents: New public housing for blacks, for example, could not be concealed, and every project threatened to arouse a storm of controversy. Despite their growing numbers and their obvious needs; therefore, blacks got very little in the way of municipal benefits throughout the 1940s and 1950s. Chicago, where the machine style was still entrenched, gave a little more; the Cook County AFDC rolls, for example, rose by eighty percent in the 1950s, and blacks were given some political jobs. But in most cities the local service agencies resisted the newcomers. In New York City and Los Angeles, for example, the AFDC rolls remained virtually unchanged in the 1950s. In many places public housing was brought to a halt; urban renewal generally became the instrument of black removal; and half the major southern cities (which also received large numbers of black migrants from rural areas) actually managed to reduce their welfare rolls, often by as much as half.[4]

Finally, when blacks entered the cities they were confronted by a relatively new development in city politics: namely, the existence of large associations of public employees, whether teachers, policemen, sanitation men or the like. The provider groups not only had a very large stake in the design and operation of public programs—for there is hardly any aspect of public policy that does not impinge on matters of working conditions, job security, or fringe benefits—but they had become numerous enough, organized enough and independent enough to wield substantial influence in matters affecting their interests.

The development of large, well-organized, and independent provider groups has been going on for many years, probably beginning with the emergence of the civil-service merit system at the turn of the century (a development usually credited to the efforts of reformers who sought to improve the quality of municipal services, to eliminate graft and to dislodge machine leaders).[5] But although the civil service originated in the struggle between party leaders and reformers, it launched municipal employees as an independent force. As city services expanded, the enlarging numbers of public employees began to form associations. Often these originated as benevolent societies, such as New York City's Patrolmen's Benevolent Association, which formed in the 1890s. Protected by the merit system, these associations gradually gained some influence in their own right, and they exerted that influence at both the

municipal and the state level to shape legislation and to monitor personnel policies so as to protect and advance their occupational interests.

The result was that, over time, many groups of public employees
managed to win substantial control over numerous matters affecting
their jobs and their agencies: entrance requirements, tenure guarantees,
working conditions, job prerogatives, promotion criteria, retirement
benefits. Except where wages were concerned, other groups in the
cities rarely became sufficiently aroused to block efforts by public
employees to advance their interests. But all of this also meant that when
blacks arrived in the cities, local political leaders did not control the
jobs—and, in cases where job prerogatives had been precisely specified
by regulation, did not even control the services—that might have been
given as concessions to the black newcomers.

Under the best of circumstances, of course, the task of integrating a
new and uprooted rural population into local political structures would
have taken time and would have been difficult. But for all of the reasons
given, local government was showing little taste for the task. As a result,
a large population that had been set loose from southern feudal institutions was not absorbed into the regulating political institutions (or economic institutions, for they were also resisted there) of the city.
Eventually that dislocated population became volatile, both in the
streets and at the polls. By 1960 that volatility forced the federal government to take an unprecedented role in urban politics.[6]

Urban blacks, who had been loyal Democrats for almost three
decades, had begun to defect even as their numbers grew, signaling the
failure of the municipal political machinery. New ways to reach and
reward the urban black voter were needed. Accordingly, the Kennedy
and Johnson administrations analysts began to explore strategies to
cement the allegiance of the urban black vote to the national party. What
emerged was a series of federal service programs directed to the ghetto.
The first appropriations were small, as with the Juvenile Delinquency
and Youth Offenses Control Act of 1961, but each program enlarged
upon the other, up until the model-cities legislation of 1966. Some of the
new programs—in manpower development, in education, in health—
were relatively straightforward. All they did was give new funds to local
agencies to be used to provide jobs or services for the poor. Thus, funds

appropriated under Title I of the Elementary and Secondary Education Act of 1965 were earmarked for educational facilities for poor children; the Medicaid program enacted in 1965 reimbursed health agencies and physicians for treating the poor; and manpower agencies were funded specifically to provide jobs or job training for the poor.

Other of the new federal programs were neither so simple nor so straightforward, and these were the ones that became the hallmark of the Great Society. The federal memoranda describing them were studded with terms like "inner city," "institutional change" and "maximum feasible participation." But if this language was often confusing, the programs themselves ought not to have been. The "inner city," after all, was a euphemism for the ghetto, and activities funded under such titles as delinquency prevention, mental health, antipoverty, or model cities turned out, in the streets of the cities, to look very much alike. What they looked like was nothing less than the old political machine.

Federal funds were used to create new storefront-style agencies in the ghettos, staffed with professionals who helped local people find jobs, obtain welfare or deal with school officials. Neighborhood leaders were also hired, named community workers, neighborhood aides or whatever, but in fact close kin to the old ward heelers, for they drew larger numbers of people into the new programs, spreading the federal spoils.

But federal spoils were not enough, for there were not many of them. If blacks were to be wrapped into the political organization of the cities, the traditional agencies of local government, which controlled the bulk of federal, state, and local appropriations, had to be reoriented. Municipal agencies had to be made to respond to blacks.

Various tactics to produce such reform were tried by national Democratic administrations, at first under the guise of experiments in "institutional change," but the experiments got little cooperation from local bureaucrats. Therefore, as turbulence spread in the northern ghettos, the federal officials began to try another way to promote institutional change—"maximum feasible participation. of residents of the areas and members of the groups served." Under that slogan the Great Society programs gave money to ghetto organizations, which then used the money to harass city agencies. Community workers were hired to badger housing inspectors and to pry loose welfare payments. Anti-poverty lawyers took municipal agencies to court on behalf of ghetto clients. The new "community action" agencies helped organize the ghetto poor to picket the welfare department or to boycott the school system.

In these various ways, then, the federal government intervened in local politics and forced local government to do what it had earlier failed to do. Federal dollars and federal authority were used to resuscitate the functions of the political machine, on the one hand by spurring local service agencies to respond to the black newcomers, and on the other by spurring blacks to make demands upon city services.

As it turned out, blacks made their largest tangible gains from this process through the public-welfare system. Total national welfare costs rose from about $4 billion in 1960 to nearly $15 billion in 1970. Big cities that received the largest numbers of black and Spanish-speaking migrants and that were most shaken by the political reverberations of that migration also experienced the largest welfare-budget rises. In New York, Los Angeles, and Baltimore, for example, the AFDC rolls quadrupled, and costs rose even faster. In many cities, welfare costs absorbed an ever-larger share of the local budget, a bigger piece of the public pie. In New York City, for example, welfare costs absorbed about twelve percent of the city's budget in the 1950s; but by 1970 the share going to welfare had grown to about twenty-five percent (of a much larger budget), mainly because the proportion of the city's population on Aid to Families of Dependent Children increased from 2.6 percent in 1960 to 11.0 percent in 1970.[7] In other words, the blacks who triggered the disturbances received their biggest payoffs from welfare,[8] mainly because other groups were not competing within the welfare system for a share of relief benefits.[9]

But if blacks got welfare, that was just about all they got. Less obvious than the emergence of black demands—but much more important in accounting for increasing service costs—was the reaction of organized whites to these political developments, particularly the groups who had direct material stakes in the running of the local services. If the new upthrust of black claims threatened and jostled many groups in the city, none were so alert or so shrill as those who had traditionally gotten the main benefits of the municipal services. These were the people who depended, directly or indirectly, on the city treasury for their livelihood: They worked in the municipal agencies, in agencies that were publicly funded (e.g., voluntary hospitals), in professional services that were publicly reimbursed (e.g., doctors), or in businesses that depended on city contracts (e.g., contractors and construction workers). Partly they were incited by black claims that seemed to threaten their traditional preserves. Partly they were no longer held in check by stable relationships with political leaders, for these relations had weakened or become uncertain or even turned to enmity: Indeed, in some cases, the leaders themselves had been toppled, shaken loose by the conflict and instability of the times. In effect, the groups who worked for or profited from city government had become unleashed, at the same time that-newcomers were snapping at their heels.

The result was that the provider groups reacted with a rush of new demands. And these groups had considerable muscle to back up their claims. Not only were they unusually numerous and well organized, but they were allied to broader constituencies by their class and ethnic ties and by their union affiliations. Moreover, their demands for increased benefits, whether higher salaries or lower work loads or greater autonomy were always couched in terms of protecting the professional standards of the city services, a posture that helped win them broad public support. As a result, even when the organized providers backed up their demands by closing the schools, or stopping the subways, or letting the garbage pile up, many people were ready to blame the inconveniences on political officials.

Local political leaders, their ties to their constituencies undermined by population shifts and spreading discontent, were in a poor position to resist or temper these escalating demands, especially the demands of groups with the power to halt the services on which a broader constituency depended. Instead, to maintain their position they tried to expand and elaborate the benefits—the payrolls, the contracts, the perquisites, and the services—of the municipal agencies.

Nor, as had been true in the era of the machine, was it easy to use these concessions to restore stable relationships. Where once political leaders had been able to anticipate or allay the claims of various groups, dealing with them one by one, now each concession was public, precipitating rival claims from other groups, each demand ricocheting against the other in an upward spiral. Not only did public concessions excite rivalry, but political officials lost the ability to hold groups in check in another way as well; unlike their machine predecessors, they could attach few conditions to the concessions they made. Each job offered, each wage increase conceded, each job prerogative granted was now ensconced in civil-service regulations or union contracts and, thus firmly secured, could not be withdrawn. Political leaders had lost any leverage in their dealings; each concession simply became the launching pad for higher demands. Instead of regular exchange relationships, open conflict and uncertainty became the rule. The result was a virtual run upon the city treasury by a host of organized groups in the city, each competing with the other for a larger share of municipal benefits. Benefits multiplied and budgets soared—and so did the discontent of various groups with the schools, or police, or housing, or welfare, or health. To illustrate, we need to examine the fiscal impact of mounting political claims in greater detail.

Rising Demands and the Fiscal Crisis

Education is a good example, for it is the single largest service run by localities, accounting for forty percent of the outlays of state and local government in 1968, up from thirty percent in 1948.[10] The huge expenditures involved in running the schools are also potential benefits—jobs for teachers, contracts for maintenance and construction, and educational services for children—all things to be gained by different groups in the local community. Accordingly, the educational system became a leading target of black demands,[11] at first mainly in the form of the struggle for integrated schools. Later, worn down by local resistance to integration and guided by the Great Society programs that provided staff, meeting rooms, mimeograph machines, and lawyers to ghetto groups,[12] the difficult demands for integration were transformed into demands for "citizen participation," which meant a share of the jobs, contracts and status positions that the school system yields up.[13]

Blacks made some gains. Boards of education began hiring more black teachers, and some cities instituted schemes for "community control" that ensconced local black leaders in the lower echelons of the school hierarchy.[14] But the organized producer groups, whose salaries account for an estimated eighty percent of rising school costs,[15] made far larger gains. Incited by black claims that seemed to challenge their traditional preserves, and emboldened by a weak and conciliatory city government, the groups who depend on school budgets began rapidly to enlarge and entrench their stakes. Most evident in the scramble were teaching and supervisory personnel, who were numerous and well organized and became ever more strident—so much so that the opening of each school year was signaled by news of teacher strikes in cities throughout the country. And threatened city officials strained to respond by expanding the salaries, jobs, programs and privileges they had to offer. One result was that average salaries in New York City, Chicago, Los Angeles, Philadelphia, Washington, D.C., and San Francisco topped the $10,000 mark by 1969, in most instances having doubled in the decade.[16] Not only did the teachers win rapid increases in salaries but, often prompted by new black demands, they exploited contract negotiations and intensive lobbying to win new guarantees of job security, increased pensions, and "improvements" in educational policy that have had the effect of increasing their own ranks—all of which drove up school budgets, especially in the big cities where blacks were concentrated.[17] In Baltimore, where the black population has reached forty-seven percent, the school budget increased from $57 million in 1961 to $184 million in 1971; in New Orleans from $28.5 million to $73.9 million in 1971; in Boston school costs rose from $35.4 million in 1961 to $95.7 million in 1971.[18] Total national educational costs which in 1957 amounted to $12 billion, topped $40 billion by 1968,[19] and the U.S. Office of Education expected costs to continue to rise, by at least thirty-seven percent by 1975. In this process, blacks may have triggered the flood of new demands on the schools, but organized whites turned out to be the main beneficiaries.

What happened in education happened in other services as well. Costs rose precipitously across the board as mayors tried to extend the benefits of the service agencies to quiet the discordant and clamoring groups in the city. One way was to expand the number of jobs, often by creating new agencies, so that there was more to go around. Hence, in New York City the municipal payroll expanded by over 145,000 jobs in the 1960s, and the rate of increase doubled after Mayor John V. Lindsay took office in 1965.[20] By 1971, 381,000 people were on the municipal payroll. Some 34,000 of these new employees were black and Puerto Rican "paraprofessionals," according to the city's personnel director. Others were Lindsay supporters, put on the payroll as part of his effort to build a new political organization out of the turmoil.[21] Most of the rest were new teachers, policemen, and social workers, some hired to compensate for reduced work loads won by existing employees (teachers won reduced class sizes, patrolmen the right to work in pairs), others hired to staff an actual expansion that had taken place in some services to appease claimant groups who were demanding more welfare, safer streets or better snow removal.[22] As a result, total state and local governmental employment in the city rose from 8.2 percent of the total labor force in 1960 to 14 percent in 1970. A similar trend of expanded public employment took place in other big cities. In Detroit state and local employment rose from 9 percent of the labor force in 1960 to 12.2 percent in 1970; in Philadelphia from 6.9 percent to 9.8 percent; in Los Angeles from 9.8 percent to 12.0 percent; in San Francisco from 12.2 percent in 1960 to 15.2 percent in 1970.[23]

Another way to try to deal with the clamor was to concede larger and larger salaries and more liberal pensions to existing employees who were pressing new demands, and pressing hard, with transit, or garbage, or police strikes (or sick-outs or slow-downs) that paralyzed whole cities.[24] In Detroit, garbage collectors allowed refuse to accumulate in the streets when the city offered them only a six-percent wage increase after the police won an eleven-percent increase.[25] In Cincinnati, municipal laborers and garbage collectors threatened a "massive civil-disobedience campaign" when they were offered less than the $945 annual raise won by policemen and firemen.[26] In Philadelphia, garbage collectors engaged in a slowdown when a policeman was appointed to head their department.[27] A San Francisco strike by 7500 city workers shut down the schools and the transit system and disrupted several other services simultaneously.[28] An unprecedented wildcat strike by New York City's policemen, already the highest-paid police force in the world, would have cost the city an estimated $56,936 a year for every policeman (and $56,214 for every fireman) if demands for salaries, pensions, fringe benefits and reduced work time had been conceded.[29] If these demands were perhaps a bit theatrical, the pay raises for city employees in New York City did average twelve percent each year in 1967, 1968, and 1969; meanwhile, the U.S. Bureau of Labor Statistics reported that the earnings of health professionals in the city rose by eighty percent in the decade, at least double the increase in factory wages. In other cities across the country similar groups were making similar gains; municipal salaries rose by seven to ten percent in both 1968 and 1969, or about twice as fast as the Consumer Price Index.[30]

The pattern of crazily rising municipal budgets was the direct result of these diverse and pyramiding claims on city services, claims triggered by political instability.[31] Accordingly, budget trends followed political trends. New York City, for example, received about 1.25 million blacks and Puerto Ricans in the years between 1950 and 1965, while about 1.5 million whites left the city. The political reverberations of these shifts weakened the Democratic party organization and resulted in the Lindsay victory on a fusion ticket in 1965. But the Lindsay government was extremely unstable, without ties to established constituents, virtually without a political organization and extremely vulnerable to the demands of the different groups, including the ghetto groups whose support it was trying to cultivate. New York also had very strong and staunch provider groups, as everyone knows from the transit, garbage, teacher and police strikes, each of which in turn threatened municipal calamity. The subsequent escalation of demands by blacks and Puerto Ricans on the one hand, and municipal provider groups on the other, produced the much-publicized turmoil and conflict that wracked the city.

To deal with these troubles, city officials made concessions, with the result that the municipal budget almost quadrupled in the 1960s. And as the turmoil rose, so did city costs: An annual budget rise of 6 percent in the 1950s and 8.5 percent in the early 1960s became an annual rise of 15 percent after 1965.[32] By the late 1960s New York spent half again as much per capita as other cities over a million (excluding educational costs), twice as much per capita as cities between 500,000 and a million, and three times as much as the other 288 cities.[33]

A few cities where the existing political organization was firmly entrenched and machine-style politics still strong were spared. Chicago is the notable example, and Chicago's political organization shows in lower welfare costs, in per-pupil expenditures that are half that of New York City, in garbage collection costs of $22 a ton compared to $49 in New York City. Mayor Daley never lost his grip. With the white wards firmly in tow, he made modest concessions to blacks earlier and without fear of setting off a chain reaction of demands by other groups. And so he never gave as much, either to blacks or to organized whites. But most other large cities showed a pattern of escalating discontent and escalating service budgets more like New York City than Chicago.[34] By 1970 the total costs of local government had risen about 350 percent over 1950.

The cities are unable to raise revenues commensurate with these expenditures; and they are unable to resist the claims that underlie rising expenditures. And that is what the fiscal crisis is all about. Cities exist only by state decree, and depend entirely on the state governments for their taxing powers.[35] Concretely this has meant that the states have taken for themselves the preferred taxes[36] leaving the localities to depend primarily on the property tax (which accounts for seventy percent of revenues raised by local governments),[37] supplemented by a local sales tax in many places, user charges (e.g., sewer and water fees) and, in some places, a local income tax.[38] The big cities have had little choice but to drive up these local taxes to which they are limited, but at serious costs.[39] New York City, for example, taxes property at rates twice the national average, yielding a property-tax roll three times as large as any other city. New York City also has an income tax, which is rising rapidly. Newark, plagued by racial conflict, ranks second in the nation in its rate of property tax.[40]

The exploitation of any of these taxes is fraught with dilemmas for localities. By raising either property or sale taxes excessively, they risk driving out the business and industry on which their tax rolls eventually depend, and risk also the political ire of their constituents. For instance, it was estimated that a one-percent increase in the New York City sales tax had the effect of driving six percent of all clothing and household-furnishing sales out beyond the city line, along with thousands of jobs.[41] A New York property-tax rate of four percent of true value on new improvements is thought by many to have acted as a brake on most new construction, excepting the very high-yielding office buildings and luxury apartments. Boston's six percent of true-value property tax brought private construction to a halt until the law was changed so that new improvements were taxed only half as heavily as existing buildings.[42] Increases in either sales- or property-tax rates thus entail the serious danger of diminishing revenues by eroding the tax base. To make matters worse, with the beginning of recession in 1969, revenues from sales and income taxes began to fall off, while the interest the cities had to pay for borrowing rose, at a time when local governments were going more and more into hock.[43]

Fiscal Constraints and Political Turmoil

In the face of fiscal constraints, demands on city halls do not simply stop. Indeed, a number of frustrated claimants seem ready for rebellion. When pension concessions to some employees in New York City were thwarted by the state legislature, the enraged municipal unions closed the bridges to the city and closed the sewage plants, while the president of Local 237 intoned that "Governor Rockefeller needs to be reminded that the teamsters are made of sterner stuff than the people of Czechoslovakia and Austria who caved in so easily to Hitler three decades ago."[44] If most groups were less dramatic in pressing their demands, it is probably because they were more quickly conciliated than these workers, many of whom were black and Puerto Rican. The political instability, which escalating demands both signify and exacerbate, rocked one city government after another. Indeed, many big-city mayors simply quit the job, something that does not happen very often in politics.

The reason they give is money—money to appease the anarchic demands of urban groups. Joseph Barr, former mayor of Pittsburgh and a past president of the United States Conference of Mayors, explained that "the main problem of any mayor of any city of any size is money...we are just choked by the taxes. The middle classes are fleeing to the suburbs and the tax base is going down and down...if the mayors don't get relief from the legislatures, God help them!...Any mayor who is not frustrated is not thinking." Arthur Naftalin, former mayor of Minneapolis and also a past president of the United States Conference of Mayors, said that the "most difficult and most important problem [is that the city] can't reach the resources. The states have kept the cities on a leash, tying them to the property tax—which is regressive. Old people and low-income people live in the city, and they catch the burden increasingly." Thomas C. Tarrington, mayor of Denver 1963–1968, when he resigned in midterm, said when he left: "I hope to heaven the cities are not ungovernable…[but] with perhaps few if any exceptions, the financial and organizational structures of most large cities are hardly up to the needs of 1969 or 1970. Our cities were structured financially when we were a rural nation and our structures of government are such that the mayors lack not only the financial resources but the authority to do the job." Ivan Allen, Jr., mayor of Atlanta since 1962: "At my age I question whether I would have been physically able to continue for another four years in the face of the constant pressure, the innumerable crises, and the confrontations that have occurred in the cities." A. D. Sillingson, mayor of Omaha from 1965: "I've gone through three and a half tough years in this racial business, and I could just stand so much." And the country's first black mayor, Carl B. Stokes of Cleveland, inter- viewed before he was reelected by the slimmest of margins in 1969, announced that the biggest challenge facing someone in his position was "obtaining the necessary money with which to meet the necessary needs of a big city."[45] Mr. Stokes declined to run again in 1971, leaving Cleve- land politics fragmented among eleven different candidates. The list of prominent mayors who threw in the sponge includes such celebrated urban reformers as Jerome P. Cavanaugh of Detroit and Richard C. Lee of New Haven. Nearly half the United States Conference of Mayors Executive Committee and Advisory Council have retired or announced their intentions of retiring after their present term, an "unprecedented" number according to a conference spokesman.

Whether the candidates were new aspirants moving in to fill the vacuum or older hands sticking it out, by 1969 big-city elections through- out the country reflected the instability of the times. Mayor Lindsay was reelected, but with only forty-two percent of the vote. The same year two Democrats ran against each other in Detroit. In Pittsburgh Peter F. Flaherty, an insurgent Democrat, won only to promptly repudiate the ward chairman who turned out the vote for him; in Youngstown, a solidly Democratic city, a Republican was elected; in Philadelphia, where regis- tration is heavily Democratic, the Democratic party was unable to block a Republican sweep headed by District Attorney Arlen Specter, putting him in line for a try at the mayor's office. Of 156 Connecticut towns and cities that held elections in 1969, forty-six municipalities switched parties. And an assembly of eighty-five representatives of federal, state and local governments, labor and religious leaders, editors and educators, meeting at Arden House in 1969, pronounced:

> America is in the midst of an urban crisis demonstrating an inadequacy and incompetency of basic policies, programs and institutions and presenting a crisis of confidence. These failures affect every public service—education, housing, welfare, health, and hospitals, transportation, pollution control, the administration of criminal justice, and a host of others—producing daily deterioration in the quality of life. Although most visible in the large cities, that deterioration spreads to suburbia, exurbia, and beyond. Frustration rises as government fails to respond.[46]

This pronouncement came not from a radical caucus but from a gathering of the most prestigious representatives of American institutions.

Those who for the time survived the turmoil were even shriller in sounding the alarm. Mayor Joseph Alioto of San Francisco said simply: "The sky's falling in on the cities; it really is. We've had six cops killed in San Francisco since I took office. We need jobs and money for the poor and haven't money for either. We can't go on like this. Even the capitalistic system's not going to survive the way we're going." Kenneth Gibson, the black mayor of Newark: "Wherever the cities are going, Newark's going to get there first.... If we had a bubonic plague in Newark everybody would try to help, but we really have a worse plague and nobody notices." Mayor Wesley Uhlman of Seattle said he was so busy putting out fires he had no time to think about anything else. Moon Candrieu, the mayor of New Orleans: "We've taxed everything that moves and everything that stands still, and if anything moves again, we tax that too.... The cities are going down the pipe and if we're going to save them we'd better do it now; three years from now will be too late." "Boston," said Mayor Kevin White, "is a tinderbox.... The fact is, it's an armed camp. One out of every five people in Boston is on welfare. Look, we raise 70 percent of our money with the property tax, but

half our property is untaxable and 20 percent of our people are bankrupt. Could you run a business that way?" And Mayor Lindsay of New
York proclaimed: "The cities of America are in a battle for survival....
Frankly, even with help in Washington, I'm not sure we can pull out of
the urban crisis in time."[47] (Not long afterwards, Governor Rockefeller
suggested that perhaps New York City's government, at least, ought not
to survive, that it might be a good idea to abolish the present city structure and begin all over.)[48]

The mayors speak of the twin troubles of scarce revenues and racial
confrontation. And it is no accident that the troubles occur together and
are most severe in the biggest cities. It was the biggest cities that experienced the most serious disturbance of traditional political relations as
a result of the influx of blacks and the outflux of many whites. In this
context, demands by black newcomers triggered a rush of new demands
by whites, especially the large and well-organized provider groups that
flourished in the big cities. The weakened and vulnerable mayors
responded; they gave more and more of the jobs, salaries, contracts and
services that had always worked to win and hold the allegiance of diverse
groups. The eventual inability of the cities to garner the vastly increased
revenues needed to fuel this process helped bring the urban political
process to a point of crisis. The fiscal crisis is indeed real—not because
of mounting "needs" for services but because of mounting demands for
the benefits associated with the municipal bureaucracies. To block the
responses of the bureaucracies to these demands for lack of revenues is
to block a process of political accommodation in the largest population
centers of the nation. The defection of the mayors was another sign of
how deep the disturbances were, not in health agencies or welfare agencies, but in the urban political structure.

Federalism as a Constraining Influence

If mayors cannot resist the demands of contending groups in the cities,
there are signs that the state and federal governments can, and will. The
fiscal interrelations that undergird the federal system and leave the cities
dependent on state and federal grants for an increasing portion of their
funds are also a mechanism by which state and federal politics come to

intervene in and control city politics. This is happening most clearly and directly through changes in state expenditures for the cities.

With their own taxing powers constricted from the outset, the mayors had little recourse but to turn to the states for enlarged grants-in-aid, trying to pass upward the political pressures they felt, usually summoning the press and the urban pressure groups for help. Since governors and legislators were not entirely immune to pressures from the city constituencies, the urban states increased their aid to the big cities.[49] Metropolises like New York City and Los Angeles now get roughly a quarter of their revenues from the state.

Accordingly, state budgets also escalated, and state taxes rose.[50] All in all, at least twenty-one states imposed new taxes or increased old taxes in 1968, and thirty-seven states in 1969, usually as a result of protracted struggle.[51] North Carolina enacted the largest program of new or increased taxes in its history; Illinois and Maine introduced an income tax, bringing to thirty-eight the number of states imposing some form of income tax; South Carolina passed its first major tax increase in a decade. Even Ohio moved to change its tradition of low-tax and low-service policies that had forced thirteen school districts in the state to close. Overall, state and local taxes rose from five percent of the Gross National Product in 1946 to more than eight percent of the GNP in 1969. Americans paid an average of $380 in state and local taxes in the fiscal year 1968, $42 more per person than the previous year, and more than double the fiscal year 1967. The rate tended to be highest in urban states: In New York the per-person tax burden was $576; in California, $540; in Massachusetts, $453. The low was in Arkansas, with a tax rate of $221.[52]

But raising taxes in Albany or Sacramento to pay for politics in New York City or Los Angeles is no simple matter, for the state capitals are not nearly as vulnerable as city halls to urban pressure groups, but are very vulnerable indeed to the suburbs and small towns that are antagonized by both higher taxes and city troubles. Besides, the mass of urban voters also resent taxes, especially when taxes are used to pay off the organized interests in the service systems, without yielding visibly better services.[53] Accordingly, even while taxes are raised, state grants to the cities are cut anyway. Thus, the New York State legislature reduced grant-in-aid formulas in welfare and Medicaid (programs that go mainly to the central cities and mainly to blacks in those cities) in 1969[54] and again in 1971 (1970 was an election year and so the governor proposed increased aid to the cities without tax increases). Each time, the cuts were effected in all-night marathon sessions of the legislature, replete with dramatic denouncements by Democratic legislators from the cities and cries of betrayal from the mayors. Despite the cuts, anticipated state spending still rose by $878 million in 1969, the highest for any single year excepting the previous fiscal year in which the rise had been $890 million. By 1970, when the proposed budget had reached $8.45 billion, requiring $1.1 billion in new taxes, the outcry was so terrific that the governor reversed his proposals and led the legislature in a budget-slashing session, with welfare and Medicaid programs the main targets.

When Governor Ronald Reagan, a self-proclaimed fiscal conservative, nevertheless submitted a record-breaking $6.37-billion budget for the 1969–1970 fiscal year, he met a storm of political protest that threatened a legislative impasse, leaving California without a budget. The next year Reagan proposed to solve the state's "fiscal crisis" by cutting welfare and medicaid expenditures by $800 million; even so, he submitted another record budget of $6.7 billion. When the long legislative battle that ensued was over, the governor signed an unbalanced budget of $7.3 billion, with substantial cuts in welfare and medicaid nevertheless.

Pennsylvania's former Republican Governor Raymond P. Shafer, in his short two years in office, managed to win the opposition of all but twenty-three percent of Pennsylvania voters as he and the legislature fought about how to raise $500 million in new revenues. At the beginning of his term in 1967 the governor was forced to raise state sales taxes to six percent, despite his campaign pledge of no new taxes, and early in 1969, with the budget $200 million short, he proposed that state's first income tax. When Shafer left office the income tax was enacted by his successor, Democratic Governor Milton Shapp, only to be voided by the Pennsylvania Supreme Court in 1971. A modified income-tax law was finally passed, but by that time the state legislature was also making spending reductions, including a fifty-percent cut in state education appropriations for ghetto districts.[55]

When Connecticut's 1969 biannual state budget proposal required a $700-million tax increase despite cuts in the welfare budget, the Democratic-controlled General Assembly rebelled, forcing a hectic special session of the state legislature to hammer out a new budget and tax program. In the tumultuous weeks that followed, a compromise package presumably agreed upon by the Democratic governor and the Democratic majority in both houses was repeatedly thrown into doubt. When the session was over, Connecticut had passed the largest tax program in its history, had borrowed $32.5 million, and Governor John N. Dempsey had announced he would not seek reelection. Two years later Republican Governor Thomas J. Meskill engaged the legislature in battle again over another record budget that the governor proposed to pay for with a seven-percent sales tax—the highest in the country. Not only the legislature, but the insurance industries, the mayor of Hartford and 5000 marchers took part in the protest that ensued, leading to a compromise tax package that replaced the sales-tax increase with a new state income tax, together with more borrowing and new welfare cuts as well. A few short months later, after new public protests, the income tax was repealed, the sales-tax increase was restored, and more spending cuts were made, mainly in state grants to municipalities and in welfare appropriations.

The New Jersey legislature, at a special session called by Democratic Governor Richard Hughes in 1969 to plead for added revenues for urban areas, rejected a new tax on banks and lending institutions—this despite the urging of the governor, who called the cities of the state "sick" and its largest city, Newark, "sick unto death," and despite the clamor of New Jersey's mayors. The legislature eventually agreed to redirect some existing urban-aid funds to pay for increased police and fire salaries—a measure made particularly urgent after Newark's firemen went on strike, forcing the city to make emergency salary arrangements. When Republican Governor William T. Cahill took office later that year he signed a measure raising the New Jersey sales tax to five percent, claiming he faced a "major state fiscal crisis" of a $300-million deficit.

Other state governments are locked in similar fiscal and political battles. Michigan began the 1972 fiscal year without authorization to spend money after the legislature had been virtually paralyzed by a six-month struggle over the $2-billion budget, which the governor had proposed to finance with a thirty-eight percent increase in the state income tax. Wisconsin cut welfare and urban-aid expenditures over Governor Ody J. Fish's protest and, having enacted a new and broadened sales tax, precipitated a march on the capital by Milwaukee poor. Not long afterward, Governor Fish resigned, imperiling the Wisconsin Republican party. In Rhode Island, Democratic Governor Frank E. Licht promised no new taxes in his reelection campaign in 1970 and two months later recommended an income tax, amidst loud voter protest. When Texas, having passed the largest tax bill in its history in 1969, faced a deficit of $400 million in 1971, Governor Preston E. Smith vetoed the entire second year of a two-year budget, which totaled $7.1 billion.

In brief, pressures from the big cities were channeled upward to the state capitals, with some response. At least in the big urbanized states, governors and legislatures moved toward bailing out the cities, with the result that state expenditures and state taxes skyrocketed. But the reaction is setting in; the taxpayers' revolt is being felt in state legislatures across the country. And as raucous legislative battles continue, a trend is emerging: The states are turning out to be a restraining influence on city politics, and especially on ghetto politics.

While, in the main, grants-in-aid were not actually reduced, they were not increased enough to cover rising city costs either, and the toll is being taken. Some municipalities began to cut payroll and services. By 1971 vacancies were going unfilled in New York City, Baltimore, Denver, and Kansas City. San Diego and Cleveland reduced rubbish collection; Dallas cut capital improvements; Kansas City let its elm trees die.[56] Detroit started closing park toilets. And some city employees were actually being dismissed in Los Angeles, Cleveland, Detroit, Kansas City, Cincinnati, Indianapolis, Pittsburgh, and New York City. "This is the first time since the Depression that I have participated in this kind of cutback of education," said Cincinnati's superintendent of schools.[57] "You run as far as you can, but when you run out of gas you've got to stop," said Baltimore's Mayor Thomas J. D'Alesandro.

But the biggest cuts imposed by the states were in the programs from which blacks had gained the most as a result of their emergence as a force in the cities. Special state appropriations for health and education in ghetto districts were being cut; nine states cut back their Medicaid programs;[58] and most important, at least nineteen states reduced welfare benefits by mid-1971, according to a *New York Times* survey. Moreover, new state measures to root out "welfare fraud," or to reinstitute residence restrictions, or to force recipients into work programs threatened far more drastic erosion of black gains in the near future.

There are signs that the federal government has also become a restraining influence on city politics. In the early 1960s the national Democratic administration had used its grants to the cities to intervene in city politics, encouraging ghetto groups to demand more from city halls and forcing recalcitrant mayors to be more responsive to the enlarging and volatile ghettos, whose allegiance had become critical to the national Democratic party. But a Republican administration was not nearly so oriented to the big cities, least of all to the ghettos of the big cities. Accordingly, the directions of the Great Society programs that the Nixon administration had inherited were shifted; bit by bit the new federal poverty agencies were scattered among the old-line federal bureaucracies, and the local agencies that had been set up in the ghettos were given to understand that confrontation tactics had to be halted. By now the Great Society looks much like traditional grant-in-aid programs; the federal fuel for ghetto agitation has been cut off. And new administration proposals for revenue sharing would give state and local governments firm control of the use of federal grants, unhampered by the "maximum feasible participation" provisions that helped to stir ghetto demands in the 1960s.

There are other signs as well. The wage freeze stopped, at least temporarily, the escalation of municipal salaries, and this despite the outcry of teachers across the country. Finally, and perhaps most portentous for blacks, the administration's proposal for "welfare reform" would give the federal government a much larger role in welfare policy, lifting the struggle for who gets what outside of the arena of city politics where blacks had developed some power and had gotten some welfare.

Nor is it likely, were the Democrats to regain the presidency and thus regain the initiative in federal legislation, that the pattern of federal restraint would be entirely reversed. The conditions that made the ghettos a political force for a brief space of time seem to have changed. For one thing, there is not much action, either in the streets or in the voting booths. The protests and marches and riots have subsided, at least partly because the most aggressive people in the black population were absorbed; it was they who got the jobs and honorary positions yielded to blacks during the turmoil. These concessions, together with the Great Society programs that helped produce them, seem to have done their work, not only in restoring a degree of order to the streets but in restoring ghetto voters to Democratic columns.

In any case, it was not ghetto insurgency of itself that gave blacks some political force in the 1960s. Rather it was that the insurgents were concentrated in the big cities, and the big cities played a very large role in Democratic politics. That also is changing; the cities are losing ground to the suburbs, even in Democratic calculations, and trouble in the cities is not likely to carry the same weight with Democratic presidents that it once did.

To be sure, a Democratic administration might be readier than a Republican one to refuel local services, to fund a grand new cornucopia of social programs. The pressures are mounting, and they come from several sources. One is the cities themselves, for to say that the cities are no longer as important as they once were is not to say Democratic leaders will want the cities to go under. Moreover, the inflated costs of the city are spreading to the suburbs and beyond, and these communities are also pressing for federal aid. Finally, there is the force of the organized producers themselves, who have become very significant indeed in national politics; the education lobby and the health lobby already wield substantial influence in Washington, and they are growing rapidly. But while these pressures suggest that new federal funds will be forthcoming, the rise of the suburbs and the parallel rise of the professional lobbies indicate that it is these groups who are likely to be the main beneficiaries.

The general truths to be drawn from this tale of the cities seem clear enough and familiar enough, for what happened in the 1960s has happened before in history. The lower classes made the trouble, and other groups made the gains. In the United States in the 1960s, it was urban blacks who made the trouble, and it was the organized producer groups in the cities who made the largest gains. Those of the working and middle classes who were not among the organized producers got little enough themselves, and they were made to pay with their tax moneys for gains granted to others. Their resentments grew. Now, to appease them, the small gains that blacks did make in the course of the disturbances are being whittled away.

There is, we think, an even more important truth, though one perhaps not so quickly recognized. These were the events of a political struggle, of groups pitted against each other and against officialdom. But every stage of that struggle was shaped and limited by the structures in which these groups were enmeshed. A local service apparatus, which at the outset benefited some and not others, set the stage for group struggle. Service structures that offered only certain kinds of benefits determined the agenda of group struggle. And a fiscal structure that limited the contest mainly to benefits paid for by state and local taxes largely succeeded in keeping the struggle confined within the lower and middle strata of American society. Schoolteachers turned against the ghetto, taxpayers against both, but no one turned against the concentrations of individual and corporate wealth in America. Local government, in short, is important, less for the issues it decides than for the issues it keeps submerged. Of the issues submerged by the events of the urban crisis, not the least is the more equitable distribution of wealth in America.

Originally published in 1973.

Notes

1. This view of the urban problem was given official status by the "Riot Commission." According to the commission:[The] fourfold dilemma of the American city [is:] Fewer tax dollars come in, as large numbers of middle-income tax payers move out of central cities and property values and business decline, More tax dollars are required, to provide essential public services and facilities, and to meet the needs of expanding lower-income groups; Each tax dollar buys less, because of increasing costs. Citizen dissatisfaction with municipal services grows as needs, expectations and standards of living increase throughout the community [*Report of the National Advisory Commission on Civil Disorders* (New York: Bantam, 1968), p 389]. Similarly, Alan K. Campbell and Donna E. Shalala write: "Most of the substantive problems flow, at least in part, from…the fact that the central cities have been left with segments of the population most in need of expensive services, and the redistribution of economic activities has reduced the relative ability of these areas to support such services" ["Problems

Unsolved, Solutions Untried: The Urban Crisis,"—in *The States and the Urban Crisis* (Englewood Cliffs, N.J.: Prentice Hall, 1970), p. 7]. The conventional wisdom is again echoed by the U.S. Advisory Commission on Intergovernmental Relations:

> The large central cities are in the throes of a deepening fiscal crisis. On the one hand, they are confronted with the need to satisfy rapidly growing expenditure requirements triggered by the rising number of "high cost" citizens. On the other hand, their tax resources are growing at a decreasing rate (and in some cases actually declining), a reflection of the *exodus of middle and high income families and business firms from the central city to suburbia* [italics in original] [*Fiscal Balance in the American Federal System: Metropolitan Fiscal Disparities* (Washington, D.C.: Government Printing Office, 1967). Vol. II, p. 5].

Politicians share this view. "In the last 10 years, 200,000 middle-class whites have moved out of St. Louis," said Mayor A. J. Cervantes, "and 100,000 blacks, many of them poor, have moved in. It costs us *eight times as much* to provide city services to the poor as to the middle-class" [italics in original] [the *New York Times*, May 22, 1970].

2. As a matter of fact, city revenues have not declined at all, but have risen astronomically, although not as astronomically as costs. Presumably, if the city had been able to hold or attract better-off residents and businesses, revenues would have risen even faster, and the fiscal aspect of the urban crisis would not have developed.

3. It should be made clear at the outset that the costs of government generally rose steadily in the years after World War II. This is the subject of James O'Connor's analysis in "The Fiscal Crisis of the State," *Socialist Revolution.* 1, 1 (January/February 1970), 12–54; 1, 2 (March/April 1970), 34–94. But while all government budgets expanded, state and local costs rose much faster, and costs in the central cities rose the most rapidly of all, especially after 1965. Thus, according to the Citizens' Budget Commission, New York City's budget increased almost eight times as fast in the five fiscal years between 1964 and 1969 as during the postwar years 1949 to 1954. From an average annual increase of 5.5 percent in 1954, budget costs jumped to 9.1 percent in 1964 and to 14.2 percent in 1969 (the *New York Times*, January 11, 1960). It is with this exceptional rise that this article is concerned.

4. For a discussion of the uses of welfare in resisting black migrants, see Frances Fox Piven and Richard A. Cloward, *Regulating the Poor: The Functions of Public Welfare* (New York: Pantheon, 1971); Chapters 7 and 8.

5. At least some of the employees in all cities with more than 500,000 inhabitants are now under civil service; in about half of these cities, virtually all employees have such protections.

6. See Piven and Cloward, op. cit., Chapters 9 and 10, on the impact of the black migration on the Democratic administrations of the 1960s.

7. *Changing Patterns of Prices, Pay, Workers, and Work on the New York Scene*, U.S. Department of Labor, Bureau of Labor Statistics (New York: Middle Atlantic Regional Office, May 1971), Regional Reports No. 20, p. 36.

8. The dole, needless to say, is a very different sort of concession from the higher salaries, pensions, and on-the-job prerogatives won by other groups. For one thing, the dole means continued poverty and low status. For another, it is easier to take away, for recipients remain relatively weak and unorganized.

9. That poor minorities made large gains through the welfare "crisis" and other groups did not is important to understanding the furious opposition that soaring welfare budgets arouse. Organized welfare-agency workers were competing for the welfare dollar, of course, but were not nearly so successful as the workers in other services, for they were not in a position to take much advantage of political turmoil. They were not nearly so numerous or well organized as teachers, policemen or firemen, and they could not use the threat of withholding services to exact concessions nearly so effectively. Unlike schoolteachers or garbage men, their services were of importance only to the very poor.

10. See *State and Local Finances: Significant Features 1967–1970*, U.S. Advisory Commission on Intergovernmental Relations (Washington, D.C.: Government Printing Office, 1969), Figure 6, p. 39.

11. Conflict and competition over the schools have been further heightened because the proportion of blacks in the schools has increased even more rapidly than the proportion of blacks in the population, owing to the youthfulness of blacks and the flight of whites to private schools. In Washington, blacks constituted fifty-four percent of the local population in 1965, but ninety percent of the school children; in St. Louis blacks were twenty seven percent of the population, but sixty-three percent of the school population; in Chicago, they were twenty-three percent of the general population, but fifty-three percent of the school population; in New York City, where blacks and Puerto Ricans make up about twenty-seven percent of the population, fifty-two percent of the children in the schools were black or Puerto Rican. Of the twenty-eight target cities in the nation, seventeen had black majorities in the school system by 1965. See *Racial Isolation in the Public School*, U.S. Commission on Civil Rights (Washington; D.C.: Government Printing Office, February 20, 1967), Table II-2.

12. The federal government was also providing direct funds to improve the education of the "disadvantaged" under Title I of the Elementary and Secondary Education Act of 1965. However, although in four years following the passage of the act, $4.3 billion was appropriated for Title I, it was widely charged that these funds were misused and diverted from the poor by many local school boards.

13. A series of training guides to such efforts, prepared with federal funds by a local poverty program known as United Bronx Parents, included a kit on "How to Evaluate Your School" and a series of leaflets on such matters as "The Expense Budget—Where Does All the Money Go?" "The Construction Budget—When the Community Controls Construction We Will Have the Schools We Need,"

as well as an all-purpose handbook on parents' rights vis-à-vis the schools. Not surprisingly, Albert Shanker, president of the teachers union in New York City, charged there was "an organized effort to bring about rule in the schools by violence," involving the use of flying squads of disrupters who went from school to school and who, he said, had been trained with government (i.e., poverty program) funds (the *New York Times*, November 16, 1970, p. 2).

14. See *Urban America, Inc., and the Urban Coalition, One Year Later: An Assessment of the Nation's Response to the Crisis Described by the National Advisory Commission on Civil Disorders* (New York: Praeger, 1969), pp. 34–35. See also Naomi Levine with Richard Cohen, *Oceanhill-Brownsville: A Case History of Schools in Crisis* (New York: Popular Library, 1969), pp. 127–128.

15. This estimate was reported by Fred Hechinger, the *New York Times*, August 29, 1971.

16. Averaging $9200 in 1970–1971, according to the National Education Association.

17. State averages reflect the political troubles in big cities. Thus, in an urban state like New York, $1251 was spent per pupil in 1969–1970, and New Jersey, California, Connecticut and Massachusetts were not far behind. This represented an increase of about eighty percent in per-pupil expenditures since 1965–1966.

18. Educational costs have also risen sharply outside the central cities, particularly in the adjacent suburban school districts. These rises are a direct reverberation of troubles in the cities. Suburban school boards must remain competitive with the rising salary levels of educational personnel in the central cities, particularly considering the high priority placed on education by the middle-class suburbs. For example, between 1958 and 1959, enrollment in the Westchester, New York, schools increased by 1.5 percent, and the operating budget by 12 percent. In Fairfield, Connecticut, enrollment increased by 5.2 percent, the budget by 13.2 percent. In Suffolk County, New York, enrollment increased by 6.6 percent, the budget by 11.6 percent. In Monmouth, New Jersey, enrollment increased by 4.4 percent, the budget by 19 percent. Moreover, there are also increasing numbers of blacks in some of the older suburbs, with the result that these towns are experiencing political disturbances very similar to those of the big cities.

19. *State and Local Finances*, op. cit., p. 39.

20. *Changing Patterns of Prices, Pay Workers, and Work*, op. cit., pp. 7–8.

21. Some 25,000 of the new jobs were noncompetitive (the *New York Times*, May 28, 1971). Not surprisingly, the governor suggested that the mayor economize by cutting these, instead of always talking about cutting the number of policemen and firemen.

22. Welfare is the main example of an actual expansion of services, for the number of welfare employees increased largely as a reflection of increasing case loads.

But so were new policemen hired to appease a broad constituency concerned about rising crime, sanitation men to answer demands for cleaner streets, and so forth.

23. *Changing Patterns of Prices, Pay, Workers, and Work*, op. cit., p. 9. Moreover, big payrolls were a big city phenomenon. A study showed that, in three states studied in detail, the ratio of public employment per 100 population varied sharply by city size, more so in New Jersey and Ohio, less markedly in Texas. See *Urban and Rural America: Policies for Future Growth*, U.S. Advisory Commission on Intergovernmental Relations (Washington, D.C.: Government Printing Office, April 1968), pp. 47–49.

24. According to Harold Rubin:

> Time lost by state and local government employees due to work stoppages climbed from 7,510 man-days in 1958 to 2,535,000 man-days in 1968, according to the U.S. Bureau of Labor Statistics. Such strikes have not been limited to those performing "nonessential duties." For example, during the first half of 1970 there have been strikes by prison guards (New Jersey), sanitation men (Cincinnati, Ohio; Phoenix, Arizona; Atlanta, Georgia; Seattle, Washington; and Charlotte, North Carolina), teachers (Youngstown, Ohio; Minneapolis, Minnesota; Butte, Montana; Tulsa, Oklahoma; Boston, Massachusetts; Newark and Jersey City, New Jersey; and Los Angeles, California; to list only some of the larger school systems involved), bus drivers (Cleveland, Ohio; Tacoma, Washington; and San Diego, California), hospital employees (State of New Jersey; Detroit, Michigan), policemen (Newport, Kentucky; Livonia, Michigan; and Winthrop, Massachusetts), and firemen (Newark, Ohio, and Racine, Wisconsin) ["Labor Relations in State and Local Governments," in Robert A. Connery and William V. Farr (eds.), *Unionization of Municipal Employees* (New York: Columbia University, The Academy of Political Science, 1971), pp. 20–21.]

25. *The New York Times*, June 13, 1971.

26. *The New York Times*, January 31, 1970.

27. *The New York Times*, February 26, 1970.

28. *The New York Times,* March 17, 1970.

29. *The New York Times*, March 15, 1971. These estimates were given to the press by the city's budget director.

30. Rising wages and pension benefits among municipal employees are frequently attributed to unionization, which has indeed spread in the 1960s, rather than to changes in city politics. Membership in the American Federation of State, County, and Municipal employees increased from 180,000 to 425,000 in one decade; The American Federation of Teachers enlarged its ranks from 60,000 members in 1961 to 175,000 in 1969. But to point to unionization as a cause simply diverts the argument, since the spread and militancy of unionism among city employees in the 1960s must itself be explained. In any case, a Brookings Institution study of nineteen local governments showed no conclusive differences between unionized and nonunionized wages; both had risen substantially.

See David Stanley, "The Effect of Unions on Local Governments," Connery and Farr (eds.), op. cit., p. 47.

31. Norton Long and others have argued that the city's economic problems are largely the result of efforts by city employees to keep up with pay scales in the private sector, despite the absence of productivity increases in public-service jobs comparable to those that justify wage increases in the private sector ("The City as Reservation," *The Public Interest*, No. 25 [Fall 1971]). This argument; however, presumes that city pay scales lag behind private scales and that city workers are merely straining to catch up. Quite the opposite has come to be true in some big cities. A 1970 study by the Middle Atlantic Bureau of Labor Statistics of pay rates in the New York metropolitan area found city pay rates to be much higher than private-industry rates. For example, carpenters, electricians and plumbers who worked for the city earned fully sixty percent more than those in private industry; painters and automobile mechanics earned thirty-six percent more; even messengers, typists, switchboard operators and janitors were substantially better off when they worked for the city. Moreover, city workers also received far better holiday, vacation, health insurance and pension benefits. It should also be noted that all but the last grouping were also much better paid in the city than in the suburbs. And so were patrolmen, firemen, sanitation man, and social workers substantially better paid in the city than in the suburbs. A similar conclusion was reached by Bennett Harrison, who compared mean weekly earnings in the public and private sector of twelve metropolitan areas, using 1966 data. His calculations reveal a sharp disparity between public and private earnings in the central cities (although in 1966 some categories of suburban earnings were higher than the central city). See his *Public Employment and Urban Poverty* (Washington, D.C.: The Urban Institute, 1971), p. 30.

32. Put another way, the average annual increase in New York City's expense budget during the last five years was $582 million, or eight times as high as the $71-million annual average increase from fiscal 1949 to fiscal 1954.

33. "Report on Financing Our Urban Needs," *Our Nation's Cities* (Washington, D.C.: Government Printing Office, March 1969), p. 21.

34. According to *Fiscal Balance in the American Federal System*:

> National aggregates for 1957 and 1962 and more restricted data for 1964–65 indicate that local government in the metropolitan areas spends more and taxes more per person than in the remainder of the country…there is a striking contrast in non-educational expenditures—which include all the public welfare, health, hospital, public safety and other public services essential to the well-being of citizens. These general government costs are two-thirds higher in the metropolitan areas than they are in the rest of the country [op. cit., Vol. II, p. 59].

Specifically, per-capita expenditures during 1964–1965 averaged $301.20 in the thirty-seven largest metropolitan areas, compared to $218.31 in small or non-metropolitan areas (*ibid.*, Table 16, p. 60). As for the central cities themselves, "central cities contained 18.6 percent of the population (in 1964–65), but accounted for almost 25 percent of all local expenditure." In per-capita terms, local government expenditure in the large central cities "was 21 percent higher than in their outside regions, and almost two-thirds above that for the rest of the nation" (*ibid.*, p. 62). Moreover, when educational costs are omitted (suburban communities spend a great deal on education), the thirty-seven largest central cities "had an outlay of $232 per capita in 1965—$100 greater than their suburban counterparts" (*ibid.*, p. 6): By 1966–1967, the disparity had become more dramatic in many cities. Per-capita general expenditures, including education costs, was $475 in Washington, D.C., compared to $224 in the Washington suburban ring; $324 in Baltimore, compared to $210 in the suburban ring; $441 in Newark, compared to $271 in the suburban ring; $335 in Boston, compared to $224 in the suburban ring; $267 in St. Louis, and $187 in the suburbs (State and Local Finances, op. cit., p. 70). Similarly, a study of fifty-five local governments in the San Francisco–Oakland metropolitan area showed that both the property-tax rate and the level of per-capita expenditures were higher in the central city. In dormitory suburbs, per-capita expenditures were only fifty-eight percent of those in the central city. See Julius Margolis, "Municipal Fiscal Structure in a Metropolitan Region," *Journal of Political Economy*, 65 (June 1957), p. 232.

35. The New York State Constitution, for example, specifies that:

> It shall be the duty of the Legislature, subject to the provisions of this Constitution, to restrict the power of taxation, assessment, borrowing money, contracting indebtedness, and loaning the credit of countries, cities, towns and villages, so as to prevent abuses in taxation and assessments and in contracting of indebtedness by them. Nothing in this article shall be construed to prevent the Legislature from further restricting the powers herein specified (Article VIII, Section 12).

Traditionally the states have granted powers of taxation to the localities only very reluctantly.

36. Not only do states limit the taxing powers of localities, but they have the authority to mandate local expenditures (e.g., salary increases for police and firemen) with or without adjusting local taxing powers to pay for them. They also have the authority to vote tax exemptions at local expense for favored groups. State legislatures are given to doing exactly that, exacerbating the financial plight of local governments.

37. This was $27 billion out of $40 billion that localities raised in revenues from their own sources in 1967–1968 (*State and Local Finances*, op. cit., Table 8, p. 31). It should be noted that property taxes are declining relative to other sources of local revenue. At the turn of the century about eighty percent of state and local budgets were financed by the property tax. Today the states hardly rely on it at all. Nevertheless, local governments still finance about half their budgets with property taxes.

38. The first city income tax was levied in Philadelphia, in 1939, when the city was on the verge of bankruptcy. The use of the income tax by big cities spread in the

1960s, with Akron and Detroit adopting it in 1962, Kansas City in 1964, Baltimore and New York City in 1966 and Cleveland in 1967. See City Income Taxes (New York: Tax Foundation, Inc., 1967), *Research Publication* No. 12, pp. 7–9. City income taxes must, of course, also be approved by the state, an approval that is not always forthcoming.

39. By 1964–1965, per-capita local taxes in the central cities of the thirty-seven largest metropolitan areas had risen to $200 per capita. In Washington, D.C., taxes were $291 per capita; in New York City $279; and in Newark $273. Overall, central-city residents were paying seven percent of their income in local taxes and in the biggest cities ten percent (*Fiscal Balance in the American Federal System*, op. cit., Vol. II, pp. 75–79).

40. By 1968 official statistics for the nation as a whole showed local property taxes totaling $27.8 billion. The annual rise since then is estimated at between $1 and $3 billion.

41. *Our Nation's Cities,* op. cit., p. 24.

42. *Our Nation's Cities*, op. cit., pp. 36–37. To understand the full impact of property taxes, one must remember that these are taxes on capital value, and not on income yielded. Thus, a three percent-of-true-value tax on improvements can easily tax away seventy-five percent of the net income that a new building would otherwise earn—a loss, economists generally agree, that tends to be passed on to consumers. See, for example, Dick Netzer, *Economics of the Property Tax* (Washington, D.C.: The Brookings Institute, 1966), pp. 40–62.

43. Local tax collections increased by 500 percent between World War II and 1967, but costs have risen ten percent faster, and the bigger the city, the tighter the squeeze. If the process were to continue, and today's growth rate of city spending vs. city revenues to continue, a recent study commissioned by the National League of Cities estimates a gap of $262 billion by 1980 (*Our Nation's Cities*, op. cit., p. 22). Measured another way, state and local indebtedness combined rose by 400 percent since 1948, while the federal debt rose by only twenty-six percent (*U.S. Fiscal Balance in the American Federal System*, op. cit., Vol. I, p. 55). In the thirty-six large central cities alone, the cumulative tax gap could reach $25 to $30 billion by 1975 (*ibid.*, Vol. II, p. 91). A special Commission on the Cities in the Seventies, established by the National Urban Coalition, concluded that by 1980 most cities will be "totally bankrupt" (the *New York Times*, September 24, 1971).

44. The statement went on to say "that which is good enough for white cops and firemen is good enough for black and Puerto Rican employees of New York City" (the *New York Times*, June 8, 1971). According to city officials, the annual cost of pension benefits, which had been $215 million in 1960, was projected to reach $1.3 billion in the next ten years (the *New York Times*, June 9, 1971).

45. The Christian Science Monitor, September 4, 1969.

46. *The States and the Urban Crisis, Report of the Thirty-Sixth American Assembly* (Harriman, N.Y.: Arden House, October 30–November 2, 1969). The Report went on, not surprisingly, to recommend increased state and federal aid for the cities.

47. James Reston, "The President and the Mayors," the *New York Times*, March 24, 1971. In another column on April 21, 1971, Reston summarized the reports of the big-city mayors as: "First, they felt the crisis of the cities was the major threat to the security of the nation—more serious than Vietnam or anything else. Second, they felt that the bankruptcy and anarchy were underestimated.... They sound like communiques from a battlefield.... They have got beyond all the questions of race or party and are looking for power and leadership to deal with the urban problem."

48. The governor said he had in mind a new structure like the London County Council. City political leaders, for their part, had been proposing to abolish city-state relations by declaring New York City a separate state.

49. By 1966–1967, per-capita intergovernmental aid was substantially higher for the central cities than suburban localities (contrary to popular impression). Per-capita aid to Washington, D.C., was $181, compared to $81 in the outlying suburbs; $174 to Baltimore, and $101 to the suburbs; $179 to Boston, and $74 to the suburbs; $220 to New York City, and $163 to the suburbs; $144 to Newark, and $53 to the suburbs; $70 to Philadelphia, and $61 to the suburbs; $88 to Chicago, and $55 to the suburbs; $126 to Detroit, and $115 to the suburbs (*State and Local Finances*, op. cit., Table 29, p. 69).

50. Arthur Levitt, controller of the state of New York, recently released figures showing that state spending had increased from $1.3 billion in 1956 to $3.9 billion in 1964, to approximately $8 billion in 1968. In the four years ending in 1968, state spending rose by an annual average of $875 million, or 18.7 percent. In 1968 the spending increase was $1.4 billion, or 22.1 percent over the previous year (the *New York Times*, April 2, 1969–July 7, 1969). During this same five-year period, state revenues from taxes and federal aid increased from $3.7 billion to $7.2 billion. In other words, spending exceeded revenues, and by greater margins in each of the successive years. The total deficit for the five-year period amounted to $2.5 billion, which, of course, had to be borrowed. A large part of this rise in New York State's budget reflects aid to localities, which increased from $622 million in fiscal 1955 to $1.04 billion in fiscal 1960, to $1.67 billion in 1965, and $3.23 billion in fiscal year 1969. State spending for aid to education has doubled in the last six years, and the state share of welfare and medicaid costs doubled in only four years.

51. By 1971 the estimated difference between revenues and outlays were in excess of $500 million in New York, California and Texas. Florida was short $120 million; New Jersey $100 million; Connecticut $200 million (the *New York Times*, January 3, 1971). A handful of rural states, however, were considering tax cuts.

52. Data provided by the Commerce Clearing House, as reported in the *New York Times*, September 27, 1970.

53. A Gallup poll in 1969 showed that forty-nine percent would not vote for more money to pay for schools if additional taxes were sought, against forty-five percent who would (the *New York Times*, August 17, 1969). Another key fact in understanding the populist character of the tax revolt is that state and local taxes consist mainly in sales and property taxes and various user charges, all of which tend to be relatively regressive. Even the state income tax, when it is used, is usually imposed as a fixed percentage of income (unlike the graduated federal income tax, which takes more from those who have more, at least in principle). In any case, fully two-thirds of state revenues were raised from sales and gross receipt taxes. [*State and Government Finances in 1967*, U.S. Bureau of the Census (Washington, D.C.: Government Printing Office, 1968), Table I, p. 7]. Consequently, the new taxes have had a severe impact on the working and middle classes, who are paying a larger and larger percentage of personal income to state and local government. In New York, state and local taxes now absorb over thirteen percent of personal income; in California, over twelve percent; in Illinois and Ohio over eight percent. As a result of rising state and local taxes (ant price inflation), per-capita disposable personal income fell considerably between 1965 and 1969. See Paul M. Schwab, "Two Measures of Purchasing Power Contrasted," *Monthly Labor Review* (April 1971). By contrast, federal taxes declined as a percent of Gross National Product between 1948–1968, during which period state and local taxes rose from about five percent to eight percent of GNP (State and Local Finances, op. cit., Figure 5, p. 29). The "tax revolt" in the states should be no surprise.

54. Most of the 1969 welfare cuts were restored within a short time, but the 1971 cuts were not.

55. *The New York Times*, February 16, 1971; June 9, 17, 19, 25, 1971; and July 2, 1971.

56. *The New York Times*, August 30, 1970; November 27, 1970; and May 25, 1971.

57. Nationally, the annual rise in teacher salaries slumped to only 5.5 percent, after rising by about 8 percent each year for several years.

58. Usually by limiting eligibility, or limiting the types of services covered, or requiring co-payments by patients. See *Health Law Newsletter* (Los Angeles: National Legal Program on Health Problems of the Poor, June 1971), p. 2.

Part III

The Assault on Contemporary Poor Relief

8

Introduction

In the 1980s and 1990s, a great furor arose in American politics over "welfare." Republicans and Democrats, governors, presidents and the Congress, competed to attack programs which provided cash or in-kind assistance to the poor. The program singled out for particular vilification was Aid to Families with Dependent Children (AFDC), a federal system of grants-in-aid to the states inaugurated in the 1930s to provide cash assistance to impoverished mothers and children. The attacks took their toll, and a range of programs for the poor lost federal funding, particularly in the early years of the Reagan presidency, and again after Republicans swept the congress in 1994. Meanwhile, the states allowed AFDC benefits to lag sharply behind inflation. Then, in 1996, with much fanfare, and with both the Democratic President and the Republican Congress claiming credit, the federal AFDC program was eliminated in favor of a new program which essentially turned cash assistance over to the states, with federal lump sum grants to make the deal attractive. The main federal requirements that remained were intended to curb state largesse, by requiring work in exchange for aid, and limiting the time span of eligibility.

These historic changes were justified by the familiar argument of perverse effects, endlessly repeated. However well-intended, it was said,

aid to the poor inevitably encouraged irresponsible behavior, which ultimately worsened the poverty the aid was intended to alleviate. The variation of this argument that generated the most political heat, but found the least empirical support, blamed the availability of welfare grants for out-of-wedlock births. The other main line of attack asserted that welfare grants fostered something called "dependency," encouraging people to drop out of the labor market in the first place, and then to stay out. This line of argument actually stood up to the facts rather better than the argument about out-of-wedlock births. It made sense to think that poor women raising children might turn to welfare if cash grants supplemented by food stamps and Medicaid paid more than a low wage job. Logically, but not in the heated and vitriolic politics created by the attack on welfare, a concern with the relationship of welfare to dependency should have directed attention to the deteriorating conditions of the low-wage labor market. After all, if there were jobs that paid living wages, and if health care and child care were available, a great many women on welfare would leap at the chance of a better income and a little social respect.

AFDC was legislated in the 1930s, but it remained a very small program until the 1960s. Meanwhile, as the migration of people displaced from agriculture in the American south and Puerto Rico continued, a great pool of impoverished people built up in the cities. Under the more permissive laws of the northern states, many of them were eligible for welfare. In the early 1960s, spurred by the black movement and the more liberal federal posture, large numbers of the urban poor began to apply for aid and, with street protests surging, welfare officials approved a higher proportion of their applications. The welfare rolls rose, reaching some three million families by the beginning of the 1970s.

Conservative commentators now say that the expansion of the welfare rolls produced the American problem of the underclass. However, they ignore the agricultural upheaval that displaced people and drove them to the cities. They ignore the changes in the urban labor market which made it increasingly difficult for unskilled people to find jobs that paid a living wage. They ignore the elemental question, What were poor people to do? Welfare was certainly not an ideal solution—grant levels were too low, the system degraded those who turned to it, and being on the dole deprived them of the social respect associated with wage work or other ways of contributing to a community. But the liberalization of welfare did allow poor women and children some kind of livelihood, in many instances by patching together income from irregular low-wage work and a welfare check.

The new legislation that "reforms" the welfare system makes that livelihood radically insecure for many families. Millions of women will be forced into "workfare" programs, or simply cut off the rolls to scramble for whatever jobs they can get. Either way, they will do work that would otherwise be done by other low-wage earners, and the glut of job seekers will probably drive wages down to even lower levels.

Sober people should wonder whether it makes much sense to force the mothers of young children into the search for work at a time when postindustrial restructuring of the labor market has already displaced many existing workers. But these policies are not driven by visions of a better collective future. They are driven by the economic and political interests that have coalesced in the assault on the social compact. In part, the motivation is simply greed. Business groups and their politician allies push for tax cuts for the best-off, and reconcile this with fiscal prudence by also pushing for cuts in spending for the worst-off. Not incidentally, the worst-off are ordinarily, in the absence of protest, least able to defend the programs on which they depend. Attacking programs for the poorest of the poor also meshes with the interests of politicians who have adapted to the new business-Christian political machine on the Republican side, and the shriveling infrastructure and constituencies of the New Deal Democrats on the other side, by resorting to a scapegoat politics which singles out the poor, especially poor women, immigrants, and minorities. The singular focus on the poor and their programs as somehow to blame for what is wrong with America has so far succeeded in distracting the attention of the mass of working people from the steady erosion of their wages and working conditions. The final irony is that the dismantling of income protections for the poor is certain to increase pressures on wages and working conditions. In other words, there is indeed a kind of diabolic rationality behind these policy initiatives.

We begin this section with an essay on the "Historical Sources of the

Contemporary Relief Debate," showing the parallels between earlier campaigns to roll back poor relief and contemporary arguments. Of course, we hoped that it would be different this time. One reason was that women were becoming more politicized. Many college-educated women worked in the social programs, so they had jobs to protect; and polls showed that women were more supportive of government social provision. We put forth this argument, and analyzed the profound institutional changes underlying the development of a distinctive women's politics, in "Women and the State," which is reproduced here. We were wrong. Not many better-off women came to the defense of poorer women, and welfare reform proceeded with little opposition. Finally, in an essay published here for the first time, we scrutinize the disappointing role of policy experts and their research in the debacle called welfare reform.

1997

9

The Historical Sources
of the Contemporary Relief Debate

Since 1970, criticism of American social welfare programs has grown more and more clamorous. Analysts compete to advance what are purported to be new insights, presumably gleaned from contemporary experience, showing that social welfare programs are in fact harmful to those whom they are supposed to help, driving them deeper into poverty. Yet for all the uproar, almost nothing new is being said. The "theory" that welfare harms the poor is centuries old, and always gains ascendancy when programs that aid the poor are under serious political assault, as they clearly are today. Indeed, the contemporary attack on social welfare is being scripted by a history of conflict over relief that goes back to the sixteenth century.

Historically, attacks on welfare were usually precipitated by sharp economic dislocations associated with periodic market downturns or with the introduction of new forms of production. Viewed from the bottom, market downturns obviously meant material hardship, as well as destruction of the resources on which community and personal life depended. Shifts in the market for goods and in methods of production had similar effects when they entailed the massive displacement of workers and the uprooting of communities and families. In the wake of such disturbances, people often mobilized to demand protection from the market forces that were destroying their way of life, and sometimes life itself. At such junctures, elites frequently responded by granting relief or welfare on a large scale.

But while maintaining social peace might require that relief be expanded, this concession was problematic from the perspective of elites precisely to the extent that it shielded working and poor people from the market. The very dislocations that precipitated protest from below often generated new opportunities for profit which relief obstructed. When working people were shielded by social provision, they were more likely to resist the hardships imposed by the changing forms of production and the changing terms of profitability.

In the past as today, the public discussion of social welfare ignored these large-scale economic dislocations, and the divergent class interests involved. Market downturns left huge numbers of the work force unemployed and drove the wages of those still working far below subsistence. Entire trades were destroyed when new machines and new ways of organizing production were introduced; families were pauperized and villages decimated. But the institutional changes that swept away the life supports of the poor, and the role of dominant classes in promoting those changes, were typically ignored, buried in a veritable barrage of reports that piously argued that relief programs were not good for the society and were even worse for the poor.

The present debate over social welfare in the United States reiterates the historical debate with remarkable exactness. As during earlier periods, high-minded and disinterested charges are being brought against welfare state programs (in our time mainly by intellectuals attached to corporate-funded think tanks). This essay places these contemporary charges against the American welfare state in the context of the long history of conflicts over social welfare.

It is only during the last half-century that the United States has become, in the modern sense, a "welfare state." This term has diverse meanings, reflecting in part different national traditions, and sometimes it is used to embrace virtually all state interventions in the economy and society. We use it here in the much narrower sense of government programs that provide income supports to groups deemed to be at risk in the market (such as the aged), or programs that protect people against specified contingencies, such as unemployment or sickness or marital breakdown.[1] Because social programs were inaugurated later here, and because expenditure levels remained lower than in most other affluent Western nations, the United States is often thought of as a welfare state laggard. Nevertheless, despite the late beginning and despite often strident opposition, the national programs first established in the depths of the Great Depression did endure, and were eventually expanded and elaborated. By the mid-seventies, welfare state expenditures accounted for 7.7 percent of the gross national product, and in 1985 the U.S. Census reported that 31 percent of the population and 47 percent of households received benefits from federal social insurance or means-tested programs.[2] Feldstein (1985: 94) estimates that social programs of all kinds cost more than $300 billion a year, compared to $19 billion twenty years ago, and account for half of all federal government spending on nondefense programs.[3]

The expansion of welfare benefit programs has reduced poverty and inequality in the United States in two ways. First, the programs directly distribute income to the poor. Tax revenues gathered from those who are at least somewhat better off fund programs that provide income and services to those who are worst off. It is true that the redistribution effected through this tax-and-transfer mechanism has been very limited (Devine and Canak 1986). Governments typically fund relief programs for the poor by taxing the middle class rather than the rich, and the United States is certainly no exception. Nevertheless, the most extreme destitution was relieved, and as social welfare spending increased, the poverty rate dropped, from 30 percent in 1950 to a low of 11 percent in 1973. Danziger and Plotnick (1982: 45) estimate that in 1976, three-quarters of those who would otherwise have fallen below the poverty line were lifted out of poverty by cash and in-kind transfers. Moreover, it is not only the very poor whose position has been improved. The expansion of the welfare state effectively counteracted a marked upward trend in the income inequality that was being generated by the market during the three decades after World War II (Reynolds and Smolensky 1977; Danziger, Haveman, and Plotnick, 1981; Plotnick and Skidmore 1975).

The other way that welfare state programs reduce poverty is by strengthening the bargaining position of working people, particularly those with little leverage in the labor market. The social programs remove people from the work force, with the result that the ranks of the reserve army of labor are thinned. We tend to overlook this effect because, once freed of the obligation to sell their labor, groups such as the aged or the disabled come to be defined as "unemployable." But before the protective programs were established, many of the aged and the disabled did work; and prior to Aid to Families with Dependent Children and the food stamp program, most impoverished mothers and their children also foraged for whatever work they could get. Programs that make it possible for millions of the old or the disabled or impoverished mothers to survive without work or the search for work obviously tighten labor markets, and thus buttress the bargaining power of those who remain in the labor force in contests over wages and working conditions.

The existence of social welfare also affects power relations in the labor market in a less direct way. When working people are made more secure by sources of income that do not depend on the market, when they know they can turn to unemployment or relief benefits, they are likely to become a little bolder and more demanding in their dealings with employers. The availability of social provision thus strengthens the position of workers by making them more secure, and this is especially important for nonunionized low-wage workers, who are otherwise close to the precipice of sheer want.

Of course, other economic and political conditions also bear on the relative power of workers and may offset the effects of welfare state programs. For example, the expansion of the welfare state in the United States in the late 1960s and early 1970s was rapidly followed by a series of sectoral and locational changes in the pattern of investment which shifted employment growth from high-wage industrial jobs to low-wage service jobs, and from the Rust Belt central cities (where many of the poor, especially the minority poor, had concentrated) to the Sun Belt and the metropolitan fringe. Moreover, the expansion of social welfare was followed rapidly by the influx of baby-boom workers and of greater numbers of women into the labor market, by the decline in union membership and strength, and by the erosion of the legislative protection of the minimum wage. Equally important, the effects of an expanded welfare state in strengthening workers have been offset by an aggressive employer campaign to drive down labor costs. Thus the welfare state has not been the sole or even the main determinant of worker power in the last two decades, but rather has helped to partially offset the factors that were eroding worker power. Even this, of course, is a major achievement.

We emphasize, however, that the achievements of the welfare state are largely the result of the fact that social welfare programs generate what are called, in the current debate, "work disincentives."[4] We underline this point because it is exactly the reverse of conservative charges against welfare state programs. As attempts to slash these programs have gained momentum in the last decade, so have public claims that they are ineffective and even worsen the poverty they are intended to alleviate, precisely because they discourage work efforts or generate work disincentives. These claims are so egregious that they might well be called the Great Relief Hoax. They are a hoax because they contradict what might other wise be obvious: that people whose labor is of little value in the market are better off when they receive income protections, and that most other workers are also better off when they no longer have to compete with such vulnerable workers. But the Great Relief Hoax is not an invention of our time. It has a very long history.

Economic Dislocation and Demands for Relief

The first relief programs that could reasonably be construed as predecessors to the modern welfare state emerged with the breakdown of traditional agricultural economies and the rise of capitalist markets. Public arrangements for the relief of the poor—arrangements the Webbs (1963: 29) called the "new statecraft dealing with destitution"—were forged in Northern Europe and England in the first half of the sixteenth century, in the wake of severe economic disturbance and social strife. The forces that would shape social provision over the succeeding centuries were already apparent. Economic dislocation and the attendant disruption of social life not only led to vagrancy and crime among the poor but sometimes made them "unruly" and demanding, and relief programs were everywhere designed to restore order by providing aid.

As capitalist labor markets spread, social strife over poor relief periodically intensified. More and more people were drawn or forced out of traditional agriculture and into wage labor, out of the villages and into the cities. They became totally dependent on market employment for their subsistence, and were thus totally exposed to the often terrible vicissitudes of the market. When periodic downturns or massive market shifts left large numbers unemployed (a term that was not even invented until markets in human labor were established on a large scale), or forced wages below subsistence, people often mobilized in threatening protests and demanded aid. Thus in the late eighteenth and early nineteenth centuries, in the aftermath of accelerating enclosure, rising grain prices, the destruction of the handloom weaving trade, and other market developments, the English countryside seethed with insurgency. And for a long time, even after capitalist markets were well established, the poor were strengthened in their demands for social protection by the precapitalist idea of a social compact between rich and poor, a compact that obligated the rich to provide for the poor at times of great need in exchange for their service and deference. This pressure from below frequently forced the expansion of relief, and in England it was sufficiently threatening to sustain relatively liberal relief-giving for long periods.[5]

Even in the United States, where the idea of a social compact was weaker, and where employers were not politically restrained by the power of an aristocratic class with roots in a traditional landed economy, pressures from below for social protection could not be ignored at times of widespread economic hardship.[6] The most dramatic of these surges appears to have occurred in the mid-nineteenth century, in the midst of the decades-long wave of immigration from famine-ridden Ireland and on the eve of industrialization. Annual reports compiled by Katz (1986: 37) from the state of New York, for example, show that the outdoor relief rolls jumped from 11,937 in 1840 to 63,764 in 1850 to 174,403 in 1860, while the poorhouse population increased as well.

The contemporary American welfare state was also initiated, and then expanded, in response to pressure from below. The massive unemployment of the Great Depression stimulated a wave of protests demanding "bread or wages." Local government authorities, their revenues depleted by the economic collapse, were both stymied in responding to these demands and fearful of resisting them. To cope with their dilemma, they lobbied in an increasingly alarmist spirit for federal emergency relief measures, until then unprecedented in the United States. In the spring of 1933, only weeks after he took office, Franklin Roosevelt pushed a relatively liberal relief program through the Congress—the first step in the creation of the contemporary American welfare state. Within eighteen months, 20 million people, fully 16 percent of the population, were receiving relief payments (Piven and Cloward 1971: chap. 2; Patterson 1981: chap. 4).

In the 1960s, there was a new upsurge from below, this time composed of blacks displaced from southern agriculture. As mass protests escalated, threatening to disrupt the precarious regional and racial accommodations on which national Democratic leaders relied, the Kennedy and Johnson administrations responded by liberalizing and expanding the programs initiated in the 1930s, as well as by introducing new programs in housing, health, and nutrition. Furthermore, a good many corporate leaders went along with this liberalization, at least for a time. Not only were they chastened by black riots in the biggest cities of the nation, but the fantastic economic expansion in the period following World War II had softened business opposition to social programs. Indeed, commentators began to refer to the emergence of a new domestic accord between capital and labor. One important feature of that accord was the acceptance of expanded welfare state programs, which some analysts began to call the "social wage" in recognition of working-class stakes in the welfare state.

Employer Opposition to Relief

Except at moments when widespread insurgency from the bottom threatened social peace, economic elites resisted the demands of the poor. For one thing, the wealthy resented the cost of relief, as evidenced by recurrent complaints about the poor rates or the tax rates. But the opposition was as deep and persistent as it was because employer groups feared that relief provided to particularly vulnerable groups—the unemployed or the aged or the very young—would have far-reaching effects on all working people. Employers understood that by shielding working people from some of the hazards of the market, social programs blunted market sanctions and thus reduced the still formidable power of employers over workers. Moreover, for just this reason, the very idea of social provision was dangerously subversive of market ideology.[7] Because the stakes were high, struggles for social protection from below were always answered by resistance from above. Accordingly, once a measure of social peace was restored, employers pressed to restrict and reshape the programs. They exerted themselves to lower benefits, to tighten eligibility criteria so fewer people would receive benefits, and to attach such punitive conditions to the receipt of aid that few people would willingly apply for it. Such measures were intended, of course, to restore the compulsion to sell labor on whatever terms the market offered.

Furthermore, new market conditions sometimes provoked employer opposition even to long-established relief programs, usually as part of a larger campaign to increase worker discipline. This was especially likely when employers were confronted by intensified competition. To maintain or restore profits, they tried to extract more from their workers, whether by speeding up the pace of work or lowering wages or both. And they tried to strip workers of social protections in order to make them acquiesce to these new conditions. Conflicts over relief, in short, have always been at the heart of broader class conflicts over power in market relations.

Even in the sixteenth century, it was apparent that a good deal was at stake in the organization of relief arrangements, that relief was not merely a modest system of redistribution, but that the extent of relief and the methods by which it was distributed affected power relations between classes. Accordingly, from the start enormous energy and inventiveness were invested in devising relief programs that carefully scrutinized and categorized supplicants (the impotent versus the able-bodied, the resident versus the vagrant), hedged in the giving of aid with elaborate conditions, subjected recipients to strict disciplinary regimens and close surveillance, and exposed them to public rituals of degradation as "paupers." Otherwise, it was feared that social provision would encourage the poor to shun work, or rather, to shun the kinds of work and the terms of work for which they were deemed fit.

Efforts to shape relief arrangements so they would not intrude on market relations virtually define the history of social welfare, or at least the history of elite efforts to shape the programs. Thus the stratagem of requiring those who received aid to enter workhouses was recurrently attempted and recurrently fell into disuse, partly because the poor themselves were outraged by these institutions (and sometimes tore them down), but also because the better off objected to the higher costs of indoor relief.[8] As the outdoor relief rolls were slashed during subsequent decades, total costs actually rose because substantial numbers remained in the far more costly poorhouses (Katz 1986: 37).[9] Moreover, costs aside, manufacturers were always wary of the possibility that the workhouse, or any organized work-relief program, would nurture nascent forms of social production to compete with the market. In effect, strident opposition by manufacturers to useful production ensured that work-relief programs would be costly, since whatever goods were produced could not be marketed. Under these constraints, after a flurry of reform enthusiasm, enforced work usually degenerated into meaningless tasks like breaking stones. And the workhouse, no matter that it was proclaimed a "House of Industry" by Benthamite reformers, became a place so unspeakably vile no one would enter it except on penalty of starvation. That, from the perspective of reformers, was in a way its virtue. As we have said elsewhere,

> What begins as a great expansion of direct relief, and then turns into some form of work relief, ends finally with a sharp contraction of the rolls.... Meanwhile, the few who [are] allowed to remain on the rolls...[are]...once again subjected to the punitive and degrading treatment which has been used to buttress the work ethos since the inception of relief. (Piven and Cloward 1971: 348)

Thus, in the 1830s, the English ruling class mobilized a largely successful attempt to eliminate outdoor relief. In part, they were reacting to the fact that the relief rolls had swelled steadily over the previous century, absorbing large numbers of the rural poor who had been displaced from agriculture. In part, they were acting to satisfy the need for a willing labor force to serve in the emerging factory system; in Polanyi's words, "industrial capitalism was ready to be started" (1957: 102). All that was required for the great industrial takeoff was an unimpeded market in human labor.

In place of outdoor relief, the New Poor Law Commissioners of 1834 called for the workhouse.

> Into such a house none will enter voluntarily; work, confinement, and discipline will deter the indolent and vicious; and nothing but extreme necessity will induce any to accept...the sacrifice of their accustomed habits and gratifications. (Piven and Cloward 1971: 33–4)

If relief was available only in places so feared and hated, then the rising manufacturing class of England could be assured that no one who could possibly work would turn to relief. Willingness to enter the workhouse was thus, in itself, an infallible test of eligibility.

A broadly similar mobilization against relief occurred in the United States in the closing decades of the nineteenth century. American communities had more or less replicated the English parish-based poor-relief system, with its combination of the workhouse or almshouse and aid to at least some of the poor in their own homes (as well as variable local arrangements for indenturing or auctioning off paupers, practices that were more likely in small towns than in big cities). With these arrangements, American communities also replicated the conflicts that pervaded the English system. Accordingly, periodic efforts to stem pauperism by replacing outdoor relief with poorhouses or workhouses began with colonial development (Mohl 1971; Alexander 1983; Katz 1986: chap. 1). These "reforms," while perhaps more successful than in England, were nevertheless limited in their application because it was widely understood by local elites that the often turbulent poor would not submit to the almshouse or the workhouse.

Beginning in the mid-1870s, in the wake of the relief expansion that had begun some three decades earlier, public outdoor relief came under sustained and concerted attack. The attack was part of a larger effort by industrialists to cope with the reckless expansion and falling prices of the period (Gordon, Edwards, and Reich 1982: 106 and passim). Moreover, these were the years of the great railroad strikes, and the specter of an insurrectionary working class loomed large. Spurred by their own need to survive in an era of fierce competition, industrialists struggled to reduce production costs, mainly by mechanizing to eliminate skilled workers and gain more control over the production process. Accordingly, they attacked unions and recruited millions of immigrants to flood the labor market, in an effort that Gordon, Edwards, and Reich characterize as the "homogenization" of the labor force. And to deter resistance to the changing terms of work, they also inaugurated—in partnership with the new charity organization societies—a largely successful campaign against public outdoor relief in most of the big cities of the country.

The corporate-funded charity organization society movement took its lead from a society established in London in 1869. Thereafter, the movement spread rapidly as similar societies were inaugurated in most big American cities.[10] The Charity Organization Society of New York, established in 1882, listed among its patrons such names as William Waldorf Astor, August Belmont, Andrew Carnegie, J. Pierpont Morgan, and Mrs. Cornelius Vanderbilt (Brandt 1908: 266). The main goal of this movement was to eliminate outdoor relief on the grounds that it supported all manner of wicked behavior among the lower orders, especially malingering. In place of outdoor relief, the charity organization societies recommended a closely controlled, scientific philanthropy dedicated to correcting the moral turpitude they believed was the cause of poverty. However, a local clergyman, writing to Frederic C. Howe, a trustee of the Cleveland Charity Organization Society, saw it rather differently:

> Your society, with its board of trustees made up of steel magnates, coal operators, and employers is not really interested in charity. If it were, it would stop the twelve-hour day; it would increase wages and put an end to the cruel killing and maiming of men. It is interested in getting its own wreckage out of sight.... Christ himself might have been turned over by you to the police department as a "vagrant without visible means of support." (Cited in Bremner 1956: 54)

While reform campaigns against outdoor relief had occurred before in the United States, never were these efforts as vigorous or uncompromising as in the late nineteenth century. Public outdoor relief was suspended in New York City in 1874, except for the provision of coal in the winter, and was simply eliminated in Brooklyn in 1878 and in Philadelphia in 1879. In the next few years, funds for relief were slashed in Providence, where expenditures dropped from $150,051 in 1878 to $7,333 a year later; in Cleveland, outlays were cut from $95,000 in 1878 to

$17,000 in 1880. Comparable cuts were made in Chicago and Washington. The New York Association for Improving the Condition of the Poor even opposed "soup houses" because they did not distinguish between those who were deserving and those who were not. By the turn of the century, public outdoor relief had virtually been eliminated in the big cities, although the campaign was less effective in many smaller towns (Mohl 1983: 41–2; Keller 1977).

Employer concern with relief mounted again in the early 1930s, as the rapid implementation of the new emergency relief program helped calm the protests that had generated it. Earlier, in the panicked months of 1932, some prominent business leaders had themselves called for national emergency relief measures (although businessmen were riled when the new federal relief agency tried to create jobs on public projects for the unemployed: they protested the added costs, and were indignant at the prospect of government intrusion into their markets"). But once the panic of 1932 subsided, businessmen and southern planters began to complain of the disruptive effects they thought federal minimum relief payments were exerting on local wage rates (Piven and Cloward 1971: chap. 3).

Accordingly, and true to the historic pattern, Roosevelt terminated emergency relief in the mid-1930s. In its place, he proposed a new work relief program for the able-bodied, as well as an intricately fashioned set of measures (incorporated in the Social Security Act) which provided benefits for some of the unemployed and for some of the old, the disabled, and orphaned children. The political pressures that shaped these measures were the same dualistic pressures that have always shaped welfare state programs. On the one hand, and especially in the still-tumultuous 1930s, there were pressures from those who were still poor, often desperately poor. As Domhoff says in his explanation of the act, "distress and discontent [were] bubbling up from the lower levels within the depression-ridden society" (Domhoff 1970: 217; see also Piven and Cloward 1971: chap. 3, and 1977: chap. 2). On the other hand, employer objections to liberal emergency relief mounted, helping to prompt new legislation.

Until this time, business had consistently rejected proposals for old-age or unemployment insurance. But once federal legislation seemed inevitable, at least some big-business leaders were willing to play a role in molding it. Some provisions of the Social Security bill originated in the work of a number of business-backed policy groups, including the Business Advisory Council of the Department of Commerce (headed by Gerald Swope of General Electric), Industrial Relations Counsellors (the consulting firm created and controlled by John D. Rockefeller, Jr.), and the American Association for Labor Legislation, which had been largely responsible for crafting the Wisconsin unemployment plan on which part of the act was modeled. Not surprisingly, a number of these "business statesmen" came from the retail sector, which had a stake in measures that promised to sustain mass purchasing power during economic downturns. A few leaders from such capital-intensive industries as oil also lent some support to the bill, since they did not depend on low-wage labor (see Ferguson 1984 for this argument).

But large manufacturers that did depend on low-wage labor, as well as smaller businesses generally, opposed the act. The chambers of commerce and the National Association of Manufacturers were adamant in their opposition, as were organized agricultural interests, particularly southern plantation owners who relied on an ample supply of cheap labor. Moreover, these southern interests carried great weight in the New Deal and particularly in the Congress, where both the House Ways and Means Committee and the Senate Finance Committee were chaired by southerners (Alston and Ferrie 1985a: 105).[12]

The intricate provisions of the Social Security Act, particularly when contrasted with the liberal federal emergency relief program it replaced (or even when contrasted with the staff recommendations on social security), can be understood as a compromise between the conflicting needs to quell unrest and to ensure a supply of low-wage labor. The legislation carefully restricted eligibility for old-age and unemployment insurance: whole categories of workers, including agricultural workers, were excluded from coverage in both programs. Among those in eligible categories, only workers with a personal history of steady employment qualified, and benefits were pegged to former earnings. Since unemployment insurance was the more market-sensitive program because it provided aid to able-bodied adults in their prime, the states were ceded considerable authority in eligibility determination, in setting benefit levels, and in specifying the duration of coverage, an arrangement that made the program more sensitive to local labor-market conditions and employer demands. The result was a system of social provision that in some ways actually underlined market sanctions and incentives while in other ways straining against them: protection against adversity was extremely modest and could be earned only through work, and the stratification of the labor market was at least partially reproduced in the schedule of program benefits.

The effort to design social programs that meshed with the market was even more evident in the "categorical programs" that provided aid for some of the impoverished not covered by old-age or unemployment insurance. The categorical programs singled out as eligible only those of the poor who were unlikely to be of much value as workers (the aged, the orphaned, and the blind). Control over the setting of benefit levels and the administration of these restricted programs was lodged in the states or localities, where local employers could use their influence to gain whatever additional restrictions were needed to ensure that the programs would mesh precisely with the requirements of local labor markets. As Quadagno says, "a 'states-rights' agenda served to maintain the confidence of the…business community" (1984: 645). Southern congressmen who packed the House Ways and Means Committee even succeeded in eliminating language requiring states to set old-age-assistance grant levels so as to provide "a reasonable subsistence compatible with decency and health." Their fear was that funds for the elderly would reach younger members of black families, who would then be less pliant workers.[13]

These carefully designed arrangements led over time to the institutionalization of a series of welfare state programs so closely "market-conforming" as to make the United States notorious among Western democracies for the narrow and niggardly protections it provided. Until the 1960s, even those of the aged fortunate enough to be covered by Social Security pensions earned through work—the Old Age and Survivors and Dependents Insurance (OASDI) provisions of the Social Security Act—received benefits so low that many of them remained in poverty, and many remained in the labor force as well.

The expansion of the welfare state that was widely considered part of the class accord in the period immediately following World War II was once again interrupted by employer opposition, this time prompted by the economic convulsions of the 1970s. Analysts dispute the reasons for the onset of rapid inflation and declining corporate profit rates. But whether the causes lay in the inflationary impact of the Vietnam War, the oil-price shocks, or the longer-term problems associated with the declining competitiveness of the American economy, it is clear that American business sought to reduce the impact of these instabilities with a renewed assault against the working class. Employers mobilized to cut wages, slash workplace protections, crush unions, and discredit the very possibility of worker power with an ideological campaign threatening capital flight if workers resisted the new demands.

As during earlier periods, the effort to restrict or eliminate welfare state protections is an important part of the business mobilization against the working class. In part, the intent is to redistribute income upward: sharp tax cuts are implemented for the rich, and the revenue losses are to be at least partly offset by cuts in the social programs. In part, the intent is to reduce the labor-market power of workers by intensifying economic insecurity.

Contemporary Employer Opposition

To better appreciate the reasons for the current mobilization against the welfare state, it is worthwhile to review some of the estimates made of the work effort that is in a sense "lost" as a consequence of the expansion of the social programs. Overall, it is clear that expansion of the programs has removed millions of people from the labor market, resulting, of course, in a "tighter" labor market than would otherwise exist. Consider the effects of Social Security payments on the work-force participation of the aged. OASDI benefit expenditures reached $182 billion in fiscal 1986, or 4.4 percent of GNP and one-third of federal outlays on nondefense items (Feldstein 1985: 102). In 1948, half of all men over sixty-five were in the labor force. As Social Security expanded, the proportion dropped to 20 percent. Meanwhile, with the enactment of optional retirement at sixty-two, the proportion of men aged sixty-two to sixty-four who were labor-force participants fell from 80 percent in 1961 to 60 percent in 1978 (Burhauser and Tolley 1978: 449–53).[14]

Social welfare measures have had similar if less dramatic effects on the labor-force participation of other groups. The expansion of the disability programs from 687,000 recipients in 1960 to 4,352,000 in 1975 appears to be correlated with a sizable drop in the labor-force participation not only of relatively older workers but even of prime-age men forty-five to fifty-four years old. Ellwood and Summers (1986) report that 4 percent of these prime-age men were out of the labor force in 1960, but 9 percent in 1980; for blacks, the percentage of nonparticipants had gone from 7 percent to 16 percent. Mead (1986: 133–4) draws on a Congressional Budget Office (1982) study to blame relatively generous benefits for the fact that the disability rolls doubled between 1969 and 1976, and that the proportion of recipients returning to work each year fell. In 1977, 28 percent of those on the disability rolls received the equivalent of over three-fifths of their prior earnings, while 14 percent actually received more than 100 percent, a result made possible by the fact that disability benefits are scaled to family size, while wages are not. Moreover, disability recipients receive Medicare, and often also receive income from other programs, such as veterans' benefits. Mead concludes, not without indignation, that the main role of disability programs has been to let poorer, older, and less skilled workers retire early.[15] Of course, these data probably also reflect the increased use of disability benefits to cope with the involuntary unemployment resulting from deindustrialization, which has left many displaced workers trapped in communities where there are no longer even low-wage jobs to be found. However—and this is Mead's point and the point of the critics generally—without recourse to programs like disability, many of these displaced industrial workers would be quicker to take whatever employment they could get.

Or consider unemployment insurance. In the decades since 1935, coverage has been extended to more workers and benefits have been liberalized, largely by congressional action extending the duration of coverage during periods of high unemployment. In the recession of 1973–74, for example, the basic 26-week period of coverage was extended to 65 weeks (and many workers displaced from jobs by foreign competition also received benefits under the Trade Adjustment Assistance Act). As a result, two out of three of the 12 million unemployed received benefits during that severe downturn. Again, there are disputes about the precise effects of unemployment insurance on work effort. However, almost all studies agree that the availability of unemployment benefits increases the length of unemployment spells.[16] Mead cites a government survey conducted in 1976 to show that unemployment benefits not only substantially extended the length of time out of work but also raised the wage expectations of the unemployed:

> The average worker who had lost or left a job was prepared to enter a new one only if it paid 7 percent more than his or her last position. While 35 percent of these jobless were willing to return to work for less than they formerly earned, 38 percent demanded more money. Even after fifty weeks out of work the average respondent persisted in expecting nearly as high a wage as in his or her old job. If the jobless demanding a wage increase were defined as voluntarily unemployed and excluded from the statistics, unemployment as officially measured would drop by more than a point, more than three points for nonwhites. (Mead 1986: 72)

Disincentive effects were also found when the federal government sponsored a series of guaranteed-income experiments. Low-income families in the experimental groups were provided with income and were compared with control groups in several locations, including New Jersey, Seattle, Denver, rural Iowa, North Carolina, and Gary, Indiana.[17] While the level of experimental benefits varied between sites and among test groups, it was relatively generous compared to the means-tested programs. And as is to be expected, the benefits reduced work effort. In New Jersey, husbands reduced work effort by 5 percent and wives by 25 percent; Seattle and Denver, which had more generous income supports, showed work-effort reduction of 9 and 20 percent by husbands and wives respectively.

By now, the research literature on work-disincentive effects is voluminous. In an exhaustive review of over 100 of these studies, Danziger, Haveman, and Plotnick (1981) concluded that the major income-transfer programs, including those for the elderly, have reduced the total annual hours of work in the economy by an estimated 4.8 percent (see also Masters and Garfinkle 1978). Lampman's estimate is somewhat higher, about 7 percent of total hours worked, and he also points out that the reduction is concentrated among groups with relatively low productivity (1979). These percentages are, however, more significant than they might at first seem. They suggest that if the programs were eliminated, and if employment did not expand faster than the work force, the increased search for jobs by former beneficiaries could raise the unemployment level by 5 to 7 percent.

The Reagan administration's efforts to slash the programs should be viewed in the light of these effects. The immediate consequence of program cuts has been to expand the number of people searching for employment, and to lower the terms on which they will accept employment.[18] The other and more pervasive consequence is to weaken workers generally in their relations with employers. Thus when the duration of unemployment benefits was slashed despite widespread industrial displace- ment, the proportion of the unemployed who received benefits fell from two-thirds to one-third—the lowest level since the Great Depression. Inevitably, those still working fear the prospect of job loss more, and because they do are more likely to concede to employer demands. Those who are already without work are forced more quickly to underbid each other in the competition for jobs. Meanwhile, the termination of the Comprehensive Education and Training Act removed 400,000 people from public service jobs, and a relentless purge of the disability rolls succeeded in removing nearly half a million people, although vigorous lobbying and litigation resulted in the restoration of 291,000 cases to the rolls.[19]

Cuts in AFDC, Medicaid, and food-stamp benefits have similar effects on many low-wage service-sector workers, particularly part-time, temporary, and home workers, who are less likely to be covered by unemployment or disability insurance. Moreover, workers with these protections turn to the means-tested programs when their unemployment benefits are exhausted or when they find their disability benefits terminated. Without these residual protections, the worker's fear of being fired that buttresses employer power is intensified. The Reagan administration has worked hard to cut the means-tested programs. It has repeatedly demanded reductions in program budgets, albeit with mixed success.[20] (In point of fact, AFDC recipients have suffered most from the failure of the states to raise benefit levels to keep pace with inflation, as we will note in the next chapter. But this process was well under way when Reagan took office.) The Reagan administration has also vigorously advocated forced-work programs for AFDC recipients, and workfare programs are now being implemented in about thirty states. And it has twice floated proposals for radically restructuring the AFDC and nutritional programs by devolving administrative and fiscal responsibility to the states. Such a move would make these programs more vulnerable to business pressures, since businessmen can and do bargain with state and local officials for tax and policy concessions as the price of locating in one place or another.[21] The original administration decentralization proposal in 1981, dubbed a "New Federalism," was allowed to die when the governors voiced loud objections. But the administration is trying again. An internal administration memo explains the current effort at decentralization with the disingenuous argument that "individual needs for public assistance can be assessed most effectively at the level of government closest to the need."

The elimination of any federal standards, which in the past lifted benefit levels particularly in low-wage and low-benefit states, is said to be justified on similar grounds: "Because individual needs vary, public assistance benefits should not be tied to a federally-determined standard." Lest this talk about individual needs lead anyone to forget the main issue, the memo takes care to reaffirm the old principle of less eligibility: "No worker should be able to better his financial condition by reducing or quitting work and collecting public assistance, and public assistance should not make a non-worker financially better off than a worker."[22] To guarantee the implementation of this principle, the administration proposes to decentralize the programs. The funds from 59 existing programs that provide services and benefits to the poor would become available for state and local experiments to "reduce dependency" on government assistance. Over time, this strategy could facilitate massive cuts in federal funding.

The persistence and shrewdness of the administration in this and other efforts to cut welfare state programs reveals its seriousness of purpose. And that purpose is an old one. The social programs are the focus of business opposition in the eighties for much the same reason they have always been. The existence of the programs, whether poor relief or unemployment insurance, provides working people with a measure of security, and therefore with a measure of power.

The Brief Against Social Provision

Whether the object is to curtail benefits recently won or to whittle away long-established protections, employer campaigns against relief or welfare must necessarily also be public relations campaigns of considerable sensitivity, particularly in the contemporary United States, where electoral-representative arrangements require that a good many working people be persuaded to support (or ignore) policies that are against their own interests. Naturally enough, such campaigns do not explain the questions of class power that are at issue, or deal with the way changing economic relations are affecting the circumstances of different classes. Instead, campaigns against social provision invariably take the form of public arguments that relief is in fact injurious to everyone, and especially to those who receive it.

The paradigmatic case against relief was developed in England in the early 1830s at a time when English manufacturing interests were slashing outdoor relief in order to force displaced agricultural workers into the newly forming industrial proletariat. Accordingly, the great liberal thinkers of the day, such as Townsend, Malthus, Bentham, and Burke, discovered that the well-being of the nation demanded that poor relief be abolished, or at least be sharply restricted.

Scholars proclaimed in unison that a science had been discovered which put the laws governing man's world beyond any doubt. It was at the behest of these laws that compassion was removed from the hearts, and a stoic determination to renounce human solidarity in the name of the greatest happiness for the greatest number gained the dignity of secular religion. The mechanism of the market was asserting itself and clamoring for completion: human labor had to be made a commodity. (Polanyi 1957: 102)

No doubt the English ruling class drew comfort from the theory that it was not the economic dislocations of the previous century which were responsible for the misery of the poor, but the giving of relief itself. As the Poor Law Commission of 1834 said, outdoor relief, by repealing the "law of nature by which the effects of each man's improvidence or misconduct are borne by himself and his family," had generated a "train of evils: the loss of self-respect, responsibility, prudence, temperance, hard work, and the other virtues that had once sustained him. It was this degradation of character, more than material impoverishment, that defined the pauper" (Himmelfarb 1985: 162–3). As in so many other matters, Alexis de Tocqueville summed up the core of the what was and continues to be the elite wisdom:

> Any permanent, regular, administrative system whose aim will be to provide for the needs of the poor will breed more miseries than it can cure, will deprave the population that it wants to help and comfort, will in time reduce the rich to being no more than the tenant-farmers of the poor, will dry up the sources of savings, will stop the accumulation of capital, will retard the development of trade, will benumb human industry and activity, and will culminate by bringing about a violent revolution in the State, when the number of those who receive alms will have become as large as those who give it, and the indigent, no longer being able to take from the impoverished rich the means of providing for his needs, will find it easier to plunder them of all their property at one stroke than to ask for their help. (1968: 25)

If these warnings have a familiar ring, so should the use to which they were put, in a "barrage of publicity and polemic." Ten thousand copies of the official report of the Poor Law Commissioners were sold, and another ten thousand distributed without charge. Similarly, the volumes of testimony the commission had collected were widely disseminated, and all this in the context of a larger publicity campaign involving "hundreds of lesser-known pamphleteers, justices of the peace, clergyman, magistrates, Members of Parliament, landowners, economists, philanthropists, and reformers" (Himmelfarb 1985: 154–5). To the accompaniment of this chorus of approval, the Poor Law Commissioners recommended, and the Parliament enacted, a series of reforms that attempted to make the workhouse the main form of relief in England. As Polanyi sums it up, "Psychological torture was coolly advocated and smoothly put into practice by mild philanthropists as a means of oiling the wheels of the labor mill" (1957: 82).

The broadly similar campaign against outdoor relief in the United States toward the end of the nineteenth century was accompanied by similar charges against social provision. The arguments were of course already familiar from earlier attacks on poor relief for fostering idleness and improvidence, as well as from the highly publicized English campaign for the New Poor Law. Still, the attack on outdoor relief that began in the 1870s was far more serious and sustained than earlier efforts to slash relief, and the rhetoric that accompanied it was more strident. This was, after all, the era of Herbert Spencer and the flowering of social Darwinism.[23] Blithely ignoring the massive disruptions associated with rapid industrialization, large-scale immigration, urbanization, and recurrent severe depressions, reformers pinpointed public outdoor relief as the source of the travails of poverty and social disorganization in late-nineteenth-century cities. They also produced the "data" to confirm it. Katz (1986: 86–8) describes a survey of 12,614 poorhouse inmates conducted by Dr. Charles S. Hoyt, secretary of the New York State Board of Charities, in 1874–75. It became the most widely quoted document on pauperism in the late nineteenth century, and purported to show that most inmates were long-term paupers, presumably destroyed by idleness and dependency. In fact, Hoyt reached this conclusion by administering his questionnaire only to the "fixed population" (and not to short-term inmates) as well as by including inmates of insane asylums and orphanages attached to some of the poorhouses in his sample, all of which greatly exaggerated the persistent use of relief and its deleterious effects.

No one expressed the outlook of the reformers better than Josephine Shaw Lowell, leader in the establishment of the New York State Charities Aid Association, member of the New York State Board of Charities, founder in 1882 of the New York Charity Organization Society, and in all these capacities, a leader in the campaign to abolish outdoor relief. In the midst of the depression of the 1880s that followed fast on the heels of the devastating depression of the 1870s, she declared relief to be responsible both for low wages and for poverty:

> All systematic dolegiving is proved not to be charitable.... Almsgiving and dolegiving are hurtful even to those who do not receive them,

because they help to keep down wages by enabling those who do receive them to work for less than fair pay. No greater wrong can be done...to all working people....

Almsgiving and dolegiving are hurtful to those who receive them because they lead men to remit their own exertions and depend on others...false hopes are excited, the unhappy recipients of alms become dependent, lose their energy, are rendered incapable of self-support.... The proof that dolegiving and almsgiving do break down independence, do destroy energy, do undermine character, may be found in the growing ranks of pauperism in every city, in the fact that the larger the funds given in relief in any community, the more pressing is the demand for them.... Better leave people to the hard working of natural laws than to run the risk of interfering with those laws in a mischievous manner. (Lowell 1972: 3–6)

Lowell also thought that each case of poverty "is to be *radically* dealt with; that in finding fellow beings in want and suffering, the cause of the want and suffering are to be removed if possible, even if the process be as painful as plucking out an eye or cutting off a limb" (1972: 6, emphasis in original). The gruesome metaphor takes on meaning when it is recalled that prominent reformers (although not Lowell herself) recommended breaking up families—for example, by institutionalizing young children so their impoverished mothers could seek employment—as a "solution" to pauperism.[24] In fact, with the constriction of outdoor relief, many impoverished families themselves tried to place their children in orphan asylums, hoping to retrieve them when times were better.

From the depression that began in 1873, the country rolled from one economic collapse to another at intervals of only a few years. In 1874, the American Iron and Steel Institute estimated at least 1 million unemployed. By 1878, labor advocate William G. Moody estimated half the work force was either wholly or partially unemployed (Mohl 1983: 36). In the 1880s, the numbers of unemployed again reached close to a million, while 5.5 million new immigrants, many recruited by commission agents for industrialists, poured into the country. Even those lucky enough to find employment remained miserably poor. Foner reports, for example, that in the 1880s a family of four needed, at the barest minimum, about $720 a year for subsistence. Many workers, even better-paid male workers, earned much less. Government data showed that the average worker earned only a little more than a dollar a day in 1883. If the worker was exceptionally fortunate and employed year round, this would yield an annual income of less than half the subsistence minimum (Foner 1955: 20).

As for relief, Katz (1985: 47–48) reports that before outdoor relief was eliminated in Brooklyn in 1878, the practice consisted of distributing meager amounts of food (flour, potatoes, or rice but no "luxuries" such as tea or sugar) or coal, but never both in the same week. The average family probably received aid for only a very few weeks each year. Similarly, in his study of poverty in Boston, Huggins (1971: 146–7) shows that during the winter of 1893–94, when a new economic crisis caused widespread desperation, an estimated $9 was distributed to each male applicant for the whole winter season. Under these conditions, it is reasonable to surmise that neither the giving nor the withholding of relief had much to do with the moral decline of the poor which so preoccupied the reformers.

These brute economic facts notwithstanding, what Keller (1977: 504) calls the "chilling social Darwinist assumptions" held sway among the reformers. It was not the economy that needed correcting. On the contrary, as a reformer reviewing the problem of unemployment in the dark year of 1894 observed:

> In this country, despite all assertions to the contrary, there is generally work enough for everybody who is willing to work, at wages which with proper economy will enable the worker to lay something aside for a rainy day (Shaw 1894: 29).

Rather, what was of concern to the reformers was interference with the natural laws—conceived in moral as well as economic terms—which demanded the survival of the fittest. "Hard times," Albert Shaw worried, "increase...the number of unworthy persons who ask aid," and he went on to assure his readers, in a review of charity society efforts in a dozen cities, that very little charity was being given at all (1894: 31). Outdoor relief, echoed the New York State Board of Charities, speaking much as did state charity boards elsewhere, is "injurious and hurtful to the unfortunate and worthy poor, demoralizing in its tendencies, a prolific source of pauperism and official corruption, and an unjust burden upon the public" (Mohl 1983: 45).

Opposition to federal emergency relief and work relief in the early 1930s sounded some of these same, by now classical, themes. In a message to Congress in 1931, as the catastrophe of the Great Depression swept through the country leaving millions unemployed, Hoover reiterated his opposition to any "government dole" with the extraordinary assertion, in the midst of a worldwide economic collapse, that the "breakdown and increased unemployment in Europe is due in part to such practices" as government relief for the unemployed (cited in Piven and Cloward 1971: 53). Similarly, in a message to Congress January 4, 1935, Roosevelt declared that emergency relief, with its relatively inclusive coverage and liberal grant levels, would be terminated. In 1935, unemployment remained at historic levels, and the economy had made only a feeble recovery. Nevertheless, Roosevelt echoed the age-old theory that relief was a major source of the malaise: "Continued dependence upon relief induces a spiritual and moral disintegration fundamentally destructive to the national fiber.... We must preserve not only the bodies of the unemployed from destitution but also their self-respect, their self-reliance and courage and determination" (Schlesinger, 1960: 267–8).

We want to remind the reader of the close resemblance between the historic antiwelfare arguments and current charges against the welfare state, pithily captured by Nathan Glazer in his pronouncement "Our efforts to deal with distress themselves increase distress" (1971: 52). Charles Murray (1984: 68) advances the identical thesis that the expansion of social provision in the sixties and seventies had the perverse consequence of increasing poverty. Kaus (1986: 68) worries about the "effect of welfare in sustaining the underclass, umbilical-cord style." The historic contentions echo repetitively through all of these contemporary complaints.

The Apparent Credibility of the Charges

Why has the argument that social welfare is injurious to the poor been persuasive even at times when the programs were so small as to make the charges dubious for that reason alone? Part of the answer is in the sheer weight of well-funded propaganda. Another part is that, whether in Tocqueville's day or ours, a crude sort of evidence can usually be found to make these charges credible simply by scrutinizing the poor. Ordinarily, patterns of life among people at the bottom do not draw much attention; they are left to cope as best they can, and their coping generally includes behavior that is "deviant" according to official society. Attacks on social provision become the occasion for publicizing these patterns of life among the poor. Thus out-of-wedlock births are "discovered" by Tocqueville in nineteenth-century rural England, or by social scientists among blacks in twentieth-century America, and proclaimed to be new pathological trends, which are then attributed to social aid.

Nor does the existence of huge and presumably neutral systems of government information make the contemporary poor less susceptible to these politically motivated "discoveries." At first glance, it might seem that virtually everything that can be counted is being counted, analyzed, and reported in any case. But not quite so; the data systems are pliant. A recent example is instructive. For many years, the Census had used a coding procedure that did not identify unmarried mothers when they lived in a larger household with their parents. With the rise of a public outcry about welfare and illegitimacy in the 1970s and 1980s, the Census coding procedures were altered so that unmarried mothers were sure to be identified, and the numbers reported doubled in two years (Bane and Ellwood 1984: 3, fn. 1).

This is not to say that the evidence of disorganization is entirely or even mainly an artifact. Symptoms of disorganization among the poor may very well escalate during periods of relief conflict, not because of the availability of aid, but as a consequence of the economic and social dislocations that led to the expansion of relief-giving in the first place. Because these disorganizing trends coincide with the expansion of relief-giving, critics can generally find the "proof" of their contention that relief is harmful to the poor.

Thus the fluctuations in the economy which lead to material hardship and demands for relief also deprive people of the basic resources needed to sustain community and personal life. Not only market downturns but also economic growth can mean rapid shifts in the kinds of workers required, or the places in which they are required. Such dislocations not only reduce wage income for many people; they can also wipe out other resources on which social life is constructed, as when enclosure eliminated the common lands in eighteenth-century England, or when downtown business leaders joined together in urban renewal projects that displaced the poor and working class from their homes and communities in twentieth-century American cities. The costs of these market developments for people at the bottom go beyond material hardship to the rupture of ties to place, kin, community, and culture which make a coherent social and personal life possible. As a result, symptoms of social disorganization do mount. While the relief that is sometimes given at such times mitigates hardship, it can hardly repair the ruptures that result from economic dislocation. But the giving of aid does provide the occasion for invoking the spurious theory that it is relief itself that causes social and personal disorganization.

In fact, while Tocqueville abhorred "legal almsgiving," his understanding of the relationship between poverty and relief was far more complicated than the use of his opinions by latter-day intellectuals such as Himmelfarb (1985: chap. 6). Tocqueville was at some pains to make clear that the root causes of poverty were not in indiscriminate almsgiving but in the destructive effects on the poor of what he called "industrialization." Poverty was the result, in other words, of the creation of a class of workers exposed to the insecurities of the market, a development that created both great wealth and great misery. His solution was a prescient call for intervention in the economy to prevent the rapid displacement of population and promote more balanced and stable economic development (1969: 26).

But perhaps the most important reason that the charges against welfare seem to make sense is the strength of the cognitive model on which they draw, a model that gives the particular charges a coherence and persuasiveness they would otherwise lack. The model is continuously alluded to by the reformers when they speak of the "natural law" that is violated by "legal almsgiving." Natural law in England and the United States is, of course, laissez-faire. It is the set of ideas that asserts that not only goods but money, land, and labor are all commodities, and as commodities must be regulated, not by governments or communities, but by the market "law" of supply and demand. To do otherwise, to intrude through public action on market processes, is to court disaster by disrupting the workings of natural law. Once this mythic conception of how society is organized gained ascendancy, it became a powerful ideological resource in the periodic campaigns against social protections.

Market-Conforming Programs and the Degradation of the Pauper

There is a final, perhaps ironic point to be made about the consequences of employer-led assaults on social provision. These assaults result in programs so punitive and stigmatizing that they do indeed come over time to produce some of the demoralizing effects attributed to the fact of social provision itself. When Tocqueville (1968: 19) declaimed about the "degraded condition into which the lower classes have fallen" as a result of relief, there was perhaps this truth in his observation: people kept in misery by penurious levels of aid, and then forced to accept the degraded identity of the pauper in exchange for that aid, are likely to be stripped of their energy and morale.

Consider, for example, the institution of the workhouse or the almshouse. The workhouse was self-consciously designed to deter people from asking for aid. The method of deterrence was simply to make conditions so repugnant that the poor would strive at virtually any cost to avoid the dreaded state of the pauper. Thus workhouses and almshouses were awful: bad and insufficient food, decrepit and filthy quarters into which all sorts of unfortunates, including the diseased and frequently the insane, were indiscriminately crowded together. The fact that the receipt of aid was conditional on incarceration, and incarceration under these vile physical conditions, also made inevitable the total social degradation of the pauper. Other rituals of the workhouse, such as the separation of family members and the strict penal regimen, virtually ensured that result. The terror inspired by the workhouse did no doubt induce most of the poor to endeavor somehow to survive by their own exertions, and probably also ensured that many did not survive at all. As for those of the very young or the crippled or the sick or the old who had no other option than "the house," their physical and social degradation became an object lesson in what it meant to fail in the labor market. "The Poor Law," says Hobsbawm, "was not so much intended to help the unfortunate as to stigmatize the self-confessed failures of society" (1968: 69). A high price was paid for this social lesson in the torment inflicted on the enfeebled people who were incarcerated. Moreover, to the extent that the able-bodied also turned to the work-house, the experience must surely have been extremely debilitating, both physically and psychologically. But the damage thus done was not attributed to the awful conditions of the workhouse or the extraordinary measures through which paupers were made into social pariahs, but rather to the insidious effects of relief itself.

Polanyi's seminal work on the English Speenhamland system has contributed to this confusion. Despite his sharp criticism of the institutional arrangements that produced a "self-regulating market" in land, commodities, and labor in the nineteenth century, and his empathy with the poor who were the victims of the campaign to commodify human labor, Polanyi nevertheless saw the spread of relief in England after 1895 as the major source of the destitution of the poor.

> Although it took some time till the self-respect of the common man sank to the low point where he preferred poor relief to wages, his wages which were subsidized from public funds were bound eventually to be bottomless, and to force him upon the rates. Little by little the people of the countryside were pauperized; the adage, "once on the rates, always on the rates" was a true saying. But for the protracted effects of the allowance system [that is, poor relief] it would be impossible to explain the human and social degradation of early capitalism (1957: 80).

Under the Speenhamland plan—which some historians claim was not in fact so widely practiced as Polanyi thought[25]—the poor-relief authorities guaranteed "the right to live" by requiring that the poor offer themselves to employers for whatever wages they could get, and by then supplementing the wages with relief benefits keyed to family size and the price of bread. As Polanyi (1957: 97) says, the Speenhamland system was "started as aid-in-wages, ostensibly benefitting the employees, but actually using public means to subsidize the employers. For the main effect of the allowance system was to depress wages below the subsistence level." The confusion in Polanyi's analysis arises from the failure to distinguish firmly between the effects on wages and morale of guaranteeing the "right to live," and the effects on wages and morale of the forced-work aspect of the Speenhamland plan. At a time when there was an enormous surplus of labor in rural England, the work demanded of those who were living on the parish must indeed have driven wages down, and this together with the general upheaval in rural life caused by the spread of markets must surely have been demoralizing. But income guarantees of themselves, stripped of the forced-work requirements, would have had quite the opposite effect. By removing large numbers of the rural population from the labor force at a time of labor surplus, relief payments unconditioned by work would have raised the price of labor and perhaps introduced a measure of stability into the life of the rural poor at a time of wrenching instabilities. Polanyi acknowledges this possibility only very indirectly when he says that had it not been for the introduction of the anticombination laws (laws prohibiting unions) at the same time as the Speenhamland system spread, its results might have been quite different. That is a reasonable supposition. But even in the absence of worker organization, relief payments themselves, had they been severed from the forced-work component of the system, would have set a floor under rural wages. It thus seems reasonable to think that it was the use of the relief system to force the rural poor to work at any wage—"work relief" in contemporary language—that caused the general deterioration in wages and morale which many observers reported in southern England, where the plan was apparently implemented more widely.

The lesson for contemporary welfare policy seems to us clear. Market-oriented relief reforms help to produce the demoralizing effects on recipients that are attributed to the fact of social provision itself. Nowhere is this more evident than in the elaborately crafted arrangements of the contemporary American "means-tested" programs. These arrangements, which reflect a history of employer opposition, do indeed debilitate and demoralize the people who receive benefits. It is not receiving benefits that is damaging to recipients, but rather the fact that benefits are so low as to ensure physical misery and an outcast social status. Even these benefits are given only under close surveillance (including, until recently, midnight raids, "suitable-home" laws, and "man-in-the-house" rules) and are conditioned on modern rituals of degradation such as publicized "hot lines" encouraging relatives, friends, and neighbors to report information on welfare recipients—all of which surely have disabling and demoralizing effects.

The history of employer-backed relief reform also casts light on the contemporary campaign to replace cash assistance with varieties of mandatory work programs. Experience suggests it is unlikely that many people will actually be employed in such programs. Costs alone, and particularly the high costs of child care for AFDC mothers, would preclude it. Forced-work programs are significant, not because they are likely to be implemented on a large scale, but because the introduction of punitive and stigmatizing workfare programs will deter people from applying for aid at all, much as the threat of the workhouse deterred people from becoming supplicants. The implications of Mead's uncompromising declaration in favor of forced work should be considered in this light:

> The solution must lie in public authority. Low-wage work apparently must be mandated just as the draft has sometimes apparently been necessary to staff the military. Authority achieves compliance more efficiently than benefits. Government need not make the desired behavior worthwhile to people. It simply threatens punishment (in this case, the loss of benefits) if they do not comply (1986: 84–5).

Even more chilling is Kaus's call for the abolition of all social welfare benefits for the poor and their replacement by subminimum-wage jobs. The New Poor Law Commissioners of 1834, who promoted a forced-work system where paupers were made to break stone or move wood-piles from one place to another in exchange for their porridge, could not have said it better.

Workfare should not be a short-term program to existing welfare clients, but a long-term program to destroy the culture of poverty. In this "hard" view, what's most important is not whether sweeping streets or cleaning buildings helps Betsy Smith, single teenage parent and high school dropout, learn skills that will help her find a private sector job. It is whether the prospect of sweeping streets and cleaning buildings for a welfare grant will deter Betsy Smith from having the illegitimate child that drops her out of school and onto welfare in the first place—or, failing that, whether the sight of Betsy Smith sweeping streets after having her illegitimate child will discourage her younger sisters and neighbors from doing as she did (Kaus 1986: 27).

Kaus is almost surely right about the deterrent effects he anticipates for his proposal. As we said fifteen years ago in *Regulating the Poor*, work relief is designed to spur people to offer themselves to any employer on any terms. And it does this by making pariahs of those who cannot support themselves. This object lesson in the virtues of work is accomplished by the terrible treatment accorded those who do not work (1971: 34). The resulting immiseration and degradation of the pauperized poor then becomes yet another justification in the campaign against social provision.

Originally published in 1987.

Notes

1. Wilensky's definition, for example, is broader: "The essence of welfare is government protected minimum standards of income, nutrition, health, housing, and education, assured to every citizen as a political right" (1975:1). However, the very sweep of this definition introduces troublesome ambiguities, for it embraces a range of public services, including education, which may or may not have the effect of ensuring minimum living standards. See Alber (1985) for a knowledgeable discussion of alternative definitions of the welfare state.

2. *New York Times*, April 17, 1985. The largest source of these benefits was, of course, the Social Security program. Consistent with these data, Caplow et al. (1982: 26–29) returned to Middletown and found that a solid majority of families receive federal benefits today, compared to only one-third even during the depths of the Great Depression.

3. After adjusting for inflation, there has been a sixfold increase in real outlays between 1965 and 1985, and an increase in the share of the GNP absorbed by the social programs from 2.9% to 7.7% (Feldstein 1985: 94).

4. See Stigler (1946) for one of the earliest contemporary formulations of this problem.

5. See Piven and Cloward (1985: chap. 2) for an extended discussion of the relationship between the displacement of people from traditional agricultural economies and the emergence of relief.

6. Much of the history of popular political struggles over poor relief in the United States before the Great Depression remains to be written. The historical studies remain sparse. See Mohl (1971) on New York City before 1825. See Katz (1986, chap. 1) for a brief overview of popular demands for relief in the United States. Some references to demands of the unemployed for relief can be found in Gutman (1976: 60–61); Foner (1947: 162); Feder (1936: 32–5, 52); and Reznick (1933: 31).

7. The meaning of the growth in the relief rolls in the mid-nineteenth century, and of subsequent attacks on relief, is sometimes muddied by the issue of the use of relief as political patronage. Thus Katz (1986: 36) writes that as the relief rolls grew, so did "a complex network linking the poor, some local businessmen and professionals, and ward politicians in an exchange of welfare, cash and votes." But this thesis should be treated with caution, given the ease with which outdoor relief was subsequently eliminated in the big cities where patronage politics was well established. By contrast, Civil War pensions, a form of social provision that tended to reach the somewhat better off, were indeed widely used as patronage, and steadily expanded in the closing decades of the century. This was during the very period in which the virtual elimination of outdoor relief in the big cities of the nation was justified by the argument that relief was susceptible to patronage abuse. On Civil War pensions, see Keller (1977: 506).

8. This problem was first delineated by T. H. Marshall (1964) some decades ago when he explored the tensions between the capitalist markets and the social rights that had come to be associated with citizenship.

9. In 1870, New York State spent an average of $109.59 for each of its 15,343 poorhouse inmates, and an average of $8.96 for each of the 101,796 people who received outdoor relief (Katz 1986: 293–4, n. 29).

10. Reznick (1956: 297) reports that by 1883 there were 25 charity societies, and the number more than doubled in the following decade.

11. See the discussion of business opposition to work relief during this period in Piven and Cloward (1971: 80–4); see Esping-Anderson (1986) for a general discussion of the sources of this opposition in aspects of the modern welfare state which promote the "decommodification" of production.

12. For a more general discussion of the role of the South in the New Deal, see Key (1984); Tindall (1965); Piven and Cloward (1977: chap. 5); Alston and Ferrie (1985b).

13. See Piven and Cloward (1971: 115–16). See also Alston and Ferrie (1985a) and Quadagno (1984: 643). See Weir (1986) for a different explanation of unemployment policy that generally emphasizes the impact of constraints arising from administrative and electoral-representative arrangements. See also James

Patterson (1967: 144–5) and Richard Bensel (1984:168) for a discussion of the conflicts generated by the patronage implications of relief expenditure.

14. For a concise review of some studies of the work-disincentive effects on the aged of Social Security benefits, see Danziger, Haveman, and Plotnick (1981).

15. Parsons (1980) and Leonard (1979) also report large disincentive effects of the disability programs. However, Haveman and Wolfe (1981) found significantly smaller disincentive effects.

16. Danziger, Haveman, and Plotnick (1981) review these studies. See also Feldstein (1974), and Garfinkle and Plotnick.

17. New Jersey, Seattle, and Denver were the largest experimental sites.

18. A study by the congressional Office of Technology Assessment found that of the 11.5 million workers who lost jobs because of plant shutdowns or relocations between 1979 and 1984, only 60% found new jobs, and of these, 45% had taken pay cuts, often sharp pay cuts (*New York Times*, February 7, 1985).

19. The criteria defining medical eligibility were eased in the 1960s and 1970s, and vocational factors were introduced in determining suitability for employment, so that, for example, functionally illiterate people were judged disabled if they were physically unable to perform manual labor. Critics charged that as a consequence the disability rolls had become populated by many people who could in fact work, and in 1980 the Carter administration obtained legislation authorizing a general case review. The Reagan administration used this legislative authorization to purge the rolls by imposing stricter medical criteria and eliminating any consideration of vocational or occupational factors.

20. After implementing the first round of administration cuts in 1981, the Congress resisted the draconian cuts subsequently proposed. The actual reductions were not anything like the crippling cutbacks the Reagan administration had demanded. A report prepared by the Urban Institute estimated that through 1984, AFDC outlays were down 14% compared to the 28% the Reagan administration wanted, and food-stamp outlays were also down 14% compared to the administration's attempted cut of 52% (Palmer and Sawhill 1984: Table 6.1). Even these more modest cuts forced hundreds of thousands deeper into poverty. See U.S. House of Representatives, Committee on Ways and Means (1985).

21. For a more extended discussion of the political significance of decentralization efforts, see Piven and Cloward (1985: 128–32).

22. These quotations are from an undated memo circulated privately by the White House Welfare Reform Task Force entitled "Public Assistance to Alleviate Poverty."

23. For a discussion of the dominant intellectual views of the time, see Haskell (1977).

24. See Bremner (1956) for the most influential study of the period. See also Katz (1986, especially pp. 72–8) for a discussion of the views of S. Humphrey Gurteen, another leader in the charity organization movement. See also Pumphrey and Pumphrey (1983) on the practice of institutionalizmg the children of impoverished mothers.

25. This is not a settled issue. See Blaug (1963) and Block and Sommers (1984).

References

ALBER, JENS. 1985. "Continuities and Changes in the Idea of the Welfare State." Paper prepared for a conference, "The Future of the Welfare State," sponsored by the New School for Social Research and the Friedrich Ebert Foundation, New York, December 5–6, 1985.

ALEXANDER, JOHN K. 1983. "The Functions of Public Welfare in Late-Eighteenth-Century Philadelphia: Regulating the Poor?" Pp. 15–34 in Walter I. Trattner, ed., *Social Welfare or Social Control? Some Historical Reflections on "Regulating the Poor."* Knoxville: University of Tennessee Press.

ALSTON, LEE J., AND JOSEPH P. FERRIE. 1985a. "Labor Costs, Paternalism, and Loyalty in Southern Agriculture: A Constraint on the Growth of the Welfare State." *Journal of Economic History* 14(1): 95–117.

————. 1985b. "Resisting the Welfare State: Southern Opposition to the Farm Security Administration." In Robert Higgs, ed., *The Emergence of the Modern Political Economy*. Greenwich, Conn.

BANE, MARY JO, AND DAVID T. ELLWOOD. 1984. "Single Mothers and Their Living Arrangements." John F. Kennedy School of Government, Harvard University, Cambridge, Mass. Mimeo.

BENSEL, RICHARD. 1984. *Sectionalism and American Political Development, 1880–1980.* Madison: University of Wisconsin Press.

BLAUG, MARK. 1963. "The Myth of the Old Poor Law and the Making of the New." *Journal of Economic History* 23: 151–84.

BLOCK, FRED, AND MARGARET R. SOMMERS. 1984. "Beyond the Economistic Fallacy: The Holistic Social Science of Karl Polanyi." Pp. 47–84 in Theda Skocpol, ed., *Vision and Method in Historical Sociology*. Cambridge: Cambridge University Press.

BRANDT, LILLIAN. 1908. *The Charity Organization Society of the City of New York, 1882–1907. Twentieth Annual Report for the Year Ending September Thirtieth, Nineteen Hundred & Seven.*

BREMNER, ROBERT H. 1956. *From the Depths: The Discovery of Poverty in the United States.* New York: New York University Press.

BURHAUSER, RICHARD V., AND G. S. TOLLEY. 1978. "Older Americans and Market Work." *The Gerontologist* 18(5): 449–53.

THEODORE CAPLOW ET AL. 1982. *Middletown Families: Fifty Years of Change and Continuity.* Minneapolis: University of Minnesota Press.

CONGRESSIONAL BUDGET OFFICE. 1982. *Disability Compensation: Current Issues and Options for Change.* Washington, D.C.: Government Printing Office.

DANZIGER, SHELDON H., ROBERT HAVEMAN, AND ROBERT D. PLOTNICK. 1981. "How Income Transfer Programs Affect Work, Savings, and the Income Distribution: A Critical Review." *Journal of Economic Literature* 19: 975–1028.

DANZIGER, SHELDON H., AND ROBERT D. PLOTNICK. 1982. "The War on Income Poverty: Achievements and Failures." Pp. 31–50 in Paul Sommers, ed., *Welfare Reform in America.* Hingham, Mass. Kluwer-Nijhoff Publishing.

DEVINE, JOEL A., AND WILLIAM CANAK. 1986. "Redistribution in a Bifurcated Welfare State: Quintile Shares and the U.S. Case." *Social Problems* 33(5): 391–406.

DOMHOFF, G. WILLIAM. 1970. *The Higher Circle: The Governing Class in America.* New York: Random House.

ELLWOOD, DAVID T., AND LAWRENCE H. SUMMERS. 1986. "Poverty in America: Is Welfare the Answer or the Problem?" Pp. 78–105 in Sheldon H. Danziger and Daniel H. Weinberg, eds., *Fighting Poverty: What Works and What Doesn't.* Cambridge, Mass.: Harvard University Press.

ESPING-ANDERSON, GOSTA. 1986. "Institutional Accommodation to Full Employment: A Comparison of Regimes." In H. Keman and H. Palokeimo, eds., *Government Responses to the Contemporary Economic Crisis.* Beverly Hills, Calif: Sage Pubns. In press.

FEDER, LEAH H. 1936. *Unemployment Relief in Periods of Depression.* New York: Russell Sage Foundation.

FELDSTEIN. MARTIN. 1974. "Unemployment Compensation: Adverse Incentives and Distributional Anomalies." *National Tax Journal* 27: 231–44.

———. 1985. "The Social Security Explosion." *Public Interest.* 81: 94–106.

FERGUSON, THOMAS. 1984. "From Normalcy to New Deal: Industrial Structure, Party Competition, and American Public Policy in the Great Depression." *International Organization* 38(1): 41–94.

FONER, PHILIP S. 1947. *History of the Labor Movement in the United States.* New York: International Publishers.

———. 1955. *History of the Labor Movement in the United States.* Vol. 2. New York: International Publishers.

GARFINKLE, IRWIN, AND ROBERT PLOTNICK. Undated. "How Much Does Unemployment Insurance Increase the Unemployment Rate and Reduce Work, Earnings, and Inefficiency?" Discussion Paper no. 378–76. Institute for Research on Poverty, University of Wisconsin, Madison.

GLAZER, NATHAN. 1971. "The Limits of Social Policy." *Commentary* 52(3): 51–58.

GORDON, DAVID M., RICHARD EDWARDS, AND MICHAEL REICH. 1982. *Segmented Work Divided Workers: The Historical Transformation of Labor in the United States*. Cambridge: Cambridge University Press.

HASKELL, THOMAS. 1977. *The Emergence of Professional Social Science*. Urbana: University of Illinois Press.

HAVEMAN, ROBERT H., AND BARBARA L. WOLFE. 1981. "Have Disability Transfers Caused the Decline in Older Male Labor Force Participation? A Work-Status Rational Choice Model." Institute for Research on Poverty, University of Wisconsin, Madison. Mimeo.

HECLO, HUGH. 1986. "The Political Foundations of Antipoverty Policy." Pp. 312–40 in Sheldon H. Danziger and Daniel H. Weinberg, eds., *Fighting Poverty: What Works and What Doesn't*. Cambridge, Mass.: Harvard University Press.

HIMMELFARB, GERTRUDE. 1983. *The Idea of Poverty: England in the Early Industrial Age*. New York: Vintage Books.

HOBSBAWM, ERIC J. 1968. *Industry and Empire: The Making of Modern English Society*. Vol. 2, *1750 to the Present Day*. New York: Pantheon Books.

HUGGINS, NATHAN IRVING. 1971. *Protestants Against Poverty: Boston's Charities, 1870-1900*. Westport, Conn.: Greenwood Publishing

KATZ, MICHAEL B. 1986. *In the Shadow of the House: A Social History of Welfare in America*. New York: Basic Books.

KAUS, MICKEY. 1986. "The Work Ethic State." *New Republic*, July 7, pp. 22–33.

KELLER, MORTON. 1977. *Affairs of State: Public Life in the Nineteenth Century*. Cambridge, Mass.: Harvard University Press.

KEY, V. O. 1984. *Southern Politics in State and Nation*. Knoxville: University of Tennessee Press.

LAMPMAN, ROBERT. 1979. *Focus* (University of Wisconsin) 4(1): 3.

LEONARD, J. 1979. "The Social Security Disability Program and Labor Force Participation." Working Paper no. 392. National Bureau of Economic Research, Cambridge, Mass.

LOWELL, JOSEPHINE Shaw, "Uplifting the Pauper." 1972. Pp. 3–11 in David Rothman and Sheila Rothman, eds., *On Their Own: The Poor in Modern America*. Reading, Mass.: Addison-Wesley Publishing Co.

MARSHALL, T. H. 1964. *Class, Citizenship, and Social Development*. Garden City, N.Y.: Doubleday & Co.

MASTERS, STANLEY, AND IRWIN GARFINKLE. 1978. *Estimating the Labor Supply Effects of Income-Maintenance Alternatives*. Madison: Institute for Research on Poverty, University of Wisconsin.

MEAD, LAWRENCE M. 1986. *Beyond Entitlement: The Social Obligations of Citizenship.* New York: Free Press.

MOHL, RAYMOND A. 1971. *Poverty in New York, 1783–1825.* New York: Oxford University Press.

————. 1983. Pp. 35–50 in Walter I. Trattner, ed., *Social Welfare or Social Control? Some Historical Reflections on "Regulating the Poor."* Knoxville: University of Tennessee Press.

MURRAY, CHARLES A. 1984. *Losing Ground: American Social Policy, 1950–1980.* New York: Basic Books.

PALMER, JOHN, AND ISABEL SAWHILL, EDS. 1984. *The Reagan Record: An Assessment of America's Changing Domestic Priorities.* Cambridge, Mass.: Ballinger Publishing Co.

PARSONS, DONALD O. 1979. "The Male Labor Force Participation Decision: Health, Declared Health, and Economic Incentives." Ohio State University, Columbus. Mimeo.

PATTERSON, JAMES T. 1967. *Congressional Conservatism and the New Deal.* Lexington: University of Kentucky Press.

————. 1981. *America's Struggle Against Poverty, 1900–1980.* Cambridge, Mass.: Harvard University Press.

PIVEN, FRANCES FOX, AND RICHARD A. CLOWARD. 1971. *Regulating the Poor: The Functions of Public Welfare.* New York: Pantheon Books.

————. 1977. *Poor People's Movements: Why They Succeed, How They Fail.* New York: Pantheon Books.

————. 1985. *The New Class War: Reagan's Attack on the Welfare State and Its Consequences.* Rev. and enl. ed. New York: Pantheon Books.

PLOTNICK, ROBERT, AND FELICITY SKIDMORE. 1975. *Progress Against Poverty: A Review of the 1964–1974 Decade.* New York: Academic Press.

POLANYI, KARL. 1957. *The Great Transformation: The Political and Economic Origins of Our Time.* Boston: Beacon Press.

PUMPHREY, MURIEL, AND RALPH E. PUMPHREY. 1983. "The Widows' Pension Movement, 1900–1930: Preventive Child-Saving or Social Control?" Pp. 51–66 in Walter I. Trattner, ed., *Social Welfare or Social Control? Some Historical Reflections on "Regulating the Poor."* Knoxville: University of Tennessee Press.

QUADAGNO, JILL. 1984. "Welfare Capitalism and the Social Security Act of 1935." *American Sociological Review* 49(5): 623–47.

REYNOLDS, MORGAN, AND EUGENE SMOLENSKY. 1977. *Public Expenditures, Taxes, and the Distribution of Income: The United States, 1950, 1961, 1970.* New York: Academic Press.

REZNECK, SAMUEL. 1933. "The Depression of 1819–1822, a Social History." *American Historical Review* 39: 28–47.

————. 1956. "Patterns of Thought and Action in an American Depression, 1882–86." *American Historical Review* 21(2): 284–307.

SCHLESINGER, ARTHUR M., JR. 1960. *The Age of Roosevelt. Vol. 3, The Politics of Upheaval, 1935–36.* Boston: Houghton Mifflin Co.

SHAW, ALBERT. 1894. "Relief for the Unemployed in American Cities." *Review of Reviews* 9: 29–37.

STIGLER, GEORGE. 1946. "The Economics of Minimum Wage Legislation." *American Economic Review* 36.

TINDALL. GEORGE B. 1965. *The Emergence of the New South.* Baton Rouge: University of Louisiana Press.

TOCQUEVILLE, ALEXIS DE. [1835] 1968. "Memoir on Pauperism." Pp. 1–27 in Seymour Drescher, ed., *Tocqueville and Beaumont on Social Reform.* New York: Harper Torchbooks.

U.S. HOUSE OF REPRESENTATIVES. Committee on Ways and Means. Subcommittees on Oversight and on Public Assistance and Unemployment Compensation. 1985. *Children in Poverty.* Washington, D.C.: Government Printing Office.

WEBB, SIDNEY, AND BEATRICE WEBB. 1963. *English Poor Law History. Pt. 1, The Old Poor Law.* Hamden, Conn.: Archon Books.

WEIR, MARGARET. 1986. "The U.S. Federal Government and Unemployment: Policy Innovation in the New Deal and the Great Society." In *Project on the Federal Social Role, Working Paper no. 8*: Unemployment. National Conference on Social Welfare, Washington, D.C.

WHITE HOUSE WELFARE REFORM TASK FORCE. Undated. "Public Assistance to Alleviate Poverty: Proposed Demonstration Program." Mimeo.

WILENSKY, HAROLD I. 1975. *The Welfare State and Equality: Structural and Ideological Roots of Public Expenditures.* Berkeley: University of California Press.

10

Women and the State:
Ideology, Power, and the Welfare State

Introduction

Much of the feminist literature evinces an almost categorical antipathy to the state. Among socialist feminists, the antipathy is signaled by the use of such terms as social patriarchy or public patriarchy to describe state policies that bear on the lives of women.[1] And among cultural feminists, it takes form in the nostalgic evocation of the private world of women in an era before state programs intruded on the family (Elshtain, 1982, 1983).

There is some irony in this. While women intellectuals characterize relationships with the state as "dependence," women activists turn increasingly to the state as the arena for political organization and influence. At least as important, the intellectual animus toward the state flies in the face of the attitudes of the mass of American women evident in survey data. While the data show most women are opposed to a defense buildup and presumably, therefore, hostile to the military aspects of state power, in domestic policy areas they evidently believe in a large measure of state responsibility for economic and social well-being, suggesting a belief in the strong and interventionist state that some feminist intellectuals abjure.[2]

Of course, activist women may be erring "liberals," and popular attitudes, including the attitudes of women, can be wrong. But in this instance, we think it is an undiscriminating antipathy to the state that is wrong, for it is based on a series of misleading and simplistic alternatives. On the one hand, there is somehow the possibility of power and autonomy; on the other, dependence on a controlling state. But these polarities are unreal: All social relationships involve elements of social control, and yet there is no possibility for power except in social relationships. In fact, we think the main opportunities for women to exercise power today inhere precisely in their "dependent" relationships with the state, and in this chapter we explain why.

Before we turn directly to this issue, we want to consider the shift in the political beliefs signaled by the gender gap, for we think it important as well as evidence of my main contentions about power. Of course, everyone agrees the gender gap is important as well as evidence of something. The media has bombarded us with information on the gap and also has given us our main explanation, attributing the new cleavage of opinion and voting behavior between men and women to the policies of the Reagan administration.[3] This is not wrong, for the Reagan policies may well have had a catalytic effect on the expression of women's political attitudes. The organized women's movement has also been given credit for generating the gap, and despite the poor match between the largely middle-class constituency of the movement and the cross-class constituency of the gap, and between the issues emphasized by the movement and the issues that highlight the gap, this is probably not entirely wrong either.[4] Nevertheless, we think a development of this scale is likely to have deeper sources than have heretofore been proposed. We will conclude that those roots are in the expanding relationships women have developed with the state and in the new possibilities for power yielded by those relationships. But because the connection between beliefs and this new institutional relationship is not simple and direct, we want first to evaluate and give due weight to other influences on the shift in political opinion that has occurred among women.

Rather than showing the imprint of the women's movement, with its clearly modernizing tendencies, the emphasis on peace, economic equality, and social needs associated with the gender gap suggests the imprint of what are usually taken as traditional female values. This oft-made observation suggests the gender gap is not a fleeting response to particular current events but has deep and authentic roots. At the same time, traditional values of themselves cannot account for this development. The caretaking values of women are old, but the sharp divergence between women and men is entirely new. However, much tradition may color the politics of women: The fact that traditional values associated with the family are now being asserted as public values is a large transformation. Or, as Kathy Wilson told a reporter on the occasion of the convening of the National Women's Political Caucus in 1983, "women are recognizing that their private values are good enough to be their public values." More than that, the beliefs associated with the gender gap are specifically about the obligations of government to protect these values. Women are asserting that the state should represent women, in their terms.

All of this suggests the possibility that a major transformation of consciousness is occurring on a scale that argues powerful historical forces must be at work, whatever the precipitating role of current administration policies. While the comparisons may seem at first glance too grand, we think the public articulation and politicization of formerly insular female values may even be comparable to such historic developments as the emergence of the idea of personal freedom among a bonded European peasantry, or the spread of the idea of democratic rights among the small farmers of the American colonies and the preindustrial workers of England and France, or the emergence of the conviction among industrial workers at different times and places of their right to organize and strike. Each of these ideological developments reflected the interplay of traditional and transforming influences. And each brought enormous political consequences in its wake.

Ideological Transformation and the Gender Gap

If the gender gap is evidence of an ideological transformation, how do we begin to explain it? It is worth observing the primitive state of our theorizing about ideology.[5] This is probably due in no small part to the treatment of ideas by the dominant sociological tradition as not requiring much explanation. It is not that ideas were unimportant in this tradition. To the contrary, consensual ideas were taken as axiomatic, as the very essence of society. In this view, ideas were not attributed to human actors but to the social structure. It seemed to follow that the emergence of deviant or oppositional ideas could be explained as the result of strains or ruptures in the social structure. This sort of reasoning tended to deflect attention away from ideology, for it was not a dynamic factor in social life. Ideology was either consensual and axiomatic, in which case it changed little or only gradually; or if the ideas of particular groups changed sharply, then it was the stresses in the social structure that had generated the deviation that deserved scrutiny. Emile Durkheim pointed the direction as he set out to develop his analysis of the causes of suicide: "Disregarding the individual as such, his motives and his ideas, we shall see, directly, the states of the various social environments...in terms of which the variations in suicide occur" (1951, p. 151).[6]

For a long time, studies of oppositional movements followed Durkheim's lead in dismissing the significance of the ideas of social actors as causes of their behavior, and in searching instead for explanations in the "social environment." Movements were not reflections of ideas, albeit deviant ideas, but rather the result of stresses or breakdowns in the social structure. The result, as Tilly, Tilly, and Tilly (1975) have pointed out (although surely not to argue the significance of ideology), was that movements came to be characterized by a mindless eruptive imagery, as in Crane Brinton's metaphor of fevers (1952). Or, when attention was paid to the ideas associated with movements, as in the work of Neil Smelser (1962), these ideas were treated not as possible causes of movements but as additional symptoms of the derangement in the social environment that alone explained the movement.

The variety of Marxist structural interpretations that gained prominence in the last decade overtook and to some extent displaced the sociological perspective generated mainly by Durkheim and Parsons. The classical Marxists, including Marx himself, at least sometimes had appreciated the importance of oppositional ideology and even had given it explanatory weight, although the issue remained ambiguous and contradictory. However, this theme remained subordinate, at least in the American Marxist revival. Instead, the Marxist structuralists sought to challenge and supplant the ideational characterization of social structure that had come to dominate sociology with a characterization of social structure as rooted in the mode of production. In doing so, they continued to focus on social structure as the overriding determinant of political action and for the most part did not accord ideology a significant role in its own right.

Only very recently, with the waning of conviction in the various structuralisms and the renewed attention to Gramsci (1971) has ideology, particularly the ideology of ordinary people, come into focus. There is at least a developing agreement that ideas pattern action, and that oppositional ideas underlie oppositional action. The signal importance of even this beginning is suggested by Lukes (1975) when he argues that if politics is reduced to structural determinants, whatever those structural determinants, the realm of the political is effectively eliminated.

Even so, a good deal of the recent interest in ideology owes more to empirical than to theoretical work, and particularly to studies of peasant movements that proliferated in the wake of the war in Southeast Asia. These studies derived much of their inspiration from the earlier historical work on peasant and preindustrial popular movements of Eric Hobsbawm (1965), E. P. Thompson (1966), and Barrington Moore (1966). We will draw on this literature, partly for its insights on ideology, and partly because we think there are certain parallels between the situation of women and peasants. As with women, the focus on the politics of the peasantry was long overdue, if only because, like women, they are so numerous and have so long been ignored. Most peasants lived at the periphery of the modern world of the market and the state. So did many women, especially those whose lives were delimited by the insular and patriarchal family system that spread in the West with industrialization. And women were like peasants in that many lived within a kind of subsistence economy, the family economy where women provided unpaid services to men in exchange for a share of the income men earned in the wider world.

The significant thrust of the literature on peasant movements is its insistence that peasants have ideas that inform their action, including revolts. This theme recurs in the work of such otherwise rather different analysts as Moore, Rudé, Womack, Wolf, and Thompson, to name only a few. Peasant ideas are traditional ideas, rooted in what Hobsbawm calls the "double chains of lordship and labour" (1981, p. 2). Peasant ideas are formed, in other words, in reflection of the centuries-old relations of deference to overlords and the centuries-old travails of wrenching a subsistence from the land. These are the ideas that Thompson (1971) calls the "moral economy of the English crowd."

Much of this may be said of women. Like peasants, women developed ideas that reflected their lived experience within the subsistence economy of the patriarchal family and that described and justified that experience. They valued the family, they celebrated maternity and the nurturing services they provided their children and their men, and they honored the family bonds that seemed to guarantee them and their children a measure of security in exchange for their services.

In other words, women also developed a traditional moral economy, a moral economy of domesticity, reflecting both their universal life tasks of motherhood, which Sarah Ruddick (1982) has, we think, rightly argued are formative in the development of a cognitive and moral orientation she calls "maternal thinking," and their more particular experience within a Western patriarchal family that made them dependent on male wages. Surely it is these large and compelling features of their circumstances—no less compelling than the double shackles of lordship and labor—that account for the startling differences in the moral development of women, with its greater emphasis on relationship, care, and obligation (Gilligan, 1982) compared to the moral development of men.

What we call the moral economy of domesticity makes many of us uncomfortable. After all, these ideas justified and helped ensure the confinement and subservience of most women within the family. If they were political actors at all, it was only within sexual and family relations where, as social inferiors and economic dependents, their leverage was limited. Accordingly, even when women in traditional situations are viewed as social actors, their action is often characterized as devious, manipulative, evasive. (Here, again, the parallel with characterizations of peasants, with slaves, and other subject groups is striking and almost surely partly true.) Dignity seems to require that we see the ideas that thus limited women and ensured their subservience as the impositions of others.

The literature on the peasantry is instructive, however, for it demands we feel more empathy for subject peoples and give them more credit as well. Peasants are the "colossal majority" of all the people who have lived on this earth, John Berger (1979) says, and yet they have rarely been treated as historically significant actors. To be an historical actor means not only to change the world by one's action—the winds and the tides do that—but to act with purpose. Purpose implies ideas. It also implies some measure of agency, however constricted, for if ideas are simply imposed, then people are victims, not actors. To see purpose, the ideas implied by purpose, and some assertion of agency in the action of ordinary people was a major step forward. We had learned that peasants were not inanimate.

Peasant ideas were formed out of the centuries-old experience of domination by rural overlords and centuries-old bondage to the soil. But even thus "shackled," peasants were not entirely powerless, and their ideas were not the ideas of utterly powerless people. In fact, many of these ideas reflect a series of political accommodations won by peasants from other more powerful groups in the peasant communities. Thus, the traditions of peasants included firm standards defining the obligations of lords, landlords, and central rulers to the peasant community.

It was, we are told, when these standards and the political accommodations they implied were violated that the peasantry became political actors. Thus, in Scott's (1976) work on Southeast Asia, in Thompson's (1971) analysis of the English food riots, in Womack's (1968) account of the Zapata wars, rebellion is provoked when others violate traditional standards: When the landlord fails to fulfill his customary obligations to reduce his rent if the crop fails; or when he demands an increased share of the peasants' crops, or seizes the peasants' historic holdings; or when magistrates fail to conform with ancient customs requiring the "fair" distribution of local food supplies during periods of shortage. In these and many other instances, transgressions against traditional standards provoked the peasantry to defiant political action. In this sense, tradition itself armed people to enter history.[7]

We can also see the strong imprint of the traditional ideas of women on their actions when they moved beyond the realm of the family, and beyond the politics of personal relations, to do battle with the large forces they perceived as threatening to destroy and transform their lives. Women, like peasants, sometimes entered history. And they did so when the traditional moral economy of domesticity, with its emphasis on the primacy of caretaking values, was violated. Women joined and even lead the food riots that swept across Europe in the eighteenth and nineteenth centuries in resistance to the "new-fangled" doctrine of the market. Women reformers in the United States and Europe at the end of the nineteenth century pioneered in the struggle for social welfare protections. In the United States in the 1960s, black women who could not feed and clothe their children asserted their right to welfare as mothers. The women who joined in the general looting during the New York blackout in 1977 might have been saying something of the same thing when they ignored the television sets and stereos in favor of baby food and canned spinach. And Polish women who joined in the Solidarity strikes explained it was because their families, and especially their children, needed food. In each instance, we can see the traditional caretaking values of the moral economy of the family that provoked the political action of women and also guided its forms, much as "the moral economy of subsistence" or the "moral economy of the English crowd" provoked and guided the political action of peasants. More than that, caretaking values sometimes armed women to challenge or defy the dominant values of the public world, and particularly the values of the market, for when women entered the public world, the moral economy of domesticity inevitably clashed with the doctrines of laissez faire.[8]

All of this is surely very appealing for the dignity it gives to simple people. And it also bears on an explanation of the gender gap, since the issues on which the polarization of the political opinions of men and women has occurred seem to be patterned broadly by the traditional values of the moral economy of domesticity. But there is a large difficulty if the matter is left there. That caretaking values are being asserted as public values, that domestic rights are being asserted as public rights, is of itself a very large change that cannot be explained by tradition alone.

Nor is an emphasis on traditional ideas by itself usually an adequate explanation of the political action of peasants and other peoples. If traditional ideas sometimes provoke people to deviant political action, these ideas can, by definition, only generate traditional modes of political action, calling for the restoration of traditional social arrangements. Much of the literature on peasant politics seems to us so enraptured by the recognition of the force of traditional ideas as to overlook or understate the elements of innovation and transformation implied by the events recounted. True, there may be instances when popular custom itself prescribes the occasions and forms of protest, as in Hobsbawm's characterization of the riots of the *menu peuple* (1965) as a virtually ritualized communication between the preindustrial urban crowd and the Prince. But tradition mainly prescribes the forms of acquiescence to prince or lord, and not the forms of rebellion. If peasant political action is guided by ideas as this literature rightly insists, then rebellion implies the existence of new ideas that cannot be ascribed to tradition alone.

Even those movements that seem to be entirely restorative often contain strong elements of innovation that are generally ignored in the literature. Thus, the extensive literature on the food riots (Rudé, 1964; Thompson, 1971; Tilly, 1975) portrays these as if literally scripted by traditions governing the distribution of food. The *actions* of the market crowds who commandeered grain or bread to sell it for a "just" price in fact challenged the growing central governments of Europe and the spread of the market. The *intentions* ascribed to the crowds, however, were to merely enforce the edicts of medieval law and custom. But they enforced tradition by breaking with it, by usurping the authority that had heretofore belonged only to local rulers. Surely this was no small thing and implied something more than traditional ideas.

The same observation can be made of the contemporary antifeminist movements. Much about the movements seems to fit the mold suggested by the study of restorative peasant movements. The women participants in these movements may well have been activated by transgressions of the traditional moral economy of domesticity. The insular and patriarchal family is eroding, jeopardizing the old rights that had guaranteed women and their children a life and a livelihood within the family. The metaphor of family breakdown usually applied to these developments is somewhat misleading, for it suggests an evolutionary development beyond the control of human actors, and people usually do not oppose developments that they do not ascribe to human agents. Peasants do not protest drought, for example, for they see it as the result of forces beyond anyone's control. They are more likely to protest new extractions by tax collectors, for they can see the human actors whose transgressions of traditional arrangements are causing them hardship. As Pearce (1982) points out, the rate of marital dissolution has in fact not increased over the past century. But where once it was mainly through death that women or men were left alone to raise their children, now it is mainly through desertion and divorce or the failure to marry in the first place, and it is mainly women who are left.[9]

If ideas guide action, then we would expect transgressions of the moral economy of domesticity to generate a restorative or reactionary politics. There is ample evidence just this happened, with the rise of movements expressing indignation at the violations of the old family norms and calling for the restoration of the old family order. But even in these most restorative of movements, there were new modes of action and therefore new ideas. Women in the pro-life and anti-ERA movements mobilized in activist and public ways to demand that the state intervene to accomplish the restoration of tradition, none of which, as a number of commentators have pointed out, was traditional at all.

The question is, then, even recognizing the great weight of past beliefs, how do ideas change? And what are the conditions in our own time that account for the changing political ideas of women? There are two main explanations in my opinion. We will call the first *idealist*, for it posits that ideologies change as a consequence of exposure to other ideologies, and the second *objectivist*, to capture the focus on change in objective socioeconomic conditions. In the idealist view, traditional ideologies are transformed by exposure to new ideas that come from some outside source. It is a popular argument, as when the stimulus for the suffragist movement is found in the abolitionists, the stimulus of the modern women's movement in the New Left. It is also an old argument. Tocqueville, for example, excoriated the men of letters of the eighteenth century for their responsibility in generating revolutionary sentiments. While the intellectuals of course disagreed among themselves, the argumentation itself had "fired the imagination even of women and peasants" (p. 139), leading them to think "what was wanted was to replace the complex of traditional customs" with rules derived from general and abstract theories.

This line of explanation has been elaborated by Rudé as the process by which the traditional or "inherent" popular culture absorbs different and (perhaps) forward-looking ideas (1980). In developing this distinction between inherent and derived ideologies, he is self-consciously drawing on Gramsci's (1971) distinction between "organic" and "nonorganic" ideologies. Rudé does not think, however, that the external influences that transform popular ideologies are necessarily the ideas of the class struggle. What he does think is that popular political struggles could not advance "without the native 'plebian culture' or 'inherent ideology becoming supplemented by…the political, philosophical or religious ideas, that at varying stages of sophistication, became absorbed in the more specifically popular culture" (1980, p. 33). This theme is also evident in other analyses of peasant or preindustrial uprisings. Thus, Hobsbawm and Rudé (1968) attribute great importance to the presence of educated shoemakers in helping to stimulate the "Captain Swing" uprisings among English agricultural laborers; Thompson (1966) makes much of the dissemination of the idea of the "rights of men" through the writings of Cobbett and others in accounting for insurgency among the English working class in the early nineteenth century; and Wolf (1969) attributes a large role to the Viet Minh who were able to draw upon traditional village patterns to "build a bridge between past and present" (p. 189).

We call this the *idealist* explanation because it seems to posit a force to ideas that is independent of the social circumstances of the people who adopt the ideas. Of course, people sometimes absorb ideas from without, and this is what peasants have done. The large and interesting question is why they are sometimes receptive and to which ideas they are receptive. Tocqueville (1955), in fact, asked this question. He wondered why, "instead of remaining as in the past the purely intellectual concept of a few advanced thinkers," the new ideas found a welcome among the masses (p. 139) and thought the answer was the dissolution of old institutions as well as a ruling class so stupid as to articulate and justify the grievances of the lower orders. Rudé (1980) also asks the question and answers that derived ideas are more likely to be absorbed when they articulate popular experience and belief (p. 29) and when, somehow, circumstances are right. This is almost surely correct and points away from a pure idealism, but it is entirely too vague.

The second, and we think more powerful explanation is an *objectivist* explanation. It is, quite simply, that new political ideas are developed in reflection of changes in objective social circumstances, although not in a simple and direct way and surely not apart from the continuing influence of preexisting ideas formed in the context of other circumstances as well as the influence of derived ideas. This way of accounting for ideological change is of course most familiar in the broad Marxist view that class situation generates class ideologies (although in the hands of some Marxists, the idealist error is reversed, and the imprint of tradition on the ideas formed in response to new circumstances, and even on the ability of people to respond to new circumstances with new ideas, is ignored). But an objectivist explanation is also implicit in the literature on the peasantry. If the traditional ideas of peasants reflect their particular social experience, then changes in those experiences should generate new ideas, albeit new ideas shaped and limited by preexisting ideological traditions. And perhaps it is in the search for ways of accounting for new conditions that peasants are likely to be receptive to ideas that come from elsewhere. To argue otherwise, to regard ideas once formed into an ideological heritage as impervious to change except as a consequence of the influence of external ideas is either to argue that peasant circumstances never change or to withdraw from them the status of historical actors, capable of reflecting and acting on new objective possibilities and constraints.

Change in the Objective Circumstances of Women

We have come this far, by such a tortured path, to posit that the gender gap simultaneously reflects the influence of women's traditional beliefs and the transformation of those beliefs in response to radical changes in the objective circumstances of American women. We turn now to a consideration of those objective circumstances, of the way changes in the family, the labor market, and the state have altered the opportunities and constraints that confront women as political actors. If ideologies are, as we contend, forged in the crucible of memory and experience, then the scale of these institutional shifts lends weight to my opening contention that a major ideological transformation is at work.

One large change is in the family. Rising rates of divorce and separation, combined with growing numbers of women who bear children but do not marry, mean that fewer and fewer women are in situations that even outwardly resemble the traditional family. Moreover, even those women who remain within traditional families now confront the possibility, if not the probability, of desertion or divorce and the near-certainty of a long widowhood. Even within those shrinking numbers of apparently traditional families, relations have been altered by the fact that many no longer rely exclusively on the wages earned by men.

Even taken by itself, we should expect this large change in circumstance to have consequences for the politics of women. The firm contours of the insular and patriarchal family narrowly limited the options for action available to women, but it also created options for action, for exercising power in family relations, no matter how convoluted the ways. Now these options are contracting. They do not exist in families where men are not present. And even when they are, the old forms of female power have almost surely been weakened if, as Ehrenreich (1983) argues, men in general are increasingly "liberated" from their obligations under the moral economy of domesticity and, thus, wield the threat of desertion or divorce.

But if the traditional family relations gave women some limited options for action, in the larger sense these relations made women dependent on men and, therefore, subject to them, even for access to the public world. It should not be surprising, therefore, that the political opinions of women followed those of men so closely in the past. The family was indeed an institution of social control, as of course all institutions are.

The shredding of marital bonds, together with the inability of families to maintain themselves on the wages earned by men, meant that more and more women, like peasants before them, were forced to enter the labor market. Women became wage workers on a mass scale. Whatever this actually meant in the lives of women, it clearly meant that women had entered the mainstream of ideas about power simply because most of those ideas are about marketplace power. There are few analysts indeed who do not think the economic resources and opportunities for organization generated by market relations are critical resources for power. In this very broad sense, the Left tradition is not different. For nearly a century, Left intellectuals have looked almost exclusively to production relations as the arena in which popular power could be organized and exercised. Production, by bringing people together as workers in mass-production industries, generated the solidarities that made collective action possible. And, once organized, workers in the mass-production industries also gained leverage over capital.

But the prospects for women generated by their mass entry into the labor market are neither so simple nor so happy. The situation is, of course, different for different women. For those who are better educated and perhaps younger, liberation from the constraints of the family has meant an opportunity to move into and upward in the realms of the market and politics. These women have tried to shake themselves free of the old moral economy of domesticity and in their place developed new ideas to name their new opportunities and aspirations. These are the ideas of the women's movement, ideas about liberation, modernization, and market success. That movement not only took advantage of burgeoning opportunities for women in government, business, law, and medicine.[10] It helped create those opportunities. In this sense, changes in objective circumstances and ideology were interactive, as we think they always are. If new ideas reflect new conditions, new ideas in turn may well lead people to act in ways that help shape those conditions.

But most women did not become lawyers, nor will they. Most women, forced to sell their labor, sold it in the expanding low-wage service sector as fast-food workers, or hospital workers, or office-cleaning women where, perhaps as a result of the influx of vulnerable women workers, wages and working conditions actually deteriorated during the 1970s (Rothschild, 1981). The stability of the ratio of female earnings to male earnings, *despite the large gains made by some women*, is striking evidence of the weak position of these workers.[11] They are located in industries where unionization has always been difficult and where those unions that did form realized few gains because widely scattered work sites made organization difficult, and a ready supply of unemployed workers weakened the strike power.

Nor is it likely that women will gradually enter the manufacturing industries where workers did succeed in unionizing, if only because these industries are shrinking. New jobs are being created not in steel, autos, or rubber, but in fast foods, data processing, and health care. Of course, even if this were not so, even if women were likely to enter the smokestack industries in large numbers, it would be too late, for international competition and robotization have combined to crush the fabled power of mass-production workers. In fact, the broad shifts in the American economy from manufacturing to services and from skilled work to unskilled work, combined with the likelihood of continuing high levels of unemployment, mean that the possibilities for the exercise of popular power in the work place are eroding for both men and women.

Women are thus losing their old rights and their limited forms of power within the family. In the marketplace, their position is weak, and prospects for improvement through individual mobility or the development of collective power are grim. These circumstances have combined to lead women to turn to the state, and especially to the expanding programs of the welfare state. Income supports, social services, and government employment partly offset the deteriorating position of women in family and economy and have even given women a measure of protection and therefore power in the family and economy. In these ways, the state is turning out to be the main recourse of women.

The relationship of women to the welfare state hardly needs documenting. Women with children are the overwhelming majority among the beneficiaries of the main "means-tested" income maintenance programs, such as AFDC, foodstamps, and Medicaid.[12] Moreover, the numbers of women affected by these programs are far greater than the numbers of beneficiaries at any one time, for women in the low-wage service and clerical sectors of the labor force turn to welfare-state programs to tide them over during family emergencies or their frequent bouts of unemployment. Older women, for their part, depend on social security and Medicare benefits, without which most would be very poor. However inadequately, all of these programs moderate the extremes of poverty and insecurity among women.

More than that, the programs that make women a little less insecure also make them a little less powerless. The availability of benefits and services reduces the dependence of younger women with children on male breadwinners, as it reduces the dependence of older women on adult children. The same holds in the relations of working women with employers. Most women work in situations without unions or effective work rules to shield them from the raw power of their bosses. Social-welfare programs provide some shield, for the availability of benefits reduces the fear that they and their children will go hungry and homeless if they are fired.

Women have also developed a large and important relationship to the welfare state as the employees of these programs. The proportion of such jobs held by women has actually increased, even as the total number of social-welfare jobs greatly expanded. By 1980, fully 70% of the 17.3 million social-service jobs on all levels of government, including education, were held by women (Erie, Rein, & Wiget, 1983), accounting for about one-third of all female nonagricultural employment and for the larger part of female job gains since 1960 (Erie, 1983). In these several ways, the welfare state has become critical in determining the lives and livelihood of women. The belief in a responsible state reflected in the gender gap is partly a reflection of this institutional reality. But will this new institutional context yield women the resources to participate in the creation of their own lives as historical actors? Can it, in a word, yield them power?

Women and Political Power

Very little that has been written about the relationship of women to the state suggests we look to it for sources of power. To the contrary, the main characterization is of a state that exercises social control over women, supplanting the eroding patriarchal relations of the family with a patriarchal relationship with the state. In our opinion, the determination to affirm this conclusion is generally much stronger than the evidence for it. Even in the nineteenth century, state policies had a more complicated bearing on the situation of women. Thus, while it is clearly true that changes in family law that granted women some rights as individuals, including the right to own property, did not overcome their subordination, that is hardly evidence that the state by these actions was somehow moving "toward a new construction of male domination" (Boris & Bardaglio, 1983, p. 75).

This kind of argument is even more strongly made with regard to welfare state programs. From widows' pensions and laws regulating female labor in the nineteenth century, to AFDC today, state programs that provide income to women and children, or that regulate their treatment in the marketplace, are condemned as new forms of patriarchal social control. Now there is surely reason for not celebrating widows' pensions as emancipation or AFDC either. These programs never reached all of the women who needed support (widows' pensions reached hardly any), the benefits they provided were meager, and those who received them were made to pay a heavy price in pride. Similarly, government regulation of family and market relations never overcame economic and social discrimination and in some instances reinforced it. But perhaps because some income would seem to be better than none, and even weak regulations can be a beginning, the definitive argument of the social-control perspective is not that the welfare state is weak and insufficient, but that involvement with government exacts the price of dependence, somehow robbing women of their capacities for political action. It seems to follow that the massive expansion of these programs in the past two decades and the massive involvement of women and their children in them is cause for great pessimism about the prospects for women exerting power and surely for pessimism about the prospects for women exerting power on the state.

In general, we think this mode of argument is a reflection of the eagerness with which we have embraced a simplistic "social control" perspective on institutional life, straining to discover how every institutional change is functional for the maintenance of a system of hierarchical relations and, therefore, evidence of the power of ruling groups. Of course, ruling groups do have power, they do try to exercise social control, and they usually succeed, at least for a time. But they are not all powerful. They do not rule entirely on their terms, they do not exercise social control without accommodations. Even then, the institutional arrangements that achieve social control are never entirely secure, for people discover new resources and evolve new ideas, and sometimes these resources and ideas are generated by the very arrangements that, for a time, seemed to ensure their acquiescence.

The critique of the welfare state developed by radical feminists was surely strongly influenced by the major Left analyses of these programs. Overall, and despite the complexities in some of their arguments, the Left disparaged social-welfare programs as functional not for the maintenance of patriarchy but for the maintenance of capitalism. Where in other arenas there was sometimes readiness to see that institutional arrangements had been shaped by class conflict, and even to see a continuing capacity for class struggle, in the arena of social welfare there was mainly social control. In part, this reflected the view, almost axiomatic among many on the Left, that the only authentic popular power is working-class power arising out of production relations. It was at least consistent with this axiom to conclude that welfare-state programs weakened popular political capacities and in several ways. The complicated array of program and beneficiary categories, combined with regressive taxation, fragmented working-class solidarity; the programs provided puny benefits but considerable opportunities for coopting popular leaders and absorbing popular energies; and the very existence of social-welfare programs distracted working people from the main political issue which, of course, was the control of capital. In this view, the welfare state was mainly understood as an imposition from above.

But we do not think the evolution of the American welfare state can be understood as the result only or mainly of a politics of domination. Rather it was the result of complex institutional and ideological changes that occurred in American society and of the complex and conflictual politics associated with these changes. Over the course of the last century, the role of government (particularly the federal government) in American economic life progressively enlarged. This development was largely a reflection of the demands of businessmen in an increasingly concentrated economy. But it had other consequences beyond creating the framework for industrial growth. As government penetration of the economy became more pervasive and more obvious, laissez-faire doctrine lost much of its vigor, although it still echoed strongly in the rhetoric of politicians. Few analysts dispute the significance of the doctrine in the American past. It was not that the actual role of government in the economy was so restricted, for the record in that respect is complicated. Rather, the doctrine of limited government was important because it restricted the spheres in which democratic political rights had bearing. Eventually, however, the doctrine became untenable. The political ideas of Americans, like the ideas of peasants, gradually changed in reflection of a changing reality. An economy increasingly penetrated by government gave rise to the wide recognition of the role of the state in the economy and a gradual fusion of ideas about economic rights and political rights (Piven & Cloward, 1982).

This shift in belief is evident in a wealth of survey data that show that Americans think government is responsible for reducing economic inequality, for coping with unemployment, for supporting the needy, for, in short, the economic well-being of its citizens. It is also evident in electoral politics, as Tufte's (1978) analyses of the efforts of political leaders to coordinate the business cycle with the election cycle make evident, as do exit poll data on the popular concerns that generated electoral shifts in the 1980 election.[13]

And as with peasants, ideas undergird political action. The emerging recognition that government played a major role in the economy, and that the democratic right to participate in government extended to economic demands, increasingly shaped the character of political movements. Beginning with the protests of the unemployed, the aged, and industrial workers in the Great Depression, to the movements of blacks, women, and environmentalists in the 1960s and 1970s, government became the target of protest, and government action to redress grievances arising in economic spheres became the program. The gradually expanding American welfare state was mainly a response to these movements. It is not by any means that the movements were the only force in shaping the welfare state. On the one hand, the success of the protestors was owed to the growing legitimacy of their demands among a broader public and the threat they therefore wielded of precipitating electoral defections if government failed to respond. On the other hand, the programs that responded to protest demands were limited and modified by other powerful interests, mainly by business groups who resisted the programs or worked to shape them to their own interests. Nevertheless, popular movements were a critical force in creating and expanding the welfare state (Piven & Cloward, 1971, 1977).

If the welfare state was not an imposition, if it was forged at least in part by a politics from below, what then will be its consequences over the longer run for the continued exercise of political force from below? This of course is the main question raised by the social control thesis, and it is of enormous significance for women given their extensive involvement with the welfare state. Thus far, that involvement is not generating acquiescence. To the contrary, the expectations of government revealed by the gender gap, as well as the indignation and activism of women's organizations in reaction to the policies of the Reagan administration, are not the attitudes of people who feel themselves helpless. Rather, they suggest that women think they have rights vis-à-vis the state and some power to realize those rights. If, however, the wide involvement of women in the welfare state as beneficiaries and workers erodes their capacities for political action, then what we are witnessing is a deluded flurry of activity that will soon pass.

But perhaps not. Perhaps this is the beginning of women's politics that draws both ideological strength and political resources from the existence of the welfare state. One sense in which this may be so is that the welfare state provides some objective institutional affirmation of women's political convictions. We said earlier that the welfare state was in large part a response to the demands of popular political movements of both men and women. These movements, in turn, had been made possible by changes in the relationship of government to the economy which had encouraged the idea that democratic rights included at least some economic rights. Once in existence, the social programs strengthen the conviction that economic issues belong in political spheres, and that democratic rights include economic rights. In particular, the existence of the social programs are, for all their flaws, an objective and public affirmation of the values of economic security and nurturance that connect the moral economy of domesticity to the gender gap.

This kind of affirmation may well strengthen women for political action. To use a phrase suggested by Jane Jenson (1983) in connection with the rise of the French women's movement, the "universe of political discourse" helps determine the likelihood and success of political mobilizations. One can see the criticality of the universe of political discourse or ideological context in determining not only the success but the scale of past expressions of oppositional politics among women. We have already suggested that the participation of women in the food riots of the eighteenth and nineteenth centuries reflected the centrality of nurturance to women (as well as their institutional access to the markets where collective action could take place). But perhaps women were able to act as they did on so large a scale because their distinctive values as women were reinforced by the traditional belief, held by men and women alike, that the local poor had a prior claim on the local food supply. By contrast, when middle-class women reformers in the nine-teenth-century United States tried to "bring homelike nurturing into public life" (Hayden, 1981, pp. 4–5), they were pitted against the still very vigorous doctrines of American laissez faire. Not only were their causes largely lost, but their movement remained small, failing to secure much popular support even from women. The situation is vastly differ-ent today. The women reformers who are mobilizing now in defense of social-welfare programs are not isolated voices challenging a dominant doctrine. The existence of the welfare state has contributed to the cre-ation of an ideological context that has given them substantial influence in the Congress as well as mass support from women.

Women have also gained political resources from their relationship with the state. One critical resource would appear to be of very long standing. It is, quite simply, the vote and the potential electoral influ-ence of women, given their large numbers. Of course, that resource is not new, and it is not owed to the welfare state. Women have been enfranchised for over six decades, but the promise of the franchise was never realized for the reason that women followed men in the voting booth as in much of their public life. Only now, with the emergence of the gender gap, does the promise of electoral power seem real.

Part of the reason for the new significance of women's electoral power is in the institutional changes we have described. The "break-down" of the family, while it stripped women of old resources for the exercise of power within the family, nevertheless freed women to use other resources. In fact, we think the breakdown of any institutional pattern of social control can generate resources for power, Tilly and other resource mobilization theorists notwithstanding. Tilly may be right to scorn the long-held view that breakdown generates Durkheimian stress or disorganization. He is wrong, however, to go on to insist that what is usually viewed as social disorganization cannot yield people resources. The disintegration of particular social relationships may well mean that people are released from subjugation to others and thus freed to use resources that were previously effectively suppressed. The breakdown of the plantation system in the United States, for example, meant that rural blacks were removed from the virtually total power of the planter class, and only then was it possible for them to begin to use the infrastructure of the black Southern church as a focus for mobilization.

Similarly, only as women were at least partly liberated from the overweening power of men by the "breakdown" of the family has the possibility of electoral power become real. The scale of the gender gap and the fact that it has persisted and widened in the face of the Reagan administration's ideological campaign suggests the enormous electoral potential of women. This, of course, is the media's preoccupation and the preoccupation of contenders in the 1984 election as well. But its importance extends beyond 1984. Women have moved into the forefront of electoral calculations because they are an enormous constituency that is showing an unprecedented coherence and conviction about the key issues of our time, a coherence and conviction that, we have argued, is intertwined with the development of the welfare state. This electorate could change American politics. In particular, it could change the politics of the welfare state, although not by itself.

The welfare state has generated other political resources that, it seems fair to say, are mainly women's resources. The expansion of social-welfare programs has created a far-flung and complex infrastructure of agencies and organizations that are so far proving to be a resource in the defense of the welfare state and may have even larger potential. The historic involvement of women in social welfare and their concentration in social welfare employment now have combined to make women preponderant in this infrastructure and to give them a large share of leadership positions as well.[14] The political potential of these organizations cannot be dismissed because they are part of the state apparatus. Such organizations, whether public or private, are part of the state, in the elementary sense that they owe their funding to government. Nevertheless, the byzantine complexity of welfare state organization, reflecting the fragmented and decentralized character of American government generally, as well as the historic bias in favor of private implementation of public programs, may afford the organizations a considerable degree of autonomy from the state. That so many of these organizations have lobbied as hard as they have against the several rounds of Reagan budget cuts is testimony to this measure of autonomy. They did not win, of course. But mounting federal deficits are evidence they did not lose either, and that is something to wonder about.

There is another aspect of the politics generated by this organizational infrastructure that deserves note. The welfare state brings together millions of poor women who depend on welfare-state programs. These constituencies are not, as is often thought, simply atomized and, therefore, helpless people. Rather, the structure of the welfare state itself has helped to create new solidarities and has also generated the political issues that cement and galvanize these solidarities. We can see evidence of this in the welfare-rights movement of the 1960s, where people were brought together in welfare waiting rooms, and where they acted together in terms of common grievances generated by welfare practices. We can see it again today, most dramatically in the mobilization of the aged to defend social security. The solidarities and issues generated by the welfare state are, of course, different from the solidarities and issues generated in the work place. But that difference does not argue their insignificance as sources of power, as the Left often argues, and especially for women who have small hope of following the path of industrial workers.

The infrastructure of the welfare state also creates the basis for cross-class alliances among women. The infrastructure is dominated, of course, by better-educated and middle-class women. But these women are firmly linked by organizational self-interest to the poor women who depend on welfare-state programs. It is poor women who give the welfare state its raison d'etre and who are ultimately its most reliable source of political support. Of course, the alliance between the organizational infrastructure and the beneficiaries of the welfare state is uneasy and difficult and sometimes over-shadowed by antagonisms that are also natural. Nevertheless, the welfare state has generated powerful cross-class ties between the different groups of women who have stakes in protecting it.

Conclusion

The erosion of the traditional family and their deteriorating position on the labor market has concentrated women in the welfare state. The future of these women, workers and beneficiaries alike, hangs on the future of these programs. They need to defend the programs, expand them, and reform them. They need, in short, to exert political power. The determined and concerted opposition to welfare-state programs that has emerged among corporate leaders and their Republican allies and the weak defense offered by the Democratic Party suggests that the situation will require a formidable political mobilization by women. The programs of the welfare state were won when movements of mass protest, by raising issues that galvanized an electoral following, forced the hand of political leaders. The defense and reform of the welfare state is not likely to be accomplished by less.

Originally published in 1985.

Notes

1. See, for example, Barrett (1983), Boris and Bardaglio (1983), Brown (1980), Eisenstein (1981, 1983), Kickbusch (1983), McIntosh (1978), Polan (1982), Schirmer (1982), and Wilson (1977). Happily, however, some of the most recent work, a good deal of it still unpublished, has begun to explore the political and ideological resources yielded by women in and through the welfare state. See, for example, Balbo (1981, 1983), Borchorst and Siim (1983), Dahlerup (1983), Ergas (1983), Hernes (1983), Rossi (1983), and Schirmer (1983).

2. Attitudes toward defense spending accounted for a good part of the difference between male and female preferences in the 1980 election. This pattern persisted into 1982, when 40% of men favored increased defense spending but only 25% of women did. However, by 1982 women had come to place concerns about defense second to their concerns about the economy (Miller & Malanchuk, 1983). Gurin (cited in Rossi, 1983) also shows an increase of gender identification among women through the 1970s. See also Schlichting and Tuckel (1983) for an examination of differences in the attitudes of married and unmarried and employed and unemployed women, which concludes that the gender gap holds regardless of marital or labor-force status.

3. Rossi (1983) reviews studies that show the beginning of a gender gap as early as the 1950s. However, exit poll data after the 1980 election revealed an unprecedented 9% spread in the voting choices of men and women. In subsequent

polls, the spread substantially widened to a 15% difference between men and women in response to whether Reagan deserved reelection in a *New York Times* poll reported in December 1983. Moreover, while male ratings of the President rose with the upturn in economic indicators and the invasion of Grenada, the unfavorable ratings by women remained virtually unchanged.

4. Attitudes about the reproductive and legal rights of women, which have been the central issues of the movement, do not differentiate male and female respondents in the surveys. Single women, however, are much more likely than men to support the "women's rights" issues.

5. Geertz (1973) made this point but it remains largely true today. The main exceptions are in those branches of social theory descended from the European-language philosophers, particularly phenomenology and hermeneutics, which are concerned precisely with intersubjective meaning systems. But these developments have remained isolated from the mainstream of social analysis because the significance of objective social reality in patterning human action, including symbolic action, is ignored or denied. See Giddens (1976).

6. If the ideas of men were inconsequential in explaining their action, the ideas of women were apparently even less consequential in Durkheim's view. Indeed, women were not even much influenced by social environment, for "being a more instinctive creature than man, woman has only to allow her instincts to find calmness and peace" (1951, p. 272).

7. This argument is actually not new. Like much else, it should probably be credited to Tocqueville who, in setting out to explain the upheavals associated with the French Revolution, also emphasized the importance of traditional ideas. He thought the peasantry were goaded to rebel because the nobility had defaulted on their obligations to the community spelled out by those traditional ideas.

8. Kaplan (1982) provides an eloquent exposition of the force and potential radicalism of traditional women's values in a series of episodes of collective protests in Barcelona early in this century. Margaret Somers's work on "collective memory and the claim to regulative liberty and narrative justice" among women in early nineteenth-century England makes a broadly similar argument (1983).

9. While it is difficult to get firm empirical evidence on this question, we are inclined to agree with Ehrenreich (1983) when she argues the breakdown of the two-parent family is the result of a kind of male emancipation from the burdens of family support. The extreme disparity in the economic circumstances of men and women in the aftermath of separation provides some support for this view, for it argues a very substantial material advantage for men in marital breakup and disadvantage for women. Weitzman (1981) shows that the available income of men rose sharply 1 year after divorce by 42%, while the standard of living of women dropped sharply, by 73%. A recent Census Bureau report helps make sense of this finding. More than one-half of divorced men default entirely or partially on court-ordered child-support payments, which averaged only $2110

in 1981. Meanwhile, the practice of alimony payments has almost disappeared. Only 15% of the 17 million divorced or separated women were awarded alimony, and less than one-half of those were actually receiving the full payments due them.

10. Where only 4% of the nation's lawyers and judges were women in 1971, women accounted for 14% in 1981. In the same period, the percentage of physicians who are women rose from 9 to 22%, and the percentage of female engineers increased from 1 to 4%.

11. See Peattie and Rein (1981) for a review of data on women's participation in the labor force that shows the persistence of part-time and irregular employment as well as the concentration of women in low paid jobs. See also Chapters 11 and 12, this volume.

12. Over one-third of female-headed families, or 3.3 million, received AFDC in 1979 (Census Bureau). An almost equal number received Medicaid, and 2.6 million were enrolled in the food stamp program (Erie, Rein, & Wiget, 1983).

13. See Burnham (1981) for an excellent discussion of the issues that determined the outcome of the 1980 election. He concludes that worry over unemployment was the critical issue leading voters who had supported Carter in 1978 to defect to Reagan in 1980.

14. Rossi (1982), in an analysis of the first National Women's Conference at Houston in 1977, reports that 72% of the delegates were employed either by government or by nonprofit social welfare organizations. See also Rossi (1983) for a discussion of "insider–outsider" coalitions made possible by government employment. This pattern exists in European welfare states as well (see Balbo, 1983; Ergas, 1983: Hernes, 1982).

References

BALBO, L. *Crazy quilts: Rethinking the welfare state debate from a woman's perspective.* 1981, unpublished paper.

BALBO, L. Untitled paper presented to Conference on the Transformation of the Welfare State: Dangers and Potentialities for Women, Bellagio, Italy, August 1983.

BARRETT, N. B. *The welfare system as state paternalism.* Paper presented to Conference on Women and Structural Transformation, Institute for Research on Women, Rutgers University, November 1983.

BERGER, J. *The peasant experience and the modern world.* New Society, 1979, 17, 376–378.

BORCHORST, A., & SIIM, B. *The Danish welfare state: A case for a strong social patriarchy.* Paper presented to the conference on the Transformation of the Welfare State: Dangers and Potentialities for Women, Bellagio, Italy, August 1983.

BORIS, E., & BARDAGLIO, P. The transformation of patriarchy: The historic role of the state. In I. Diamond (Ed.), *Families, politics, and public policy*. New York: Longman, Green, 1983, pp. 70–93.

BRINTON, C. *The anatomy of revolution*. Englewood Cliffs, N.J. Prentice-Hall, 1952.

BROWN, C. Mothers, fathers and children: From private to public patriarchy. In L. Sargent (Ed.), *Women and revolution*. Boston, Mass.: Southwood Press, 1980, pp. 239–267.

BURNHAM, W. D. The 1980 earthquake: Realignment, reaction, or what? In T. Ferguson & J. Rogers (Eds.), *The hidden election: Politics and economics in the 1980 presidential campaign*. New York: Pantheon Books, 1981, pp. 98–140.

DAHLERUP, D. *Feminism and the state: An essay with a Scandinavian perspective*. Paper presented to the conference on the Transformation of the Welfare State: Dangers and Potentialities for Women, Bellagio, Italy, August 1983.

DURKHEIM, E. *Suicide*, Glencoe, Ill.: The Free Press, 1951.

EHRENREICH, B. *The hearts of men*. New York: Anchor Books, 1983.

EISENSTEIN. Z. *The radical future of liberal feminism*. New York: Longman, Green, 1981.

EISENSTEIN, Z. The state, the patriarchal family, and working mothers. In I. Diamond (Ed.), *Families, politics, and public policy*. New York: Longman, Green, 1983, pp. 41–58.

ELSHTAIN, J. B. Feminism, family and community. *Dissent*, 1982 (Fall), 442–450.

ELSHTAIN, J. B. Antigone's daughters: Reflections on female identity and the state. In I. Diamond (Ed.), *Families, politics, and public policy*. New York: Longman, Green, 1983, pp. 298–309.

ERGAS, Y. *The disintegrative revolution: Welfare politics and emergent collective identities*. Paper presented to the conference on the Transformation of the Welfare State: Dangers and Potentialities for Women, Bellagio, Italy, August 1983.

ERIE, S. P. *Women, Reagan and the welfare state. The hidden agenda of a new class war*. Paper presented to the Women's Caucus for Political Science, Chicago, Illinois, September 14, 1983.

ERIE, S. P., REIN, M., & Wiget, B. Women and the Reagan revolution: Thermidor for the social welfare economy. In I. Diamond (Ed.), *Families, politics, and public policy*. New York: Longman, Green, 1983, pp. 94–123.

GEERTZ, C. *The interpretation of cultures*. New York: Basic Books, 1973.

GIDDENS, A. *New rules of sociological method: A positive critique of interpretive theories*. New York: Basic Books, 1976.

GILLIGAN, C. *In a different voice*. Cambridge. Mass.: Harvard University Press, 1982.

GRAMSCI. A. *Prison notebooks*. New York: International Publishers, 1971.

HAYDEN, D. *The grand domestic revolution.* Cambridge, Mass.: The MIT Press, 1981.

HERNES, H. M. *The role of women in voluntary associations.* Preliminary study submitted to the Council of Europe, Steering Committee of Human Rights (CDDH), December 1982.

HERNES, H. M. *Women and the welfare state: The transition from private to public dependence.* Paper presented to the conference on the Transformation of the Welfare State: Dangers and Potentialities for Women, Bellagio, Italy, August 1983.

HOBSBAWM, E. J. *Primitive rebels: Studies in archaic forms of social movements in the 19th and 20th centuries.* New York: W. W. Norton, 1965.

HOBSBAWM, E. J. *Bandits.* New York: Pantheon, 1981.

HOBSBAWM, E. J., & RUDÉ, B. *Captain Swing.* New York: Pantheon, 1968.

JENSON, J. *"Success" without struggle? The modern women's movement in France.* Paper presented to a workshop at Cornell University on the Women's Movement in Comparative Perspective: Resource Mobilization, Cycles of Protest, and Movement Success, May 6–8, 1983.

KAPLAN, T. Female consciousness and collective action: The case of Barcelona, 1910–1918. *Signs: Journal of Women in Society and Culture,* 1982, 7, 545–566.

KICKBUSCH, I. *Family as profession—profession as family: The segregated labor market and the familialization of female labor.* Unpublished paper. Copenhagen, 1983.

LUKES, S. *Power: A radical view.* London: Macmillan, 1975.

McINTOSH, M. The state and the oppression of women. In A. Kuhn & A. Wolpe (Eds.), *Feminism and materialism.* London: Routledge and Kegan Paul, 1978, pp. 254–289.

MILLER, A. H., & MALANCHUK, O. *The gender gap in the 1982 elections.* Paper presented to the 38th Annual Conference of the American Association for Public Opinion Research, Buck Hill Falls, Pennsylvania, May 19–22, 1983.

MOORE, B. *Social origins of dictatorship and democracy.* Boston, Mass.: Beacon, 1966.

PEARCE, D. M. *Farewell to alms: Women and welfare policy in the eighties.* Paper presented to the American Sociological Association Annual Meeting, San Francisco, September 1982.

PEATTIE, L., & REIN, M. *Women's claims: A study in political economy.* Unpublished manuscript, 1981.

PIVEN, F. F. Deviant behavior and the remaking of the world. *Social Problems,* 1981, 28, 489–509.

PIVEN, F. F., & CLOWARD. R. A. *Regulating the poor: The functions of public welfare.* New York: Pantheon, 1971.

PIVEN, F. F., & CLOWARD, R. A. *Poor people's movements: Why they succeed, how they fail.* New York: Pantheon, 1977.

PIVEN, F. F., & CLOWARD, R. A. *The new class war: Reagan's attack on the welfare state and its consequences.* New York: Pantheon, 1982.

POLAN, D. Toward a theory of law and patriarchy. In D. Kairys (Ed.), *The politics of law: A progressive critique.* New York: Pantheon, 1982, pp. 294–303.

ROSE, H. In practice supported, in theory denied: An account of an invisible urban movement. *International Journal of Urban and Regional Research,* 1978, 2, 521–537.

ROSSI, A. S. *Feminists in politics: A panel analysis of the first national women's conference.* New York: Academic Press, 1982.

ROSSI, A. S. Beyond the gender gap: Women's bid for political power. *Social Science Quarterly,* 1983, 64, 718–733.

ROTHSCHILD, E. Reagan and the real America. *New York Review of Books,* February 5, 1981, 28.

RUDDICK, S. *Preservative love and military destruction: Some reflections on mothers and peace.* Paper presented to the Annual Meeting of the American Political Science Association, Denver, Colorado, September 1982.

RUDÉ, G. *The crowd in history.* New York: Wiley, 1964.

RUDÉ, G. *Ideology and popular protest.* London: Lawrence and Wishart, 1980.

SCHIRMER, J. G. *The limits of reform: Women, capital and welfare.* New York: Shenkman, 1982.

SCHIRMER, J. G. *Cut off at the impasse: Women and the welfare state in Denmark.* Paper presented to the conference on the Transformation of the Welfare State: Dangers and Potentialities for Women, Bellagio, Italy, August 1983.

SCHLICHTING, M., & TUCKEL, P. *Beyond the gender gap: Working women and the 1982 election.* Paper presented to the 38th Annual Conference of the American Association for Public Opinion Research. Buck Hill Falls, Pennsylvania, May 19–22, 1983.

SCOTT, J. C. *The moral economy of the peasant: Rebellion and subsistence in Southeast Asia.* New Haven, Conn.: Yale University Press, 1976.

SMELSER, N. J. *Theory of collective behavior.* London: Routledge and Kegan Paul, 1962.

SOMERS, M. R. *Personal communication,* 1983.

THOMPSON, E. P. *The making of the English working class.* New York: Vintage Books, 1966.

THOMPSON, E. P. *Moral economy of the English crowd in the eighteenth century. Past and Present,* 1971, 50, 76–136.

TILLY, C. Food supply and public order in modern Europe. In C. Tilly (Ed.), *The formation of nation states in Western Europe.* Princeton, N.J.: Princeton University Press, 1975, pp. 380–455.

TILLY, C., TILLY, L. A., & TILLY, R. *The rebellious century*. Cambridge, Mass.: Harvard University Press, 1975.

TOCQUEVILLE, A. DE. *The old regime and the French revolution*. Garden City, N.Y.: Doubleday, 1856/1955.

TUFTE, E. R. *Political control of the economy*. Princeton. N.J.: Princeton University Press, 1978.

WEITZMAN, L. J. The economics of divorce: Social and economic consequences of property, alimony, and state support awards. *UCLA Law Review*, 1981, 28, 1183–1268.

WILSON, E. *Women and the welfare state*. London: Tavistock, 1977.

WOLF, E. R. *Peasant wars of the twentieth century*. New York: Harper & Row, 1969.

WOMACK, J. *Zapata and the Mexican revolution*. New York: Vintage Books, 1968.

II

The Politics of Policy Science

Political regimes change. As new power blocs assume control of the state, they advance an ideology about the relation between state, society, and economy, and about the social policies that government should therefore promote, including the policies to ameliorate poverty.

Generally speaking, liberal regimes attribute poverty to institutional conditions, especially conditions in the labor market, and they promote income-maintenance programs of one sort or another to relieve the worst suffering. But these same programs are then said by conservatives to themselves be the cause of poverty because they weaken family and work incentives.

Of course, the social scientists who do "policy science" are, like other social scientists, a diverse lot, committed to quite different perspectives on social policy as on other matters. Their prospects for status and financial rewards depend on the fit between their perspectives and the ideology of the regime in power. When regimes change, policy analysts identified with the earlier regime lose favor and support, while analysts identified with the new regime are elevated in status and support. As for those cast out, they are under tremendous pressure to adapt if they are to retain their position and resources, and therefore voice.

Think, for example, of the shift in the social policy research establishment from the 1960s to the 1970s and 1980s. In the earlier period, under the influence of a liberal Democratic regime that was being shaken by the social movements of blacks, youth and women, the policy scientists located the causes of poverty in larger institutional arrangements. They traced the consequences of agricultural displacement, structural unemployment and low wages, and an inadequate safety net, and produced arguments and findings that justified the expansion of social programs. In the 1970s and 1980s, under the influence of Republican administrations and a mobilized business community, a different cohort of policy scientists located the source of poverty in social welfare programs. They revived the paradigmatic case against outdoor poor relief which was developed by eminent 19th century English social thinkers who summoned learned arguments to show that giving bread to the poor does harm both to the larger society and to the poor themselves, thus justifying "welfare reform."[1]

Policy scientists themselves, however, appear to have a different view of what they do. No matter the growing sophistication elsewhere in the social sciences about the manifold ways in which social and political influences penetrate and shape scientific inquiry, the view of the policy science establishment seems fixed in an earlier era of unbridled confidence that science is science, and politics is politics, and never the twain shall meet. As for how science should be used in the formulation of social policy, the view is easy to summarize, based as it is on a simple model of rational decision-making. Presumably the objective, which is shaped by politics, is to alter some condition deemed a social problem, whether poverty, or insecurity, or dependency, or social disorganization. The task of policy science is to identify the key variables or chains of variables that bear on this politically determined objective, and to measure the effect of manipulating those variables. The effort is of course complicated, as researchers try to cope with multiple intervening and interactive variables and with difficult problems of measurement. But complexities aside, the social scientist uses multivariate analysis in the effort to identify and measure ostensible cause- and-effect relations which are then the basis for scientifically informed interventions by government to alleviate social problems.

This dominant, rationalistic model was not without its critics. For several decades, thoughtful social thinkers argued that this model rests on an impossibly simplified view of real world policy decision-making. In brief, the core of this criticism is that the simplification demanded by empirical research into cause and effect relations is inevitably incommensurate with the complexity and fluidity of the factors that are taken into account in real world policy decisions.[2] The point is perhaps especially apt in matters of social policy, where complexity is compounded by the importance 3of informal and discretionary implementation.[3]

Still, the futility of the policy science effort as rational decision-making is not to our mind the sole or even the main problem distorting the use of social science in social policy. Indeed, this discussion is often besides the point because social science is far less important as a decision-making tool in the rational pursuit of politically agreed upon goals, than as a resource employed by different participants, but especially by powerful participants, in the politics of social policy.

Decisions about social policy are of great moment to many groups, not only because they involve the expenditure of billions of dollars with large implications for taxation and government borrowing, and not only because those expenditures have widespread reverberations on capital and labor markets, on communities, and on the multiple providers of social services, but also because the policy process is political theater, played to wide audiences, and increasingly important to politicians trying to sway voting publics.

The dominant policy science model treats political context as mainly external to policy science investigations. Politics occurs when the goals of a policy are decided, when the desirability or undesirability of the consequences of different interventions are assessed. To be sure, policy scientists are often advocates of one or another course of intervention. But the basis for their advocacy is presumably their knowledge of cause and effect, which is what policy science is about. Policy analysts think they are doing science, not politics. However, this separation of means and goals,of policy science and politics, does not match real world policy politics where the goals of major contenders are typically unacknowledged, as well as conflictual and ambiguous, and in any case different from the proclamations which count as officially articulated

245

goals. Moreover, key actors may be less interested in the ultimate consequences of policy alternatives than in the multiple consequences of actions undertaken in the process of promoting and implementing the policy, including the mere opportunity to proclaim themselves author of a major new initiative. In other words, in real world politics, means are in fact goals, and goals are always also means.

These rather obvious observations about the complex and often unacknowledged factors involved in policy-making are part of the reason for the usual skepticism about the uses of social science as a tool of rational decision-making. But neither politicians nor social scientists are deterred. Policy science is, if anything, more prominent than ever in the policy process. The reason has less to do with social science research as a tool of rational decision making than as a tool of politics. The variable relationships which are treated by the social scientist as causal sequences bearing on valued goals or outcomes are strategies in the play of performance and power that shapes policy. The cause and effect relations between government interventions and desired outcomes which are framed as questions by the researcher become the stories told to promote a particular policy direction. In other words, policy science, the investigation of cause and effect, is not mainly a strategy to aid rational decision-making in the manner the policy scientist imagines. Rather, it comes to be used as political strategy, providing arguments or stories to elicit support from among those in a wider public whose participation can influence the outcome in a political contest.[4] In the process, the cause and effect arguments provided by the policy analyst become political claims, used for some audiences under some conditions, and perhaps not for others, and concealing the intentions of particular power groups as much as they reveal intentions.

The human endeavor to understand the social world, whether scientifically or otherwise, is always deeply and pervasively shaped by social influences. That acknowledged, we can try to specify some of the distinctive ways that policy research is shaped to buttress the claims made by a dominant regime. The contemporary reliance on multivariate analysis to explore causal relations is important, not because multivariate analysis is more susceptible to political use and abuse than other forms of inquiry, but because it is susceptible in distinctive ways. For one thing, while all social analysis is selective, multivariate analysis demands a sharply selective use of data. A narrow range of variables is identified and investigated, treated as independent or intervening or dependent variables, and represented by selected empirical measures. Meanwhile, most other "variables," or other facets of social life, are ignored, including those that are difficult to observe and measure, but including also those that do not suit the dominant political argument of the regime.[5] Given these limitations, variables derived from a liberal perspective tend to produce liberal correlations; conservative variables produce conservative correlations.

Another part of the problem is that while everyone knows that correlations do not establish causality, policy scientists, and the politicians that call on the authority of policy science findings, tend to overlook this elementary truth. Indeed, the whole point of the political exercise is to proclaim correlations as causes. This is especially significant in the area of welfare policy because the paradigmatic case against social spending for the poor usually gains force in the wake of a rise in such spending (e.g., the great rise in the welfare costs beginning in the 1960s), itself the result of a chain of events which includes economic dislocation and distress (e.g., the building up of pools of extremely poor families in the cities in the wake of southern agricultural modernization and migration), and the social disorganization which often follows in the wake of uprooting and dislocation. With sufficient methodological sophistication, everything is available to correlate with everything.[6] Of course, all efforts to understand the social world are inherently limited, and multivariate analysis is probably not worse. Our point is only to make explicit the ways that these limitations facilitate the adapting of research to suit the dominant political argument of the era.

In the 1960s, most social policy researchers, like most social scientists, followed the liberal political drift in searching for systemic or institutional causes for problems associated with inequality, from poverty to ill health to educational deficits to social disorganization to crime to mental illness. Research projects were launched, books and articles published, which singled out as independent variables bearing on poverty and associated social problems such factors as labor market conditions, indicators of institutionalized discrimination, distortions in housing markets, and so on. Some researchers even began to examine the complex interplay between such government policies as military spending or highway construction, and patterns of industrial and urban growth, tracing out the implications of these developments for labor markets and housing patterns, and ultimately for poverty and social marginalization. Moreover, when liberal researchers did turn to the study of welfare arrangements themselves as the cause of poverty and associated problems, they tried to show that the failure to provide adequate benefits or services was a key source of poverty.

But in the 1970s, as the social movements which had given the 1960s their liberal cast subsided, a combination of white backlash and business mobilization turned the political wheel. The liberalization of social policies came to a halt, and then, gradually, the cutbacks began. As this happened, the liberal intellectual direction of the policy science establishment was attacked and undermined, and everything shifted into reverse.

Of course, the policy science establishment in the universities and research institutes could not refashion itself on a dime: theories and findings had been published, reputations established, and big research projects were underway. Nevertheless, the intellectual transition began, catalyzed in the early 1970s by the creation or rapid expansion of conservative think tanks funded by business. The American Enterprise Institute, the Hoover Institution, the Cato Institute, the Heritage Foundation, the Manhattan Institute, all were created or expanded in the 1970s. These think tanks then became the incubators for new policy scientists like George Gilder or Charles Murray or Robert Rector or Marvin Olasky, who proclaimed that it was the liberalization of social policy in the 1960s that was to blame for social problems ranging from poverty to ill health to crime and so on. This was, of course, the "hypothesis of perverse effects." Instead of reducing economic hardship and sustaining families, welfare policies and practices were themselves important causes of poverty and family breakdown, mainly because welfare generates ostensible work and family disincentives. A new political regime provided resources for a new group of policy scientists whose task it was to fashion a contemporary version of the ancient argument that relief-giving has deleterious consequences.

The turn in the political wheel also carried along the older liberal policy scientists, and younger liberal policy scientists coming of age. In order to compete for recognition and research funds, they conceded key ground to conservatives. The research findings they produced, however qualified and ambiguous, as we will soon explain, nevertheless contributed importantly to the new consensus that welfare was the cause of poverty and not the solution. They abandoned studies of macroeconomic forces, even of those forces contributing to worsening conditions in the low-wage labor market. And in this way, they helped prepare the way for the dismantling of 60 years of social policy.

Competition for fame and funds was surely not the only reason for the turn by liberal policy scientists. Much of the research conducted in the 1970s and 1980s by liberals was in a sense defensive, provoked by increasingly strident attacks on social policies with which they were identified. To blunt these attacks, liberal researchers focussed on the bearing of different aspects of social policy on the family-related decisions of poor women, on their employment behavior, on their income, on the well-being of their children, and so on. These questions were investigated with the aid of the enormous data sets now maintained by government and research institutes which record empirical measures of family organization, income, employment, school achievement, crime, and so on. However, as any graduate student knows, empirical data are not self-revealing. The theoretical framework which organizes the inquiry, which specifies variables and suggests their relationship, is what matters. And in this period the theoretical framework was the hypothesis of perverse effects. Conservatives were trying to buttress it, and liberals were trying to undermine it, but everyone was studying it. For all practical purposes, liberal policy scientists abandoned their own analysis and reiterated the hypothesis of perverse effects. In this way, the real debate about the difficult theoretical issues dealing with the causes of poverty and changes in family forms was simply elided.

To be sure, a good many of the researchers involved in the literally hundreds and hundreds of studies that were undertaken, at least those located in universities or at the liberal research institutes, expected that their findings would prove the hypothesis substantially wrong, or at least overstated.[7] Their research findings would therefore constitute a sort of

answer to the rising chorus of critics of welfare. In effect, the findings of
policy science would be used to shore up the social programs in the political world, perhaps with minor reforms to remedy whatever disincentive
effects were identified. And a decade or so ago, we ourselves thought
that the very existence of a research establishment tied to the welfare
state would provide some reasoned defense for the social programs
against the growing conservative assault.[8] But these expectations did not
take sufficient account of the limits of multivariate analysis framed by
politically motivated questions, whether liberal or conservative.

In any event, beginning with the guaranteed income experiments of
the mid-1970s,[9] a vast body of research was produced investigating the
impact of existing welfare practices on family decisions, and particularly
on the incidence of out-of-wedlock births and single parent family formation. Presumably, the interest in such research was prompted by the
broad coincidence between the expansion of welfare and the rise of out-
of-wedlock births, although closer scrutiny showed no such straightforward relationship over time.[10] In fact, although the number of children
living in out-of-wedlock households has been rising steadily, from 5.3 to
28 percent of all births between 1970 and 1990,[11] the purchasing power
of welfare benefits which presumably were the incentive for this trend
had fallen steadily, dropping nearly 40 percent in the two decades,[12]
during which time the fraction of out-of-wedlock children living in
AFDC households also fell.[13] Moreover, comparisons between states
with sharply varying benefit levels did not fare much better. While there
was some evidence that divorce and separation rates were modestly
influenced by benefit levels, and even some evidence that out-of-wedlock births to white women were influenced by state benefit levels,[14]
overall out-of-wedlock birth rates did not appear to be influenced by
welfare policy.[15] No matter. As these sorts of findings accumulated over
a period of more than two decades, the failure to produce definitive correlations between AFDC receipt and family formation decisions only
prompted more research with more methodologically sophisticated
techniques to study the same hypothesis of perverse effects. And so the
main political story line, that welfare leads to out-of-wedlock births,
was kept alive and intact.

The political fracas over the New Jersey "family cap" experiment illustrates how much more powerful is the force of the storyline implicit in selective variables than the mere empirical findings of correlational analysis. Several years ago, the New Jersey legislature pioneered one of the first proposals to deny AFDC families a benefit increase after the birth of a child conceived while the mother was on welfare. The Clinton Administration granted New Jersey the waiver that was required to implement this departure from the Social Security Act. This occurred with a good deal of press attention and the legislator from Trenton who championed the proposal became something of a public figure. Meanwhile, since waivers are supposed to be scientifically evaluated demonstrations, Rutgers University was given a contract to study the impact of the experiment on rates of out-of-wedlock births to AFDC recipients. In the time since, the Rutgers researchers have released several reports on their findings, which show family benefit reductions have little or no impact on rates of conception by welfare recipients.[16] No matter. Negative findings had none of the force of the proposition that welfare benefits are an incentive for out-of-wedlock births and its logical corollary, that reducing benefits will discourage such births. The family cap has since surfaced in numerous other state waiver plans, and in virtually every congressional welfare proposal. (Meanwhile, we know of no effort to evaluate the impact of the resulting benefit cuts on the well-being of recipient families who are the subjects of this experiment.)

Research on the impact of welfare incentives on the work behavior and earnings of welfare recipient families followed much the same pattern. The guaranteed income experiments of the 1970s had shown a modest work reduction effort, particularly among women in two parent households, when cash payments were guaranteed. In a way, this was an almost commonsense finding: if government cash benefits are increased and made secure while earnings from work are not, some people will work less, in this case women who were already working in the home. Subsequent studies went beyond this purely economistic argument to explore what might be called the dependency thesis, that welfare receipt psychologically disables recipients and especially their children for labor market participation. Findings tended not to support the thesis that welfare caused "intergenerational" welfare dependency.[17] A parallel line of research made use of large longitudinal data sets to study patterns of welfare utilization over time, with findings that showed most women were relatively short-term users of welfare, although repeat spells were common.[18]

Only recently have some policy researchers (all of them women) broadened the inquiry by shifting the focus away from the impact of welfare utilization on labor market participation and income, and toward the impact of labor market conditions, especially conditions in the low wage labor market, on the utilization of welfare.[19] The results of this modest but important shift reveal the great influence which the hypothesis of perverse effects had had on earlier studies. For one thing, the positing of welfare and work as mutually exclusive alternatives by the policy science establishment misrepresents the real behavior of recipients. At least 40% of adult recipients work while they are on welfare, and they work on average as much as other women with children. For another, we are learning what should have been obvious, that the presumably perverse incentive effect attributed to welfare could as well be labeled the perverse incentive effect of a low wage labor market that pays too little, too irregularly, with too few work-related benefits such as health care, for families to survive. Some years earlier, Ellwood and Bane had interpreted multiple spells of welfare as evidence of a dependency syndrome. But some researchers are now beginning to interpret the evidence that women move back and forth from work to welfare as evidence of the insecurity of much low wage work. Or, as Harris says, "Work among poor women should be viewed as the problem rather than the solution" (1996, 424).

Meanwhile, still another line of policy research focussed on the consequences for labor market participation and earnings of manipulating welfare practices in a variety of reform schemes designed to move women from welfare to work. The package of interventions is familiar: supervised job search or training or workfare assignments on the one hand, and sanctions in the form of benefit reductions or cutoffs for non-compliance on the other hand. Much of this research was conducted under the impetus of a series of "workfare" programs inaugurated over the past two decades as opposition to cash welfare escalated. And much of the more recent research, conducted by the Manpower Development and Training Corporation, actually attempted an experimental design, comparing recipients exposed to the "experimental" reforms with control groups who were not. Research on these welfare-to-work programs now extends back over twenty-five years, and the overall results argue the programs have only trivial effects in public policy terms. To be sure, a handful of the programs show *statistically* significant effects, but it is hard to see how statistically significant aggregate increases of 5 or 6% in hours worked or earnings among the experimentals make sense in policy terms. Even the purportedly most successful program of all, in Riverside California, only brought the average earnings of participants to $286 a month.[20] Moreover, as in the case of reforms designed to reduce out-of-wedlock births, there were few studies indeed of the consequences of the benefit reductions or welfare terminations experienced by the women who are sanctioned by the programs (some proportion of whom, it would seem reasonable to presume, failed to show up for job clubs or workfare for the simple reason that they were already working).[21] Instead, the governors of the states that introduced the harshest programs were left free to crow that declining state caseloads proved the programs were succeeding.

The ongoing debacle over welfare policy illustrates another deep flaw in the policy science model, which arises from misunderstanding of the role of lofty public goals in the policy process. In politics, professed goals are not first principles guiding action, as they are in the policy science model. Rather, the articulation of goals is itself a political strategy, a maneuver in the effort to win support and deflect opposition in a complex and conflict-ridden terrain. The role of David Ellwood, eminent welfare expert and government policy advisor, in the calamity of welfare reform illustrates this point.

Ellwood, like other liberal analysts, has been doing research for many years on the impact of welfare practices on work and family behavior. His 1988 book, *Poor Support*, outlined a series of policy reforms, presumably based on his research, which would ostensibly eliminate the perverse disincentive effects of existing welfare policy, largely by making work pay. The proposals included universal medical protection, an increased minimum wage, comprehensive child support payments backed up by government, and guaranteed minimum wage jobs. Ellwood also advocated time limits on the receipt of cash benefits, presumably to eliminate the perverse incentive of welfare, and to make the policy package palatable to an American public that believed in work and self-reliance.

In other words, this was a proposal based not only on policy science, but on a *political* science of a sort that policy scientists seem to favor, perhaps because it matches their simplified model of the decision process. Policy science justified proposals for universal health care, wage and other (non-welfare) income improvements, and so on, because these proposals were derived from presumed causal relations between policy and the behavior of the poor. But it was a judgment about politics that justified joining these benign recommendations with a proposal for time limits since the expectation was that tough time limits would generate public support for the entire package.

But the real political world in which social policy is fashioned works differently, and certainly it is not dominated by "the policy reformer" and "the public." For one thing, as social policies unfold, they have important economic consequences through their impact on labor markets and tax levels, and the anticipation of those economic consequences activate organized business interests. And most importantly in this instance, policy initiatives are carried forward by politicians, not experts, and politicians bring to any reform effort a preeminent concern not with a particular social policy, but with the uses of a particular policy initiative in coping with the politician's central preoccupations—with appeasing investors, garnering campaign contributions, and appealing to voters. As for the voters themselves, their preferences are not firm and knowable and they do not drive policy. Rather, voter preferences are in most policy areas ambiguous and shifting, and susceptible to political manipulation, especially on policy matters of which people have little direct knowledge. But popular attitudes are not merely the reflection of manipulation. There is also a deep reservoir of antipathy for the poor and for welfare in American culture, which is not necessarily revealed by polls asking whether people think government should assist the poor. And that antipathy can be activated when doing so seems to meet a political purpose, solve a political problem.

This is why the foray of social scientists into welfare reform turned out so badly, indeed calamitously. Reform turned into its opposite, as politicians competed to trumpet the AFDC program as a major and growing problem for American society, and proposed cutbacks in benefit levels, draconian sanctions for disapproved behaviors, the elimination of federal responsibility in favor of the states, and of course, time limits on the receipt of benefits. These major structural changes had little basis in the volumes of policy science research accumulated over three decades regarding the consequences of welfare disincentives on the behavior of the poor. What they did have to do with was an escalating competition between Democrats and Republicans to claim the leadership in welfare reform.

Clinton, very likely influenced by Ellwood's *Poor Support*, fired the opening shot with his 1992 campaign promises to "end welfare as we know it" with "two years and off to work."[22] On taking office, the President recruited Ellwood, and Mary Joe Bane, both policy analysts variously associated with the Kennedy School, to join HHS Secretary Donna Shalala on a team to design welfare reform. The talk was of new programs in job training and job creation, health care and day care, all of which would presumably smooth the path to work (and all of which would presumably be evaluated according to the most sophisticated canons of policy science). But services and jobs cost money, much more money than AFDC. This no one who mattered intended. As the estimated costs mounted, the service and job provisions shrank. In the end, the important feature of the Clinton plan was a proposed two year lifetime limit on cash assistance.

This outcome may have seemed fortuitous from the perspective of the policy scientists, but subsequent events suggest that it was inevitable given the power constellations in the contest over welfare that emerged. Almost immediately after the 1994 congressional election, the victorious Republicans tried to take the welfare issue back from Clinton, proposing to eliminate federal responsibility for cash assistance to poor families in favor of block grants, giving the states much more latitude in deciding how federal money should be spent, and even whether it should be spent on welfare at all. This was coupled with strict time limits and rigid work requirements. Cuts were also proposed in food stamp and nutritional programs, as well as low income housing, child protection services, and in the child care and job training funds that had been an important justification for the original Ellwood proposal for time limits. Many of these provisions became law in the summer of 1996 when Clinton signed The Personal Responsibility and Work Reconciliation Act, commonly called "welfare reform."[23]

As the contest for front position on welfare escalated, the President maneuvered for position. True, he responded to liberal advocacy groups by vetoing the draconian block grant proposal that emerged from the Congress in the winter of 1995-96, claiming it did not do enough to ensure that recipients worked. But he exerted himself to regain the initiative. He had learned from the 92 campaign, if he did not already know, that bashing politically powerless welfare recipients while celebrating family values struck a chord with the electorate. And so, as the slogan "it's the economy stupid" dissolved in the failure of a feeble economic stimulus package, as profits rose but wages stagnated, as the scandals and missteps of his administration piled one on the other, Clinton approved one state waiver request after the other for programs which essentially mimicked the Republican welfare cutbacks, and mimicked the rhetorical argument, of Clinton and the Republicans alike, that a too lenient welfare system was leading to worsening poverty and social pathology.

By mid-1996, Clinton had approved waiver programs in 37 states. State initiatives included not only time limits, but benefit cuts and sharp sanctions for a variety of disapproved behaviors, and quickly resulted in a ten percent drop in the welfare rolls. As Douglas Besharov commented at an American Enterprise Institute meeting in April 1996, "Based on what happened in the last year, President Clinton can justifiably claim he has ended welfare as we know it [by state waivers]. He had accomplished, Besharov said, "welfare reform on the cheap" without an increase in spending for child care or "a penny for job training." The "revolutionary" result was "an end to personal entitlement."[24]

What did policy science have to do with any of this? Certainly, it did not provide empirical evidence of the consequences which could be expected from these new initiatives. If anything, the weight of the evidence suggested that slashing benefits would have negligible influence on out-of-wedlock pregnancy rates, for example. (It is another irony that some of that evidence had been provided earlier in much cited work by Ellwood and Bane themselves.[25]) And the evidence that slashing or eliminating benefits would increase work effort and earnings also appeared to be a statistical mirage. What policy science provided was not evidence to justify the waiver proposals as serious policy experiments, but the mystification of scientific evaluation research to justify the programs in the terms specified by Section 1115(a) of the Social Security Act, as "experimental, pilot, or demonstration pilot project[s]."[26]

As for the main administrative thrust of these reforms, ceding administrative and fiscal responsibility to state governments, almost nothing was known, at least nothing was known that followed the policy science model of basing decisions on empirical knowledge of cause and effect relations.[27] It should be pointed out, however, that a good deal was known (albeit not in the policy science mode of multi-variate analysis) about the history of state administration of relief. Almost all of what was known was in fact alarming, including the record of state and county administration of poor relief programs prior to the passage of the Social Security Act, and subsequent state and county administration of residual programs for those not covered by federal assistance, known as "general assistance." Scarcely any research had been done on the consequences of cutoffs, or on the consequences of benefit reductions entailed by sanctions for non-compliance with new program requirements. No one, but no one, policy scientist or politician, had any empirical basis for predicting what would happen to the women and children affected. No matter, the reforms have gone forward. As for the policy scientists, it is hard to see what role they played, except for lending an aura of scientific authority to initiatives shaped by a partisan contest for front position in the politics of scapegoating the benighted poor.

A number of important points seem to us to emerge from this recent social policy research experience. First, most of the policy research focussed on narrowly selective policy variables as "causes" of the family and work behavior which were presumably of concern. But the justification for this preoccupation in the larger body of social science theory seems extraordinarily weak. Why, given what we know about the historic persistence of family forms over time and throughout the world, would social scientists look mainly at a relatively small welfare program as the cause of the transformation of established family forms in a generation? Moreover, how can this narrow focus be justified when we also know that family forms are changing among all classes, and in all western societies? At the very least, the policy establishment should have complemented their preoccupation with welfare policy with a search for other deep and enduring influences on family formation decisions arising from changes in the larger culture, in social organization, and in the economy.

Second, why did an extraordinarily sophisticated policy science establishment allow correlations to be treated as causes? True, there was a broad if crude correlation of welfare expansion and family change. But that correlation paralleled multiple other changes which social theory would suggest were more significant. And if correlations were to be treated as causes, then why assume, as in the case of the inquiry into the relationship between welfare availability and labor market behavior, that the direction of causation ran from welfare to the labor market and not the other way round?

Third, there is the question, in a sense the ultimate question, of whether research mattered, one way or the other. This is a difficult query. Overall, the findings were ambiguous or insignificant. The response to small or ambiguous findings was to call for more research, more complex multivariate analysis. In the process, the story told by the research *question*, and by the selective variables the question demanded, became what was politically important. Research was significant not because applied social science was a component of rational policy decisionmaking, but because the causes and consequences investigated by the policy scientists became in politics stories about who or what was to blame for family changes and poverty. Even weak and ambiguous findings seemed to work to confirm the main politically influenced storyline about the perverse effects of welfare.[28]

What if there had been theoretically broader and more complex research? Would it have made a difference? Well, no one can be sure. Still, maybe it would have mattered if the policy establishment had directed public attention to the broad changes in the culture, community and economy which were leading to deepening hardship and disorganization. As it was, advertently or inadvertently, the social researchers reinforced the argument that welfare actually harmed, perhaps a little, perhaps a lot, the people it was designed to help.

Finally, we are struck by the historical naivete of the entire research enterprise. After all, the preoccupations of this generation of social policy scientists were, good intentions aside, closely similar to the 19th century social critics who a century ago justified the draconian cutbacks of poor relief demanded by a new class of industrial capitalists by worrying endlessly and publicly about the perverse effects of a too generous poor relief on the family and work behavior of the poor. They did not worry about the cruel consequences of the elimination of relief.

As for the question of why policy scientists go along, the answer is too obvious to bear telling. Perhaps an anecdote showing what happens when they don't go along will make the point. When the state of Wisconsin introduced one of the first "learnfare" programs some years ago, they required a federal waiver since it was a violation of the Social Security Act to reduce AFDC benefits, in this case as a penalty for teenage truancy. To comply with federal requirements this was to be a social policy experiment to be tested in several counties, and the rather feisty Employment and Training Institute at the University of Wisconsin at Milwaukee got the contract to evaluate the impact of family benefit cuts on the school absences of teenage children. When early findings showed that truancy in fact increased instead of decreasing, the state government terminated the research contract, and continued the learnfare program.[29] Then, in May of 1996, when state officials requested new federal waiver authority for a plan that would essentially eliminate the right to cash assistance in favor of work and training programs, they included a request to extend the learnfare program statewide.

And that's the way it is.

1997

Notes

1. See the collection of essays in Reuschemeyer and Skocpol 1996 for a series of historical accounts of the intimate connection between the rise of contemporary social science and modern social policies. See also Schram, 1996, for a sharply critical perspective on this relationship.

2. For a discussion, see Merton, 1957.

3. On this point, see Brodkin 1995.

4. On this point, of the role of the audience in deciding the outcoming of political conflicts, see Schattschneider.

5. Charles Lindblom's (1990:197 *passim*) perceptive observation that while social scientists may increase our competence as a society in some respects, they reduce our competence in other respects, and importantly because they close off some avenues of thought and inquiry.

6. This point is discussed in Piven and Cloward, 1987, chapter 1.

7. The important research centers were The Institute for for Social Research at the University of Michigan, the Institute for Research on Poverty at the University of Wisconsin, the John F. Kennedy School of Government at Harvard, and the Urban Institute at Northwestern University. Also the Urban Institute, Washington, D.C.

8. See Piven and Cloward 1087, chapter 2. Even so, however, we were sharply critical of the narrow questions which framed the main research endeavors.

9. See, for example, Plotnick and Skidmore, 1975.

10. See Piven and Cloward 1987, 54-58 for a discussion of the formidable measurement problems that have been largely ignored in counting single parent families and out-of wedlock births.

11. Acs, 1995.

12. 1994 Green Book, 324.

13. See Ellwood and Summers 1983, 3; see also Greenstein, 1985 and Parrott and Greenstein 1995.

14. See O'Neill, Wolf, Bassi, Hannan, 1984.

15. On out-of-wedlock births, see Cutright 1973; Fechter and Greenfield 1973; Winegarden 1974; Moore and Cauldwell 1977; MacDonald and Sawhill 1978; Ellwood and Bane 1986; Rank 1994; Blank 1995. On divorce and separation rates, see Hoffman and Holmes 1976; Ross and Sawhill 1975; Lane 1681; Bishop 1980; Wilson and Neckerman 1986; Rank 1994.

16. See Michael C. Laracy, "If It Seems Too Good To Be True, It Probably Is," Report by the Annie E. Casey Foundation, June 21, 1995.

17. See for example, Hill and Ponza 1984, Duncan and Hoffman, 1986, Freeman and Holzer 1986, Haveman and Wolfe, 1994.

18. See Rein and Rainwater 1978, Coe 1981, Bane and and Ellwood 1983, O'Neil et al. 1984, Duncan 1984, Ellwood 1986, Duncan and Hoffman 1986, Blank 1989.

19. See Edin 1994, Harris 1996, Spalter-Roth and Hartmann, 1994.

20. See Jason De Parle, "The New Contract With America's Poor," *New York Times*, Week in Review, July 28, 1996.

21. For an exception, see I. Wolock et al., 1985-86. Most efforts to track the fate of AFDC recipients removed from the rolls appears to have been undertaken mainly by advocacy organizations. See for example, National Employment Law Project, March 26, 1996; Carlson and Theodore, 1995; Pawasarat and Quinn, 1995; Leon, July 1995; Children's Defense Fund, 1996; O'Neil, 1996. There have also been some studies of the fate of those affected by earlier state cutbacks in the general assistance program. See for example Danziger and Kossoudjii, 1995; and Nichols and Porter, 1995.

22. Splitting the difference, one presumes, in Ellwood's proposal for a time limit of between 18 months and three years.

23. The law also included provisions which excluded legal immigrants from a variety of assistance programs.

24. See Center on Law and Social Policy, May 16, 1996.

25. See Ellwood and Bane, 1986.

26. See Center for Social Welfare Policy and Law, July 9, 1996.

27. See Lurie, 1996.

28. See Schram 1995 on this point.

29. See Pawasarat et al., 1992; and Quinn, 1995.

References

Acs, Gregory. "Do Welfare Benefits Promote Out-of-Wedlock Childbearing?" in *Welfare Reform. An Analysis of the Issues*, ed. Isabel V. Sawhill, The Urban Institute Press, Washington D.C., 1995.

Brodkin, Evelyn Z. "The State Side of the 'Welfare Contract': Discretion and Accountability in Policy Delivery. n Working Paper no. 6, SSA Working Papers Series, University of Chicago School of Social Service Administration, November 1995.

Carlson, Virginia L. and Theodore, Nikolas C. "Are There Enough Jobs? Welfare Reform and Labor Market Reality." Job Gap Project, Office of Social Policy Research, Northern Illinois University, 1995.

CENTER FOR LAW AND SOCIAL POLICY, *CLASP Update*, Washington D.C. May 16, 1996.

CENTER ON SOCIAL WELFARE POLICY and Law, "Comment Opposing Granting of Waiver for Wisconsin Works ("W-2" Demonstration Projected, Submitted to Donna Shalala, Secretary, Department of Health and Human Services, July 9, 1996.

DANZIGER, SANDRA K. AND KOSSOUDJI, SHERRIE A. "When Welfare Ends: Subsistence Strategies of Former GA Recipients: Final Report of the General Assistance Project." University of Michigan School of Social Work, February 1995.

EDIN, KATHRYN. "The Myths of Dependency and Self-Sufficiency: Women, Welfare, and Low-Wage Work. n Working Paper No. 67. Center for Urban Policy Research, Rutgers University, Princeton, New Jersey.

ELLWOOD, DAVID T. AND BANE, MARY Jo. "The Impact of AFDC on Family Structure.." *Research in Labor Economics* 7, 1986.

HARRIS, KATHLEEN MULLAN. "Life After Welfare: Women, Work, and Repeat Dependency." *American Sociological Review*, vol. 61, June 1996.

LINDBLOM, CHARLES. *Inquiry and Change: The Troubled Attempt to Understand and Shape Society*, Yale University Press, 1990.

LURIE, IRENE. "The Impact of Welfare Reform:More Questions Than Answers," *Symposium on American Federalism: The Devolution Revolution,* Rockefeller Institute Bulletin, 1996.

MERTON, ROBERT. "Role of the Intellectual in Public Bureaucracy," in Robert Merton, *Social Theory and Social Structure*, p. 217.

NATIONAL EMPLOYMENT LAW PROJECT, "Statement Submitted to Council of the City of New York Oversight Hearing on the Human Resource Administration's Work Experience Program (WEP) and its Impact on the City Workforce." March 26, 1996.

NICHOLS, MARION AND PORTER, KATHRYN. "General Assistance Program: Gaps in the Safety Net." Center on Budget and Policy Priorities, March 14, 1995.

O'NEILL, JUNE A, WOLF, DOUGLAS A., BASSI, LAURIE J., AND HANNAN, MICHAEL T. "An Analysis of Time on Welfare." Washington, D.C.: Urban Institute, 1984.

PARROTT, SHARON AND GREENSTEIN, ROBERT. "Welfare, Out-of-Wedlock childbearing, and Poverty, What is the Connection?" Center on Budget and Policy Priorities, Washington, D.C., January 1995.

PARSONS, TALCOTT.

PAWASARAT, JOHN ET AL. "Evaluation of the Impact of Wisconsin's Learnfare Experiment on the School Attendance of Teenagers Receiving AFDC," University of Wisconsin-Milwaukee Employment and Training Institute, February 5, 1992.

_____ AND QUINN, LOIS, "Integrating Milwaukee County AFDC Recipients Into the Local Labor Market, n University of Wisconsin- Milwaukee Employment and Training Institute, November, 1995.

PLOTNICK, ROBERT, AND SKIDMORE, FELICITY. *Progress Against Poverty*. New York, Academic Press, 1975.

POLANYI, MICHAEL. *The Graet Transformation*. Boston, Beacon Press, 1957.

QUINN, LOIS. "Using Threats of Poverty to Promote School Attendance: Implications of Wisconsin's Learnfare Experiment for Families." Journal of Children and Poverty, vol. 1, no. 2. Summer 1995.

_____ AND MAGILL, ROBERT S. "Politics versus Research in Social Policy," *Social Service Review*, December 1994.

RUESCHEMEYER, DIETRICH AND SKOCPOL, THEDA, *States. Social Knowledge. and The Origins of Modern Social Policies*, Princeton University Press, 1996.

SCHRAM, SANFORD, *Words of Welfare: The Poverty of Social Science and the Social Science of Poverty*, University of Minnesota Press, 1995.

_____ "'Poor' Statistical Accounting: Rewriting the Boundaries of Social Science and Politics in the Public Sphere of Cyberspace." Unpublished manuscript, June 1996. Spalter-Roth, Roberta M. and Hartmann, Heidi I. "Dependence on Men, the Market or the State: The Rhetoric and Reality of Welfare Reform." *Journal of Applied Social Sciences* 18, 1994.

WOLOCK, I., ET AL., "Forced Exit From Welfare: The Impact of Federal Cutbacks on Public Assistance Families," *Journal of Social Service Research*, 9, 1985-86.

Part IV

Disruption: Movements and Their Electoral Impact

12

Introduction

The American social compact was forged in response to the protest movements of the 1930s and 1960s. Now, after two decades of relative quiescence by the poor and the working class, the programs are under sustained attack. Unless new protest movements emerge, the victories of the thirties and sixties will be rolled back, indeed are already being rolled back.

We think poor people win mainly when they mobilize in disruptive protests, for the obvious reason that they lack the resources to exert influence in conventional ways, such as forming organizations, petitioning, lobbying, influencing the media, buying politicians. By disruptive protest, we mean acts such as incendiarism, riots, sit-ins and other forms of civil disobedience, great surges in demands for relief benefits, rent strikes, wildcat strikes, or obstructing production by stopping assembly lines.

We first made the disruption argument in an article written more than three decades ago, in 1963, entitled "Low Income People and the Political Process." It still represents our ideas about poor people and power as well as anything we wrote later, and it is reproduced as the first article in this section.

Many political scientists, analysts of social movements, and grassroots organizers emphasize organization as the source of power. They define us as advocating "mass turmoil" and something akin to anarchy. Several articles in this section—our interchange with Gamson and Schmeidler, and "Normalizing Collective Protest"—are part of this debate.

We can now look back over the whole industrial period in the United States and ask, What did poorer people win? And what did they have to do to win it? The answer, as we see it, is stark. There were two main periods in which poor people made some gains through the political system. Labor rights and social welfare legislation were won in the 1930s; civil rights and additional social welfare legislation were won during the 1960s. And what it took to win these victories was unparalleled turmoil, both at the polls and in the streets. Indeed, all of the labor, civil rights, and social welfare legislation of consequence in the industrial era was enacted in just two turbulent five-year periods: 1933-1937 and 1963-1967 (with the exception of the Supplemental Security Income legislation in 1972, which was a delayed congressional reaction to the state and local fiscal burdens resulting from the great rise in the relief rolls which began in the early 1960s). What was won was won all at once, as disruptive industrial strike waves, unemployed marches, and riots came to a head in the first period, and civil disobedience campaigns and riots came to a head in the second.

These are inconvenient data for organizational theories of the power of poor people. They strongly suggest that it is mass protest, not poor people's organizations, that wins whatever is won. Furthermore, popular protest more or less erupts, flowers for a moment, and withers. It never lasts; it is episodic.

It is equally inconvenient that the poor people's organizations which form on the crest of these eruptions also do not last, or at least they only persist as leadership shells with a few members. Once insurgency among blacks subsided in the late 1960s, SNCC disappeared; for all practical purposes, so did CORE; and SCLC persisted largely in name only. We do not know of any organization of poor people in the 1940s and 1950s, or any after 1970, that had more than a few thousand active members, if that. Vigorous poor people's organizations, in short, are not alternatives to disruptive protest; they are instead the creatures of protest movements.

Mass disruption, both its emergence and its successes, is closely related to electoral politics, as we explain in "Movements and Dissensus Politics." On the one hand, poor people do not ordinarily rise up if they sense no support from at least a significant fraction of regime leaders, as is likely to be the case when the dominant party is secure. Then poor people are likely to be treated roughly, or ignored. When a regime is insecure, however, it is more likely to bargain actively for support, and may then issue appeals which signal its vulnerability to demands from the bottom.

Poor people may thus make gains when a dominant coalition is coming into being, or when it is eroding. In the 1930s, Democratic leaders bargained for the support of the industrial working class, and the result was legislation that established the right to organize, bargain collectively, and strike, as well as the social programs of the New Deal. In the postwar period, Democratic leaders at first tried to hold both southern white and northern black loyalties, but then having lost the South, they bargained for black support and the results were the huge advances in civil rights, as well as the social program initiatives of the Great Society.

Mass disruption not only reflects electoral instabilities; it also contributes to them. At the beginning of the Great Depression, for example, mass demonstrations by the unemployed helped to ignite the anger that led working-class voters to desert the Republican party; subsequently, huge strike waves kept Democratic party leaders insecure about the realignment that brought them to power in 1932, thus keeping them under pressure to make concessions to the working class. In the post-World War II decades, the electoral instabilities which led Democratic leaders to vacillate between encouraging civil rights demands and encouraging white southern resistance were greatly worsened by the black civil disobedience campaigns in the South, with the result that southern whites abandoned the Democratic party, leaving Democratic leaders little choice but to enfranchise blacks.

Once protest movements and electoral dissensus subsided in each period, the victories won were eroded. The power of the strike, for example, was encapsulated by new legislation in the 1940s. And labor rights, civil rights, and social programs for the poor were weakened after the 1970s. These losses are not likely to be reversed easily. To save the social programs, it is likely to take protests at least on the scale it took to win them. Some signs of mass protest have emerged in other advanced capitalist countries—in France, Germany, Italy, and Canada, for example. The question is whether such protest will continue and spread, even to the United States.

1997

13

Low-Income People and the Political Process

In the early 1960s, as protests by low-income blacks escalated, a certain brand of righteous criticism also escalated that claims to sympathize with the grievances of the poor, but not with their disruptive tactics. What poor blacks ought to do, according to this critique, is to seek redress like proper Americans, informing themselves about the institutional practices which are the source of their grievances, negotiating with institutional managers for change and backing up these negotiations with informed and disciplined pressure at the polls. In sum, the critique assumes that the resources required to engage in regular modes of political influence are freely available to all people—to the poor as well as to the rich, to blacks as well as to whites. We think this argument wrong. The disruptive tactics used by blacks were in fact their only resource for political influence. The analysis which follows is intended to show why.

The Distribution of Political Resources

We mean by "political power" the ability to control actions of the body politic (i.e., actions of the community expressed through its political institutions). We mean by "political resources" the attributes by which individuals or groups gain power, or exert influence, in these community actions. Such attributes may pertain to individuals or to organizations, and may reside in objective conditions of political action or in subjective states of the political actors.

Considered abstractly, apart from any given political system, political resources include anything that can be used by the political actor to induce others in the collectivity to make choices in a preferred direction: the offering or withdrawal of material goods, social prestige, normative authority, knowledge, personal persuasiveness, or coercive force.[1] And, considered abstractly, apart from any given political system, the entrepreneurial use of any of these attributes tends naturally to a pyramiding of resources. We take for granted that people can increase their wealth by employing it. Similarly, prestige, knowledge, authority, or persuasiveness can often be capitalized upon to bring more of these or other assets, which in turn constitute resources for additional influence. One would expect, therefore, that just as the rich get richer, so do the powerful become more powerful, and, of course, so can the rich become more powerful.

However, the institutionalized arrangements by which political activity is carried on modify the use and effectiveness of various resources and in addition generate resources distinctive to political institutions. Thus, democratic political institutions are marked by electoral arrangements for succession to positions of collective authority, and by the wide and equal distribution of the vote as a resource for controlling the use of that authority. In democratic principle the vote permits each and every citizen to exercise his due influence on decisions of the collectivity, either through direct referendum or by selecting the officials who make decisions. Each and every citizen is also, however, subject to a variety of inducements in the use of his vote. The full range of resources by which men and women can sway each other in their choices are therefore also political resources, tempering the egalitarian distribution of the vote.

To illustrate we need only point to some structural features of a formally democratic polity. The authority to make given kinds of decisions for the collectivity is fixed in designated positions in government. Since the occupants of these positions are—more and less directly—subject to removal by the electorate, they are influenced in their decisions by the preferences, expressed or anticipated, of electoral groups. These officials are, however, also subject to influence by other groups on grounds which make other resources effective.

First, resources for influence are in a general way interchangeable. Electorate control of officials depends on the singular effectiveness of the inducement of continued political power, but officials are obviously subject to other inducements. (Only when these are clearly inappropriate to official roles do we speak of corruption.) And even insofar as they seek power, officials depend on the votes of men and women who can, in turn, be influenced by a variety of inducements, whether honorific, symbolic, or material. Accordingly, political leaders will always be on the lookout for ways to increase their stockpile of such voter inducements, and will respond to opportunities to trade in influence with those who have the wealth, social standing, or popular appeal out of which to cull voter inducements.

Second, authority in government is fragmented, and often not even commensurate with policy responsibility. Officials often require certain cooperative acts from each other, and from nongovernmental groups, in order to effectuate any policy. One of the primary resources for an official's influence is the decisions within his formal jurisdiction. Reciprocal bargaining and accommodation with special groups, with the substance of public-policy decisions as the means of influence, therefore characterize official decision-making. Finally, the inevitable voter apathy on many issues, and the ambiguity of voter preferences, will result in slackened control, permitting officials to respond to those who offer non-electoral inducements without suffering losses in voter support.

Political influence can be viewed, therefore, in terms of analytically distinct systems resting on different resources. The formal system, dependent on the vote, tends toward an egalitarian distribution of influence. It is only one aspect, however, of the total system of influence in which a range of unequally distributed social and economic resources are effective. This abstracted and simplified analysis suggests that political influence will tend to distribute along lines consistent with the general distribution of resources in a society. Can electoral arrangements offset this tendency for the accumulation of political power? This question has guided a considerable body of empirical investigation by sociologists and political scientists.

Studies of Community Power Structure

How does the pattern of influence actually develop in American communities? Who really rules? Two major schools of thought have emerged among the students of community power structure, the one generally labeled "stratificationist," the other "pluralist."

The stratification theorists are primarily sociologists, and most of their work was done between 1929 and 1956. According to their view, local communities are characterized by a closed monolithic structure of political power, joined with and derived from the structure of social and economic power in the community. This view of power concentrated at the apex was depicted most vividly in Hunter's study of Atlanta and the Lynds' studies of Middletown. It was elaborated by Warner's studies of Yankee City, Hollingshead's study of Elmstown, and Baltzell's of Philadelphia, and was crowned by C. Wright Mills's sweeping depiction of a national power structure in *The Power Elite*.[2]

More recent studies by political scientists have reached a rather different conclusion, notably Robert Dahl's study of New Haven, Banfield's study of Chicago, and the Sayre and Kaufman study of New York City.[3] Political power in local communities is depicted as relatively dispersed. Not only are a range of actors said to affect any policy decision, but different actors predominate in different policy areas, employing different resources in the process. An urban-renewal decision may arouse builders and the residents designated for dislocation, a school-site decision may arouse competing parents' groups, or a highway decision may arouse construction unions and the homeowners in the path of demolition. Each of these groups may have different channels to influence, whether personal contacts with officials, party affiliations, or access to the media. And each may be influential through different inducements: the votes they represent, the publicity they threaten, or the legitimation they confer. Power is thus said to be dispersed, for it is based on a great variety of resources, widely distributed through a community. The uncertain and entrepreneurial process through which effective influence is organized under these circumstances is said to make for a relatively open political system. The conclusion, qualified to be sure, is that those who *want* to influence generally *can* influence.

However, the question of who does not participate in political decisions, and why they do not, is not frontally addressed. This is partly attributable to the principle methodology the pluralists employ (and which Polsby justifies as the only methodology for the study of power that conforms to the strictures of empirical science). The method is to focus on selected contests or issues, to identify the contestants and the means of influence they employ, and then to observe who prevails. Those who win have influence. Whatever the usefulness of this method in generating knowledge of the relative influence of identified contestants in a given issue, it falls far short of yielding knowledge of community power structure in several ways. Most to the point for our analysis, this method can tell us nothing directly about the influence, actual or potential, of those groups who do not become involved in the selected contests. The pluralists tend to be satisfied, however, that nonparticipants are those who are not interested in the issue.

Limited information regarding nonparticipants may inhere in the methodology that the pluralists insist upon, but their sometimes breezy dismissal of this matter is made possible by an implicit conceptual assumption about the nature of Political Man—a concept somewhat analogous to the rationalistic Economic Man of laissez-faire theorists. The political actor, whether an individual or an organized group, is treated virtually as Man-in-Space, uninfluenced by a social environment, and discrepancies between what he does and what he is able to do, between his actual and potential influence, tend to be regarded only as qualifications which follow in a less than perfect world.

But surely such an assumption is untenable, reviewed in the light of even the most elementary knowledge of social stratification. It is obvious that some groups in a community are without material resources to offer as political inducements to decision-makers. Some groups are separated by social location from the possibility of exercising personal influence on decision-makers. And some groups suffer educational disadvantages so that they have less knowledge of political issues and are less expert at political strategy. It is equally obvious that these political deficits are not randomly distributed. Those who are without material resources are also those who are without personal access to decision-makers or other resources for influence. Finally, those who are without power feel and think themselves to be powerless and act accordingly.

Dahl's study of New Haven, arguing essentially the pluralist perspective, nevertheless presented evidence showing that participation increases with income, with social standing, and with formal education. Participation was greater among professional, business, and white-collar occupations than among working-class occupations, and greater in better residential areas than in poorer areas.[4] Dahl takes pains to point out that since there are so many more "worse-off" citizens, their aggregate participation is still considerable—a circumstance which does not quite satisfy democratic norms, however. Further evidence on the relationship between effective influence and social class can be drawn from the forms which participation took among the "worse-off." They were most active in the footwork of campaigning—a kind of participation which is not usually recompensed with public-policy concessions. On the other hand, the "worse-off" appeared least frequently in the classification showing the highest index of local activity, the group that also might be expected to be politically most effective.

It does not seem reasonable, therefore, to ascribe the low level of participation among the poor to lack of political interest or lack of political will. It is more likely due to a lack of political power. The syndrome among the poor that some call apathy is not simply a state of resignation; it is a definite pattern of motivated inaction impelled by objective circumstances. People who know they cannot win do not often try.

In short, while sociologists and political scientists differ regarding the structure of power in American communities, their disagreement is actually about the question of how influence is distributed within the middle and upper levels of the social order. The pluralists may have succeeded in casting some doubt on simple conceptions of a monolithic community power structure, but the evidence that they present demonstrates at most the lateral dispersion of influence among the upper and middle classes. Whether or not such lateral dispersion exists, it argues nothing about the power of the lower class. If our analysis so far suggests that the poor have few resources for regular political influence, the weight of empirical evidence surely does not dispute it.

The Role of Organizations in the Political Process

Our discussion so far has been conducted in terms of a quaint, but not very useful, artifice. We have examined the capacity of low-income people for regular political influence by discussing the attributes of individuals and groups. But the political process does not consist primarily in the relations between disparate individuals and official decision-makers.

Large, rationalized organizations have come to dominate both governmental and private spheres, each development reinforcing the other. And for a whole range of issues that are not precipitated into public prominence so as to become significant electoral issues, the political dialogue is carried on between organizations. A planning commission deals with organizations or realtors and homeowners; a board of education with teachers' unions and parents' associations; a department of commerce with chambers of commerce. Similarly, on the federal level, regulatory agencies negotiate with the industries they regulate; the Department of Labor negotiates with unions; and the Department of Health, Education and Welfare with professional and scientific societies and philanthropic federations.

Large organizations bring to the political process a superior capability for influence; they have the resources to engage in regular surveillance of the processes of government and to initiate issues.[5] Where individuals are aroused to political action only at periodic elections or through the occasional congruence of awareness and interest, rationalized organizations are able to maintain a steady watch on the political process and to maintain the resources for regular participation and influence. Large organizations are capable of rationalizing and capitalizing the use of resources for influence, both among their participants and over time, thus developing capabilities commensurate with a complex and bureaucratic society and a complex and bureaucratic government. They can keep abreast of the maze of actual and proposed legislation and procedures, decipher their implications and exploit many informal and formal occasions for negotiation and bargaining. They have the ability to generate public issues through regular organizational liaisons and to gain access to the media and political parties. In addition they can offer public institutions the support and technical capability of their own organizations, permitting them to become regular contributors to governmental action and thus extending both the occasions and the means of influence.

Lower-class people have not developed large-scale formal organizations to advance their interests. The reasons are not mysterious. To be poor means to command none of the resources ordinarily considered requisites for organization: money, organizational skill and professional expertise, and personal relations with officials.[6] The instability of lower-class life[7] and the character of lower-class beliefs also discourage the poor from organizational participation.

But of far greater importance, most organizations are generated by the functions they perform in the economic structure, functions having to do with the protection and enhancement of either profits, property, or occupational roles. Engagement in the economic structure makes interaction and association—whether through a labor union, a merchants' association, or a professional society—profitable or potentially profitable. Most of the poor, being more or less out of economic structures, are not in a position either to create such organizations or to profit from them. It is thus not simply that the poor do not have the necessary attributes for participation in organizations; more to the point, they are not located in economic institutions which facilitate interaction and organization, nor would they have much to gain from participation in organizations not linked to the economic structure.

One of the chief historical examples of low-income organization is the industrial union. Unions developed by exploiting features distinctive to the factory structure in order to secure adherents and to force in their name certain institutional accommodations, first in private spheres and then through the electoral process during the New Deal. It is our view that this organizational form is not available to the contemporary poor.

One feature that made union organization possible and enabled leaders to sustain it was the structural context of the factory itself. Men and women were already assembled and regularly related to each other. The factory was thus a framework for organizing activity which directly paralleled the scope of common grievances and potential benefits for which men and women were being induced to join together. Moreover, once the union was established in the factory, the shared and structured work setting considerably lessened the task of sustaining the organization. The union could bring to bear group sanctions on the worksite to insure participation by workers (and subsequently the legal sanction of the union and closed shops), and dues could be collected through the factory payroll department. Because union organizational structure paralleled factory structure, it could utilize the formal and informal processes of the functioning factory to its own advantage. As a consequence, only limited participation by workers was actually required in the union itself. The union could be sustained without intensive investment in organizing activity which characterized the early days of the industrial union movement and the initial organization of each factory. Thus, not only was the initial assertion of union power possible because men and women were already engaged together in a common structure and could, therefore, be organized, but the initial task of organizing did not have to be repeated for successive assertions of power to be made. The union was able to regularize its organization on the basis of limited contributions from participants, and it was able to do this by relying on the developed structure of the factory system itself.

By contrast, today's poor are relatively dispersed, without patterns of regular interaction. Without such interaction, a sense of common group problems and common group interests is much less likely to develop, especially among a mobile and culturally heterogeneous poor. And even when such shared perspectives do emerge, they are not likely to result in regular participation. Factory workers were first drawn together by the factory; it is a moot question whether organizers could have done it by themselves. Today's poor have to be drawn together by sheer organizer grit, and the group can be sustained only by enormous investments of organizing effort.

Another feature of the factory situation that made organization possible was that union membership paid off in material benefits. The unions developed in the context of profitable enterprises. Workers were essential to these enterprises; their labor was therefore a source of potential leverage with owners and managers. If organized, workers could bring the factory to a halt, and press for improvements in wages and working conditions which management was in a position to grant. It was the expectation of material incentives that led men and women to join the union, and the continued ability of the union to produce these incentives that led workers to stay in the union.

The contemporary poor, however, are not located in positions that can yield economic incentives. They do not fill roles essential to profitable enterprises. If they work at all, it is in marginal jobs, often for employers who are themselves marginal. They therefore would have little leverage to force economic concessions, even if they were organized.

Efforts to organize a rent strike in 1964 in New York City illustrate the difficulties of creating and sustaining an organization when a structural context promoting regular interaction is lacking and when there are few concrete gains to be made. The rent strike was initiated by activists, many of whom were drawn from or inspired by the civil-rights movement. They attempted to develop organizations among people who, although living together in the same physical locale, were not otherwise engaged in much regular interaction. On the face of it, the rent strike seemed to offer a compelling strategy: It singled out the landlord as a clear-cut and inciting target of action; it took place in the ideological glow of the civil-rights movement; and it promised concrete improvements in housing conditions. Nor was there a great deal of risk in rent strikes. In New York, tenants could not be legally evicted if they followed the procedures in which the organizers instructed them.

An enormous organizing task was required, however, to compensate for the absence of an existing substructure of interaction among the tenants. Nor, as it turned out, were housing improvements easy to achieve, for slumlords operating on narrow profit margins used every legal and illegal evasion to avoid investments in repair and, if all else failed, simply deserted their buildings. In spite of considerable public sympathy for the rent strikers, the movement was soon exhausted. It was exhausted by the unceasing and overwhelming efforts required to organize in the absence of any existing substructure, and in the absence of economic incentives.

It is difficult to identify an actual or latent structure of interaction which might be exploited to organize today's poor. Many of the poor are unemployed, or employed in irregular jobs in small and marginal enterprises. They will not, therefore, be heirs to the unions which secured both economic benefits and political influence for some of the poor of an earlier era. Lacking substantial economic incentives and an institutional context of interaction, the vague promise of benefits from organized political action will probably not be sufficient to overcome historic barriers to group cohesion within America's lower class: race and ethnic tensions, geographical mobility (increased by renewal and dislocation in our cities), the actuality and ideals of occupational mobility, a style of elite rule that is conciliatory and encased in democratic ritual, and, surely not least important, hopelessness—hopelessness based on the realities of power, for poor people do not stand to gain very much from the frail organizations they form.

The Electoral Process

What emerges so far in this review of the distribution of political resources is the conclusion that whatever capacity low-income people may have to influence public policy through regular political processes must rest singularly on the formal mechanism of the vote. Votes must be organized in large and disciplined blocs around policy issues for effective influence. To what extent, then, have the voting resources of low-income groups been organized successfully for this purpose?

Historically, the chief example of low-income electoral organization has been the political machine. The machine was characterized by the use—or misuse—of public power by political leaders to provide private rewards, which in turn served to elicit the votes by which public power was gained and retained. Workers on the machine payroll lent the immigrant poor a sympathetic ear, helped them out when they were in trouble with the police, provided occasional jobs and services—and registered them to vote for machine candidates. Given the deprivations of the immigrant slum, such private rewards were extremely effective in organizing votes. Since these votes were traded for private rewards, however, and not for the substance of public policy, the impact of the "river wards" on policy was small. The poor got something, to be sure, but what they got also vitiated their potential for political influence, ensuring they would not get more. Machine leaders grew rich on the public treasury, and so did the business interests to whom they gave away the city's franchises and contracts. Meanwhile, low-income constituents made their primary mark on public life through the rise of ethnic representatives to government positions.

The nature of the political machine is, however, now largely an academic question; its decline has been widely remarked upon and generally applauded. But the decline was hardly a gain for low-income people. The machine's exploitation of the public domain for private ends strained the interests of the growing middle class and "respectable" business groups in the city, while satisfying, if in private terms, low-income groups. Battles for "reform" generally revealed lower-class wards on the side of the machine, in opposition to more prosperous segments of the community. Over time, reform won out.

The urban political parties which were the successor to the machines rely on a variety of methods to organize voters. The important characteristic of the party in this context is that it strives to maintain the coalition of diverse interests and groups whose support is required for the accession to power. The parties strive, therefore, to select issues for public airing that will permit them to maintain the broadest possible coalition of supporters.[8]

Public-policy issues that reflect low-income interests, however, tend to be divisive. They are divisive partly because the contemporary poor are isolated and marked off as deviant by a predominantly middle-class political culture. Such issues are also divisive because they are thought to be compensatory in character, taking from some groups in the community and giving to others. The parties will therefore tend to avoid issues which reflect the interests of the poor, preferring to deal in policies that can be interpreted as being to the mutual benefit of a wide array of groups. The votes of the poor are no longer bought with private rewards, and they are not solicited with public rewards either.

Disruption As Political Influence

The chief point that emerges from this analysis is that low-income people have no regular resources for influencing public policy. It is obvious that they are without power as individuals. Nor are they significant participants in the large formal organizations that keep watch on government, bringing to bear the leverage made possible by organizational stability, staff, and money. Nor did the machine, nor its remnants that survive in some of our larger cities, nor the political parties, provide an effective vehicle for low-income political influence.

What political options then exist? When discontent about public policy from time to time arises among the poor, new resources and channels must be created—an imperative that inevitably leads to aggressive and deviant action, if it leads to any action at all. This is illustrated by developments in the civil-rights movement, and particularly by the tactics of the younger and brasher leaders who draw some support from low-income groups. The ideological appeals through which these leaders attract followers reflect many of the precepts attributed to the lower-class view of the society: The emphasis is on the "power structure," and the use of pressure to move the power structure; the motives of those in power are impugned; problems which in other circles are said to be complicated are said to be very simple; and an almost total irreverence is shown for professional and bureaucratic concerns. The strategies of these leaders also reflect the limited resources of their lower-class following. They rely on demonstrations, on calling out large numbers of people. Not only does their influence as leaders depend on the support of large numbers of people, but the unstable character of this support is such that it must be made visible—it cannot merely be represented to the power structure as a roster of organizational memberships.

These tactics of demagoguery and demonstration are not without precedent—particularly in the street politics of black ghettos—and politicians have occasionally risen to power by their use. The careers of such politicians as Adam Clayton Powell reveal, however, the strains between the tactics of "the street" and the requirements of regular political stratum in which they come to participate.

Even more striking and revealing than street-style politics is the use of tactics of disruption. Some "extremist" leaders have gone beyond rallies and denouncements of the power structure and have mobilized militant boycotts, sit-ins, traffic tie-ups, and rent strikes. The effectiveness of these tactics does not depend only on dramatic presentations. They are intended to command attention and to win concessions by the actual trouble they cause in the ongoing operations of major institutions—by interfering with the daily business of city agencies or with the movement of traffic or the profits of businessmen. Such disruptions cause commotion among bureaucrats, excitement in the media, dismay among influential segments of the community, and strain for political leaders.

When people sit in, or refuse to pay the rent, they are breaking the rules. This means that effective disruption depends on the ability of leaders to induce people to violate norms of conduct that are ordinarily deeply ingrained. Somehow the normal pieties, and the normal mechanisms of social control that enforce these pieties, must be overcome. Moreover, to break the rules ordinarily involves some danger; people must be induced to run the risk of provoking coercive and repressive forces.

All of which is to say that it is probably only at certain times in history that the legitimacy of regular political processes is so questioned that people can be mobilized to engage in disruption, for to do so is to violate the implicit "social contract" of major institutions and often to violate the explicit social contract of the law as well. That people are sometimes led to this, and to run the risks involved, only signifies the paucity of alternatives. If our analysis is correct, disruptive and irregular tactics are the only resource, short of violence, available to low-income groups seeking to influence public policy.

Originally published in 1963.

Notes

1. See Robert A. Dahl, *Who Governs? Democracy and Power in an American City*, p. 226, for another "common sense" listing. (New Haven, 1961.)

2. See Floyd Hunter, Community Power Structure, Chapel Hill, University of North Carolina Press, 1953; Robert S. Lynd and Helen M. Lynd, Middletown, New York, Harcourt Brace, 1929; Robert S. Lynd and Helen M. Lynd, Middletown in Transition, New York, Harcourt Brace, 1937; W. Lloyd Warner et al., Yankee City Series, 1–5, New Haven, Yale University Press, 1941, 1942, 1945, 1947, 1959; August B. Hollingshead, Elmtown's Youth, New York, Wiley, 1949; E. Digby Baltzell, Philadelphia Gentlemen, Glencoe, Free Press, 1958; C. Wright Mills, The Power Elite, New York, Oxford University Press, 1956.

3. Dahl, op. cit., Edward Banfield, *Political Influence*, Glencoe, Free Press, 1962; Wallace L. Sayre and Herbert Kaufman, *Governing New York City*, New York, Russell Sage Foundation, 1960. The controversy has also generated a consider-

able body of critical literature. Two of the best are by Nelson Polsby and Peter H. Rossi. Polsby presents an examination of the logic and method of the stratification theorists. His main argument speaks to the impossibility of summoning empirical evidence to bear on the main propositions of stratification theory. If stratification theorists are global in their purview, however, and depend upon processes which are not accessible to research, it is also true that the pluralist approach of studying the participants and outcomes of selected contests produces knowledge far short of describing community power as such. Rossi makes the case for more extensive comparative studies in order to identify some of the bases for differences in conclusions. (See Nelson W. Polsby, *Community Power and Political Theory*, Yale University Press, 1963, and Peter Rossi, "Community Decision-Making," *Administrative Science Quarterly*, March 1957).

4. Dahl, op. cit., pp. 284–301.

5. Edward Banfield, in a study based on Chicago, concluded that civic controversies "are not generated by the efforts of politicians to win votes, by differences of ideology, or group interest, or by the behind-the-scene efforts of a power elite. They arise, instead, because of the maintenance and enhancement needs of large formal organizations" (op. cit., p. 263).

6. For a discussion of the requirements for organizational influence in city affairs, see Wallace L. Sayre and Herbert Kaufman, op. cit., pp. 481–515. Sayre and Kaufman identify the following means by which nongovernmental groups influence public officials in the resolution of issues: appearances at public hearings; informal consultations; personal relations with group leaders and officials; the provision of advice and services of expert character; conducting studies or making reports; influencing party nominations or invoking party intervention (largely through the inducement of donations and publicity, or by means of personal relations with party leaders); arousing public opinion, mostly through the mass media (and therefore available primarily to the newspapers themselves or to groups with professional staff); and recourse to the courts.

7. Instability in occupational and family life has frequently been the criteria used to distinguish the lower class or the poor from the working class. See, for example, S. M. Miller, "The American Lower Classes: A Typological Approach," in *Mental Health of the Poor: New Treatment Approaches for Low-Income People*, edited by Frank Reissman, Jerome Cohen and Arthur Pearl, Free Press, 1964, pp. 139–154; also S. M. Miller and Frank Reissman, "The Working-Class Subculture: A New View," *Social Problems*, IX (Summer, 1961), pp. 86–97.

8. Party organizations are also able to a degree to neutralize policy interests by converting public power to private rewards. They do this far less effectively or extensively than the machine, however, and so must take account of policy interests in holding together voter coalitions.

14

Movements and Dissensus Politics

Social movements unfold within a larger political context dominated by electoral politics. Recently, a number of analysts have puzzled over the question of how this context influences the rise and evolution of movements.[1] In this article we reverse the inquiry and examine the impact of social movements on electoral politics. We think the evidence suggests that movements play a large role, perhaps a determining role, in the periodic electoral dealignments and realignments that bring new regimes to power and usher in new public policy eras in American history.

Social movements thrive on conflict. By contrast, electoral politics demands strategies of consensus and coalition. We will argue that movements have the impact they do on electoral politics mainly because the issues they raise and the strife they generate widen cleavages among voter groups. We call this "dissensus politics" to differentiate it from the usual process of building electoral influence by recruiting adherents and assembling coalitions, or what might be called "consensus" politics.

Of course, other conditions must also be present before movements can cause destabilizing cleavages. Movements are not likely to have much impact unless economic and social conditions are already eroding established electoral allegiances and coalitions. But then it is also the case that significant change-oriented movements are not likely to emerge except during periods of economic and social instability.

To understand the significance of dissensus politics, we need to go back to the common and taken-for-granted model of popular influence through electoral politics because we think there is a gap in this model that points to the critical role of movements. Ordinary people are said to have influence in democratic systems because their assent at the voting booth is a condition for gaining or retaining state power. Numerous analysts have pointed out, however, that even apart from the perennial problems of corruption and manipulation, the wide distribution of the franchise cannot guarantee that majorities will prevail so long as voters remain disorganized. If voters are atomized, casting their ballots as disconnected individuals, politicians need muster only small minorities to prevail.[2] For democratic majorities to prevail, voters must be organized, a task that falls to political parties. Parties make voters effective by delineating and publicizing a limited number of alternative policies and candidates, on the one hand, and by mobilizing and aggregating voters for one or another of these alternatives on the other hand.

Once the role of parties in electoral democracy is acknowledged, so is the likelihood of a host of systematic distortions of voter preferences, owing to the influence of wealth, the capacity for symbol manipulation and the control of public information, and the organized and often legal corruption of the election process. However, these problems are widely discussed, and in any case are not our subject here. To understand the importance of movements in electoral politics, we must appreciate not only the influences that distort the essentially democratic mission of organizing voter majorities, but the deeply conservative tendencies of electoral politics even apart from such distortions, especially in a two-party system. To win state office, party leaders and their candidates must build broad majorities. They strive to do this by holding the allegiance of those who voted for them in the past while also attracting marginal voters from the contending party. To do this, they try to avoid conflict and search instead for the consensual appeals and promises that preserve and if possible enlarge existing voter coalitions.[3] (Campaign ads that try to recruit voters with shots of beaming families and beautiful sunrises are only the ludicrous ultimate expression of this tendency.) The operatives in a two-party system where majorities must be constructed in the face of diversity are necessarily the conservators of coalitions.

There are, however, eras in which established electoral coalitions break apart and new coalitions form, producing "realignments." These realigning periods are usually treated as the key turning points in American electoral history, both because of the large electoral shifts that occur and because these shifts in turn bring new governing regimes to power and inaugurate new policy eras.[4] Thus the stasis and immobility bred by a two-party system has in the past been at least partly overcome by the periodic convulsions called realignments. This view of the role of realignments in overcoming the conservative tendencies of the American party system is consistent with Walter Dean Burnham's account of electoral realignments as an expression of the accumulated political tensions that result from the failure of the party system to respond to the problems generated by a dynamic capitalist economy. So far, so good.

Still, something is missing. There is a marked tendency in the literature on realignments toward reification or even mystification, as if realignments were an inherent and natural feature of American politics, occurring with an inevitable regularity at thirty-year intervals or so. But why? Unless we revert to a sort of mystical naturalism connoted by the idea of cycles, we need to understand what or who makes realignments happen. The discontinuities between social experience and electoral politics that result from a static party system may well set the stage for realignment. And signs of electoral discontent may even prompt some rhetorical shifts in campaign appeals by major party operatives. Still, overall, political leaders remain timid and conservative, trying to suppress the potential for realignment by bridging potential cleavages with general symbols and vague promises. Under these confusing conditions, discontented voters may be as atomized and ineffective as all voters are said to be in the absence of parties.

Just as people have to be mobilized to support parties and the issues and candidates they put forward, so do they have to be mobilized to desert them. Social movements are often the mobilizers of disaffection. In particular, we think social movements are politically effective precisely when they mobilize electoral disaffection. (We hasten to add that while movements win what they win as a result of their divisive impact on electoral coalitions, electoral dissensus does not necessarily guarantee victories, and such victories as are won may not last, as we will explain.)

If parties worked as they are supposed to, they would play the role we claim for social movements. Periodic elections would spur the party out of power to mobilize the potentially disaffected. Or third parties would emerge in response to the limited options offered by the major parties. Obviously, some of this does happen. However, the role of parties in generating conflict and mobilizing the disaffected is less than the principles of party competition would suggest. A fragmented governmental system in the United States means that the opposition party usually continues to control some part of the government apparatus, and so it is itself constrained by the need to hold together a majority by promoting consensus. As for third-party efforts, it has often been pointed out that they are made difficult in the American system by majority-take-all electoral arrangements, which require that a fledgling party produce instant majorities in a district to win the representation and patronage that sustains the party for another effort. Other procedural barriers to third-party efforts include obstructive registration laws that narrow participation, particularly among the lower classes, rigged ballot access laws, and the enormous cost of campaigning, particularly in this century. These obstacles to third-party organizing as popular undertakings help explain why the task of mobilizing electoral disaffection has often fallen to social movements and why such third-party efforts as do emerge are themselves often dependent on energizing social movements. From the abolitionists to the populists to the civil rights movement to the pro-lifers, social movements and third-party efforts have been intertwined, so that a firm distinction between the electoral impact of movements and third parties is difficult to draw.[5]

To appreciate the role of social movements in helping to precipitate electoral convulsion and realignment, we have to pay attention to the distinctive dynamics of social movements that enable them to do what party politicians do not do. Elsewhere, in connection with our studies of "poor peoples' movements," we emphasized the defiant and disruptive strategies of protest movements that arise among lower strata groups that have few regular political resources. We think the argument we are making here helps account for why disruptive protests, such as strikes or riots, sometimes force reform responses from the state. But we think our argument about the interplay of movements and electoral politics applies to social movements generally, including movements that enlist the middle strata and those that eschew the tactics of institutional disruption.

Social movements, even movements that are not particularly disruptive, can do what party leaders and contenders for office in a two-party system will not do: They can raise deeply divisive issues. In fact, social movements thrive on the drama and urgency and solidarity that result from raising divisive issues. If conflict is deadly to the strategy of a party trying to build a majority coalition, it is the very stuff that makes social movements grow.

Moreover, social movements tend to emerge at moments when the electoral system itself signals the emergence of new potential conflicts. Signs of increased volatility appear in electoral politics, usually traceable to changes in the economy or social life that generate new discontents or encourage new aspirations. The evidence of voter volatility in turn may prompt party leaders to do what they characteristically do, to attempt to hold together their coalition. Only now they will employ a more expansive rhetoric, acknowledging grievances among their constituents that are ordinarily ignored or naming and thus perhaps fueling aspirations that are only beginning to emerge. Even the threat of defections that jeopardize a majority can prompt electoral leaders to make the pronouncements that contribute to the climate of change and possibility that nourishes movements.

But politicians are not the only communicators. The conflicts that movements generate often lend them considerable communicative force. This is no small thing. Ordinarily, political communication is dominated by political leaders and the mass media, who together define the parameters of the political universe, including understandings of which sorts of problems should properly be considered political problems and which sorts of remedies are available. Just how deeply this communication penetrates popular understandings is disputed.[6] But whatever the hidden beliefs of people, it is hard to dispute the monopoly by the powerful on public and political communication, at least in the absence of movements.

Movements can break that monopoly, at least for a brief moment.

Movements mount marches and rallies, strikes and sit-ins, theatrical and sometimes violent confrontations.[7] The inflammatory rhetoric and dramatic representations of collective indignation associated with these tactics project new definitions of social reality, or definitions of the social reality of new groups, into public discourse. They change understandings not only of what is real but of what is possible and of what is just. As a result, grievances that are otherwise naturalized or submerged become political issues.

Movements do what Schattschneider long ago said had to be done to change the outcome of political contests. Movements raise new issues, and when new issues take center stage of politics, the balance of political forces changes, in two ways. First, by raising new issues or articulating latent issues, movements activate groups that might otherwise remain inactive.[8] Second, new issues are likely to create new cleavages, with far-reaching consequences for the balance between contending forces. Cleavages are what electoral politicians seek to avoid, but they are the key to understanding the impact of movements on electoral politics and, in particular, to understanding why movements sometimes win victories.

Ordinarily, movement strategists explain their activities in terms similar to electoral organizers, as efforts to mobilize adherents and even to mobilize voters and voter majorities. The dramatic projection of movement issues can activate followers, to be sure; and in rare instances, as in the case of the nuclear freeze movement, the consensual causes advanced by the movement are of a kind that arouse little overt opposition. But most often movements polarize while they activate. Typically, the processes that mobilize hitherto inactive groups to the movement's cause also mobilize an opposition. Moreover, because movements raise new issues, they frequently polarize groups along different axes than those that organize and divide the major parties. The new cleavages create problems for electoral leaders trying to hold together voter majorities, forcing reluctant politicians to make choices on issues they would otherwise avoid. Movements wrest concessions from reluctant political leaders when concessions are seen as a way to avert threatened defections, or to staunch the flow of defections already occurring, or sometimes when concessions are viewed as a way to rebuild an already fragmented coalition by enlarging or solidifying support from one side of the cleavage line.

Of course, the choices between constituent groups that are forced on electoral leaders by movement-generated conflict may well continue to fuel conflict and therefore threaten a new wave of electoral defections. Under these conditions, movement victories may be short-lived. The opposition provoked by the movement, and goaded and perhaps strengthened by its victories, may thus eventually prevail in intraparty contests. Or the electoral fragmentation that nourished the movement in the first place, and that the movement in turn worsened, can lead to the defeat of the party that is both the target and the social base of the polarizing movement.

In sum, movements grow when electoral leaders, prodded by signs of instability in their coalitions, communicate new possibilities to hold together their majorities. But as movements grow, nourished by the mood of hope generated by efforts at conciliation, they become the agents of widening cleavages, even dividing or shattering electoral coalitions. In this sense, movements mobilize electoral dealignments. The conflicts movements generate may also set in motion the voter shifts that eventually result in new electoral alignments.

We think the dissensual politics provoked by the interaction of movements and the coalition builders of the two-party system is illustrated by a number of twentieth century movements, including the labor movement of the 1930s, the civil rights movement of the 1960s, and the "new social movements" of the 1970s, particularly the dual movements focused on gender roles: the feminist movement, on the one hand, and the allied pro-life and Christian right movements on the other.

The emergence of the New Deal realignment is typically traced to the election of 1932, when Franklin Delano Roosevelt won office after a long period of Republican domination of the national government.[9] In this version of the story, dealignment and realignment in the 1930s were a simple voter response to economic catastrophe. It is no doubt true that economic collapse prompted many voters to turn against the majority Republican Party, setting dealignment in motion. And Roosevelt tried to take advantage of the discontent generated by economic hardship in his campaign rhetoric denouncing economic royalists and celebrating the common man. However, when the 1932 returns were in, there was little pattern to the Roosevelt sweep. He had carried all but a few states in the Northeast and had won among all income groups. In other words, economic collapse had shattered the old Republican majority, but the electoral coalition of the New Deal era had not yet emerged.

In fact, Roosevelt came to office oriented toward measures that would revive business and bring order to the financial markets. It was escalating protests among the unemployed and workers, protests fueled by hardship and the sense of political possibility that Roosevelt's rhetoric communicated, that changed FDR's course, forcing him to inaugurate extensive emergency relief and public works measures. Later, Roosevelt tried to conciliate growing demands among workers for government protection of the right to organize, demands that had been encouraged if not precipitated by New Deal promises encoded in the National Industrial Recovery Act. Throughout 1934 and 1935, the administration tried to pick a path between growing worker anger at the failure of the administration to enforce the right to organize and growing business indignation at the disruptive strikes staged by workers encouraged by federal appeasement. As the strike movement escalated, a series of administration halfway measures only backfired, encouraging worker demands precisely because appeasement revealed the political vulnerability of the regime. Meanwhile, federal conciliation and the strike wars it seemed to encourage drove a substantial segment of the business leadership virtually to declare war on the administration and in the 1934 election to go so far as to launch a short-lived third-party effort. Finally and reluctantly, Roosevelt was forced to choose between escalating worker demands and an enraged business community. With the 1936 election approaching, Roosevelt threw his support behind the National Labor Relations act, despite "bitter and sustained opposition to the act by employers before and after its passage."[10]

The polarizing impact of the labor movement had forced Roosevelt's hand. It also helped to shape the New Deal coalition that emerged from the interplay of movements and electoral politics, to which movements among the aged and farmers contributed. The shapeless—and class-less—Democratic majority of 1932 was steadily reconstituted, and by the late 1930s the pattern was clear. Workers, especially less skilled workers, were identified with the Democrats, and business and professional strata tilted sharply to the Republicans.[11] The New Deal realignment had taken form, and the conflicts generated by the movements of the era had helped to form it.

While the electoral realignment that emerged from the 1930s was defined in part by class, it was just as importantly defined by section. Working-class voters in the urban North were linked in an electoral alliance with the Democratic white South. This regional coalition was not entirely new, since the Democrats had been the party of both big-city machines and the one-party South since the nineteenth century. And the coalition had not always held together, as was evident in the elections of the 1920s, and particularly in the election of 1928, when the Democratic alliance had temporarily shattered on the shoals of sectional religious and cultural conflict. But in the 1930s New Deal conciliation of the South, together with the temptations and rewards of national power, brought the southern political stratum home to the national Democratic Party and, for a time, kept it loyal.

These rewards, however, contributed to the ultimate fragmentation of the coalition. New Deal policies promoted the industrialization of the South and also subsidized a more capital-intensive agriculture. Economic development, in turn, had political repercussions that first weakened and then destroyed the coalition. In that process, movements that were themselves a reflection of economic change and the ensuing electoral repercussions played a critical role.

The economic modernization of the South had two main effects that bear on the role of movements in the ultimate fragmentation of the New Deal coalition. First, modernization changed the class structure of the South, spurring the growth of a new middle class, including a professional middle class, who in the 1950s became natural recruits for a resurgent southern Republicanism.[12] Second, a more capital-intensive agriculture led to the displacement of millions of black and white share-croppers and tenants, as well as small farmers whose land was gobbled up by large owners who were mechanizing with federal subsidies and who were better able to make use of federal subsidies for idle land. Most of the displaced whites gravitated to nearby towns and small cities, where they were not unwelcome. But displaced blacks tended to migrate to the big cities of the South and North, where ghetto neigh-borhoods established earlier provided a kind of protective haven. In the cities, they became voters and increasingly important constituents of the urban and northern wing of the Democratic Party. And because segre-gation had thus concentrated their numbers, blacks became a potentially critical voter bloc in the industrial states with the largest number of elec-toral votes.

The events that followed reveal first the role of third parties as agents of electoral dissensus, and then the similar and in this case more defini-tive role of social movements. As the 1948 election approached, Harry Truman, the Democratic incumbent, confronted Henry Wallace's third-party challenge from the left, which threatened to attract black (and labor) voters. This explains Truman's attempt to conciliate blacks before the 1948 election by appointing a U.S. Commission on Civil Rights and then by incorporating some of the commission's recommen-dations into the Democratic platform.

With that, the blow was struck that revealed an emerging fissure in the New Deal coalition. Four Deep South delegates bolted the nominat-ing convention, and angry southern politicians formed a States Rights Party with Strom Thurmond as their candidate. Truman won the elec-tion, but the Democratic percentage of the southern white vote plum-meted, to 53 percent from FDR's 85 percent in 1936.

Once the Henry Wallace threat evaporated, the Democrats tried to conciliate the South. But the forces unleashed by southern moderniza-tion now had a momentum of their own. Each gesture of recognition of civil rights from northern liberals fueled the anger of southern whites even as it sparked the hopes of urban blacks in both the South and the North. Many observers treat the 1954 Supreme Court *Brown* decision striking down the "separate but equal" doctrine in public education as the instigator of this conflict. Certainly it was an important trigger, per-haps comparable to the "right to organize" announced in the National Industrial Recovery Act of 1933.[13] In the wake of the decision, southern whites mobilized in a movement of "massive resistance" led by the polit-ical leaders of the southern states. And with this new legitimation from the highest court in the land, the southern black movement for civil rights began in earnest with the Tallahassee and Montgomery boycotts.

In the campaigns of 1952 and again in 1956, Democratic nominee Adlai Stevenson tried earnestly to soothe an alarmed white South with talk of "states' rights." The Deep South did in fact return to Democratic columns, but in the more industrial states of the outer South, the Republican trend among middle class voters accelerated, encouraged of course by the popularity of Eisenhower.[14]

Moreover, to worsen Democratic troubles, heretofore loyal black voters began to defect from the Democratic Party in the 1956 election. The extraordinary excitement that must have been generated by early civil rights protests, combined with Stevenson's less-than-heroic efforts to placate the white South, spurred marked defections among urban blacks, among whom Democratic voting fell from 80 percent in 1952 to 60 percent in 1956. And black turnout fell as well, especially in northern cities.[15] This last development was also a warning of growing racial conflict within the party's ranks in the big cities, which was immobilizing Democratic mayors who might otherwise have worked to recruit black voters.

In the 1960 campaign, Kennedy confronted these troubles in the party and, influenced one suspects by Stevenson's sorry record in the South, decided to try to win back defecting black voters by reviving the civil rights promises of Harry Truman in his platform (and by the widely publicized telephone call from Robert Kennedy to Coretta King when Martin Luther King was jailed in Atlanta during the campaign). The strategy scored a modest success. Despite losing much of the South— Florida, Tennessee, and Virginia, as well as Alabama and Mississippi, whose electors were unpledged—Kennedy won a narrow victory. A modest upturn in the black Democratic vote, from 60 to 68 percent, was part of the reason.

But necessarily, party leaders trying to hold majorities together are not brinksmen. After he took office, Kennedy tried to heal the growing fissure in the party by avoiding civil rights initiatives and conciliating the white South. The escalating civil rights movement and the tide of support it generated in the North, especially among black voters, and escalating white southern anger and resistance, forced his hand. By the summer of 1963, in the wake of the turbulent Birmingham civil rights demonstrations and Governor George Wallace's flamboyant personal

confrontation with federal officials to bar two black students from entering the University of Alabama, Kennedy finally moved on his promises
of 1960, sending major civil rights legislation to the Congress, which
Lyndon Johnson pushed through after Kennedy's assassination.[16] A year
later, as the civil rights demonstrators were again locked in combat with
Governor Wallace at Selma, Johnson called on Congress for a voting
rights act, which was signed into law in August 1964, even as civil rights
demonstrations escalated.

As everyone now agrees, the party that finally and reluctantly conceded these historic civil rights victories was badly damaged by them,
and its chances to win the presidency were especially damaged. The
solid South, which had kept the Democratic Party alive as a national
party during the lean years of Republican domination before 1932, and
had been its most reliable base after 1932, was gone. As early as 1964,
George Wallace made a primary bid in the presidential contest and did
alarmingly well in the early primaries in Indiana and Wisconsin,
although his candidacy in the South was blocked by southern leaders
who were now ready to support Republican nominee Barry Goldwater.
Wallace ran again in 1968, this time as a third-party candidate. In the
aftermath of the debacle of pitched battles between police and demonstrators at the 1968 Democratic convention, he drew support not only
from the white South but from previously Democratic working-class
whites in the North who felt themselves besieged by mounting black
demands over jobs, housing, welfare, schools, and for a share of local
political power, on the one hand, and by the student antiwar movement
and its class and cultural provocations on the other hand.

Republican strategists had taken note of the fracturing impact of race
conflict on the Democratic Party, and they maneuvered to take advantage of it, beginning in the early 1960s with the creation by the Republican National Committee of its own "Operation Dixie" campaign to build
a Republican Party in the South.[17] Later, as race conflict spread to the
North, turning black and white Democratic constituencies against one
another, the Nixon administration added fuel to the flames with the
"Philadelphia Plan," which called for affirmative action in the construction trades,[18] and it used the Justice Department to secure the court
orders for school busing that precipitated virtual race war in many cities.

When the black movement subsided and the dust settled, the South had become the most solidly Republican section in the nation, and a majority of the white working class had joined the ranks of "Reagan Republicans."

So, if there is a final reckoning, it must be that the civil rights movement won, but in the process badly damaged the electoral base of the party that yielded it victories, helping to bring a Republican administration to power for most of the past quarter century. Still, it is hard to see how the movement had much of a choice. The southern wing of the Democratic Party had been the implacable foe of black political and economic aspirations for a century. Only as the southern political establishment was being driven out of the party were national Democratic leaders willing to act on black demands. Democratic leaders resisted this hemorrhaging, trying by delay and evasion to hold their coalition together. But the combined impact of movements and third parties in galvanizing voters doomed their efforts, so the divisions widened, civil rights victories became possible, and except in the aftermath of Watergate, the party that ceded them did not regain the presidency for a quarter of a century.

The black movement had not yet subsided before a series of other movements emerged focusing on peace, environmental, and gender issues, which have come to be called the "new social movements." Certainly these movements took heart, strategy, and in some cases activists from the civil rights movement and also from the student antiwar movement of the 1960s. And they were similar to the black movement in contributing to the conflicts that continued to beset the Democrats in 1972 when, after a chaotic Democratic convention, George McGovern was defeated by Richard Nixon in a landslide, an outcome foreshadowed in the 1968 election when the Wallace and Nixon candidacies together had claimed an emerging Republican majority of 57 percent. [19]

But the strand in the complicated interplay of movements and electoral politics that we want to try to disentangle here has to do with gender and with the movements focusing specifically on gender issues that emerged in the tumultuous late-1960s and early 1970s. We think a good case can be made that as much of the movement activity of this era subsided, the gender-focused movements actually escalated and were especially important in the dissensus politics of the past two decades.

The gender politics advanced by social movements of the right and the left first added to the fracturing of the Democratic Party that race conflict had begun, helping to keep a new Republican majority in power. But gender conflicts continued, and even escalated, particularly as the pro-life movement gained courage and momentum from the conciliatory stance of Republican leaders. By the end of the 1980s, the stage was set again for a new period of electoral dissensus and dealignment, this time working its way through the Republican majority coalition.

The movements that forced gender issues to the fore of national politics in the 1970s were expressions of profound and long-term changes in American society, including the loosening of family forms, the entry of women into the labor market, and the rise in the 1960s of an era of cultural permissiveness. These developments in turn helped give rise to a liberatory movement among women, especially among better-educated and better-placed women positioned to take advantage of the relaxation of old restrictions in the family and the labor market. The "women's liberation" movement that emerged fought on a number of fronts for enlarged economic and political opportunities for women, and movement activists naturally fought for these liberal causes within the Democratic Party. But these particular battles were framed by a larger one: the movement both directly and by implication challenged the most ancient of subordinations, the subordination of women to men that had always been understood as rooted in biology and therefore as inevitable and fated.

A social movement that strikes at such primordial understandings inevitably provokes strong reactions, especially among people skill rooted in traditional relationships and traditional communities who feel that their very identities are at risk.[20] In fact, there is a strong parallel between the civil rights and women's movements that is not often recognized, since both dared to challenge deeply imprinted identities rooted in ideas about biological destiny. No wonder both movements provoked counter movements of intractable fury. And no wonder that the pro-life movement and the Christian right to which it was allied, by reasserting the sanctity of traditional gender roles, of childbearing, and of "family values," emerged as the most significant protest movements of the 1980s.

Both civil rights and gender issues also contributed to the fracturing of the Democratic Party, which had formerly housed the constituencies who were now aroused and at war. True, the conventional wisdom attributes little significance to gender conflict, ascribing the fracturing of the Democratic Party mainly to race conflict and to a lesser extent to the "new class" activists in the new social movements. But conflict over gender roles was also cleaving the party, probably along the same or similar fault lines. The white southerners and white working-class northerners who were initially incensed by racial challenges were only a few years later reacting against the threat to traditional gender roles posed by the modernizing women's movement.

Or so Republican strategists clearly thought. How else explain the centrality given to symbolic gender issues by the Republican leadership, beginning in 1980? The elimination from the Republican platform that year of the traditional Republican endorsement of the ERA is one example. Then there is the use of *Roe v. Wade* as a virtual litmus test for Supreme Court nominations. The hard-line positions against abortion publicized by Republican presidents and presidential contenders is another example. Consider the international furor created when the administration refused to fund family-planning programs that included abortion in the third world. Or the notoriety generated here by the "gag rule" prohibiting the provision of abortion information in U.S. family-planning agencies that received federal funds.

These highly publicized moves by Republican national leaders begin to make sense when we view them as a strategy to worsen the cleavages that had been created within the Democratic Party by the deeply conflictual issues of the feminist and pro-life movements. It was within the Democratic Party that the women's movement's demands for an emancipatory understanding of gender were played out, and it was primarily among traditional Democratic constituencies that these issues had provoked anguish, fear, and partisan defection. For more than a decade, the Republican leadership worked both to exacerbate and assuage these anxieties, creating the odd spectacle of the powerful leaders of the richest and most technologically advanced country in the world in the grip of an anachronistic fundamentalism.

The election of 1992 and the campaign that preceded it suggests, however, that the majority coalition forged in part by conflict over gender politics is itself vulnerable to the continuing conflict and fragmentation caused by the dualistic movements advancing gender politics. The Republicans continued to stress their appeals to the traditionalist movements. Their 1992 convention was virtually given over to a theatrical celebration of a gender traditionalism and the celebrities associated with it, a kind of mirror image of the Democratic convention of 1972 where social movement activists also seemed to have a commanding role. But as the pro-life and Christian right movements escalate, forcing more strident affirmation of traditional gender roles, they may well be generating new cleavages, this time within the Republican coalition. This is what the Democrats seemed to hope for, styling a convention and campaign that was modern and socially liberal, pro-choice, and in which women politicians figured prominently. The 1992 election returns suggest the outcome of the issues raised by the dual gender movements and the fissures they generated. It is not so much that the Republican candidate lost, for that outcome has many causes. Rather, what bears on our argument about the role of social movements in generating dissensus politics is the shift of women voters away from Republican columns, especially the single mothers and working women who, whether through circumstances or choice, are not traditionalists.

In sum, we think a good deal of light can be cast on both movements and electoral politics by examining their interaction, and particularly by examining the contribution of movements to moments of electoral convulsion. The conflicts that give rise to movements, and that movements in turn escalate, sometimes overcome the stasis inherent in two-party electoral politics. Movements raise issues and generate conflicts that spur dealignment and realignment. In the process they may win victories from party leaders straining to hold majorities together. We think that the great domestic reforms of the twentieth century—from labor rights to civil rights to reproductive rights—were forced on party leaders who used reform to avert or stem voter defections.

But whether victorious or defeated, social movements are short-lived. The usual explanations point to the co-optation of movement leaders or to the exhaustion of movement participants, who grow weary of the taxing forms of political action that movements demand, both of which surely happen. More to the point of our argument here, however, social movements subside precisely because they transform the electoral context that brings them into being and nourishes them for a time. The conflicts promoted by social movements and the electoral shifts they set in motion tend to fragment and defeat the dominant party whose latent cleavages both made social movement politics possible and became the arena of movement action. That process unfolded in the Republican electoral coalition as the 1980s came to a close and helped to account for the defeat of the Republican contender in the presidential election of 1992, and of course in 1996.

What can movement leaders do then? During each of the historical episodes we have described, there was a moment when hope flourished that the mutual limits of movement and electoral politics could be overcome. Growing movements and the electoral instabilities they created combined to nourish the idea that something more enduring was possible than the perennial convulsive encounters between transient movement politics and intransigent electoral politics. The movements should turn to electoral politics, enter the party, and reform it, as when Bayard Rustin, standing at the cusp of the civil rights movement in 1965, called for a turn from "protest to politics."[21] As the civil rights movement lost momentum, its leaders did indeed move into electoral politics. SNCC leaders ran for local offices or for Congress, just as women are now doing and as they did in the 1920s, in the wake of winning the franchise.[22] So too, at least in a general way, did union leaders turn to electoral politics when they entered the inner councils of the Democratic Party some fifty years ago. But the record of these efforts in the past argues that the hope for a synthesis of party and movement is likely to be disappointed. When movement leaders become electoral politicians, they necessarily leave behind the distinctive movement power born of conflict. The imperatives of coalition building that shape electoral politics in a two-party system demand that leaders shun conflictual issues in order to build majorities. And, as former movement agitators bend to the dictates of electoral politics, the hope of reform necessarily awaits the next social movement and the next period of dissensus.

Originally published in 1968.

Notes

1. See for example Frances Fox Piven and Richard A. Cloward, *Poor People's Movements: Why they Succeed, How they Fail* (New York: Pantheon Books, 1977); Doug McAdam, *Political Process and the Development of Black Insurgency, 1930–1970* (Chicago: University of Chicago Press, 1982); Sidney Tarrow, *Power in Movement: Social Movements, Collective Action, and Politics* (New York: Cambridge University Press, 1994); Anne Costain, *Inviting Women's Rebellion* (Baltimore: Johns Hopkins University Press, 1992).

2. See for example E. E. Schattschneider, *Party Government* (New York: Rinehart and Co., 1942).

3. Theodore Lowi even suggests that the major parties collaborate with each other in a "tacit contract to avoid taking important issues to the voters." See his "The Party Crasher," *New York Times Magazine*, August 23, 1992.

4. See V. O. Key, "A Theory of Critical Elections," Journal of Politics 17 (February 1955); James Sundquist, *Politics and Policy* (Washington D.C.: Brookings Institution, 1973); Walter Dean Burnham, *Critical Elections and the Mainsprings of American Politics* (New York: W. W. Norton, 1970); Benjamin Ginsberg, "Critical Elections and the Substance of Party Conflict, 1844–1968," *Midwest Journal of Political Science* no. 16 (1972); Richard L. McCormick, *The Party Period and Public Policy* (New York: Oxford University Press, 1986).

5. For historical accounts of third-party efforts in the United States see Richard Hofstadter, *The Age of Reform: From Bryan to F.D.R.* (New York: Alfred A. Knopf, 1955); Keith J. Polakoff, *Political Parties in American History* (New York: Alfred A. Knopf, 1981); Lawrence Goodwyn, *Democratic Promise: The Populist Movement in America* (New York: Oxford University Press, 1976); Steven J. Rosenstone, Roy L. Behr, and Edward H. Lazarus, *Third Parties in America: Citizen Response to Major Party Failures* (Princeton, N.J.: Princeton University Press, 1984).

6. See James C. Scott, *Weapons of the Weak* (New Haven, Conn.: Yale University Press, 1985).

7. On the dramaturgical strategies of movements, see Robert Benford and Scott A. Hunt, "Dramaturgy and Social Movements: The Social Construction and Communication of Power," *Sociological Inquiry* 62 (February 1962).

8. On the relationship of issues to cleavages, see E. E. Schattschneider, *The Semisovereign People* (New York: Holt, Rinehart and Winston, 1960).

9. Some analysts, however, date the beginnings of realignments in the election of 1928, when the candidacy of Catholic Al Smith made religion the pivotal—and polarizing—issue of the campaign, attracting new voters from among Catholics and driving Southern voters out of Democratic columns.

10. The quote is from William G. Domhoff, *The Power Elite and the State: How Policy Is Made in America* (New York: Aldine de Gruyter, 1990), 65. On the political forces responsible for the NLRA, see also Piven and Cloward, *Poor People's Movements*, chapter 3, and *Why Americans Don't Vote* (New York: Pantheon Books, 1988), chapter 5; Irving Bernstein, *The Lean Years: A History of the American Worker, 1930–33* (Baltimore: Penguin Books, 1970); Michael Goldfield, "Labor's Subordination to the New Deal. Part One: The Influence of Labor on New Deal Labor Legislation" (paper delivered at the annual meeting of the American Political Science Association, New Orleans, 1985); Thomas Ferguson, "From Normalcy to New Deal: Industrial Structure, Party Competition and American Public Policy in the Great Depression," *International Organization* 38 (Winter 1984).

11. By 1936, "businessmen switched to Landon while workers went the other way." See Richard Jensen, *The Winning of the Midwest: Social and Political Conflict, 1888–1896* (Chicago: University of Chicago Press, 1981), 212. Among high-income voters, Roosevelt ran 29 percentage points behind the Republican candidate. For responses to a Gallup poll on party identification in 1940, see James Sundquist, *Dynamics of the Party System: Alignment and Realignment of Political Parties in the United States* (Washington, D.C.: Brookings Institution, 1973), 202.

12. On this development, see Thomas Sugrue, "The Origins of White Backlash in the Urban North" (prepared for delivery at the annual meeting of the American Political Science Association, Chicago, September 3–6, 1992).

13. The decision itself however was the culmination of a long series of efforts by the NAACP, aided by civil rights lawyers in the Department of Justice. See Richard M. Valelly, "National Parties and Racial Disenfranchisement," ed. Paul E. Peterson, *Classifying by Race* (Princeton: Princeton University Press, 1985).

14. In 1948, the Democrats lost Alabama, Louisiana, Mississippi, and South Carolina. In 1952 and 1956 they recaptured these states, only to lose Florida, Virginia, Tennessee, and Texas, and Louisiana as well in 1956.

15. This discussion draws from Piven and Cloward, *Poor People's Movements*, chapter 4. On black voting patterns in 1956, see Henry Lee Moon, *Balance of Power: The Negro Vote* (Garden City: Doubleday, 1948), 221; Samuel Lubell, *White and Black*, 2d ed. rev. (New York: Harper Colophon Books, 1966); and Oscar Glantz, "The Negro Voter in Northern Industrial Cities," *Western Political Quarterly*, no. 13 (December 1960).

16. On the impact of the civil rights movement on presidential decision making in this period, see Mark Stern, "Calculating Visions: Civil Rights Legislation in the Kennedy and Johnson Years," *Journal of Policy History* 5 (1993); Arthur Schlesinger, Jr., *A Thousand Days* (Boston: Houghton Mifflin, 1965); Theodore Sorenson, *Kennedy* (New York: Harper & Row, 1965); and Sundquist, *Politics and Policy*.

17. See Philip A. Klinkner, "Race and the Republican Party: The Rise of the Southern Strategy in the Republican National Committee, 1960–1964" (paper deliv-

ered at the annual meeting of the American Political Science Association, Chicago, September 3–6, 1992).

18. See Jill Quadagno, *Unfinished Democracy: Rights, Race and American Social Policy* (New York: Oxford University Press, 1994).

19. This is of course the title of Kevin Phillips's 1969 book.

20. For interpretations of these "existential" screams, see Jane Sherron De Hart, "Gender on the Right: Meanings behind the Existential Scream," *Gender and History* 3 (Autumn 1991): 261; Kristen Luker, *Abortion and the Politics of Motherhood* (Berkeley: University of California Press, 1984); and Jane Mansbridge, *Why We Lost the ERA* (Chicago: University of Chicago Press, 1986).

21. Bayard Rustin, "From Protest to Politics," *Commentary*, no. 39 (February 1965).

22. For a discussion of the failed electoral strategy of the suffrage movement, see Anna L. Harvey, "Uncertain Victory: The Electoral Incorporation of Women into the Republican Party, 1920–1928" (paper delivered at the annual meeting of the American Political Science Association, Chicago, September 3–6, 1992).

15

Organizing the Poor:
An Argument with Frances Fox Piven and
Richard A. Cloward's *Poor People's Movements*

WILLIAM A. GAMSON AND EMILIE SCHMEIDLER

One unintended consequence of the movements of the past twenty years has been a shift in the angle of vision from the academy. By long tradition, social movements had been viewed with suspicion and disdain by academic social scientists.[1] The dominant theories debunked the motives of participants or reduced them to hapless victims of social forces that produced stress and social breakdown. The main intellectual task in the study of social movements was an analysis of the structural conditions that produce this symptom of social pathology.

The movements of the 1960s and 1970s changed this outlook. An earlier generation had been traumatized by the rise of fascism and the mobilization of various right-wing groups. Their view of the Left was refracted through the postwar red scare and the Cold War lens. Fear and disdain, not admiration, drew them to the study of social movements.

The successes of the civil rights movement, the anti-war movement, the women's movement, and the environmental movement attracted a new generation of social scientists. When they did not themselves actively participate in such movements, they supported the aspirations of participants. And this was especially true for what Piven and Cloward call "poor people's movements." Accounts of farm-worker struggles, of tenant unions, of welfare-rights efforts, of dissident movements within unions, were invariably written by sympathizers, if not participant observers.

Inevitably, this shift in sympathies produced a different theory of social movements. Attention turned from the social forces and conditions that produce movements, to the question of how movements produce their success. Students of social movements focused on issues of strategy and tactics, looking at the problem from the vantage of those engaged in purposeful efforts at social change. A new set of questions animated studies of social movements: How does one parry repression and other, gentler efforts at social control? How does one generate and maintain commitment and loyalty to groups engaged in collective action? How does one avoid factional splits that weaken the capacity for united action? How does one exploit the vulnerabilities and schisms of antagonists?

Resource mobilization theory represents the clearest articulation of this alternative view.[2] The theory explains how challengers, lacking routine access to the polity, are able to gain collective control over the resources of some constituency and to use them in some form of rebellious collective action. The interplay between the efforts of challengers to bring about change and the efforts of their targets at social control provides the central dynamic.

To find a literature that analyzed the strategy of collective action, resource-mobilization theorists were forced to look outside the academy. They found inspiration in the writings of political activists and revolutionaries and in the historic debates on the Left about organization and strategy. The competing arguments of Marxists, syndicalists, and anarchists; the great revisionist debate in the German Social Democratic Party; Marx's analysis of the French Revolution of 1848; Lenin's *What Is To Be Done?*; Trotsky's *History of the Russian Revolution*; Michel's *Political Parties*—these are the canons. From more contemporary sources, resource-mobilization theorists draw on the writings of community organizers such as Saul Alinsky and Si Kahn, as well as on various manuals for direct action and organizing by movement activists.[3]

Solidarity and organization receive central places in the theory. Some organization is necessary to carry a challenge, but the argument is not for a particular form. There is no special brief in the theory for centralized, bureaucratic, mass-membership organizations over loosely organized networks of local action centers. The type of organization that works best is treated as an empirical issue. One must specify the conditions under which one type of organization is better than another, rather than search for a universal form.

But organization, in a more generic sense, is necessary. Tilly treats it as one of the four central components of collective action, along with interests, mobilization, and opportunity. By organization, he means the degree of common identity and unifying structure. The extent of a group's collective action is a function, in part, of the intensity of its organization.[4]

Oberschall argues that "For sustained resistance or protest, an organizational base and continuity of leadership are...necessary." He discusses different forms of organization and concludes that "If the movement can successfully build up a centralized organizational structure accepted by all, the choice of leaders and collective decision-making can become regularized and the resources of the members fully exploited for the pursuit of the movement's goals."[5]

Most of these writers emphasize the imperatives that a challenger must face because it operates in an intense conflict situation. Gamson summarizes a chapter on "combat readiness" by arguing that "Challenging groups are involved in political conflict. They are ready for such combat if they maintain a structure of specific commitments on the part of members that enables them to conduct routine tasks between battles so that they are ready for action when necessary." He concludes that "there are definite advantages for a challenging group...to organize itself for facility in political combat."[6] McCarthy and Zald note that "because resources are necessary for engagement in social conflict, they must be aggregated for collective purposes.... Resource aggregation requires some minimal form of organization."[7]

It is more infrastructure than a particular form of organization that is emphasized in resource mobilization theory—particularly structures of solidarity and communication. Collective action is a craft, there are skills and routines for carrying it out. The presence of an infrastructure, generally maintained by an array of organizations, makes it easier to aggregate resources and to use them in collective action.

Enter *Poor People's Movements*

In the midst of this revision in the academy, Piven and Cloward published a major treatise, *Poor People's Movements* (1977). Their book contains both a general argument and a detailed case analysis of four
American movements: unemployed workers and industrial workers in
the 1930s, civil rights and welfare rights in the 1960s.

The relationship between *Poor People's Movements* and resource mobilization theory is a curious one. Piven and Cloward have nothing but
obloquy for social-movement organizations. These entities are not
responsible for the successes that are achieved. "Whatever influence
lower-class groups occasionally exert in American politics does not
result from organization, but from mass protest and the disruptive consequences of protest.... Protest wells up in response to momentous
changes in the institutional order. It is not created by organizers and
leaders.... Protest movements are shaped by institutional conditions,
and not by the purposive efforts of leaders and organizers" (36–37).[8]

Not only do movement organizations deserve no credit for successes
but, worse, they are an impediment to it. "Our main point," they write
in their introduction, "is not simply that efforts to build organizations
are futile. The more important point is that by endeavoring to do what
they cannot do, organizers fail to do what they can do. During those
brief periods in which people are roused to indignation, when they are
prepared to defy the authorities to whom they ordinarily defer,...those
who call themselves leaders do not usually escalate the momentum of
the people's protests.... All too often, when workers erupted in strikes,
organizers collected dues cards.... Organizers not only failed to seize
the opportunity presented by the rise of unrest, they typically acted in
ways that blunted or curbed the disruptive force which lower-class
people were sometimes able to mobilize.... Organization-building
activities tended to draw people away from the streets and into the
meeting rooms" (xxi–xxii).

With such a different view of organization, one might expect Piven
and Cloward to be at swords' points with resource-mobilization theorists. In fact, this has not happened at all. *Poor People's Movements* has sev-

eral quotations from the resource-mobilization literature that was available at the time Piven and Cloward wrote. In all cases, they draw on this body of work sympathetically, emphasizing points that buttress their arguments. There is no critical reference or expression of disagreement.

Reviews of *Poor People's Movements* in the leading American political science and sociology journals were written by scholars with a resource-mobilization perspective. Lipsky, writing in the *American Political Science Review*, called it an "influential and important book" and found many reasons to applaud their effort. Jenkins, in a review essay in *Contemporary Sociology*, described it as "certainly the most provocative, if not the most important political study to appear in years," and as a member of that "distinctive genre of works that combine clear-headed analysis with practical commitments to social change." Both reviews go on to raise questions and critical points about the central argument, but there is no polemic here.[9] Resource mobilization work published since 1977 finds points of agreement with *Poor People's Movements* and, when disagreeing, does so in mild, comradely terms.

How can we account for the mutual respect and lack of antagonism between two schools whose ideas on organization seem so fundamentally at loggerheads? First, each school is attempting to exorcise a different devil. For the resource-mobilization theorists, the unfriendly spirit is in the academy, looking at movements from outside with fear and disdain. The intellectual scaffolding they were attempting to dismantle emphasized the expressive and reactive nature of social movements, stimulated by structural strains and social breakdowns.

For Piven and Cloward, the unfriendly spirit is not in the academy but in the meeting room of leftist organizations. *Poor People's Movements* is haunted by apparatchiks, mouthing platitudes about the importance of organization building, while the opportunities for direct action fritter away. Resource-mobilization writers feel no need to defend such a target. Who loves apparatchiks? Most of them have had their own wearying experiences with those who allow organizations to become an end in their own right, at the expense of movement goals. Piven and Cloward's polemic cannot help but strike some sympathetic chords. They, in turn, have no reason to defend traditional collective-behavior theory, and they certainly do not share the fear and disdain that lies behind it. As we will argue below, they depend on it and share its premises more than they realize, but this is through assumptions that they do not make explicit.

Both schools write from the vantage point of movement participants, in contrast to traditional collective-behavior theorists. For resource-mobilization theorists, Piven and Cloward are in their camp, asking the same sort of questions about what it takes for movements to succeed. Shared political sympathies make disagreements seem narrower and more technical. Piven and Cloward are warmly sympathetic to the aspirations of the movements they describe and, in the case of the welfare-rights movement, were important and influential participants as well. Both schools are interested in the special problems of relatively powerless groups, operating outside of the pluralist bargaining system.

Finally, there are many specific points on which the arguments of the two schools converge. No resource-mobilization theorist would quarrel with Piven and Cloward's argument that organizers do not control the larger social forces that create opportunities for mass defiance and rebellion. Even such redoubtable disciples of organization as Lenin and Trotsky readily concede the point. "Insurrection must rely upon a revolutionary upsurge of the people," counsels Lenin. "Without a guiding organization," Trotsky argues, "the energy of the masses would dissipate like steam not enclosed in a piston-box. But nevertheless what moves things is not the piston or the box, but the steam."[10]

An even more important affinity is their mutual emphasis on the efficacy of disruption as a strategy for relatively powerless groups. For Piven and Cloward, the power of disruption is at the center of their argument. "It is our judgment," they write (24), "that the most useful way to think about the effectiveness of protest is to examine the disruptive effects on institutions of different forms of mass defiance, and then to examine the political reverberations of those disruptions."

Resource mobilization theorists are more eclectic about strategy, considering various forms of collective action appropriate under different circumstances. But there is also a strong emphasis on the instrumental character of disruptive strategies—including violence—and the effectiveness of disruption for groups outside the polity. *Poor People's Movements* cites Gamson's *Strategy of Social Protest*, which "argues convincingly that rational calculations of the chances of success underlie the use of violence" (19). Tilly, in a similar vein, suggests a series of reasons why one should hesitate "to assume that collective violence is a sort of witless release of tension divorced from workaday politics: its frequent success as a tactic, its effectiveness in establishing or maintaining a group's political identity, its normative order, its frequent recruitment of ordinary people, and its tendency to evolve in cadence with peaceful political action." Gamson presents evidence that "unruly groups, those that use violence, strikes, and other constraints, have better than average success." When Piven and Cloward argue for the impact of mass defiance and disruption, they clearly converge with central strands of resource mobilization theory.[11]

Disagreements

We applaud this comradely spirit. There is no departure from it in acknowledging central points of disagreement. Piven and Cloward are writing primarily for an audience of Left intellectuals and political activists. They are inveighing against what they see as a tendency among some of their comrades to exaggerate the benefits of formal organization and to underestimate its costs. "In the main, the Left has held that formal mass-membership organizations are the correct vehicles by which the working class can drive toward power, at least in nonrevolutionary situations. This view is so deeply imprinted on the tradition of the left that debates about political strategy have been virtually confined to the question of how to build such bureaucratically structured membership organizations. The strategic usefulness of this organizational form, its effectiveness as a vehicle for influence, has been treated as axiomatic" (xv).

This is certainly overstated. Historically, there has been a continuing debate on the Left on this issue, among anarchists and Marxists, for example. Some traditions on the Left have emphasized such organizations but they have had ample skeptics and critics over the years. And it is certainly not axiomatic among resource-mobilization theorists who have their own internal debates about centralization versus decentralization and the optimum form of organization in varying political situations.

Piven and Cloward blur the issue of organization by assuming a particular form—bureaucratic, centralized, and mass membership. In fact, they pay little attention to the many possible forms, turning their argument into what appears as a general polemic against deliberate organizing efforts. Organizations, per se, are antithetical to insurgency, generally impeding it rather than aiding it. The influence of one is contrasted with the other. "Whatever influence lower-class groups occasionally exert in American politics does not result from organization, but from mass protest." In discussing the ineffectiveness and inadequacies of the old AFL unions in major industries during the 1930s, they note that "organization failed, and perhaps for that reason, the workers' movement grew."

Poor People's Movements is wrong in arguing that organization inevitably or usually dampens insurgency. On the contrary, it is a critical component in sustaining and spreading it. Certainly, some established organizations will act to tame and contain it but, in successful movements, others or new ones will be built to perform the necessary organizational functions. They will frequently act to inflame and spread defiance, particularly in the early stages of a movement. Typically, these mobilizing organizations will make use of an existing infrastructure of older organizations and informal networks.

Piven and Cloward are wrong in assuming that organizations must draw their primary resources from outside the constituency they are attempting to mobilize and represent. They argue (xxi) that "The flaw [in the organizational model] is, quite simply, that it is not possible to compel concessions from elites that can be used as resources to sustain oppositional organizations over time." In fact, the successful movements they studied built their collective action on indigenous resources, drawn from their own constituency, not from elites. These movements were able to extract social changes from elites that made possible their continuing control over their resource base, but this does not imply that elites were the source of these resources. We grant that some organizations may later become dependent on elites, once their constituency has demobilized. Cooptation by elites without any real change has certainly been the fate of some challengers, but it is far from inevitable.

Finally, *Poor People's Movements* offers no satisfactory substitute for organizations in explaining the insurgencies that play so central a role in their argument. In place of explanation, they offer the old war horses of historical inevitability and the dislocation and breakdown produced by social change. "Protesters win, if they win at all, what historical circumstances have already made ready to be conceded," they tell us. "Protest wells up in response to momentous changes in the institutional order" (36). As Jenkins observes, the particular version of breakdown theory on which they rely is close to the mass-society theories of the 1950s. "The loss of work and the disintegration of communities meant the loss of the regulating activities, resources, and relationships on which the structure of everyday life depends, and thus the erosion of the structures that bound people to existing social arrangements," Piven and Cloward write (11), in explanation of the institutional conditions for mass insurgency. Resource-mobilization theorists would agree that changes in the institutional order are critical in explaining protest, but they focus on the opportunities for mobilization that are created thereby instead of on the altered psychological state of the challengers.

We share with Piven and Cloward their conclusion that the civil-rights movement and the industrial-workers movement of the 1930s won important and continuing changes. But their animus against organization has led them to obscure the positive role movement organizations played in these successes. Their fealty to their argument has led them to present the history of these movements selectively, omitting important evidence that contradicts their interpretation. We confront the difference between us by reexamining these two movements here, taking a closer look at the evidence on the role of organization in the initial acts of insurgency that brought the movements to national prominence.

The Industrial Workers' Movement

Industrial workers are not exactly poor. With unionization, their median income became substantially higher than the national median. Even in the 1930s, the period that concerns us here, they were (as Piven and Cloward clearly recognize) a limiting case. Their structural position gave them a power to disrupt the economy that no other lower-class group had. The moral that Piven and Cloward draw from the success of the movement is that the "unorganized disruptions of industrial workers in the 1930s produced some political gains, but the organized electoral activities of the unions could not sustain them."

Just how unorganized were these disruptions? *Poor People's Movements* contains a thoroughly convincing account of the ineptitude of the old AFL unions in the major mass production industries in America during the early 1930s. It is undeniable that these older unions played little role in the spread of wildcat strikes and sit-downs during this period. Unplanned sit-downs were frequently stimulated by management speedups and other specific grievances.

We will reexamine two important strikes of the period, both of which Piven and Cloward discuss. For one of these strikes, the so-called "Battle of Toledo" in 1934, they offer evidence that seems clearly to contradict their central thesis. For the other, the great Flint sit-down strike at General Motors in the winter of 1936–37, they present incomplete evidence and ignore important organizational contributions that undermine their thesis.

Toledo, Ohio, had been badly hit by the depression. Unemployment in the city was high, and the employed were largely ununionized. However, Toledo was a stronghold of A. J. Muste's radical Unemployed Leagues. When a major strike for union recognition broke out at the Electric Auto-Lite Company, the company hired strikebreakers in an attempt to keep the plant open and reach full production.

With large numbers of unemployed to serve as potential strike breakers, the company was apparently in a strong position to break the union. However, the Musteites, Piven and Cloward tell us, mobilized large numbers of unemployed workers to reinforce the picket lines. When the company got a court order to limit picketing and to prohibit it altogether by League members, "the Musteites decided to violate the restraining order, and some local Communists joined in with the slogan 'Smash the Injunction by Mass Picketing' " (121–22).

It was these organizational cadres that began the picketing and returned to the picket line after being arrested and released. Emboldened by their example, as Piven and Cloward acknowledge, the picket lines grew and further arrests and court injunctions only stimulated more growth. Ultimately, Auto-Lite was forced to close the plant and the strike ended with an employer agreement to a 22 percent wage increase and limited recognition of the union. The role of organization here hardly seems one of blunting or curbing insurgency. On the contrary, as Piven and Cloward themselves acknowledge, these organizers "took the lead in encouraging strikers...to defy the courts."

In the Toledo case, Piven and Cloward present the evidence to undercut their own thesis, but they are more selective in presenting the details of the sit-down strike at General Motors in Flint, Michigan. They emphasize the relative spontaneity of the strike and point out that the union could claim as members only a small minority of Flint workers.

To understand the subtle interplay between spontaneity and organization in this act of mass defiance, it is worth examining the events that led up to it in some detail. It is true that the GM plants in Flint were largely unorganized. Fine estimates the paid-up membership in the United Automobile Workers (UAW) in Flint as 150 or less at the end of October 1936. An important incident occurred on 13 November at GM's Fisher Body Plant number 1, and by the end of the month, UAW membership in Flint had grown tenfold.[12]

A few days earlier, a local UAW organizer, Robert Travis, had met with forty UAW members. Travis discussed with them how to act in case of surprise developments, how they were to come together at a given spot in each plant, reach a quick decision, and take appropriate steps. Each of the men was given a "volunteer organizer" card with the Union's international seal. The UAW organizers were aware of the mood of defiance among their fellow workers and the wave of sit-down strikes that had been sweeping the country. They were preparing themselves to take advantage of the moment when it would happen in Flint.

They didn't have long to wait. Three nonunion welders at the Fisher 1 plant came on their shift on 12 November and discovered that one worker had been removed from the team. They simply stopped working and allowed a sizable job gap to develop before they were persuaded to go back to work. The next day, when they reported to work, two brothers on the team named Perkins found that they had been fired. They took their back pay and left without protest, but they did show their red cards (termination notices) to some of the union activists during the short lull before the next shift began. One of the union men,

Bud Simons, took the initiative by running through the main welding and soldering department yelling, "The Perkins boys were fired! Nobody starts working!"

The foreman tried to get the line moving again and, in frustration, grabbed a man named Joe Urban, the remaining member of the team of welders who had stopped the line the day before in spontaneous protest. As he was dragging him off to the office to fire him, he was challenged by the union activist, Simons, who yelled, "Come on, fellows, don't let him fire little Joe!" A dozen men responded, blocking the foreman's way. He quickly dropped Urban and went seeking help from the assistant plant manager.

The assistant plant manager approached Simons, who suggested that the workers get a committee together to see the plant manager. Simons made sure he had other union stalwarts on the committee, although he was not able to exercise complete control over those included. In the meeting with the plant manager, Simons served as spokesman for the group. "We've organized ourselves into a union," he told the plant manager. "It's the union you're talking to right now."

Simons insisted that the fired workers be rehired immediately, before work was resumed. The plant manager agreed that they could return later, but Simons held to the original demand. With the negotiations unsettled, the committee went back to the shop floor to hold an impromptu meeting, which ended with strong support to sit down until the fired men were back at work. One brother took several hours to locate before he returned to "a deafening cheer that could be heard in the most distant reaches of the quarter-mile plant."[13]

Throughout this incident, the presence of self-conscious organizational cadre played a crucial role. They didn't start the original sit-down, but they called the strike in response to the firing of those who did, they challenged the authority of the foreman, they acted as spokesmen during the negotiation, and they conducted the meeting that produced the critical strike vote backing the union line in the negotiation.

It is true that they were interested in signing up members but this did not mean that they discouraged defiance. By leading the strike, they were able to assert the claim of the union as the appropriate vehicle for rebellious collective action. And many workers responded to their militancy and success by joining the union. Within six weeks of this incident, the great GM sit-down strike of 1936–37 was underway. This strike, which Fine calls "the most significant American labor conflict in the twentieth century," had its strongest sustained support among the workers of Fisher 1.

It is true, as Piven and Cloward claim, that the Congress of Industrial Organizations (CIO) did not create the strike movement of industrial workers. But the ability of steel workers to threaten employers with credible strikes was greatly increased by the 433 organizers whom the CIO assigned when they launched the Steel Workers Organizing Committee. In sum, we see little evidence that organizers and leaders of the industrial workers movement tried to reduce the momentum of the people's protest and plenty of evidence that they contributed substantially to the successes that were won.

Nor were the movement organizers forced to become dependent on the resources of elites for survival. By mustering enough power to gain not only recognition but the automatic checkoff of union dues by employers, unions were able to stabilize and maintain their organizations with the resources of their own constituency.

The Civil Rights Movement

Like industrial workers, the Southern civil rights movement was not exactly a movement of poor people. Ministers and college students provided the critical cadre—that is, middle-class elements within the black community. Nevertheless, the southern black community as a collectivity was politically, socially, and economically dominated, held in check by repressive forms of social control.[14] If we allow "poor" to become a synonym for "powerless," and interpret it to include what resource mobilization theorists call "challengers," then the civil rights movement clearly qualifies.

The civil-rights movement succeeded in breaking the political and social domination of the Southern black community, although it failed to break the economic domination. Piven and Cloward acknowledge the successes but give little credit to organizations. When they discuss critical incidents in the movement, organizations remain hidden in the

319

background, and their language suggests a spontaneous hostile outburst.

When *Poor People's Movements* discusses the Montgomery bus boycott in 1955, an implied lack of organization runs through the account. "As word of the arrest [of Rosa Parks] spread, a remarkably instantaneous mobilization of the black leadership took place" (208). When they discuss the spread of sit-ins after Greensboro, North Carolina in 1960, they write that "The sit-in movement swept like a brush fire from one locale to another" (221). After the successful campaign in Birmingham, Alabama in 1963, they write, "protests burst forth across the country" (243). Much of the civil-rights movement appears, in their account, as a spontaneous eruption of black defiance.

Writing on the bus boycott, Piven and Cloward identify Rosa Parks as a "seamstress in a local department store," and describe one of the major leaders, E. D. Nixon, as a "well-known activist." They neglect to mention that E. D. Nixon had been state president of the National Association for the Advancement of Colored People (NAACP) for many years and that Rosa Parks had been his secretary there. Nixon activated the ministers who were to play such a critical role.

As Morris makes clear in his work describing the infrastructure of the civil-rights movement, the Montgomery bus boycott built on existing organizations in the black community. The Montgomery Improvement Association (MIA), the organization created to coordinate the boycott, was a local church-based organization. Furthermore, it mobilized the resources of existing secular organizations including the Women's Political Council, Progressive Democrats, Citizen's Committee, and the local NAACP.

The Montgomery bus boycott was one of a growing series of protests. Boycotts in Columbus, South Carolina and Baton Rouge, Louisiana, had occurred as early as 1953, and some MIA leaders were well aware of them. By the end of the Montgomery boycott, similar protests—typically led by a local minister and organized through the churches—were occurring or threatened in about thirty communities. It was the leaders of these boycotts who, along with other southern clergy, organized the Southern Christian Leadership Conference (SCLC) in 1957, attempting to accomplish across the South what the MIA had in Montgomery. The emergency of MIA and SCLC, Morris writes, "reflected the dominant role that churches began to play in confrontational politics by the late 1950s." The churches "supplied the movement with money, organized masses, leaders, highly developed communications, and relatively safe environments where mass meetings could be held to plan confrontations."[15]

After the successful conclusion of the Montgomery bus boycott, Martin Luther King published Stride Toward Freedom and traveled widely, speaking about the struggle. SCLC, the network of black churches, and other organizations spread the story of the boycott as a model of exemplary protest. The Fellowship of Reconciliation (FOR), for example, produced a short film, a comic book, and other material about the boycott that was widely used in black schools and colleges. Some 200,000 copies of the comic book were distributed.[16]

The NAACP contributed to this insurgency in major ways, particularly through its Youth Councils. They were part of the same movement network, linked through local movement centers that provided a nexus for civil rights organizations, black colleges, and movement churches. Many activists had more than one of these organizational bases, increasing the density and connectedness of the network.

By the time the 1960 sit-in occurred in Greensboro, North Carolina, there had been sit-ins in at least fifteen cities. Morris found that civil rights organizations initiated sit-ins in fourteen of the fifteen. The NAACP initiated sit-ins in nine of them, and the Congress for Racial Equality (CORE) played an important initiating role in seven cities. "The majority of these sit-ins," Morris writes, "were (1) connected rather than isolated, (2) initiated through organizations and personal ties, (3) rationally planned and led by established leaders, and (4) supported by indigenous resources."[17]

The Greensboro sit-in, while not the first, greatly intensified movement activity. Within two months, major sit-ins and related activity took place in at least sixty-nine cities in fourteen states throughout the South. Deliberate organizational activity had a lot to do with this rapid spread. The four college students who sat in at Greensboro and sparked the mass spread of the movement had all been members of the local NAACP Youth Council. At least two had read the FOR account of the Montgomery boycott. Within three days, the president of the local

NAACP chapter called the CORE national office for help. CORE rushed to take advantage of the opportunity, sending staff there and organizing sympathy boycotts in the North.[18]

The leaders of the Greensboro sit-in with the aid of the staff from CORE's national office, made contact with movement centers throughout North Carolina, South Carolina, and Virginia, urging them to train students for sit-ins. In April, the student participants created their own organization, the Student Non-Violent Coordinating Committee (SNCC), receiving help in the form of office space and money from existing organizations. The movement churches through SCLC, provided the base for training and planning. As Morris concludes, "The sit-ins spread across the South in a short period of time because activists, working through local movement centers, planned, coordinated, and sustained them".[19]

In their account of the Birmingham campaign, Piven and Cloward acknowledge the extensive planning involved, but they do little to illuminate the contribution of movement organization and infrastructure to mobilizing and sustaining mass defiance and the role of careful planning in making protest more effective. SCLC organized the campaign self-consciously in an effort to force a response from the federal government. Its strategy was built around a series of protests that systematically increased the level of confrontation.

Birmingham, Alabama, was widely known as a particularly brutal city. SCLC expected the police commissioner, "Bull" Connor, to react viciously to demonstrators. This would expose and symbolize southern racism in its most virulent form. Since Birmingham was increasingly an industrial center with northern ties, a mass confrontation there would produce a crisis affecting northern industrial interests who would help pressure the federal government to act.

SCLC believed it could mobilize a protest in Birmingham because it had strong connections through which to organize there and a relatively unified black community. Boycotts by SCLC's Birmingham affiliate during 1962 had already persuaded local merchants to agree to desegregate. Advance planning began as early as the fall of 1962, as SCLC began mobilizing resources through local and national movement networks. The challenge would come during the Easter season, six months later, to allow adequate time for preparation, to capitalize on the religious significance of the holiday, and to maximize the effectiveness of a boycott during a major buying season.

SCLC recruited local people willing to demonstrate and go to jail, organized workshops on nonviolence and direct action, and made detailed plans for specific demonstrations (for example, counting seats at lunch counters). In January 1963, Martin Luther King made a speaking tour to organize support through SCLC affiliates in many cities. SCLC contacted other movement organizations: the NAACP, CORE, SNCC, and the Southern Regional Council.

During the incubation period, SCLC conferred with its own lawyers and those of the NAACP's Legal Defense Fund about their planned defiance of anticipated court injunctions against demonstrations. When SCLC scheduled a major march for Good Friday and the city obtained an injunction that prohibited virtually any demonstration, SCLC was prepared. They defied the injunction and marched, and many were arrested and jailed as anticipated. The leader of the march, King, was kept in solitary confinement, producing the beginning of a federal response when President Kennedy called King's wife, Coretta Scott King, to assure her of his concern.

To preserve the momentum, SCLC devised a new tactic: disrupting downtown routines with thousands of young people because they would be less susceptible to economic retaliation than adults. SCLC staff recruited and trained several thousand students ranging from elementary school to college age. Shortly after Easter weekend, hundreds of students, in groups of ten to fifty, penetrated police lines and gathered to demonstrate downtown. When the demonstrations continued and grew in spite of arrests, the police used dogs, hoses, and clubs to prevent the youths from getting beyond the black section of town.

By this time, national media attention was focused on Birmingham. The Kennedy Administration sent Justice Department officials to Birmingham to mediate and contacted corporations with branches in Birmingham to urge them to press for a settlement. As the dance of demonstrations and attempted repression continued, federal pressure for a settlement increased. Local white civic and business leaders met with black leaders and Kennedy Administration representatives and, ultimately, a settlement was reached, ratifying a major victory for the civil-rights movement. A month later, President Kennedy sent legislation to Congress that eventually became the 1964 Civil Rights Act.

SCLC recognized that Birmingham was part of the newly industrializing South, and, hence, that a crisis there would not be localized. The presence of a repressive police commissioner made it highly likely that peaceful, nonviolent demonstrations would produce such a crisis. SCLC planned and focused the mass defiance that took place, making use of existing organization within the movement and the black community. It drew on familiar forms of solidarity such as nightly church meetings and preaching. SCLC escalated the confrontation rather than blunting it.

Nor were civil-rights organizations forced to become dependent on the resources of elites to sustain them. By breaking the pattern of social subordination and destroying the legal structure of Jim Crow laws that sustained it, the movement was able to stimulate black pride and permanently increase the capacity for collective action. By winning the enfranchisement of black voters in the South, many former movement activists were able to build a continuing political base in the black community. These accomplishments don't rest on some continuing dole of resources from a no-longer frightened elite.

Of course, not every existing organization in the black community encouraged insurgency. Some ministers were frightened by it and did not use their churches to help it along. The national office of the NAACP did not back the Greensboro sit-ins, nor did it provide lawyers to defend those arrested. But it is impossible to conclude from the overall evidence that the role of organization in the civil rights-movement was to dampen insurgency and discourage defiance.

Conclusion

Piven and Cloward aimed to be provocative, but they did so by badly overstating their argument. They are too fair-minded to ignore completely the contribution and courage of organizers in these movements. In spite of their thesis, they pay occasional obeisance to movement organizers and exemplars. "There were nevertheless organizers in these [labor] struggles," they acknowledge. "Some of these organizers were insurgents from the rank and file; others were radicals whose vision of an alternative future helped to account for their exemplary courage. Wherever these organizers came from, their vision helped goad workers into protest, and their courage gave workers heart and determination" (148).

Nor can they ignore the role of organizational activists in the civil-rights movement. They seek exemption from the implications of this activity by noting that these organizations were not much concerned with building formal membership and were "cadre organizations." But the idea of cadre organizations doesn't appear in the index, is introduced in an ad hoc manner to preserve their argument, and is never developed.[20]

When *Poor People's Movements* goes from general thesis to specific case analysis, the argument becomes less provocative but more reasonable. Apparently, it is not every organization that discourages insurgency, aspires to create a mass membership and hierarchical bureaucracy, and is willing to sell its birthright for a mess of elite pottage. Some movement organizations stimulate anger and defiance, and escalate the momentum of the people's protests. Some use their communication networks to spread disruptive forms of collective action and their organizational planning to chart strategy and timing, and to increase the effectiveness of collective action. Some institutionalize their dependence on their own constituency rather than come to rely on elite resources for survival. If some militant organizations later become tame and abandon their oppositional politics, other formerly docile organizations sometimes become centers of militancy—as the black churches and colleges did in the Southern civil rights movement.

The intellectual task becomes the more exacting one of figuring out what types of organization are likely to facilitate insurgency or abandon their oppositional politics under different historical conditions. *Poor People's Movements* might be interpreted as providing one kind of answer to this question, an argument against mass-membership organizations. This is certainly a much less dramatic and provocative thesis. But in the end, an analysis of the advantages and disadvantages of different forms of organization is a great deal more useful to students of social movements than the anti-organizational phillipic that the authors offer us.

Originally published in 1984.

Notes

1. We speak of the academy in North America. The European experience has parallels as well as important differences, but they are not relevant to our argument here.

2. Representative theoretical statements and empirical works include Michael Lipsky, "Protest as a Political Resource," *American Political Science Review* 62 (1968): 1114–58, Anthony Oberschall, *Social Conflict and Social Movements* (Englewood Cliffs, N.J.: Prentice-Hall, 1973), William A. Gamson, *Power and Discontent* (Homewood, Ill.: Dorsey, 1968), idem, *The Strategy of Social Protest* (Homewood, Ill.: Dorsey, 1975), John D. McCarthy and Mayer N. Zald, *The Trend of Social Movements in America* (Morristown, N.J.: General Learning Press, 1973), idem, "Resource Mobilization and Social Movements: A Partial Theory," *American Journal of Sociology* 82 (1977): 1212–34, Edward Shorter and Charles Tilly, *Strikes in France, 1830–1968* (Cambridge: Cambridge University Press, 1974), Charles Tilly, *From Mobilization to Revolution* (Reading, Mass.: Addison-Wesley, 1978), Mayer N. Zald and John D. McCarthy, *The Dynamics of Social Movements* (Cambridge, Mass.: Winthrop, 1979), and J. Craig Jenkins, "Sociopolitical Movements," in *Handbook of Political Science*, ed. Samuel Long (New York: Plenum, 1981).

3. See Saul Alinsky, *Rules for Radicals* (New York: Random House, 1971), and Si Kahn, *How People Get Power: Organizing Oppressed Communities for Action* (New York: McGraw-Hill, 1970), as well as Michael Walzer, *Political Action: A Practical Guide to Movement Politics* (Chicago: Quadrangle, 1971), George Lakey and Martin Oppenheimer, *Manual for Direct Action* (Chicago: Quadrangle, 1965), O. M. Collective, *The Organizers' Manual* (New York: Bantam, 1971), and Donald K. Ross, *A Public Citizen's Action Manual* (New York: Grossman, 1973).

4. Tilly, *From Mobilization to Revolution*, 62–69.

5. Oberschall, *Social Conflict and Social Movements*, 119, 144.

6. Gamson, *Strategy of Social Protest*, 107–108.

7. McCarthy and Zald, "Resource Mobilization and Social Movements," 1216.

8. Page references to *Poor People's Movements* are to the 1979 Vintage paperback reprint.

9. Michael Lipsky, review of *Poor People's Movements*, by Frances Fox Piven and Richard A. Cloward, *American Political Science Review* 73 (1979): 597–98; and J. Craig Jenkins, "What Is To Be Done: Movement or Organization?" *Contemporary Sociology* 8 (1979): 222–28.

10. V. I. Lenin, *Selected Works* (New York: International, 1967), 2: 365; and Leon Trotsky, *The History of the Russian Revolution* (New York: Monad, 1980), 1: xix.

11. Charles Tilly, "The Chaos of the Living City," in *Violence as Politics*, ed. Herbert Hirsch and David C. Perry (New York: Harper & Row, 1973); and Gamson, *Strategy of Social Protest*, 87.

12. Sidney Fine, *Sit-Down: The General Motors Strike of 1936–1937* (Ann Arbor: University of Michigan Press, 1969), 117.

13. Quoted from Henry Kraus, *The Many and the Few* (Los Angeles: Plantin, 1947, 54. For a fuller analysis of the entire incident, see William A. Gamson, Bruce Fireman, and Steven Rytina, *Encounters with Unjust Authority* (Homewood, Ill.: Dorsey, 1982), 1–5.

14. For a theoretical analysis of the mobilization of dominated groups, see Aldon Morris, *Origins of the Southern Civil Rights Movement* (New York: Free Press, 1984), chap. 11.

15. *Ibid.*; and idem, "Black Southern Sit-In Movement: An Analysis of Internal Organization," *American Sociological Review* 46 (1981): 744–767, at 751–752.

16. William Robert Miller, *Martin Luther King, Jr.: His Life, Martyrdom and the World* (New York: Weybright & Talley, 1968), 47, 52, 65–66.

17. Morris, "Black Southern Sit-In Movement," 758.

18. Miller, *Martin Luther King*, 86–87; and August Meier and Elliot Rudwick, *CORE: A Study in the Civil Rights Movement, 1942–1968* (New York: Oxford University Press, 1973), 102–3.

19. Morris, "Black Southern Sit-In Movement," 758.

20. In their account of the National Welfare Rights Organization, Piven and Cloward advocate a cadre organization, modelled on the successes of the civil-rights movement and of SCLC in particular (*Poor People's Movements*, 282–85).

Acknowledgments

We are grateful to Aldon Morris and Mayer N. Zald for their comments and suggestions on an earlier draft of this article.

327

16

Disruption and Organization: A Reply to Gamson and Schmeidler

Gamson and Schmeidler reiterate two familiar and related criticisms of our work on protest movements. One is that we have not fully converted to the new faith: to explain the origins of protest movements, we still invoke the "old war horses of dislocation and breakdown produced by social change." We are not convinced, it is true, that social movements can be reduced to explanations framed mainly in terms of solidarities and networks. Nor are we so sure that those who propose new interpretations need to justify them by demanding, as a test of faith, that all previous interpretations be declared obsolete. Social life is complex, and those who try to explain it have little reason to be confident of their success. Resource mobilization analysts think the discontents to which dislocation and breakdown theories attribute protest movements are a ubiquitous feature of social life, and protest movements are not. They insist instead that it is communal and economic solidarities that make movements possible. But solidarities of some kind are also a virtually ubiquitous feature of social life. At the very least, something is missing. The resource mobilization school has yet, for example, to give serious theoretical attention to the role of ideas in motivating people to action. And they have also been too quick to dismiss the social disorganization tradition in its entirety, as we will presently explain.

The second criticism is that we exhibit "animus" toward organization. Since resource mobilization analysts emphasize the centrality of organization and social infrastructure in movements, this charge suggests a serious point of disagreement. But it is not. We have been preoccupied for two decades with the question of how movements of the poor can exert political influence, and that is partly a question of how they are organized. We think some ways may be more effective than other ways, as we have tried to explain in our writing. The dispute is not about organization versus no organization; it is about the political effectiveness of different kinds of organization.

The issue of movement organization cannot be separated from the issue of power, and it is here that an authentic difference does arise. Resource mobilization analysts are not always clear about what they think power is. However, they appear to share the common conception that power inheres in the possession of valued things or traits. In his 1983 review essay on resource mobilization theory, Jenkins speaks for the school:

> Any scheme that ignores the intrinsic features of resources is...of limited value. In response, most analysts have simply listed the assets that are frequently mobilized by movements [e.g., McCarthy & Zald's (1977) money, facilities, labor, and legitimacy; or Tilly's (1978: 69) land, labor, capital, and technical expertise]. Freeman (1979: 172–5) has offered a more useful scheme, distinguishing tangible assets such as money, facilities, and means of communication from the intangible or "human" assets that form the central basis for movements.[1]

At first glance, this definition of power seems unobjectionable, if only because it is so familiar. And much of the time it works fairly well in explaining our experience: those who have land, capital, and technical expertise do indeed prevail most of the time in contests with those who have few or none of these things.

But most of the time is not all of the time. The study of protest movements necessarily focuses on just those occasions when an understanding of resources for power as valued things or traits becomes demonstrably inadequate. Sometimes in the course of protest movements people without land or capital or technical expertise nevertheless compel those with such resources to do what they would not otherwise have done. If we are to understand why those with fewer resources occasionally prevail, we need a different way of thinking about power.

In *Poor People's Movements*, the initiating question was precisely about power, and not about organization. The subtitle, *Why They Succeed, How They Fail* was meant to highlight that question. How could low income people exert influence in the American electoral-representative system? The power of those who are ordinarily powerless does not derive from the valued assets or traits they control; by definition, they control few of these things. It derives from the patterns of interdependence that characterize all of social life, and from the leverage that inheres in these interdependent relations. Power, in other words, is interactional; it is embedded in patterns of social relationship. People without valued things or traits can sometimes make others do what they want because those others depend upon them, and the more so in a society of intricately interdependent relations. It follows that people at the bottom exercise power on those occasions when they mobilize to withhold the contributions they make to institutional life. As workers, they can withhold labor; as tenants, they can withhold rent; as savers, they can withhold savings; as consumers, they can withhold purchases; and as citizens, they can withhold obedience to the rules governing civil society. This is what we mean when we assert that the power of the poor is the power to disrupt (which is not the same as the appearance of disorder connoted by terms like "unruliness" used by resource mobilization analysts).

Most of the time poor people do not disrupt the institutional relationships in which they are involved. They obey the rules that ensure their cooperation, and thus do not use what power they have. Partly they obey because they come to think the rules are right. But people reconcile themselves to thinking the rules are right because the fact of interdependence also means they are vulnerable to economic and social sanctions if they break the rules. At least as important, they are also vulnerable to state force. It was in trying to identify the conditions under which masses of people were nevertheless able to join together and use their disruptive power that we emphasized the importance of the deregulating effects of large-scale institutional change.

The brief compiled by resource-organization analysts against breakdown theories is directed against the depiction of collective action as an essentially non-rational and explosive reaction to social changes that generate strain and fragment social bonds.[2] We also plainly abjure the depiction of movements as irrational eruptions, so that is not at issue. What is at issue is the significance we attribute to the deregulating effects of social change in accounting for the emergence of movements. We do not see social infrastructure simply as lateral networks facilitating mobilization, which often seems to be the main resource-mobilization version of social life. Social infrastructures are also hierarchical and controlling, and, insofar as they are, they inhibit protest.

Resource-mobilization theorists, being astute observers, also have not been oblivious to the empirical fact that social infrastructures can inhibit as well as facilitate social protest. This is what Ash meant when she associated the "deroutinization" of life with the eruption of protest, and what Oberschall meant when, following Floyd Hunter, he argued that civil-rights protests were possible because the breakdown of the plantation system and mass migration to the cities had freed many blacks from the essentially feudal controls of the Old South, just as de Tocqueville thought the movement of the French nobility to Paris in the eighteenth century undermined their authority over the peasants.[3] And Barrington Moore also suggested that the different patterns of ties between overlord and peasant determine the possibilities of rebellion.[4] In other words, social change, especially economic change, may weaken hierarchical controls, and that is surely significant. The difficulty is that observations such as these have not been theorized. If they were, the general brief against breakdown theories would have to be sharply qualified because, by releasing people from subjugation to others, social disorganization may free them to use disruptive resources.

We also thought large-scale social change important in accounting for the occasional vulnerability of political leaders to movements. The question of whether movements succeed or fail usually is not determined simply by the effects of disruptive protests on institutions, taken alone. Rather it depends on the responses of state leaders to disruption. In the United States, these responses are governed partly by electoral calculations. Whether political leaders are free to ignore or repress protest, or are forced to conciliate the disruptors, depends very much on patterns of electoral allegiance and alignment. The periods in American history characterized by the eruption of poor people's movements were also periods of electoral instability, of shifting allegiances and surges in voter participation. And it was our point that the same economic and social changes that free people to use disruptive resources may also generate the electoral instabilities that weaken a regime's legitimacy, thus making it vulnerable to institutional disruptions and increasing the likelihood of conciliatory rather than repressive responses. It is for this reason that we tried to show the complex interactions between the emergence of movements and the institutional and electoral context in which they run their course.

Finally, this perspective on power helps account for the transitory character of disruptive movements. Most of the time, as we noted earlier, people do not defy the rules that govern their participation in institutional life. And when they do, the responses to the disruptions that result eventually restore a measure of stability. Repression may produce that consequence; so may conciliatory measures, either by placating the protestors or by absorbing their leaders, or both. And sometimes it is enough simply to ignore protesters, and wait them out.

This was our main argument, and our analysis of organizational forms flowed from it. Every political movement confronts a series of difficult decisions regarding the type of organization best suited to mobilizing the particular resources available to potential followers. But a singular focus on the organizational question is misplaced, because organizational form is necessarily a contingent and derivative issue, and thus a secondary one. The choice of a particular mode of organization implies assessments of the particular political resources available to a movement, and the strategies through which those resources can be activated and aggregated. Organizational decisions, in other words, reflect calculations of the nature of a movement's potential power.

To show the close connection in our thinking between types of power and types of organization, it may be useful to reconstruct the actual political context in which the argument was formed. Our preoccupation with disruptive strategies and the organizational vehicles by which to implement them dates from the early 1960s. It was a heady time. Southern blacks were mobilizing in sit-ins, boycotts and marches, and filling the jails in cities like Albany and Birmingham. Protests were beginning to erupt in the Northern cities as well: boycotts, marches, traffic tie-ups, rent strikes and then riots. Everywhere there was intense discussion among sympathizers and activists of the course the movement should follow. There was no question about the legitimacy of the protests; the injustices were there to be seen, and overcome. It was a time of hope bordering on delirium, and all the more so because many activists thought they saw the chance of building a mass movement of the poor that could transform American society. But there was a good deal of question and complaint about strategy, and much of it focused on the failure of protest leaders to build formal mass membership organizations.

Although the "organizational question" had been fiercely debated on the European Left during the first part of the twentieth century, little of that debate had entered Left thinking in the United States. Instead, American activists tended to take for granted that the organizational vehicle most suitable to the exercise of power by those at the bottom was the mass-membership organization, as exemplified particularly by labor unions. The Workers' Alliance of America in the 1930s was just such an effort to form the unemployed into a national union. Alinsky, who had been associated with John L. Lewis, helped spread this model to neighborhood organizing in the post-war period, In the 1960s, tenant organizers and welfare-rights organizers attempted to fashion a national tenants union and a national welfare-rights union. (And in the 1970s, "citizen action" organizers would attempt to build the same kinds of organization among working and middle-class groups.) Whether organizing the unemployed, or tenants, or welfare recipients, the goal was to build stable membership organizations at the local level and then unite them through a national structure.

This conviction about organization was, in turn, inextricably tied to a more fundamental conviction that real and sustained political leverage depended not on disruptive protests, but on bringing large numbers of people together in formal organizations that would represent their interests. It was a difficult argument to counter, for it was buttressed not only by the view that this, after all, was how the working class had organized, but more importantly by deeply engrained convictions about the potential effectiveness of democratic representation. True, activists in the 1960s did not think the poor were in fact adequately represented. But they thought that was because no one until then had had the wit or the will to bring a sufficient number of the poor together in organizations. In turn, the electoral influence of such organizations could compensate for the manifest disparity in political resources between the poor and other groups. Or course, organizers could hardly be faulted for these views; they were simply reflecting the pluralistic consensus that dominated interpretations of American politics at the time.

But while few activists could articulate an alternative to this dominant view, a good many nevertheless were acting otherwise. They were organizing demonstrations and confrontations, not membership organizations. We thought that implicit in this development was an alternative to the mass-membership model, and to the pluralist analysis on which it rested. But the alternative remained submerged because there was no intellectual construct to explain and justify it. In 1963, we tried to say that these protests made sense because low-income people had no other way to exert power: "The point is that low-income people have no regular resources for influencing public policy. It is obvious that they are without power as individuals. Nor are they significant participants in the large formal organizations that keep watch on government, bringing to bear the leverage made possible by organizational stability, staff and money. Nor did the political machine, or its remnants, or political parties, provide an effective vehicle for low-income political influence."[5] For low-income people, the chief political option was the use of "tactics of disruption" in just "the militant boycotts, sit-ins, traffic tie-ups, and rent strikes" that were then spreading:

> The effectiveness of these tactics does not depend only on dramatic presentations. They are intended to command attention and win concessions by the actual trouble they cause in the ongoing operations of major institutions—by interfering with the daily business of city agencies or with the movement of traffic or the profits of businessmen. Such disruptions cause commotion among bureaucrats, excitement in the media, dismay among influential segments of the community, and strain for political leaders.[6]

If effective disruption depended on the ability of leaders to induce people to break the rules, and to run the risks involved, we also thought the opportunities for such mobilizations were transitory:

> [I]t is probably only at certain times in history that the legitimacy of regular political processes is so questioned that people can be mobilized to engage in disruption, for to do so is to violate the implicit "social" contract of major institutions, and often to violate the explicit social contract of the law as well. That people are sometimes led to this, and to run the risks involved, only signifies the paucity of alternatives. If our analysis is correct, disruptive and irregular tactics are the only resource, short of violence, available to low-income groups seeking to influence public policy.[7]

Events strengthened these convictions. The rent strike that emerged in New York City in late 1963 and collapsed in early 1964 is an example. Organizers thought they could exert continuing and effective influence over public policies governing housing if they could build a tenants union. Their strategy was simple enough: induce people to affiliate by promising court-ordered repairs. But the implementation was not so simple. One reason, we said at the time, was the "absence of an existing substructure of interaction among the tenants" owing, among other things, to high rates of residential mobility. To compensate, we thought "an enormous organizing task was required."[8] A similarly large organizing effort was required to follow the official rules for the redress of grievances over housing conditions:

> The law prescribed an elaborate bureaucratic course, and the courts interpreted the law rigidly. Judges admitted only the inspection records of the Department of Buildings as evidence of hazardous violations. To obtain those records, organizers had to fill out forms and arrange and follow-up appointments for inspections; check agency files to make sure that hazardous violations had been posted; and meanwhile see that rents withheld by tenants were being collected and deposited in a private escrow account. (If the tenants lost in court, these funds were turned over to the landlord; if they won, the money was turned over to the clerk of the court, to be given to the landlord after repairs were made.) Finally, organizers had to shepherd tenants through the courts. And all of this turned out to require enormous effort and expertise.

336

At the outset, rent-strike cadres were not dismayed by these elaborate procedures. Indeed, they defined them as a means of educating tenants and building tenant associations. Canvassing door-to-door to discover housing violations was a way of making contact with tenants; filing "multiple form" complaints was a way of stimulating building meetings; assigning tenants the responsibility for collecting rents and managing escrow accounts was a way of strengthening building committees and developing leadership. And through these tenant groups, organizers believed the poor could be educated to the larger political issues underlying slum housing. Such "radicalizing" of tenants was presumably to produce mass associations capable of exerting regular influence on government; each arduous bureaucratic task would contribute to the creation of a permanent " 'peoples' organization'...."

But the bureaucratic rites by which repairs were to be exacted, and tenants educated, exhausted organizers and bewildered tenants. To cope with agency procedures required precisely those resources of money and expertise which are scarcest among the poor. Meanwhile, landlords exploited bureaucratic intricacies and corruptibility to evade or overcome the challenge. Even occasional tenant victories in the courts yielded only minor and temporary repairs. Unable to produce repairs quickly and to multiply them widely, tenant affiliation did not expand, and the strike developed little political force. Thus the movement began to subside a few months after it formed.[9]

There was not much of a strike, and no disruption, because the rules of the public agencies had dictated the tactics of the movement, and landlords simply recovered their rents in court. But we thought tenants did have potential disruptive power. That power depended on large-scale rent withholding that could bankrupt the slum property system, and which, in the political context of the 1960s, would have exerted pressure for government policies to improve slum housing conditions. "The key to a disruptive rent strike," we said, "is for tenants to pocket the rent, not place it in escrow.... The main job of organizers would be to expand the strike by exciting indignation and urging tenants to spend their rent money for other needs."[10] Only in this way could the disruptive power of the constituency of this movement have been mobilized.

But a "spend the rent" campaign could succeed only if evictions were forestalled, and that would require planning, coordination and, communication—in other words, organization. We suggested a more centralized but less-structured mode, or what we began to call "cadre organizations":

> The spread of rent-strike action must be controlled. If those withholding rent are dispersed over too wide an area, the logistics of resisting evictions may become overwhelming. It is probably preferable for organizers to work intensively on a few blocks at first, concentrating their energies to ensure complete coverage of eviction threats. As the area of strike action expands, organizers will need to make sure that a viable communications system exists, and that there are neighborhood cadres capable of resisting evictions. In addition, reserve forces—perhaps sympathetic students—should be available for quick mobilization to protect a particular block if public officials decide to try to break the strike by a dramatic show of force....
>
> The key problem in this phase is to develop a neighborhood communications system for reporting evictions. One way is to leaflet a neighborhood, asking tenants threatened by eviction to call a central telephone number so that organizers can be dispatched to watch the apartment. Another way is to have organizers hang around on the block, telling people to let them know the moment the marshal appears in the vicinity."

A similar debate over strategy and movement organization welled up during this period in the civil-rights movement. One source of dissatisfaction stemmed from the fact that much of the actual protest—and particularly the more disruptive forms of protest, such as the civil disobedience in the South and the street actions in the North (traffic tie-ups, for example)—was not resulting in the growth of an organized mass base among the black poor. People were not being recruited as organization members; they were only being recruited for collective defiance of caste rules. This disagreement over strategy and movement organization divided the movement. There were some in SNCC, for example, who turned away from dramatic demonstrations that, they thought, left nothing in their wake, and hunkered down in the southern ghettos to begin the longer-term task of building membership organizations of the black poor.

We disagreed. The movement won because its confrontational tactics worsened the "cleavage in the North-South Democratic coalition.... The legislative concessions of 1964 and 1965 owed less to the numbers of people committed to the civil rights movement—whether blacks or their white allies—than to the sharply divisive impact the movement had upon an already strained North–South Democratic partnership."[12] In other words, as confrontations in the South provoked violence, and public opinion became inflamed, the Democratic ranks in the South were rapidly eroded by white racist defections to a resurgent Republican party, leaving the national Democratic party without much choice but to concede legislation to dismantle the caste system and enfranchise blacks in order to rebuild its southern wing.

Moreover, it was not the established, formally-structured civil-rights organizations which were at the forefront of protest. They were too integrated with elites, too oligarchic, too fearful of risk, and too cumbersome to move. SNCC, SCLC, and CORE led the direct action phase of the movement. They were "leadership" organizations, or "organizations of organizers," rather than membership organizations. And they activated people through institutions and networks (e.g., churches, colleges) where they were already "organized." To distinguish these kinds of organization, we said that formal mass-membership organizations are "organized" but disruptions are "mobilized," and they are best mobilized by cadre organizations that activate preexisting networks.[13]

These ideas about disruption and the organizational requirements for the mobilization of disruption were central to our 1966 proposal calling on organizers to develop a "welfare rights movement." We thought it might be possible to create effective political pressure for the enactment of federally guaranteed minimum-income legislation by mobilizing hundreds of thousand of poor families to disrupt state and big-city finances by applying for relief benefits. We thought "cadres of aggressive organizers from the civil rights movement and the churches, from militant low-income organizations...and from other groups on the Left" could mobilize such a movement by activating leaders of important networks in which poor people were already involved, such as "leaders of social, religious, fraternal, and political groups in the slums...to recruit the eligible to the rolls."[14]

However, when George A. Wiley resigned as associate national director of the Congress of Racial Equality to organize a welfare-rights movement, he and the organizers on whom he relied for advice decided it was first necessary to build a national mass-membership organization of welfare recipients. Wiley said at the time that he wanted to succeed where the civil-rights movement had failed: namely, to build a "national union" of poor people. And he did just that, at least for a time, complete with constitution and an elaborate structure of elected leaders at the local, state and national levels. In other words, he accepted the conventional organizing wisdom that only a formal mass-membership organization, even one composed of welfare recipients, could become an effective lobbying force in the halls of congress.

But Wiley and other organizers also believed that a national organization of the welfare poor could be a vehicle for disruption. Once constructed, it could turn to mobilizing millions of eligible but unaided families to flood the local welfare rolls. In other words, a mass-membership organization could simultaneously pursue both conventional and disruptive strategies. At the time, we were less sure, but we did not press the point; disagreements about movement organization seemed less important than opportunities to activate the poor around welfare issues. As time passed, however, the resources of the National Welfare Rights Organization and the energies of recipients were increasingly turned away from the streets and welfare centers to testifying, lobbying, lecture circuits, and other conventional strategies for the exercise of influence. Moreover, the established leaders even resisted expanding the membership base to include recipients from other relief categories because that could lead to competition for leadership.

These experiences formed part of the basis for our critique of the organizational model favored by activists, and by many intellectuals who thought about these questions, and it was partly to present that critique that we wrote *Poor People's Movements*. We thought the formally-structured mass-membership organization was unsuited to marshalling disruptive resources, that in fact the model was predicated on very different resources for influence that were not available to low-income people. Whether right or wrong, we had by then become convinced that low-income groups only exert influence through disruption, that social dislocations had much to do with the release of those disruptive resources, that cadre organizations were best suited to mobilizing those resources, and that the periods in which disruptions could be mobilized never lasted because disruptions are, virtually by definition, transitory, if only because they precipitate government responses (whether repressions, concessions, or both) that effectively demobilize the poor. We therefore thought it made little sense for organizers to attempt to build enduring membership organizations of the poor, especially if the effort drained organizing resources away from the mobilization of the disruption itself. In other words, a certain kind of organizing doctrine may help frustrate such power as the poor can occasionally exert.

Chapter I of *Poor People's Movements* set out our basic analysis of the disruptive power of protest movements, together with a discussion of the social patterns that "shape movements by shaping the collectivity out of which protest can arise. Institutional life aggregates people or disperses them, molds group identities, and draws people into the settings within which collective action can erupt."[15] The successive case studies of protest movements in the 1930s and 1960s were intended to provide evidence in support of those propositions, and to examine the bearing of alternative modes of movement organization on the course of movements. In the discussions of both the unemployed and workers' movements in the 1930s, we repeatedly observed that established organizations (such as the AF of L unions) did not mobilize insurgency, and pointed to the crucial roles played by "small Communist nuclei" and others who "served as key centers of agitation and mobilization."[16] Moving ahead to the 1960s, we said this about the civil rights movement:

> [T]he direct-action organizations which developed during the civil rights struggle were cadre organizations. The cadres—whether in SNCC or CORE or SCLC—at first engaged in exemplary actions [e.g., civil disobedience followed by arrests].... Such exemplary actions, in turn, inspired a mass mobilization.... This mobilization took place mainly through segregated institutions where people were already "organized": the black colleges, churches, and ghetto neighborhoods....[17]

And when recounting the debates over power and organization in the welfare rights movement, we included a major section, entitled "A Proposal to Mobilize an Institutional Disruption," containing subheadings called "Conflicting Theories of Political Influence" and "Mobilizing versus Organizing," the latter of which contains this passage:

> To mobilize a crisis, we thought it would be necessary to develop a national network of cadre organizations rather than a national federation of welfare recipient groups. This organization of organizers—composed of students, churchmen, civil rights activists, anti-poverty workers, and militant AFDC recipients—would in turn seek to energize a broad, loosely-coordinated movement of variegated groups to arouse hundreds of thousands of poor people to demand aid. Rather than build membership roles, the purpose would be to build the welfare rolls. The main tactics should include large-scale "welfare rights" information campaigns; the enlisting of influential people in the slums and ghettos, especially clergymen, to exhort potential recipients to seek the aid that was rightfully theirs, and the mobilization of marches and demonstrations to build indignation and militancy among the poor.[18]

Finally, we concluded the introduction to the paperback edition of *Poor People's Movements* with this thought:

> If we acknowledge [weaknesses in the received doctrines about organization which are revealed by historical experiences], we may...then begin to consider alternative forms of organization through which working-class people can act together in defiance of their rulers in ways that are more congruent with the structure of working-class life and with the process of working-class struggle, and less susceptible to penetration by dominant elites. The mass-membership bureaucracy was, after all not invented by the Left, but is rather a form through which the Left emulates the modes of organization that exist in the capitalist society the Left seeks to transform. That it should be defended so uncritically seems odd.[19]

It must be said, in closing, that our outlook provoked a good deal of excited opposition among both activists and movement analysts. The emphasis on disruption was scorned: "Create a crisis and pray," activists said;[20] "blind militancy," Hobsbawm said.[21] And our emphasis on the transitory character of disruptive protest together with criticism of the mass-membership model was taken as further evidence of an alleged tendency in our work to celebrate anarchy. These responses reflect a crude polarization of political alternatives, and caricature our views.

Gamson and Schmeidler simply reiterate these misinterpretations. They have no warrant to characterize our outlook as "an anti-organizational phillipic," and to instruct us, after we have spent two decades making the same point, that "The intellectual task [is] the more exacting one of figuring out what types of organization are likely to facilitate insurgency or abandon their oppositional politics under different historical conditions." Nor have they proved anything by providing some further anecdotes showing the role of "structures of solidarity and communication" in two of the movements we analyzed, since we had already provided considerable evidence in support of the same contention. That protest movements are something other than inchoate uprisings among anomie masses is not a point of difference between us and the resource-mobilization school, and it never was.

Originally published in 1984.

Notes

1. Jenkins, J. Craig., "Resource Mobilization Theory and the Study of Social Movements," *American Sociological Review* 9 (1983): 533.

2. Tilly, Charles, Louise Tilly, and Richard Tilly, *The Rebellious Century* (Cambridge, Massachusetts: Harvard University Press, 1975).

3. Ash, Roberta, *Social Movements in America* (Chicago: Markham Publishing Company 1972), 164–67; Oberschall Anthony, *Social Conflict and Social Movements* (Englewood Cliffs, New Jersey: Prentice-Hall, 1973).

4. Moore, Barrington, *Social Origins of Dictatorship and Democracy* (Boston: Beacon Press, 1966).

5. Piven, Frances Fox, "Low Income People and the Political Process," 1963, reprinted in Richard A. Cloward and Frances Fox Piven, *The Politics of Turmoil* (New York: Pantheon Books, 1974), 85.

6. *Ibid.*, 86.

7. *Ibid.*, 85–6.

8. *Ibid.*, 82 and 83.

9. Piven, Frances Fox, and Richard A. Cloward, "Rent Strike: Disrupting the Slum System," 1967, reprinted in Cloward and Piven, *The Politics of Turmoil* 153–54.

10 *Ibid.*, 156.

11. Piven, Frances Fox, and Richard A. Cloward, "Disrupting City Services to Change National Priorities," *Viet Report: A Special 64 Page Report on Urban America in Revolt.* Summer 1968, 29.

12. Cloward, Richard A., and Frances Fox Piven, "Dissensus Politics: A Strategy for Winning Economic Rights," 1968, reprinted in Cloward and Piven, *The Politics of Turmoil*, 161.

13. Piven, Frances Fox, and Richard A. Cloward. *Poor People's Movements* (New York: Pantheon Books, 1977), 284–85.

14. Cloward, Richard A., and Frances Fox Piven, "A Strategy to End Poverty," 1966, reprinted in Cloward and Piven, *The Politics of Turmoil*, 95.

15. Piven, Frances Fox, and Richard A. Cloward, *Poor People's Movements*, 21.

16. *Ibid.*, 151.

17. *Ibid.*, 221–24.

18. *Ibid.*, 275–88.

19. Piven and Cloward, *Poor People's Movements*, xvi.

20. *Ibid.*, 282.

21. Hobsbawm, Eric J., "Organizing the Poor," *The New York Review of Books*, March 23, 1978.

Normalizing Collective Protest

Over the past two decades, resource mobilization (RM) analysts have emphasized the importance of institutional continuities between conventional social life and collective protest.[1] There is much about this interpretation with which we agree. It is a corrective to some of the malintegration (MI) literature in which movements are portrayed as mindless eruptions lacking either coherence or continuity with organized social life. Nevertheless, we shall argue that RM analysts commit a reverse error. Their emphasis on the similarities between conventional and protest behavior has led them to understate the differences. They thus tend to normalize collective protest.

Blurring the distinction between normative and nonnormative forms of collective action is the most fundamental expression of this tendency, as if rule-conforming and rule-violating collective action are of a piece. To be sure, RM analysts are obviously aware that some forms of protest violate established norms and are therefore illegitimate or illegal. Indeed, a good deal of their work deals with electrifying examples of defiance of normative structures. Nevertheless, in the course of examining the institutional continuities between permissible and prohibited modes of collective action, they often allow this distinction to disappear. But an exposition of the similarities between the structure of everyday life and the structure of protests if not an explanation of why people sometimes live their everyday lives and other times join in collective defiance. And it is, of course, precisely this theoretical problem that is central to the MI analyses which RM disparage; it is nonnormative collective action—disorder and rebellion—that MI analysts want to explain.

Other problems in the RM literature are consistent with this normalizing tendency. Protest is often treated by RM analysts as more organized that it is, as if conventional modes of formal organization also typify the organizational forms taken by protest, as if the processes of influence set in motion by collective protest are no different than those set in motion by conventional political activities.

These criticisms, which are discussed in this article, do not detracts from the generalization that institutional arrangements pattern both conventional and unconventional collective action. Still, the differences must be explained. And once the problem of explaining differences is brough back into view, the wholesale rejection of the MI tradition by RM analysts may be seen as premature.

Normative and Nonnormative Collective Action

In his recent appraisal of theories of civil violence, Rule says RM analysts define violent actions as "simply a phase in other forms of collective action, caused by the same forces that move people to other, 'normal' assertions of collective interest" (1988: 170-71). Thus the Tillys object to "sociological interpretations of protest, conflict, and violence that treat them as occurring outside of normal politics, or even *against* normal politics" (1975: 240; emphasis in original). It is true, as the Tillys say, that protest is a form of politics. But does it really make sense to treat protest and violence as if they were simply "normal" politics? To do so is to ignore the powerful role of norms in the regulation of social life, including relations of domination and subordination.

Ongoing struggles for power continually stimulate efforts by contenders to promulgate and enforce rules which either proscribe the use of specific political resources by their antagonists, or define conditions limiting their use (e.g., the conditions under which labor can be withheld in industrial conflict, or sexual access withheld in mating conflict).

346

Thus conceived, rule-making is a strategy of power. Moreover, it is a strategy which creates new and lasting constraints on subsequent political action. Once objectified in a system of law, the rules forged by past power struggles continue to shape ongoing conflicts by constraining or enhancing the ability of actors to use whatever leverage their social circumstances yield them. That is why new power struggles often take the form of efforts to alter the parameters of the permissible by challenging or defying the legitimacy of prevailing norms themselves (Piven, 1981). Nevertheless, protest is indeed "outside of normal politics" and "against normal politics" in the sense that people break the rules defining permissible modes of political action. Of course, the distinction between normative and nonnormative is not always easy to draw because norms themselves are often ambiguous, and no more so than when they become the focus of conflict and renegotiation. Still, a riot is clearly not an electoral rally, and both the participants and the authorities know the difference.

There are several important ways in which some RM analysts direct attention away from rule-violations. One is to treat collective protest as if it were merely interest group politics, a proclivity which marks the work of McCarthy and Zald (1977; cf. Also McCarthy, Wolfson, Baker, and Mosakowski, on citizen organizing against drunk driving). Another is to conflate the normative and nonnormative. In his study of crowd behavior, McPhail (1991) not only conflates political gatherings (e.g., urban riots) with such other collective "actions" as sports and religious events, but does not consider it important to explain why the crowd which is the audience for a sports event is sometimes transformed in to a riotous mob. Even Tilly, whose work shows appreciation of the distinctive features of protest, frequently lumps normative and nonnormative collective action together. His definition of "contention" covers all "common action that bears directly on the interests of some other acting group," such as collective violence ("that sort of contention in which someone seizes or damages persons or objects"), and conventional political action, such as electoral rallies and campaigns (1986, 381-82). His classification of contemporary forms of collective political action includes:

> Strikes
> Demonstrations
> Electoral rallies
> Public meetings
> Petition marches
> Planned insurrections
> Invasions of official assemblies
> Social movements
> Electoral campaigns (1986: 393).

A similar conflation occurs in the survey essay on "social movements" prepared by McAdam, McCarthy, and Zald for Smelser's *Handbook of Sociology* where they define virtually all forms of collective action as "social movements"—from mass civil disobedience to "burial societies" and "PTAs" (1988: 704).[2]

A still further expression of this normalizing tendency occurs when analysts focus on those aspects of protest that are normative and ritualized (thereby illuminating the continuities between everyday institutional processes and collective protest) but then make much less of the non-normative aspects (thereby obscuring the discontinuities between everyday institutional processes and collective protest). Here, for example, is Tilly's characterization of preindustrial food riots:

> If we ignore the intimate relation of the food riot to the politics of the old regime, we shall neglect the coherent political action the riot represents. Far from being impulsive, hopeless reactions to hunger, bread riots and other struggles over the food supply took a small number of relatively well-defined forms.... The work of the crowd embodied a critique of the authorities, was often directed consciously at the authorities, and commonly consisted of the crowd's taking precisely those measures its members thought the authorities had failed their own responsibility to take—inventorying grain in private hands, setting a price, and so on. (1975, 386)

But as this description makes clear, humble villagers did not just act in the traditional role of the authorities; they usurped their powers. Surely this feature of their action demands explanation.[3] Yet even when Tilly and his collaborators provide such dramatic examples of defiance, it is the socially patterned character of such protest events that commands their theoretical attention.

Finally, consistent with their predisposition to think of collective violence as normal politics, some RM analysts characteristically deemphasize violence by protesters and instead single out violence by the authorities. On the basis of their historical studies, the Tillys claim that most

> collective violence will ordinarily grow out of some prior collective action which is not intrinsically violent: a meeting, a ceremony, a strike.... To an important degree, the damage to objects and, especially, to persons consisted of elite reactions to the claims made by ordinary people: troops, police, and thugs acting under instructions from owners and officials attacked demonstrators, strikers, and squatters. (Tilly et al. 1975, 49 and 288)

Similarly, Snyder and Tilly conclude that "where governments have substantial force at their disposal, in fact, these specialists ordinarily do the major part of the damaging and seizing which constitutes the collective violence" (1972, 526). This leads to their generalization that "collective violence should rise and fall with the nonviolent political activity" (527). Granted that government is the main perpetrator of violence, this does not warrant the implication that people themselves do not engage in various forms of nonnormative collective action, including violence against persons and property. And if that is so, then governmental repression should also rise and fall partly in reflection of the amount of defiant behavior in which protesters themselves engage.

The Pace and Timing of Collective Protest

A critical reason for calling attention to these normalizing tendencies is that they invalidate much of the work by RM analysts that deals with the prerequisites of protest—with the conditions under which people are led to defend or advance their interests by taking defiant actions that violate rules and risk great reprisals. We first criticize the grounds on which RM analysts have rejected traditional MI explanations of protest origins;

349

then we show that the RM explanation, which emphasizes socially structured opportunities for protest, is inadequate.

Grievances and Protest

One insignia of RM work is the argument that there is little or no relationship between variations in relative deprivation and the pace and
timing of collective protest. Oberschall asserts that "grievances and
disaffection are a fairly permanent and recurring feature of the historical landscape" (1978, 298), suggesting a "constancy of discontent"
(McAdam et al. 1988) that in turn justifies shifting "from a strong
assumption about the centrality of deprivation and grievance to a weak
one" in explanations of collective protest (McCarthy and Zald 1977,
1215). It is largely on this ground that RM analysts claim to have won the
debate with MI analysts: "Useless Durkheim," Tilly says (1981, chap.
4).[4]

    The empirical basis for this claim rests in no small degree on the
widely accepted evidence presented by Tilly and his collaborators, especially their time-series studies of the relationship between breakdown
variables, such as intensified hardship or rapid urbanization, and the pace
and timing of collective protest. But MI analysts do not claim that breakdown is a necessary precondition of normative forms of group action.
What they emphasize instead is that breakdown is a precondition of collective protest and violence, of riot and rebellion. Any effort to test
breakdown theories must therefore employ a dependent variable in
which normative and non-normative forms of collective action are disaggregated, which Tilly and his collaborators do not do. In effect, the MI
tradition is being dismissed for an argument it never made.

    Shorter and Tilly's study of strike frequencies in France illustrates this
problem. They claim that strike rates correlate with good times and not
with economic downturns, thus presumably invalidating the hardship
variant of the relative deprivation version of the MI tradition. But strikes
were legal in France beginning in 1865 (Tilly et al. 1975, 73) and thus for
the entire 1865–1965 period of the Shorter and Tilly study. Or at least
Shorter and Tilly do not separate out legal strikes from strikes that
include illegal activity (e.g., violence and sabotage or other strike

actions initiated by workers that violate government regulations or wildcat strikes that violate union contracts). Taken as a whole, this corpus of research does not answer the question of the conditions under which ordinary people do in fact resort to violence or defiance, and the findings cannot therefore be taken to refute the MI perspective.

We quickly acknowledge that time-series studies that distinguish between normative and nonnormative action will be more difficult to conduct. Not only is the distinction itself sometimes elusive, but norms change over time, in part as the result of successive challenges that produce new balances of power, reflected in new structures of rules. Forms of collective action impermissible in one period may be permissible in another, or the reverse. Moreover, caution has to be exercised in aggregating collective actions that occur in different institutional contexts, simply because different norms may apply, as when land occupations by urban squatters acquire tacit legitimacy and factory takeovers usually do not.

This problem and the obfuscation it creates is worsened by the fact that normative collective action occurs much more frequently than non-normative action, and perhaps more so in the modern period with the granting of political rights and the vast increase in permissible forms of conflict. The sheer quantity of conventional political action overwhelms the episodic incidents of unconventional protest. Electoral rallies occur with great frequency, for example, but riots are infrequent. For this reason, unless normative and nonnormative forms are disaggregated, the conventional will overwhelm the unconventional, thus blotting out any possible relationship between breakdown and collective protest. The point is that collective violence and defiance must be operationalized in ways that are true to the MI argument, however difficult that may be, if the relevance of MI ideas to the origins of collective violence and defiance is to be fairly tested.

A second and equally fatal source of confounding results from a criticism we made earlier—the failure to distinguish between violence initiated by protesters and violence initiated by the authorities. The MI tradition seeks to predict violence by the former, not violence by the latter. Consider Lodhi and Tilly's time-series analysis of collective violence in France between 1830 and 1860, which has generally been accepted as puncturing MI explanations by showing that the pace and timing of collective violence does not increase with "the rate at which social ties are being dissolved" through urbanization (1973, 316). Their dependent variable includes "771 incidents of collective violence occurring in France from 1830 to 1860, consisting of every event involving at least one group of 50 persons or more in which some person or object was seized or damaged over resistance" (305). But Lodhi and Tilly do not go into "the nature of the actions" that compose their grand totals of collective violence," limiting themselves instead to "aggregate levels...of collective violence" (305) measured by "the number killed, wounded or arrested" (298–99). And these data, they say, "measure, in effect, how rigorously police and troops put down protests and demonstrations" (306). The same problem arises in the Snyder and Tilly time-series study on hardship and collective violence in France during the same years. Again, the dependent variable is "the extent of governmental repression" (1972, 520), indicated by the number of killings and arrests by the authorities. The question, then, is what is being measured? Is it resort to violence by ordinary people, or is it violence inflicted by the authorities? But this question cannot be answered because the dependent variable is clearly not an uncontaminated measure of the extent to which people themselves initiated violence prior to governmental responses.

In sum, given both the failure to disaggregate normative and nonnormative collective action and the failure to distinguish between the perpetrators of violence, none of these studies can be taken as refuting the MI tradition. Hardship and dislocation may yet be shown to correlate with what Kerbo calls "movements of crisis" (1982; see also Kerbo and Shaffer, 1986). Moreover, malintegration ideas are now enjoying a certain renaissance among some RM analysts. What seems to be provoking this shift is the contradiction between the theoretical dismissal of the breakdown tradition, on the one hand, and the empirical descriptions of the actual conditions preceding protest episodes that RM analysts themselves describe, on the other. Their accounts almost always begin by identifying precisely the sorts of antecedent conditions to which MI analysts attribute stress. These conditions—far from being recurrent, permanent, and ubiquitous, as RM analysts usually insist—are often awesome, new, and fearsome. For example, preindustrial food rioters, land squatters, and machine smashers were reacting to social and economic forces of such transforming scale as to threaten the destruction of their way of life. And perhaps for just this reason, some RM analysts are now breaking ranks over this issue. Thus there is a growing tendency in the RM literature to reintroduce terms like "intensified grievances" and "suddenly imposed grievances" (Walsh 1981), together with renaming traditional concepts such as legitimacy and delegitimacy with terms like "cognitive liberation" (McAdam 1982) and "ideological anger" (Exum 1985, 14).

Lateral Integration and Protest

We come now to the RM quarrel with the social disorganization strand in the MI tradition. Because protest grows out of everyday social organization, which creates collective capacities, RM analysts claim that it is normal. Tilly takes this argument to its logical extreme. Following White's use of the term *catnet* to define *organization*—that is, the degree of organization depends on the extent to which categories of people (e.g., blacks) are bound together by internal networks (e.g., religious)—Tilly argues that the more categories are laced with networks, the more they can "in principle, mobilize" (1978, 64). Hence, one of the RM school's most fundamental causal propositions: "The greater the density of social organization, the more likely that social movement activity will develop" (McAdam et al. 1988, 703).

But even as social integration is exalted in explanation of protest, so too is its absence. Protest is attributed sometimes to the fact that people are integrated in the social order and sometimes to the fact that they are not. On the one hand, if social categories of people lack a "veritable lattice work" of internal networks (McAdam et al. 1988, 711), their "infrastructure deficits" impede mobilization (McCarthy 1987). On the other hand, multiple group memberships impose role obligations, thus raising the costs of participation in movements. Consequently, McCarthy and Zald (1973) direct attention to the disproportionate participation in the movements of the 1960s by persons with few social ties, or what are called the "biographically available": students and "autonomous" professionals, for example. Students in particular are singled out because their preexisting ties to the social order are no longer binding, nor have they formed new and enduring ties. Thus students could be drawn to the Freedom Summer project during the civil rights movement because they were "remarkably free of personal constraints that might have inhibited participation" (McAdam, 1988, 83). Much the same point could be made for ghetto rioters who were predominantly young and at best loosely involved in the usual array of marital, occupational, and related roles.

The proposition that the probability of protest varies directly with the degree of lateral integration is badly flawed for another reason: although collective defiance is episodic and infrequent, the lateral integration requisite to protest is ubiquitous. By not seeing this, RM analysts end by using a double standard in evaluating the MI tradition. On the one hand, they fault MI analysts for failing to concede that grievances do not necessarily lead to protest. Thus the Tillys accuse relative deprivation analysts of using a constant to explain a variation, since they give in to

> the temptation…to ignore the places, times, and populations in which nothing happened. When conflict is at issue, why waste time writing the history of harmony? The simple answer: an explanation of protest, rebellion, or collective violence that cannot account for its absence is no explanation at all; an explanation based only on cases where something happened is quite likely to attribute importance to conditions which are actually quite common in cases where nothing happened. That is the characteristic defect of many theories being bandied about today which treat rebellion as a consequence of frustrated rising expectations without specifying how often (or under what conditions) rising expectations are frustrated without rebellion.
> (1975, 12)

On the other hand, RM analysts also use a constant to explain a variation, since they too "ignore the places, times, and populations in which nothing happened." Tilly (1986) has culled four centuries of French history for episodes of collective protest, but he has not told us about those that should have erupted but did not. Here is a population of people; they had sufficient solidarity to act on their grievances, and protest might not have been met with outright repression; nevertheless, they remained inert. Surely such occasions were numerous. But the opposite impression is conveyed when these four centuries of French protests, or a century of protests in Italy, Germany, and France (Tilly et al. 1975), are compressed between the covers of a single book. Gamson's (1975) study of "challenging groups" in America suffers from the same defect. He tells us about those groups who protested but not about those who could have but did not.

This illogic pervades the RM literature. Wilson and Orum claim that "conventional psychological theories," such as relative deprivation, do not explain the ghetto riots of the 1960s, and that instead "social bonds...i.e., friendship networks, drew many people to become active participants" (1976, 198), but they do not wonder why riots before the 1960s were so rare or why there have been so few since, despite pervasive friendship bonds in both periods. Similarly, McAdam, McCarthy, and Zald suggest that the concentration of students in institutions of higher education has created the "organizational potential for chronic student movements...even if [the student movement of the 1960s] has presently waned" (1988, 712). The student movement certainly did wane; it has turned out to be anything but chronic. Most of the time most people try to make their ordinary lives, not to make history (Flacks 1988).

These analysts are led away from this problem because they overstate the structural requisites of protest. To be sure, people have to be related to one another; they must have some sense of common identity, some sense of shared definitions of grievances and antagonists, some ability to communicate, and so on. But these requisites do not depend on the dense and enduring lateral relationships posited by the RM school. On this point, Oberschall agrees: "collective protest actions...are possible even in a state of disorganization....the minimum requirements for collective disturbances are shared sentiments of collective repression and common targets of oppression" (1973, 133). Consequently, some forms of protest are more or less universally available. Arson, whether in the fields of the preindustrial world or in the streets of the urbanized world, requires technological rather than organizational resources, and not much of the former, either. Riots require little more by way of organization than numbers, propinquity, and some communication. Most patterns of human settlement, whether the preindustrial village or modern metropolis, supply these structural requirements. In fact, the movements of the

355

1960s and 1970s often mobilized people who were previously only weakly or fleetingly related to one another, whether student activists or direct action participants in the peace and environmental struggles. And the ghetto rioters may not have been riffraff, but neither were they drawn from the highly integrated sectors of the black community.

Moreover, the minimal structural requirements for protest are likely to be available even during the periods of rapid social change to which Durkheimians attribute breakdown and collective disorder. In this sense, RM analysts may have overstated breakdown ideas, as if what is meant is the total shredding of the social fabric, making it akin to complete atomization. Durkheim spoke of the way the suicide rate varies with degrees of cohesion (rural versus urban; married versus single, widowed, and divorced; and so forth). Bonds are strong, moderate, or weak; whether Durkheim also meant to suggest that bonds can disappear altogether is debatable. But whatever he intended, the point is that total atomization, if it ever exists, is at most a fleeting phenomenon: where there are human beings, there are networks. Because people are averse to being alone, they construct relationships even under the most disorganized conditions, and they do so rapidly. In short, lateral integration, however fragile, is ubiquitous, thus making opportunities for protest ubiquitous.

These observations also suggest that the generalization that the forms of protest change as societies change is overstated, and for the same reason: the requisite degree of lateral integration is overstated. The Tillys claim that urbanization and industrialization caused the small-scale, localistic, and diffuse modes of preindustrial collective protest to give way to large-scale, associational, and specialized forms. Thus from the eighteenth "to the nineteenth century either in Europe or America, we discover significant further changes in the prevailing forms of contentious gatherings. We notice the food riot, machine breaking, invasions of common fields, and their companion forms of collective action peaking and then disappearing. We find the demonstration, the strike, the election rally, the public meeting, and allied forms of action taking on more and more prominence" (Tilly 1981, 99). The main generalization follows: "The organizational revolution reorganized violence" (Tilly et al. 1975, 49).

Since at least some forms of protest require only minimal integration, however, these protest forms display remarkable continuity. "The riot," for example, "is the characteristic and ever-recurring form of popular protest" (Rude 1964, 6). More generally, preindustrial food riots, grain seizures, land invasions, and machine smashing have rough parallels in the modern period with urban riots, mob looting, squatting, sit-downs, sit-ins, rent strikes, and industrial sabotage. This suggests that Tilly's argument that repertoires of protest change as societies change—old forms out, new forms in—needs qualification. Even as changing modes of social organization bring into being new forms of protest, certain persisting features of social organization facilitate continuities in other protest forms.

Finally, the predictive value of lateral integration is weakened because the same structural capacities provide people with more than one way of reacting to their lot in life. The factors to which RM analysts attribute various forms of contention—interests, organization, mobilization—are also associated with the rise of religious movements, for example, or of organized racketeering. Consider the social bonds of friendship: Wilson and Orum (1976) attribute ghetto riots to them, and Ianni (1974) notes that blacks, lacking the ethnic-familial solidarities that make the Italian Mafia possible, nevertheless developed a Black Mafia because of friendship solidarities forged in street gangs and prisons. And perhaps there is even an interactive effect between crime and protest: the rise and spread of organized networks of drug entrepreneurship and consumption may help explain the low level of protest in the black ghettos since the 1960s. In other words, social integration does not dictate that people will seek solutions to felt grievances in politics at all, whether by conventional or unconventional means.

In general, then, organizational capacity does not predict anything—except that the violation of rules might take collective form and, if collective, that it might take political form.[5] We have elsewhere referred to this as the problem of "indeterminancy"—that given objective conditions, such as structural opportunity, do not necessarily determine given behavioral outcomes (Cloward and Piven 1979, 654; 1989). Plainly, the question of the correlates of the pace and timing of collective protest remains open.

V.I.

Vertical Integration and Protest

People who are organized laterally are also typically connected to other groups vertically. But hierarchical bonds usually constrain collective protest, and that is still another reason lateral integration does not predict protest. Tocqueville noted that it was only with the weakening of ties between nobility and peasantry that the French Revolution became possible. Moore subsequently analyzed variations in the "institutional links binding peasant society to the upper classes" and argued that weaker linkages were more conducive to peasant revolution (1966, 477–78). Oberschall also follows this line of thinking by suggesting that protest potential is enhanced when societies are "segmented" so that lower-stratum collectivities have "few links and bonds" to higher-stratum groups—for example, when landlords are absentee owners, or when forms of colonial rule generate "few links between colonizer and colonized," or when self-contained farm belts are "cut off from the power centers...except for market relations." In contrast, Oberschall

continues, if there are strong "vertical social and political bonds between upper and lower classes, mobilization into protest movements among the lower classes is not likely to take place" (1973, 119–20).[6]

Because hierarchical integration is more the rule than the exception, the important problem is to identify the conditions under which its constraining influence weakens. On this point, the ideas of MI analysts may be relevant. Vertically integrated institutions probably become settings for protest only under exceptional conditions—when grievances intensify or when linkages weaken.

Prior to the advent of the RM school, the black church, with its "other-worldly" oriented clergy who were dominated by white influentials, was thought to divert people from political action, as indeed it did. But RM analysts have since rehabilitated the black church by arguing that it provided a crucial nexus for the civil rights mobilization, and indeed it also did that. The same point can be made for the Catholic church in Latin America whose centuries-long alliance with the landed oligarchies has only recently begun to give way. And a similar shift of the church's role occurred in Poland. It was probably constituency discontent that forced the shift to activist theologies by the black churches in the South and by the Catholic churches in Latin America and Poland. Otherwise, church leaders risked the loss of legitimacy in the eyes of their parishioners. Similarly, the shift by white Protestant fundamentalist clergy in the United States from a theological doctrine prescribing the separation of religion and politics to one calling for secular political protest in the name of maintaining religious values (e.g., civil disobedience at abortion clinics) may reflect, at least in part, rising discontent among many parishioners in the face of threats to their traditional way of life raised by greater cultural permissiveness (Ginsberg 1989; Piven 1984).

Electoral institutions also illustrate the dual effects of institutional integration. The ideology of democratic political rights, by emphasizing the availability of legitimate avenues for the redress of grievances, delegitimizes protest; and the dense relationships generated by electoral politics also divert people from protest. Rising popular discontent, however, sometimes sets in motion a process that, at least temporarily, transforms electoral politics itself. For instance, when deteriorating economic circumstances produce voter volatility, the short-term concerns of political leaders with reelection may lead them to cope with unstable majorities by symbolically identifying with the grievances of discontented groups, thus fueling anger and legitimating protest (Piven and Cloward 1977, 18).

In many situations, protest becomes possible only when vertical controls weaken owing to large-scale processes of social change. In the 1930s, the craft unions associated with the dominant American Federation of Labor (AFL) issued charters to industrial workers who were clamoring for unions, but the AFL oligarchs were less than enthusiastic in welcoming their new constituents. Given their level of discontent and their loose ties to the AFL, industrial workers broke free, and strike waves followed. A similar process occurred in company unions that had been established to inhibit protest, particularly in the steel industry. And only as strikes escalated did a few enterprising union leaders, sensing the possibilities of the moment, create organizing committees to form industrial unions (Piven and Cloward 1977, 153). On this point, Hobsbawm agrees: "Mass union organization, in the United States of the 1930s as in all analogous 'explosions' of labor unionism with which I am familiar, was the result of worker mobilization and not its cause" (1978).

359

Another example of breakout is provided by the postwar drives by public employees for the right to unionize and strike. They gained this right only after the historically close ties between civil service associations and local political parties had weakened (Piven 1969). And the postwar black protest movement was not imaginable until the modernization of the plantation system led to mass evictions of blacks from the land and from a system of semifeudal controls (Oberschall 1973; Piven and Cloward 1977).[7] In short, breakdown is often prerequisite to breakout. Perhaps Durkheim is not so useless after all.

Normalizing Protest Organization

Some among the Durkheimians tend to think of collective protest as purposeless disorder, but RM analysts think it has purpose, and that it is political—the effort to exercise power in contests with other groups. In this large sense, protest is normal because politics is normal, as we would agree. In recasting collective protest as politics, however, RM analysts have normalized both the organizational forms typically associated with protest, especially with lower-stratum protest, and the political processes generated by protest.

Both of these tendencies appear in Tilly's work and are linked to his understanding of historical change as progress. Thus, in the preindustrial world, the possibility of exerting influence depended on "the willingness of [challenging groups] to inflict and endure harm," but the "grant of legality [to many previously proscribed forms of political action] lowers the group's costs of mobilization and collective action" (Tilly 1978, 167). Consequently, what now "tells more" than inflicting and enduring harm is "the group's capacity to organize, accumulate resources, and form alliances," especially within the electoral system (Tilly et al. 1975, 285). The implication is that ordinary people can now form organizations to pursue their goals through normal politics.

This conclusion strikes us as altogether too sweeping. True, with the grant of legality, the risk of repression no longer inhibits many forms of mobilization. At the same time, however, legalization increases the costs of mobilization because it imposes additional resource requirements. Tilly himself implies as much in his discussion of the way legalization transformed strikes: elements of "standardization," "routinization," and "bureaucratization" were introduced, and "spontaneity" declined (1978, 161). Moreover, legalization "muzzles" or "encapsulates" strike power (Piven and Cloward 1977, 155–75), as McCammon reminds us in her update of the way U.S. labor relations law "severely crippled, if not negated," the power of the strike (1990, 225). In other words, to use conventional methods of influence effectively, people have to be able to muster the resources both to organize bureaucratically and to overcome the influence of other groups in regular political contests. Those resources, Tilly says, are "the economist's factors of production: land, labor, capital, and perhaps technical expertise as well" (1978, 69). By these criteria, however, lower-stratum challengers are obviously left with serious resource deficits (Piven 1963).

Although RM analysts have tried to solve this problem in two ways, each method has failed. One approach has been to treat formal organization as if it compensates for lack of political resources. Unfortunately for lower-stratum groups, organization is a pale substitute for resources. Gamson's check list of what it takes for a group to become "combat-ready" shows why. Since the antagonists are bureaucratically organized, challengers must create parallel organizations with three characteristics: (1) a constitution, (2) an internal division into officers, committees, and rank and file, and (3) a formal membership list. In addition, it is important that there be sufficient centralized authority to quell factionalism in the group or, if the group is more decentralized, some other mechanism to control internal dissension. "Each of these variables—bureaucracy, centralization of power, and [the limiting of] factionalism—makes a contribution to success.... There are, then, definite advantages for a challenging group, inevitably engaged in conflict with an organized antagonist, to organize itself for facility in political combat" (1975, 108).

Gamson derives these conclusions from his study of fifty-three challengers in American history between 1800 and 1945, all of which were formally organized groups existing on an average of eight years. Two-fifths of them were occupationally based, mainly unions; one-third were assorted reform groups, including abolitionists, political parties, civil rights organizations, and peace groups; another fifth were socialist groups, such as the International Workingmen's Association; and the remainder were Right-wing or nativist groups, such as the German-American Bund (1975, 20).

Protest actions that were not sponsored by formally organized groups did not turn up in the sample.[8] "Perhaps that tells us something," Gamson says, thereby implying that collective protest episodes are always sponsored by organizations (personal communication). But even the most casual perusal of collective action events—whether the ghetto riots in the American cities of the 1960s or the mass demonstrations in Eastern Europe or the food riots in Latin America—makes clear how dubious that thesis is, and especially how dubious it is for the kinds of collective protest and disorder that are of concern to Durkheimians. (Of course, formal organizations do often come to be associated with protest events in various ways, sometimes because outside observers erroneously attribute these events to preexisting formal organizations and sometimes because protests stimulate the founding of organizations by social movement entrepreneurs who are then given credit retroactively for the protests themselves.)

Protest is also depicted as overorganized in a good many RM case studies. The rise of movements is signified by organizational paraphernalia, such as the formation of social movement organizations with leaders who make demands and call for demonstrations or lobbying. Absent these manifestations, RM analysts often do not recognize the existence of movements. Thus the two major recent RM accounts of the civil rights movement barely touch on riots: Morris (1984) does not mention them (except for a brief reference to the riot in Birmingham), and McAdam (1982) ignores the question of why they occurred. Similarly, in a survey of the social movement literature by McAdam, McCarthy, and Zald (1988), riots are mentioned only once, nor do many other modes of disruptive protest figure much in their survey. Their discussion of social movement organizations ranges across such issues as inclusivity and exclusivity, federation and chapter structures, and competition within social movement industries, which exerts pressure for "product differentiation." The "professional social movement organization" is singled out; in "pure" form, its distinguishing characteristic is that it "communicates with adherents or members through the mails or the mass media" (1988, 716–18).

These portrayals may well have validity for groups that have the resources to construct enduring formal organizations and still further resources that can be converted into political power. But can those with few resources form influential organizations successfully? Indeed, do they even have the resources to form stable formal organizations, influential or not? Lower-stratum groups often act as though they think so, and they do their best to adopt constitutions, elect officers, divide responsibilities among committees, compile membership lists, hold conventions, seek alliances, and garner external financial and expert resources. But such formal organizations cannot be wished into existence; it takes resources to create them and especially to sustain them. Labor organizations solve this problem with mechanisms to coerce membership and contributions—such as the union shop and dues check-off—but lower-stratum groups typically lack the capacity to coerce participation. Consequently, efforts by lower-income people to build formal organizations generally fail, as the most cursory reading of the history of poor people's organizations reveals. Naison's account of tenant organizing in New York City during the 1930s ends by noting that the citywide structure that coordinated local tenant organizations "proved fragile":

> Never did City-Wide's fund-raising produce over one thousand dollars per year.... The slum tenants...lacked the resources to subsidize it, or the political skills and inclinations to build the kind of stable organizations that could give City-Wide real permanence. City-Wide survived on the politically-motivated idealism and skills of underemployed professionals, both of which were vulnerable to shifts in political climate and improvements in the economy. (1986, 127)

The same point can be made for welfare rights organizing in the 1960s: the National Welfare Rights Organization lasted only about five years because local groups throughout the country could not sustain themselves once external resources from the antipoverty program, such as organizers drawn from the ranks of VISTA volunteers, began to contract. A serious defect of Gamson's sample is that the vast number of failed organization-building episodes by lower-stratum people is not represented, since most such efforts never resulted in fully formed organizations, or the resulting organizations were so puny and short-lived that they were not available to be sampled. Had there been a way to sample these episodes, Gamson might not have been so quick to advance a formal organization prescription, especially for lower-stratum groups. In short, the resources necessary to develop permanent mass-based bureaucratic organizations are not equally distributed in the class structure. The preoccupation with formal organization thus inadvertently contributes to the class bias in the work of RM analysts that has been remarked upon by Kerbo (1982).

The RM analysts have also tried to solve the problem of lower-stratum resource deficits by emphasizing the importance of coalition politics in which "third parties" make up for resource deficiencies.[9] Here the problem is not so much that lower-stratum groups lack resources to form stable organizations as that their organizations, even when formed, command few of the kinds of resources that can be converted into regular political influence. Organization, in short, is not necessarily a source of power.

The role of third parties in making up for the lack of political influence by lower-stratum groups was highlighted by Lipsky in his analysis of the 1963–64 New York City rent strike (1968, 1970). He concluded that the essence of the politics of protest is "showmanship" or "noise" in which leaders curry sympathy and support from potential "reference publics." His findings, which have been widely accepted, are summarized by the Tillys: "Lipsky makes a strong case that the strike movement owed what success it had (which was not enormous) to the fact that dramatic protests activated powerful third parties who then put pressure on responsible authorities to respond to the grievances of the protestors" (1975, 294). None of this was true. The so-called rent strike movement consisted of a mere flurry of rent-withholding activity between November 1963 and March of the next year. The only sense in which the episode was "dramatic" was that Jesse Grey, the citywide strike leader, knew how to attract press coverage by announcing (inaccurately) that thousands of buildings were about to go on strike and by conducting tenement tours for sympathetic reporters who wrote stories deploring housing conditions. As a factual matter, no powerful third parties put pressure on anyone (Piven and Cloward 1967).[10]

How then can people without conventional political resources exert influence? In our own work on unemployed and labor movements, rent strikes, welfare rights organizing, and the civil rights movement, we have tried to show that lower-stratum protesters have some possibility of influence—including mobilizing third-party support—if their actions violate rules and disrupt the workings of an institution on which important groups depend.[11] When lower-stratum groups form fragile formal organizations and employ conventional political strategies, they can easily be ignored. But institutional disruptions cannot so easily be ignored: they provoke conflict, they arouse an array of third parties, including important economic interests, and they may even contribute to electoral dealignment and realignment. To restore institutional stability and to avoid worsening polarization, political leaders are forced to respond, whether with concessions or with repression. To suppose that normal or conventional political strategies can have these effects is to underestimate the maldistribution of political resources and to trivialize the consequent realities of power.

Even when the resources are available to create them, formally organized groups are not likely to undertake disruptive protests. Gamson's formal organization prescription ignores the problems that disruptive or rule-breaking protests create for formal organizations. It is not that disruption and violence are never employed by formally organized groups; it is that, in general, organization constrains such tactics. Protests can provoke severe repression, which formal organizations will not usually risk (secret or underground organizations are better positioned in this respect). This is a point made by E. P. Thompson when he speaks of the English crowd's

> capacity for swift direct action. To be of a crowd or a mob was another way of being anonymous, whereas to be a member of a continuing organization was bound to expose one to detection and victimisation. The 18th century crowd well understood its capacities for action, and its own art of the possible. Its successes must be immediate, or not at all. It must destroy those machines, intimidate those employers or dealers, damage that mill...before troops come on the scene. (1974, 401)

Scott puts the same point this way: "Mob action...may represent a pop- ular tactical wisdom developed in conscious response to political con- straints realistically faced. Spontaneity and a lack of formal organization then become an enabling mode of protest rather than a reflection of the slender political talents of popular classes" (n.d.). And Oberschall again breaks with the main RM currents of thought to argue that "the degree of organization varies inversely with the magnitude of violence in con- frontations" (1973, 340).

Protest is also inhibited by constraints that result from the vertical integration upon which organizational maintenance by relatively resourceless groups often depends. Thus McAdam, McCarthy, and Zald claim that "a principal goal of [RM analysts] is understanding how emer- gent movement organizations seek to mobilize and routinize—fre- quently by tapping lucrative elite resources of support—the flow of resources, which ensures movement survival" (1988, 697), without acknowledging that this dependency generally turns movement organi- zations away from protest. This is a problem we have tried to address in our own work (1977, especially the introduction to the paperback edi- tion), but McAdam dismisses as "pessimistic" our conclusion that orga- nization (in the sense of formal organization) tends to militate against the use of disruptive tactics (1982, 54). Nevertheless, McAdam con- cludes his own discussion of these issues in words that could have been our own: "the establishment of formal organizations...sets in motion...the destructive forces of oligarchization, cooptation, and the dissolution of indigenous support...[all of which] tames the movement by encouraging insurgents to pursue only those goals acceptable to external sponsors.... The long list of movements that have failed to negotiate these obstacles attests to the difficulties inherent in the effort" (1982, 55–56).

Normalizing Political Influence

In democratic polities, whether protesters win or lose depends on the interaction between disruptive political tactics and electoral politics. But the influence resulting from the interaction between institutional disruptions and the electoral system cannot be understood by the usual mode of analysis that focuses, as the Tillys do, on the forming of alliances (1975, 285).

Lower-stratum disruptive movements tend to emerge at junctures when larger societal changes generate political volatility and dealignment and new political possibilities. On this point, we agree with the line of analysis in much RM literature that attributes protest from below in part to the opportunities generated by the fragmenting of elites and by realigning processes. Still, the impact of protest during these periods is not simply that it contributes to subsequent coalition building and realignment. What needs to be understood is that disruptive protest itself makes an important contribution to elite fragmentation and electoral dealignment. Indeed, we think the role of disruptive protest in helping to create political crises (or what we have called "dissensus politics") is the main source of political influence by lower-stratum groups (Cloward and Piven 1966, 1968; Piven and Cloward 1967, 1977, chap. 4; Piven and Cloward 1988, introduction).

The sharp contrast between our dissensus politics analysis and a good number of RM analyses can be illustrated by examining explanations of civil rights successes. For example, McAdam correctly emphasizes that a "significant disruption of public order" was essential to ensure federal responses to the civil rights movement (1982, 221). Despite this promising beginning (and despite its clear difference from Lipsky's "noise" and "showmanship"), McAdam goes on to explain federal responses in the usual coalitional terms: protesters won because of the growing influence of the black vote coupled with the support of sympathetic northern white liberals. Something like this coalitional process did indeed happen. It was not more important, however, than the fact that the tactics of the civil rights movement helped cleave the Democratic party's North-South alliance. This alliance was already weakening owing to southern opposition to New Deal labor and social welfare policies and owing to the expansion of the white middle class generated by economic modernization in the South during the postwar period. The result was to stimulate neopopulist movements and to revive the southern wing of the Republican party. Democratic leaders tipped decisively toward supporting civil rights legislation only when it became clear that black protests were also helping to swell the volume of southern white defections to the Republican party. With the white South alienated, it was finally in the interests of the national Democratic party to enfranchise blacks in an attempt to rebuild its shattered southern wing. For McAdam, however, the Democratic party's southern regional base was "a relatively small, politically expendable segment of the population" (1982, 215), which did not figure in the calculations of national Democratic party strategists. Of course, the South was not expendable and national Democratic party leaders knew it was not, which is why they resisted civil rights concessions for as long as they did. But civil rights protests—by activating northern liberals and the growing concentrations of black voters in the northern cities, and especially by enlarging the tide of southern white defections—changed the political calculus. Generally speaking, then, disruptive tactics force concessions not by enlarging and consolidating coalitions but by exacerbating electoral dissensus during periods when electoral divisions are already widening (Cloward and Piven 1966, 1968; Piven and Cloward 1967, 1977, chap. 4; Piven and Cloward 1988, introduction).

After two decades of work by analysts associated with the RM school, protest by lower-stratum people is as marginalized and deviant as it ever was. Despite a substantial volume of work on the civil rights movement, for example, we know little more than we did before about the riot of May 11, 1963, in Birmingham—perhaps the single most important episode in the black movement to that date—or of the subsequent riots in which 169 were killed, 7,000 wounded, and 40,000 arrested, except that the participants were not "riffraff."

When RM analysts talk about these riots, they reveal the biases of a normalized, overorganized, and conventionalized conception of political protest. The riots are not so much analyzed as regretted. McAdam considers that Jacobs and Landau "accurately summed up the situation" when they explained that "neither SNCC nor any other group has found a form of political organization that can convert the energy of the slums into political power" (quoted in McAdam 1982, 191). But if such efforts to organize the black lower class had been undertaken—at least if they had been undertaken early enough and forcefully enough in the 1960s—there might have been no riots. As it was, the main role played by various social movement leaders during the rioting was to try to quell it, and

RM analysts unfailingly approve. Morris says that when riots broke out in Birmingham in June 1963, civil rights leaders "hit the streets at once in order to persuade members of the black community not to engage in violence" so as to "save the agreement" with the economic elites of Birmingham. With the rioters subdued, "the agreement stood, and the planned exercise of 'people power' had been successful" (Morris 1984, 273). McAdam correctly notes that the early riots triggered a veritable northward stampede by movement leaders to establish organizational footholds in the ghetto as a means of regaining control over a movement that was "slipping away from them" (1982, 191). And Oberschall expresses the same outlook when he concludes that "the single most important failure of the middle-class blacks and the civil rights organizations was their failure to mobilize and to organize the lower-class community" (1973, 213).

So there we have it again. Like many malintegration analysts before them, resource mobilization analysts have also reduced lower-stratum protest politics to irrational and apolitical eruptions.

Originally published in 1984.

Notes

1. This contemporary development in the literature on protest follows a similar but much earlier development in the literature on property crime, or crimes against persons with income as the goal. Consider that Edwin H. Sutherland thought that "the processes which result in systematic criminal behavior are fundamentally the same in form as the processes which result in systematic lawful behavior" (1939, 4) and thus that "criminal behavior is a part of human behavior, has much in common with non-criminal behavior, and must be explained within the same general framework as any other behavior" (1947, 4). For a comparative analysis of these kindred but sequential theoretical perspectives in the study of crime and protest, see Piven and Cloward, "Crime and Protest" (forthcoming).

2. Rule is quite critical of the work on collective behavior by Park (1921), and especially by Turner and Killian (1957) for failing to "distinguish between collective and 'normal' behavior" (1988:102). He also claims that the problem of distinguishing "collective behavior from the rest of social life" is one of two central questions with which he will be preoccupied in his book (1988: 115). But in his extensive and sympathetic discussion of RM work, Rule does not note that RM analysts also blur this distinction.

3. Elsewhere, Tilly acknowledges this extraordinary normative violation: "The frequent borrowing—in parody or in earnest—of the authorities' normal forms of action...often amounted to the crowd's almost literally taking the law into its own hands" (1981, 161). Nevertheless, it is the role of norms in shaping the modes of defiance, not the defiance of norms as such, that is emphasized.

4. This overall conclusion seems illogical even within the RM framework that postulates continuity between normal and defiant political activity. It is well established, e.g., that worsening economic conditions lead to voting shifts, imperiling incumbents and sometimes causing dramatic political realignments (see, e.g., Tufte 1978). Since economic deterioration produces changes in conventional political behavior, the logic of the RM analysis would lead one to expect a similar correlation between worsening economic conditions and protest.

5. And even if people are in fact inclined to seek solutions to their problems through politics, variations in social integration may predict the forms of protest better than the incidence of it: e.g., disciplined civil disobedience occurred more often in the South and rioting occurred almost exclusively in the North during the 1960s. A possible explanation is that northern ghettos were less cohesive than southern black communities, making it more difficult to promote disciplined protest, especially in the face of provocations by the police.

6. On this point, see also Eric Wolf's (1969) discussion of the constraining effect of clan ties that crossed class lines in prerevolutionary China.

7. For further examples of this general point and the literature bearing on it, see Kerbo (1982, 652).

8. "In theory," Gamson says, "a collective behavior listing might have yielded a challenging group, in the absence of any other appropriate organizational listing, but this, in fact, never occurred. Thus all of our final sample listings are organizations" (1975, 156).

9. Morris (1984) has taken exception to this view in his discussion of the civil rights movement by summoning evidence of the substantial resources the black community itself supplied, but his own data make clear that these internally generated resources, including especially leadership resources, were contributed mainly by middle-class blacks.

10. The strike failed to rally significant third-party support because the organizers followed Gamson's prescription: they first built tenant committees. Then, together with tenant leaders, they tried to induce tenants to use the procedures for legal redress laid out by the housing agencies. They canvassed apartments for housing violations, filled out official forms, scheduled visits by building inspectors to record hazardous violations, checked to be sure the inspectors actually filed these forms, arranged for rents to be placed in escrow, contacted lawyers, and shepherded tenants through the courts, not once but over and over again in the face of delaying tactics by landlords. And for all that, only a

few victories were won. As tenants and organizers were increasingly over-whelmed and worn down by these procedures, the strike faltered and then collapsed only a few months after it began (Piven and Cloward 1967).

11. The essential importance of institutional disruptions for the exercise of political influence by resourceless groups is set out in Piven (1963) and in Cloward and Piven (1966). For theoretical elaborations and applications to particular social movements, see Piven and Cloward (1967, 1977) and Cloward and Piven (1968). The role of disruption is debated in Gamson and Schmeidler (1984) and Cloward and Piven (1984).

References

CLOWARD, RICHARD A., AND FRANCES FOX PIVEN. 1966. "A Strategy to End Poverty." Nation, May 2. Reprinted in Richard A. Cloward and Frances Fox Piven, *The Politics of Turmoil*. New York: Pantheon, 1974.

—————. 1968. "Dissensus Politics: A Strategy for Winning Economic Rights." New Republic, April 20. Reprinted in Richard A. Cloward and Frances Fox Piven, *The Politics of Turmoil*. New York: Pantheon, 1974.

—————. 1979. "Hidden Protest: The Channeling of Female Innovation and Resistance." *Signs* 4:41.

—————. 1984. "Disruption and Organization: A Rejoinder to Gamson and Schmeidler." *Theory and Society* 13:587–99.

—————. 1989. "Why People Deviate in Different Ways." In *New Directions in the Study of Justice, Law and Social Control*, ed. the Arizona State University School of Justice Studies Editorial Board. New York: Plenum.

EXUM, WILLIAM H. 1985. *Paradoxes of Black Protest: Black Student Activism in a White University*. Philadelphia: Temple University Press.

FLACKS, RICHARD. 1988. *Making History: The Radical Tradition and the American Mind*. New York: Columbia University Press.

GAMSON, WILLIAM A. 1975. *The Strategy of Social Protest*. Homewood, Ill.: Dorsey.

GAMSON, WILLIAM A., AND EMILIE SCHMEIDLER. 1984. "Organizing the Poor: An Argument with Frances Fox Piven and Richard A. Cloward, Poor People's Movements: Why They Succeed, How They Fail." *Theory and Society* 13:567–85.

GINSBERG, FAYE. 1989. *Contested Lives: The Abortion Debate in an American Community*. Berkeley: University of California Press.

HOBSBAWM, ERIC J. 1978. "Should the Poor Organize?" *New York Review of Books* 25, no. 4 (March 23).

IANNI, FRANCIS A. J. 1974. *Black Mafia: Ethnic Succession in Organized Crime*. New York: Simon and Schuster.

KERBO, HAROLD R. 1982. "Movements of 'Crisis' and Movements of 'Affluence': A Critique of Deprivation and Resource Mobilization Theories." *Journal of Conflict Resolution* 26, no. 4 (December).

KERBO, HAROLD R., AND RICHARD A. SHAFFER, 1986. "Unemployment and Protest in the United States, 1890–1940: A Methodological Critique and Research Note." *Social Forces* 64:1046–56.

LIPSKY, MICHAEL. 1968. "Protest as a Political Resource." *American Political Science Review* 62:1144–58.

————. 1970. *Protest in City Politics: Rent Strikes, Housing and the Power of the Poor.* Chicago: Rand McNally.

LODHI, ABDUL QAIYUM, AND CHARLES TILLY. 1973. "Urbanization and Collective Violence in 19th-Century France." *American Journal of Sociology* 2 (September).

MCADAM, DOUG. 1982. *Political Process and the Development of Black Insurgency, 1930–1970.* Chicago: University of Chicago Press.

————. 1988. *Freedom Summer: The Idealists Revisited.* New York: Oxford University Press.

MCADAM, DOUG, JOHN D. MCCARTHY, AND MAYER N. ZALD. 1988. "Social Movements." In *Handbook of Sociology*, ed. Neil J. Smelser. Beverly Hills, Calif.: Sage.

MCCAMMON, HOLLY J. 1990. "Legal Limits on Labor Militancy: Labor Law and the Right to Strike since the New Deal." *Social Problems* 37, no. 2.

MCCARTHY, JOHN D. 1987. "Pro-Life and Pro-Choice Mobilization: Infrastructure Deficits and New Technologies." In *Social Movements in an Organizational Society*, ed. Mayer N. Zald and John D. McCarthy. New Brunswick, N.J.: Transaction Books.

MCCARTHY, JOHN D., MARK WOLFSON, DAVID P. BAKER, AND ELAINE M. MOSAKOWSKI. In press. "The Foundations of Social Movement Organizations: Local Citizens' Groups Opposing Drunken Driving." In *Ecological Models of Organization*, ed. Glenn R. Carroll. Cambridge, Mass.: Ballinger.

MCCARTHY, JOHN D., AND MAYER ZALD. 1973. *The Trend of Social Movements in America: Professionalization and Resource Mobilization.* Morristown, N.J.: General Learning Press.

————. 1977. "Resource Mobilization and Social Movements." *American Journal of Sociology* 82:1212–41.

MOORE, BARRINGTON. 1966. *The Social Origins of Dictatorship and Democracy: Lord and Peasant in the Making of the Modern World.* Boston: Beacon Press.

MORRIS, ALDON D. 1984. *The Origins of the Civil Rights Movement.* New York: Free Press.

NAISON, MARK. 1986. "From Eviction Resistance to Rent Control: Tenant Activism in the Great Depression." In *The Tenant Movement in New York City, 1904–1984*, ed.

Ronald Lawson, with the assistance of Mark Naison. New Brunswick, N.J.: Rutgers University Press.

OBERSCHALL, ANTHONY. 1973. *Social Conflict and Social Movements*. Englewood Cliffs, N.J.: Prentice-Hall.

————. 1978. "Theories of Social Conflict." In *Annual Review of Sociology*, 4. Beverly Hills, Calif.: Sage.

PIVEN, FRANCES FOX. 1963. "Low-Income People and the Political Process." A report published by Mobilization for Youth. Reprinted in Richard A. Cloward and Frances Fox Piven, *The Politics of Turmoil*. New York: Pantheon, 1974.

————. 1969. "Militant Civil Servants." Transaction 7, no. 1 (November). Reprinted in Richard A. Cloward and Frances Fox Piven, *The Politics of Turmoil*. New York: Pantheon, 1974.

————. 1981. "Deviant Behavior and the Remaking of the World." *Social Problems* 28, no. 5:489–508.

————. 1984. "Women and the State: Ideology, Power and the Welfare State." In *Gender and the Life Course*, ed. Alice Rossi. New York: Aldine.

PIVEN, FRANCES FOX, AND RICHARD A. CLOWARD. 1967. "Rent Strike: Disrupting the Slum System." New Republic, December 2. Reprinted in Richard A. Cloward and Frances Fox Piven, *The Politics of Turmoil*. New York: Pantheon, 1974.

————. 1977. *Poor People's Movements*. New York: Pantheon.

————. 1988. *Why Americans Don't Vote*. New York: Pantheon.

————. Forthcoming. "Crime and Protest: Discovery and Rediscovery."

RUDE, GEORGE. 1964. *The Crowd in History*. New York: Wiley.

RULE, JAMES B. 1988. *Theories of Civil Violence*. Berkeley: University of California Press.

SCOTT, JAMES. N.d. "The Hidden Transcript of Subordinate Groups." Department of Political Science, Yale University.

SHORTER, EDWARD, AND CHARLES TILLY. 1974. *Strikes in France, 1830 to 1968*. New York: Cambridge University Press.

SNYDER, DAVID, AND CHARLES TILLY. 1972. "Hardship and Collective Violence in France, 1830–1960." *American Sociological Review* 37.

SUTHERLAND, EDWIN H. 1939. *Principles of Criminology*. 3d ed. Chicago: University of Chicago Press.

————. 1947. *Principles of Criminology*. 4th ed. Philadelphia: Lippincott.

THOMPSON, E. P. 1974. "Patrician Society, Plebian Culture." *Journal of Social History* 7, no. 4.

TILLY, CHARLES. 1975. "Food Supply and Public Order in Modern Europe." In *The Formation of National States in Western Europe*, ed. Charles Tilly. Princeton: Princeton University Press.

——. 1978. *From Mobilization to Revolution*. Reading, Mass.: Addison-Wesley.

——. 1981. *As Sociology Meets History*. New York: Academic Press.

——. 1986. *The Contentious French*. Cambridge, Mass.: Harvard University Press.

TILLY, CHARLES, LOUISE TILLY, AND RICHARD TILLY. 1975. *The Rebellious Century*. Cambridge, Mass.: Harvard University Press.

TUFTE, EDWARD R. 1978. *Political Control of the Economy*. Princeton: Princeton University Press.

WALSH, EDWARD. 1981. "Resource Mobilization and Citizen Protest in Communities around Three Mile Island." *Social Problems* 29:1–21.

WILSON, KENNETH L., AND ANTHONY M. ORUM. 1976. "Mobilizing People for Collective Political Action." *Journal of Political and Military Sociology* 4:187–202.

WOLF, ERIC. 1969. *Peasant Wars in the Twentieth Century*. New York: Harper and Row.

Part V

Power and Political Institutions

18

Introduction

The breaking of the social compact is being achieved in part by restructuring government, especially the national government. Some functions are being shunted upward to supranational organizations, while other functions are being devolved to state and county governments, or contracted out to private organizations. Other changes have the effect of constricting the revenue-raising capacity of the national government, or limiting its regulatory authority. These developments occurred one after the other in rapid-fire order in the 1990s. They reveal a deep truth about the close bearing of institutional arrangements on power.

  Institutions reflect power, and they enhance power. Patterned rules and practices are constructed by those who have power, with the aim of stabilizing power over time. Thus the organization of state decision-making authority and the rules by which that authority is constrained reflects the exercise of power by some people to enhance their power over other people. But while power is solidified by institution-building, it is not frozen. As the resources and goals of power blocs shift, or as new power blocs emerge, calls are issued for the reform of governmental rules and practices in an effort to routinize the exercise of power under new conditions, or to routinize the exercise of power by new groups.[1]

A notable current in American political history explores the significance of the structure of the American state in just these terms. Thus, much is often made of the separation of powers in the national government, an arrangement which Schattschneider thought was "designed to make parties ineffective...[because they] would lose and exhaust themselves in futile attempts to fight their way through the labyrinthine framework."[2] And since political parties were necessary to make atomized voters effective, weak parties ensured the weakness of democracy. Nor was this unintentional, since the founders were leery of the democratic passions which the revolution itself had helped arouse.

The essays which follow draw on this perspective to probe the political significance of another dimension of American state structure, the decentralization of governmental authority, and the complex and changing pattern of intergovernmental relations to which it has led. As has often been noted, the American governmental system is uniquely decentralized, with decision-making authority and revenue-raising capacity dispersed among federal, state and local governments. This complex pattern of intergovernmental relations became the target of reform efforts by Democratic presidents in the 1960s, and by Republican leaders in the decades that followed.

The usual assumption is that centralized authority is more accessible to elites, and decentralized authority more accessible to ordinary people. In a moment we will explain why we think this idea is misleading. First, however, we need to explain the grounds for the belief. The creation of a national government in 1789 was in part an effort by postrevolutionary elites to create a level of authority that would override popular demands emerging in the state legislatures for the reduction of confiscatory taxes or high prices or mortgage lending rates. A national government would check what Hamilton called the "the imprudence of democracy" not only because imprudence would be chastened by checks and balances of the new government, as well as by the new constitutional guarantees against interference by the states with trade or currency policy, but because a national government would be more accessible to elites and less accessible to the common people. And until well into the twentieth century, the pattern more or less held. Popular politics tended to remain local. Of course, much business politics was also necessarily local in a decentralized economy. However, when business policies were jeopardized by opposition on the local level, business lobbyists moved to the state or even the federal level where they were likely to prevail.

This trend toward centralization notwithstanding, local governments remained exceptionally vigorous in the United States, because localities did indeed do many things. They ran the schools, organized local services, policed the streets, and hired the people and raised the taxes that made these activities possible. What local government did was visible, of direct importance in the daily life of most people, and the officials in charge of these activities were relatively accessible. Local governments, and the local party organizations they spawned, were at the very ground level in politics, and they played a large role in sustaining the allegiance of democratic publics to the political system in general, and to the political parties as well.

The massive migration of blacks to the cities in the post–World War II period put this role at risk, at least in the big cities that were crucial to national Democratic victories. Imprisoned within an increasingly bureaucratic municipal apparatus, and paralyzed by the ferocity of race hatreds among their older constituents, city politicians responded slowly or not at all to the newcomers.

This sclerosis in the cities posed large problems for national Democratic leaders, and prompted them to initiate a new form of federal intervention in the big cities. The Great Society programs provided new monies for inner city services and spawned new inner city agencies. The aim of all this was to bribe or prod city governments to become more responsive to urban blacks whose votes and grievances were growing in tandem, promising trouble for national Democratic administrations.

The local character of popular politics, encouraged by American state structure and political organization, helps explain why the intense conflicts of the 1960s and 1970s often took form in the cities. Conflicts inevitably were registered in claims on municipal budgets, by community groups and municipal unions, real estate operators and civil rights groups, helping to explain the perennial urban fiscal crises of the 1960s and 1970s. Democratic national governments responded to these fiscal problems by increasing federal aid to the cities. But under Republican presidents beginning in 1968, the direction of federal spending shifted, as the grant-in-aid system was used by a new regime to promote constituency-building in the suburbs and elsewhere outside of the old cities. This shift, and the complex conditions which influenced it, are discussed in "Federal Policy and Urban Fiscal Strain."

The much discussed troubles of the national Democratic party also reflect the influence of the structural decentralization of the American government. In particular, the authority retained by the states in the American constitutional system helps to account for the political vigor of the Democratic party's southern section. Unlike the big cities, whose party organizations had been weakened by decades-long campaigns for municipal reform, the southern state parties were undergirded by the sturdy patronage base yielded by state and county revenues and authority. Even Franklin Delano Roosevelt's effort to challenge some of the southern power brokers in 1938 was broken because of the independent resources which southern politicians continued to control, including even the patronage resources generated by federal programs channeled through the state grant-in-aid system.

If a weak party system reflected the structure of the American state, it was weakened further by the large role of interest groups who promoted the post–World War II redevelopment policies which led to the growth of the suburbs and the new cities in the Sunbelt, at the expense of the older industrial centers. This pattern was of course disastrous to the long term fortunes of the Democratic party, but a weak party without a center had no capacity to consider long term consequences. We discuss these issues, and the influence of other structural features of American government on party development, in "Structural Constraints and Political Development: The Case of the American Democratic Party."

A final cautionary word before we turn to these essays. No simple generalization is adequate to describe the bearing of centralization and decentralization on power in the American system. Schattschneider was again closer to the truth when, writing in 1941, he commented that one of the remarkable recent developments in American politics is that all levels of government now are "*doing the same kinds of things* in large areas of public policy, so that it is possible for contestants to move freely from one level of government to another in an attempt to find the level at which they might try most advantageously to get what they want."[3]

Recent developments suggest that neither simple generalizations about centralization and decentralization, nor even Schattschneider's view of the contingent relationship of the intergovernmental system to the successful exercise of power, are adequate. There is a crucial dimension of state structure slighted in these emphases, and that is the relationship of states to markets. Localities were the locus of popular politics for much of American history, but local and state governments were sharply constrained, not by only by the occasional intervention of central government, but by the ability of mobile investors—and well-off taxpayers—to move or threaten to move beyond the boundaries of a given locality or state. This also was a structural constraint on democratic politics, and a very important one.

From this point of view, the gradual and incomplete centralization of popular programs from the 1930s on was an important democratic gain, because it freed these programs from the power that mobile investors and taxpayers wielded over state and local governments. For just this reason, efforts to "devolve" authority to the states ought to be viewed with suspicion. True, the notion that the states are "closer to the people" resonates, because it reflects something about our history, and something also about the closeness of local politics to daily life. But it ignores what is more important, that in an economy in which investors can play states and localities against one another with threats of disinvestment, decentralization is likely to greatly increase the leverage of business over government policies, including the policies of the social compact.[4] In other words, the current effort to restructure public authority would not be understood simply as an attack on government, but as an effort to restructure government as as to increase, in enduring ways, business power in American politics.

1997

Notes

1. Korpi, Walter. "Institutions, Interests, and Identities: The Development of Welfare State Institutions. Draft Chapter for eds. Walter Korpi and Joakim Palme, "Contested Citizenship: A Century of Social Policy Development in the Western World." Presented at the Conference on The Welfare State at the Crossroads, Sigtuna, Sweden, January 9-12, 1997.

2. Schattschneider, E. E. *Party Government*, New York: Rinehart and Co., 1942 p. 7.

3. Schattschneider, E. E. *The Semi-Sovereign People*, New York: Holt, Rinehart and Winston, 1960, p. 10. Emphasis in original.

4. For a fuller discussion, see "Welfare and the Transformation of Electoral Politics" in Part I.

19

Federal Policy and Urban Fiscal Strain

Most observers have attributed the fiscal crises that have affected many of our major urban centers in the 1970s to a variety of market shifts in the American economy. According to the prevailing explanation, the decline in the fiscal capacity of cities was the inevitable result of the decreased economic attractiveness of urban centers. Government policies and underlying political exigencies have been deemed secondary causes, necessarily subordinate to market forces.

This article will show that the market explanation for fiscal strain is incomplete and misleading. While market forces are important, government policies, shaped by political as well as economic exigencies,[1] are also important. The assertion that governmental actions are necessarily subordinate to the market is an ideological one, designed to reduce the realm of the political by definitional fiat.[2]

Part I of this article demonstrates that a series of federal policies helped stimulate the exodus of capital and population in the post–World War II period that eroded the revenue base of the older industrial cities. At the same time, other federal policies were serving to fuel demands for compensatory social programs for urban residents. Together, these policies precipitated the fiscal difficulties of the older industrial cities.

Part II shows that the American polity contains distinctive structural features that help to account for the inconsistent federal policies which generated urban fiscal strain.[3] These arrangements include the tendency for investor-oriented and popularly-oriented policies to be located at different levels of the federal system and in different agencies of a fragmented governmental structure.

Finally, Part III addresses current policies and politics, postulating that policy initiatives of the Reagan administration will shape both the local politics and future prospects of urban fiscal strain. The impact of the new policies is partly redistributional; there has been a dramatic shift toward investor-oriented federal programs. More importantly, however, the new policies are evidence of an effort by the Reagan administration to alter the structural arrangements which permitted the emergence of the politics underlying compensatory urban social welfare programs.

I. The Causes of Urban Fiscal Strain

A. The Federal Policies Leading to Diminished Municipal Resources

The prevailing explanation of the fiscal strain that has bedeviled many older large American cities emerges from the reports of Presidential commissions, the work of numerous academics, and the popular press.[4] It is easy to summarize. In response to lower taxes, lower labor costs, and other locational incentives, investors abandoned the central cities, first for the suburbs and later for the Sunbelt and international markets. Disinvestment inexorably eroded the sources of municipal revenues; not only were there fewer employers and employees to be taxed, but as prosperity waned, so did the sales and property values that were the main sources of municipal revenue.

A decline in public revenues only generates fiscal strain, however, when public officials do not make corresponding reductions in expenditures.[5] The evolving fiscal strains of the cities are not merely the result of a contracting municipal economy. They are also a result of expanding municipal expenditures. In the face of shrinking resources, city officials permitted city budgets to balloon.[6]

While fiscal strains have been endemic in the history of American cities, this particular explanation of fiscal strain has gained prominence only in the last decade. The explanations advanced prior to the recent spate of local fiscal crises were distinctly different. Some focused on the fragmentation of municipal governments, which prevented jurisdictions with expenditure needs from capturing the necessary revenues. Others stressed the misallocation of functional responsibilities among local jurisdictions that caused the mismatching of costs of providing facilities and services with revenue capacities of beneficiaries. While both of these earlier diagnoses were superficial, they did point to problems in the organization of government, and problems in the organization of government can be ameliorated by political action.

The explanation which has now become fashionable is markedly different. It is grander, and more somber. It echoes the worldview of 19th century Social Darwinism by invoking a species of natural law to explain the troubles of our cities. This natural law is the law of the market, and is presumably inexorable in its judgments. When capital disinvests from our older central cities, it does so in accord with the workings of market law. City governments and their populations must also accede to this law, and settle for less. In the words of a 1982 Reagan administration report on urban policy:

> Too often the Federal Government has been called upon to intervene to insulate individuals, businesses and communities from the consequences of changes brought about by evolving technology, shifting market conditions, and altered social attitudes. Intervention can do more harm than good by slowing the process of individual and collective adjustment to changes.[7]

In some variations of this argument, the Malthusian worldview emerges even more boldly; it is said that cities, like other natural creatures, must die when their time has come—the only question being whether government policies will enable them to die gracefully.[8]

While the economic base of many older central cities has indisputably eroded, and with it the revenue capacity of their municipal governments, the explanation for this development advanced by the prevailing school of thought is far from indisputable. One aspect of urban decline was the movement of industry, commerce, and wealthier urban residents to the suburbs.[9] The prevailing view attributes suburbanization to the unfolding of the law of the market as investors and citizens alike maximized their self-interest by leaving the central cities. Industries relocated in the suburbs largely because post-World War II linear industrial construction led investors and developers to seek the more ample space afforded by suburban locations. Residents left because the prosperity of the post-World War II period permitted them to indulge their preferences for home ownership and sideyards. Commercial investors left in response to the new and more prosperous market thereby created, and to acquire the large spaces demanded by the new style of automobile shopping. All of these developments are depicted as market phenomena, proceeding through the individual decisions of rational actors seeking to maximize their material self-interest.

Grand and somber though it may be, the dominant explanation of troubles in the big cities ignores as much as it explains. It ignores the role of government and politics not only in responding to economic life, but also in forming economic life. Would the industrial investors have relocated as readily without highway, water, and sewer grants made available by federal policies? Or without federal tax laws that provided incentives for investment in new facilities rather than the refurbishment of old ones?[10] Would as many have moved, or as quickly? Would so many urban residents have been so eager to become suburban homeowners without the enormous advantage of government constructed highways?[11] Or without the price advantages yielded by federal low cost mortgages and federal income tax benefits?[12] Without highway programs, and the population shifts they encouraged, would the retail trades have been attracted to suburban locations on so large a scale? Alternatively, suppose an entirely different pattern of federal subsidies had emerged, generating large incentives for the refurbishment of older housing, mass transit, and the service infrastructure of the cities. Is it conceivable that this would have been without effect? In other words, were the developments to which urban economic decline is attributed produced by individual rational actors seeking to maximize their self-interest in relation to other rational actors, or were they produced by the same rational actors seeking to maximize their self-interest in the context of new conditions created by state policies? Was it economics or politics that produced the urban fiscal crisis? Or, more reasonably, was it the interaction of economics and politics, in a society in which economy and polity have become ever more densely intertwined, each both cause and effect of the other?

Consider also the more recent shift of investment to the Sunbelt. This is another development often attributed to a market calculus. To be sure, labor costs and tax costs were typically lower in Sunbelt locations. The long-term movement of labor-intensive manufacturing, beginning with the relocation of the textile industry at the end of the 19th century, is easily understood in these terms. But even that historic trend cannot be isolated from key government policies which helped to account for regional disparities in labor costs. In particular, the use of cheap labor in the South owed much to the caste system, and the caste system was as much an expression of politics as of economics. Blacks were kept in place by state and local laws which disenfranchised and segregated them,[13] and by state and local government violence which curbed challenges to caste boundaries. Furthermore, the caste policies of the southern states survived for nearly a century because they were tacitly and sometimes explicitly endorsed by the national government.[14]

National labor policy has played a similar role in ratifying regional disparities in labor costs. As the unionization of industrial workers spread in the aftermath of the passage of the National Labor Relations Act in 1935, states in low-wage regions undermined the rights granted labor under the Act with state right-to-work laws, which were then sanctioned by the national government in the Taft-Hartley Act of 1947.[15] The predictable result was that unionization was impeded in the South, and wages consequently remained lower. The effects are still evident today.[16]

The impact of these longstanding trends in regional economic development has been perceptible since the turn of the century, when the textile mills of New England began to move south to take advantage of lower labor costs and a more docile labor force. While the effects on particular towns were sometimes considerable, the departure of some low-wage and intensely competitive industries was offset for a long period by the fantastic expansion of other industries. Only with the slowdown of industrial expansion in the late 1960s was the impact of

regional shifts on the older cities felt more deeply. New national policies, especially the expansion of defense related industries in the South,
the concentration of military installations in the sunbelt, and the growth
of the aerospace and electronics industries, accelerated the trend. All of
these industries are critically dependent on the government policies that
support them and promote their regional concentration.[17] Furthermore,
the ease with which industries less directly dependent on government
expenditures shifted investment to the sunbelt owed much to the fact
that a costly public infrastructure, particularly highways and water projects, was being financed by the federal government.[18]

The combined effect of federal programs has been a decline in the
components of cities' fiscal capacity. Manufacturing jobs in the central
cities have dropped sharply, a drop only partially offset by the expansion
of the service sector. Meanwhile, manufacturing jobs in non-metropolitan areas and in the South have continued to increase.[19] Population and
personal income have shifted in a parallel pattern, marking a trend that
the 1980 census indicates is accelerating.[20]

The federal government has become so involved in the American
economy that it is no longer possible to account for any major economic
development without reference to public policy. The economic base of
the older cities is contracting, and with it the revenue capacities of central city governments. But this development cannot be understood
entirely as the consequence of market processes, operating according to
market laws. There were market actors, to be sure, but these actors
made their decisions in the context of an economy in which government programs had come to play an enormous role. In that sense, the
market had come to be penetrated by government, and therefore by
politics. Nor was it simply that market actors took advantage of
govern-ment policies. Assuming that they were, as the market perspective tells us, rational and self-seeking, then it is reasonable to pre-
sume that they also promoted the policies which gave them economic
advantage.[21]

While these were market actors, they had moved from a sphere
where action is viewed as governed by economic laws to a sphere where
action is understood as voluntarist. Moreover, state leaders were not
merely reactive in this process. They were actors in their own right, fil-

tering their responses to the demands of market interests in terms of their own distinctively political objectives.[22] The conception of this complex interplay of politics and markets as merely the playing out of market forces is not only analytically deficient, but also intensely ideological. By defining politics as economics, the prevailing view attempts to define the policies which shaped the circumstances of our cities as beyond the reach of democratic political influences.

B. The Logic of Increased Compensatory Programs

The other aspect of urban fiscal strain acknowledged by the prevailing explanation concerns patterns of municipal expenditure that failed to adjust to diminishing municipal resources. A contracting tax base alone would produce a multitude of problems for the people of a city, as municipal jobs and services were cut back. Declining revenues only produce fiscal problems, however, when jobs and services are not correspondingly reduced, and expenditures outrun revenues. Expenditures in the older cities obviously did outrun revenues, typically even rising while the tax base was contracting. Within the framework of the dominant explanation of the urban fiscal crisis, this phenomenon is viewed as perverse, since avowedly economic realities were ignored by political actors. In other words, the facts of contracting municipal resources are seen as economic facts, and therefore rock-hard and inexorable. By contrast, the perversity which led cities to spend more than they took in reflects merely political facts, and political facts are depicted as "soft" because they derive from willful human decisions.[23]

That expenditures reflected politics is neither remarkable nor reprehensible. The public budget allocates both public funds and public authority, which represent the means to power, wealth, security, and/or survival for different groups. Thus, it is always the focus of group contention.[24] What was remarkable was not that expenditures reflected politics, but rather that new groups—mainly blacks and Hispanics—were entering the contest, and pressing for increased municipal expenditures. The new groups had become significant political actors because changes in the southern agricultural economy—stimulated by still other federal policies—had thrust them first into the cities and then into the electoral representative system. These new contestants were the people who ultimately bore the brunt of the shifts in investments spurred by federal policies.

Economic change typically generates population movements as well as shifts in the circumstances of populations, with the result that new political groupings and new political claims emerge. This pattern characterized the American experience in the post-World War II period. American agriculture, particularly the historically labor-intensive agriculture of the South, threw off excess laborers who, having been economically displaced by modernization, had little alternative but to migrate to the big cities.[25]

Like all major contemporary economic developments in the United States, these developments in agriculture did not occur simply as a result of market and technological processes. Federal subsidies and loans had much to do with the advance of mechanization.[26] Mechanization, in turn, not only rendered much agricultural labor superfluous, but also stimulated the enlargement of agricultural holdings so that small farmers were also displaced.[27] Meanwhile, federal supports for idle land aggravated the tendency toward labor surplus, since profits could be made without cultivation.[28] Federal welfare policies gave the agricultural states license to effectively refuse income supports to the local unemployed,[29] helping to ensure that displaced tenants, farmers and sharecroppers would make their way to the cities. These conditions combined to accelerate the migration of the displaced agricultural workforce, largely black and southern, to the older cities whose economies could not absorb them. Between 1940 and 1966, 3.7 million blacks left the South for the industrial North, most of them going to the large central cities.[30] By the end of this period, blacks were the most urban people in the United States.[31]

The vast migration of blacks, and of Hispanics who were being displaced during the same period, occurred at the same time that millions of older urban residents were leaving the central cities for the suburbs in response to the overall shift of investment. The enormous turnover in population was bound to cause political repercussions, simply because large shifts in population always undermine existing patterns of political organization. Older patterns of leadership weaken as established constituents shrink in numbers and influence, while new groups bring new demands and different styles of organization and action.

American cities have always had to cope with the instabilities generated by massive population change. In the 19th century, a distinctive and remarkable mode of political organization developed to deal with the potentially unsettling effects of generations of new migrants: the big city political machine. Machine politics meant that some of the authority and wealth of a municipality could be converted into favors, friendship, and representation that cultivated the allegiance of diverse immigrant groups. By World War II, however, most big city machines had been greatly weakened or even destroyed as a result of the efforts of municipal reformers and the subsequent influence of federal grants-in-aid. City governments had by and large become "clean" as bureaucratic politics replaced machine politics. The reform battles that resulted in the elaboration of bureaucratic structures and rules weakened machine bosses by depriving them of control of municipal jobs and municipal policies, and therefore of the patronage on which they depended.[32] But bureaucratization also meant that the jobs and services which had earlier been used to cultivate allegiance among newcomers were no longer easily dispensed to new groups. The operation of the bureaus became constrained by civil service regulations, and later by union contracts. The protracted conflict in New York City between minority groups and the school system in the 1960s and particularly between minority groups and organized teachers, for control of school jobs and school policy illustrates this development. The challenge by minorities was necessarily a challenge to the rules of the educational bureaucracy, and to the contract of the United Federation of Teachers.[33] It was not that the bureaucratization of the goods, services and honors controlled by city governments had depoliticized municipal administrations. Rather, bureaucratization provided a set of devices which protected the stakes of groups who were already the beneficiaries of municipal largesse, and thus impeded the use of municipal resources to integrate the post-World War II black and Hispanic newcomers.

Political problems of this scale in the big cities inevitably reverberate upward to the federal government. The mechanisms of transmission are not mysterious. Urban business interests lobby, and urban political leaders carry weight because of their influence on the votes of organized urban constituencies in national elections. The first main response of the federal government to the pressures generated by the economic shifts that were weakening the urban economy on the one hand, and bringing agricultural migrants to the cities on the other hand, was the urban renewal program,[34] a response that suited the interests of both downtown businessmen and city mayors. Federal subsidies were made available for the acquisition of land in "blighted" central city areas; this land was subsequently resold to private developers at below market rates.[35] That urban renewal came to be known as "black removal" was not an accident, for the designation of blighted areas for commercial or residential redevelopment was frequently influenced by the poverty and the race of the residents of these areas. Downtown businessmen and mayors could unite around a program which would return wealthier customers and taxpayers to the urban core. At the same time, urban renewal would remove the newcomers whose enlarging presence threatened to accelerate white flight and cause fissures in urban political organizations that could not easily incorporate the minorities, yet could not, as their number grew, continue indefinitely to exclude them either.

Given the powerful economic forces and large government programs that were combining to transform the cities and their populations, urban renewal was not equal to its task. Indeed, urban renewal exacerbated the political problems of municipal officials. On the one hand, it did not reverse the patterns of in- and out-migration that were weakening the big city political organizations. On the other hand, renewal itself became a major source of grievance to the largely black and Hispanic populations who were displaced. Political instabilities in the nation's largest cities took form in the electoral defections by blacks from the Democratic Party in the presidential elections of 1956, and their rather reluctant return in the election of 1960.[36] This development signalled that the newcomers were becoming a political force, pressing their own claims in city and national politics. But both the claims they made and the responses they received were shaped by complex conditions that were not of their own choosing.

If the continued incumbence of local political leaders was best secured by excluding the newcomers, the political fortunes of the national

Democratic party were not, for the national party depended on large pluralities from the biggest cities to carry the industrial states. Accordingly, the Democratic regimes of the 1960s tried to cope with the signs of eroding support in their big city strongholds with a series of programs that compensated for municipal political rigidities and a weakening economy with federally funded services and jobs oriented to the new and politically volatile populations. Beginning in 1962, a series of new programs were proposed by the White House and passed by the Congress, each designed to ameliorate some social problem, such as juvenile delinquency, community mental health, poverty, educational deprivation, or blighted neighborhoods.[37] These programs gave the already hard-pressed cities new monies, but most of the funds were tagged for the creation of new municipal jobs or services and thus actually increased municipal expenditures, albeit with the benefit of federal grants-in-aid.[38]

The broad anti-poverty and anti-racist rhetoric associated with the federally initiated programs ensured that the demands of ghetto populations would not remain neatly confined to those programs, however. A number of the programs, particularly those included in the Economic Opportunity Act of 1964 and called "the war on poverty," were backed by only limited funds, but they provided significant federal ideological legitimation of minority group claims. This legitimation was used by the new groups to press their claims for services, jobs, and honors against traditional municipal agencies. The much-maligned federal policies which provoked this response came to be known as the Great Society.[39]

To compensate for the failures of municipal politics turned out to be no simple matter, however, because those failures were not simply the vestigial results of bureaucratic arrangements. Rather, these bureaucratic arrangements reflected still active and significant local political forces. Federal policies provided compensation for new groups and prodded them to make demands on the regular apparatus of city government. Older groups with entrenched claims, particularly civil service employees whose interests were directly challenged by concessions to blacks, inevitably responded with contending claims. Demands on city governments escalated from all sides, and insecure urban political officials acceded to demands on all sides. Contention undermined urban regimes, and the ensuing weakness of urban governments in turn incited

393

and strengthened the claimants. Consequently, contending claims on municipal budgets escalated rapidly.[40]

The rise of new popular claimants did not stem the tide of concessions to traditional beneficiaries of city government largesse, such as the real estate and construction industries. Indeed, instability may well have increased the number and size of tax concessions and subsidies granted to local business supporters. Insecure politicians are more eager, not less, for business sector support and contributions.[41] Continuing federal subsidies for urban renewal also committed municipal governments to provide "in-kind" contributions in the form of city services, capital improvements, and property tax rebates. Such drains on municipal budgets generally attracted less public fanfare than the expansion of jobs and services. Even where opposition to redevelopment provoked publicity, municipal contributions to urban redevelopment could be seen as eminently reasonable, explained and perhaps understood as expenditures which would ultimately yield higher tax revenues. As it turned out, however, these revenue increases rarely offset municipal investments. Furthermore, the leverage exerted by such investment interests over city officials increased precisely because the municipal tax base was contracting. In the context of ongoing large scale capital flight, the threat of disinvestment became an even more powerful political weapon to wield for tax and subsidy concessions.[42]

Federal policies therefore again intruded on municipal politics, this time on a very large scale. These policies, known as the Great Society, were different from those that had previously undermined urban economies and promoted rural migration to the cities. The new policies were an effort to respond to the disturbances and demands generated by the victims of economic change. These policies increased local fiscal capacities through grants-in-aid for expanded public jobs, income transfers, and social services rather than by increasing the cities' ability to raise revenues from their own sources. The federal policies were designed to compensate urban governments and urban residents for economic decline. At the same time, however, they stimulated greater demands on revenue-poor city governments.[43]

From a fiscal perspective, the policies of compensation had perverse effects on municipal budgets. But from a political perspective, it was the investment policies that had perverse effects on municipal and national politics. Government policies that support investment are often assumed also to support the economic growth that redounds to the benefit of the entire population by generating jobs and income. When investment has these effects, the policies which suit investors also work to win votes.[44] But the policies which promoted new investment in recent decades also caused disinvestment in older urban centers. This, in turn, led to the contraction of employment and income in the population centers that were the main base of the Democratic Party. Several of these policies promoted disinvestment from the United States itself, as capital took advantage of a stable international monetary framework and favorable tariff laws by moving overseas. The result was a shift of capital's job and income-generating capacity beyond the boundaries of the national state.[45]

On their face, these developments were perverse. It is not that the compensatory programs were illogical, as some critics have charged.[46] They were very logical; it is just that the logic was political. The blacks and Hispanics who bore the costs of regional economic change caused by federal policies exerted sufficient pressure on the government to force the creation or expansion of public programs that moderated some of the costs of economic change. There was also a political logic underlying the programs that promoted economic relocation and development. But if each set of policies was in some sense logical, in combination they were illogical. As both sorts of government policy developed, the results made little fiscal sense, and even brought some cities to the brink of bankruptcy.

II. Political Structure and Fiscal Crisis Politics

Analyzed apart from the concrete institutional arrangements of any particular polity, the competing political interests which gave rise to such different lines of state policy could be expected to do battle. Each political interest group was struggling to push policy in a direction antagonistic to the interests of the other. In another type of polity, the contradictory effects of investor policies and compensatory policies might have produced political conflict between a mobile capital and its diverse victims. In the American polity, however, open conflict did not emerge. Instead, the urban political battles that erupted were conflicts among the diverse groups of victims—among blacks, Hispanics and whites, or among employees of municipalities, residents of urban ghettoes, and taxpayers. The potential for broader conflict was blunted by the numerous concessions made on both sides of the main fault lines of the conflict. These concessions in turn placed a severe fiscal burden on the older cities.

What accounts for this particular pattern of demand and response in American politics, a pattern that produced considerable fiscal strain, but little political conflict? Elsewhere, we have proposed that certain long-standing structural features of the American polity help to account for the peculiarly fragmented, even incoherent, pattern of political demands.[47] One such feature is the historic tendency toward the centralization of policies crucial to investors when these policies become the object of popular challenge in the localities. This centralization is coupled with a tendency toward the decentralization of popularly oriented policies, even when they are initiated by the federal government. Some of the underlying reasons for this dual pattern were apparent as early as during the creation of a national government by post-revolutionary elites in the 18th century. The Founders were anxious about popular mobilizations occurring in the states, particularly over the demand for cheap money and a moratorium on the collection of debts. As one commentator has written, "[w]hat bothered the Federalists most about the state governments was their failure to protect the rights of property, and in particular the rights of creditors."[48] The creation of a strong national government solved this problem because ordinary citizens could not organize effectively on the national level, while commercial banking and landowning elites could. The usefulness of a multilevel federal structure in promoting business interests was again evident in the late 19th and early 20th centuries when businessmen reformers, stymied at the municipal level by political machines, obtained the policies they needed at the state level. To some extent, then, the historic tendency toward the centralization of business politics reflected the greater capacity of business elites for supra-local influence, a capacity exercised when business interests were threatened by popular local mobilizations. Corporate interests were following the classic strategy of centralizing to increase their influence.

As the American economy expanded, and as American corporations began to operate in national markets, however, another motive for centralization emerged. Businessmen required consistent national policies to facilitate far-flung business operations. The need for consistency was a fundamental motive underlying the movement of corporate influence to Washington in the Progressive period. They used their influence with the federal government to overturn state laws regulating the railroads and granaries won in states where farmer populists were strong.[49]

Meanwhile, government programs oriented toward ordinary voters, including most neighborhood and social welfare programs, were typically decentralized. Authority to run these programs remained with local and state governments, at least as long as the political reverberations of popular discontent was largely confined to the local polity. Accordingly, the localities remained the main focus of popular politics because the existence of these programs attracted and organized popular political participation. Even when the massive political instabilities and local revenue shortfalls of the Great Depression generated sufficient national political pressure to force the inauguration of new federal support programs, much of the administrative authority was ceded to local and state governments.[50]

However, despite the concentration of mass political participation on the local level, local governments are also vulnerable to business pressures. Historically, in fact, they have been acutely vulnerable to threats of capital flight precisely because such governments are territorially bounded, while capital is not.[51] But the potential for sharp conflicts over policies stemming from this vulnerability of local governments to both investors and voters has been dulled by the progressive organizational fragmentation and bureaucratization of local governments. Not only are investment-oriented policies housed in different structures than popularly oriented policies, but these agencies have, over time, been largely removed from electoral influence. The model is the Authority or the Special District, financed by legally protected revenue sources and administered by officials who do not stand for election. The emergence of these structural arrangements is not mysterious either, for they were created during the last century in response to the political efforts of businessmen reformers who sought to shield from popular interference the government programs on which they depended.[52]

These structural arrangements preceded the contemporary period of urban fiscal strain. But they shaped both the political demands that generated strain, and government responses to those demands. The policies that promoted regional economic shifts were principally federal policies, for the federal government had become the focus of political activity by the most important national economic interests. Meanwhile, the politics of the victims of regional economic change remained largely localized, played out mainly in the cities where they lived and worked, when they worked. The structure of American federalism generated this vertical segmentation of politics. This helps to account for the fact that the demands of diverse claimants in the cities were never joined, so that the conflict between investor interests and the interests of victims of investor-oriented policies did not emerge.

Nevertheless, the federal government could not ignore the disturbances emerging in the cities. Certainly, these disturbances could not be ignored by the Democratic administrations of the 1960s, for they depended on the capacity of the big city political organizations to promote Democratic voter allegiance. Therefore, national Democratic leaders promoted policies designed to "bail out the cities" with federal revenues given under federal terms.[53] But if these new programs blurred the vertical segmentation of American politics and policy, they nevertheless followed the outlines of horizontal fragmentation. Urban populations and urban governments were appeased not by modification of the main outlines of the national policies which were promoting disinvestment from the cities, but rather by an expansion of the range of popularly oriented programs that we call social welfare. The federal programs were used to prod local governments into expanding the traditional battery of popularly oriented municipal jobs and services, with the effect of escalating demands on municipal budgets.

These structural arrangements made possible the dual and illogical policies which led to urban fiscal crisis. Disinvestment from the older urban economies continued without challenge, while local political concessions—and consequent fiscal problems—proliferated. The eruption of "fiscal crisis" suggests there are indeed limits on these unique arrangements for accommodating conflict.

There are signs of other limits as well. The expansion of federal policies that were intended to compensate the urban victims of national investment policies eroded the vertical segmentation which had in the past muted conflict in the United States. Many of the federal programs were channelled through local government agencies, but others were not. Even when they were, the sheer scale of federal involvement, and the publicity that was necessarily attached to the federal role in order for the funds to do their political work, made the federal government's role in popularly oriented programs highly visible. This development was extremely significant, for popular politics were becoming nationalized. This tendency did not begin in the 1960s; it owed much to the experience of the Great Depression, and perhaps even to the Progressive Period. It also owed a great deal to the steady expansion and increasing visibility of the federal government's role in the national economy in deference to investor interests. The Great Society programs, and the expansion of national social welfare programs with which they were associated, however, contributed substantially to the nationalization of popular politics. In other words, while fiscal crisis on the local level reveals one limit to the illogic of the policies which produced urban fiscal strain, the erosion of some of the institutional arrangements which permitted the simultaneous pursuit of illogical policies suggests another limit.

III. The Future Evolution of Fiscal Crisis

The Reagan administration gave the outlook associated with prevailing explanations of urban fiscal woes a new prestige and scope by invoking a species of the very same argument to justify a series of radical national policy shifts.[54] To restore economic growth, the administration argued, the profitability of private investment had to be improved. Therefore, large tax cuts for business and the affluent were required. If government revenues were to be forfeited in this fashion, however, other expenditures had to be reduced. There is no choice, and certainly no room for politics. Investors act not as political entities and not in relation to governmental policy, but merely in accord with market law. It is only government social programs, not government investor programs, that intrude on the market.

An ideology which unabashedly subordinates government to business at the national level stems in part from a decrease during the last decade in investment in new domestic productive capacity. This development—and the Reagan administration response—suggests that the historical vulnerability of local and state governments to the threat of disinvestment has now emerged as a major factor in national politics.

Armed with its ideological justification, the Reagan administration rapidly altered federal policies in ways that accelerated the pattern of disinvestment from the cities. The defense build-up clearly directed new investment and new employment toward the Southwest and away from the older cities.[55] Moreover, the relaxation of antitrust policies gave a green light to corporate mergers. This shift in policy encouraged investment in less labor-intensive industries like petrochemicals rather than the labor-intensive industries commonly found in older cities.

Meanwhile, there was little reason to expect that the Economic Recovery Tax Act of 1981, which reduced taxation on higher income households and the largest corporations, would spur investment in the older industrial cities.[56] First, declining rates of investment in new plant capacity over the past decade occurred despite steadily declining rates of corporate taxation.[57] Second, some analysts argue that tax cuts which favor the very largest corporations stimulate growth in those national and international firms which have the greatest locational discretion. Third, a tilt in tax incentives toward the largest corporations is a tilt toward those firms which generate less local employment, income, and local public revenues in proportion to their capital.[58]

Other policy changes are more complicated in their effects. Federal grants-in-aid for public infrastructure, which helped generate the post-World War II pattern of economic growth and decline, have been sharply reduced. Some of these cuts—in water and sewer facilities grants, for example—are being felt by growing as well as declining metropolitan areas. Other infrastructure cuts, however, such as the elimination of federal support for state and local roads in favor of the Interstate Highway Program, are harder on declining areas. While it is difficult and perhaps premature to disentangle the effects of these complex shifts in the pattern of federal infrastructure supports, it is likely that the overall impact is being felt most acutely in declining areas. Disinvestment in these areas is already far advanced and hard-pressed state and local governments will not have the revenues to compensate for reduced federal funding.

The monetary policy of the federal government has simultaneously undermined the capacity of municipalities to borrow on the capital markets, as high interest rates crowd out municipal bonds. This effect has been aggravated by a number of provisions of the Economic Recovery Tax Act. Since most of these bonds are now purchased by individuals, the sharp cut in top income tax rates reduces the incentive to purchase tax-exempt municipals, as does the introduction of tax-free "All-Savers" certificates. Consequently, municipalities are now paying higher interest rates in comparison to federal and corporate interest rates. Because debt service costs much more, municipalities are borrowing less.[59] Finally, the federal tax cuts have eroded the revenues of some thirty state governments that tie their tax rates to federal tax rates.

Despite the upturn in the American economy, in combination the Reagan policies foretold the continued long-term economic decline of many of the older central cities. Even in the event that economic growth continues, the Reagan policies increased the incentives for disinvestment from the older cities, which had led to the further reduction of local revenues.[60]

If some of the Reagan policies were understood as accelerating the broad pattern of regional disinvestment, still other of the administration's policies were clearly intended to reduce the scale of the federal programs that compensated city politicians and city residents for some of the effects of economic disinvestment. The jobs component of the Comprehensive Employment Act was eliminated, as was the Trade Adjustment Assistance Program, which provided supplementary unemployment payments to some workers. Sharp cuts were made—and even sharper cuts attempted—in food programs, Medicaid, housing subsidies, unemployment insurance, and Aid to Families with Dependent Children.[61] These cuts were implemented even as the cities of the industrial belt of the Midwest and Northeast were reeling from the precipitous contraction of their industries in the 1981-82 recession.

The combined results were to increase greatly the number of people living below the officially defined poverty line, and to widen income inequality.[62]

The Democratic administrations that introduced or expanded the compensatory programs had contrived to soften the impact of shifting investment patterns because they were vulnerable to the voters of the affected areas. The Reagan administration, in part because it was less politically vulnerable to these voters, failed to follow the customary pattern of expanding compensatory programs, but instead been trying to slash them.[63] These policies not only worsened the circumstances of large numbers of residents of the older industrial cities; they also redounded negatively on city revenues. In cities where disinvestment is far advanced, income subsidies have become a prop for the local economy. In poor neighborhoods, income transfers generate a significant portion of local sales, and also support local real estate values by the rent payments they make possible. In this way the federal programs were the ultimate source of a certain portion of local sales and property tax revenues. With the programs cut, not only are city residents worse off, but municipal coffers are being further depleted.

A less obvious Reagan administration effort was to reduce the effectiveness of popular political demands which once made compensatory programs necessary. In part this aim was pursued through the ideological campaign already described. The problems of urban residents and urban governments were redefined so that they were no longer understood as actionable through politics. The effort to blunt the political pressures which generated the need for compensatory programs was not only ideological; it was also programmatic. The Community Services Administration, the legatee of the poverty program which was the centerpiece of the Great Society, was eliminated,[64] and with it some of the resources and legitimation yielded by that program to promote claims on city government (as well as the federal government) by impoverished minority groups disappeared. The attempt to eliminate the Legal Services program, made with notable stridency and determination, can similarly be understood as an effort not only to curb the flow of resources to the victims, but also to reduce the political resources ceded to the victims by the Democratic administrations of the 1960s.[65] Since these resources were typically directed to promoting demands on city governments, this would also reduce pressures for local expenditures.

Finally, the Reagan administration attempted a structural shift in the American polity that would, had it succeeded, partially restored the vertical segmentation of business policies and popular policies that has been undermined by twentieth century developments. The administration attempted to decentralize significant social welfare programs. The "New Federalism" proposal harkens back to the Nixon administration's revenue sharing proposals, launched with vaguely similar rhetoric about "returning power to the people." Revenue sharing shifted authority for the allocation of some federal expenditures to the states and localities, although only a much watered-down version was implemented by a balky Congress.[66]

The Reagan administration was more determined. It too was partly thwarted in the first round of congressional action on its "block grant" proposals, with the result that less federal authority was relinquished than the White House had proposed. But in 1982, the administration tried again, in effect proposing that the AFDC and food stamp programs be ceded to the states. The new proposals were dropped when they provoked an uproar among state and local officials. It is instructive to note they went much further toward decentralization then revenue sharing or block grants, for the new proposals coupled a transfer of program authority with a shift in revenue raising responsibility.

These decentralization proposals were attempts to implement structural changes. Like all structural changes, they would have affected patterns of political organization and influence, thereby improving the capacity of some groups to make claims on the polity, and blunting the capacity of other groups. Decentralization is an attempt to reverse the nationalization of the politics of urban victims of economic change. It would accomplish this simply by fragmenting and displacing the national organizations and constituencies which emerged in past decades, forcing these political groups to scramble instead to try to influence developments in fifty states. At the same time, competition among groups intensified as they competed with each other for limited revenues on the state level.[67]

Options for responding to these demands at the state level are limited, however. State governments only have feeble influence over patterns of investment, but they are very vulnerable to investor influence. Investors can and do bargain with state and local governments over desired policies and tax rates as the price for investing their money. This kind of pressure might well result in sharp reductions in AFDC and food stamp benefits, which employers perceive as eroding work incentives and raising taxes. Indeed, investor pressure, considered alone, might well drag benefit levels and eligibility criteria down to the levels prevailing in the lowest benefit and wage state, thus reversing an equalizing effect of federal social welfare programs on the states and localities evident since the Depression.

Decentralization could have another familiar effect by increasing fractionalism among the victims of national economic policy. The considerable leverage of investors on state governments accounts in large measure for a pattern of state taxation that is relatively regressive.[68] A pattern of regressive taxation, in turn, can be expected to heighten hostility toward income support programs among the part of the population that does not depend on the programs (such as blue-collar workers), but is made to pay for them.

Most important, were decentralization to succeed, the federal government itself would be spared the pressures of increasingly competitive politics among the populations hurt by disinvestment. Popular demands would be deflected downward in the federal system, even though national policies have become far more important than state and local policies in generating patterns of economic investment. The Reagan administration was not in fact proposing decentralization. It was merely trying to restore the pattern which limits popular politics to localities.[69]

Will the political pressures generated by the victims of economic policies be blunted by these efforts? Merely to outline the potential effects of the Reagan initiatives so baldly is to make such an outcome seem less than credible. Popular ideas, and the political expectations associated with those ideas, are not so easily transformed by the ideological fulminations of a national leadership, particularly when those fulminations are contradicted by other leaders and when the ideological message denies a good portion of contemporary experience, including the experience of ordinary people. It will not be easy to persuade resi-

404

dents of big cities that the public expenditures on which they depend must be reduced because they intrude upon the market, at a time when a range of very large intrusions by the national government in the economy have become so visible.[70] The degree of federal government intervention in economic life has exposed the government, at least symbolically, to popular accountability for ensuring a measure of economic well-being. Debate over the extent of this accountability has marked every national presidential campaign for the last fifty years, and is surely one of the most striking features of contemporary American electoral politics.[71]

IV. Conclusion

Government policies were deeply implicated in the developments that led to the emergence of the period of urban fiscal strain. These policies were rooted in politics. The domestic policies of the Reagan administration, which had a large impact on urban fiscal strain, were also rooted in politics, albeit of a different kind. By denying the importance of the role of willful human actors and focusing on the importance of anonymous market processes the prevailing analysis does not reduce the role of politics in urban development; rather, it merely reduces the number of participants in the politics of urban development.

Furthermore, this article has argued that a distinctive kind of politics, shaped by long-established structural features of the American polity, muted conflict by proliferating concessions. Over time these structural arrangements weakened, conflict escalated, and spread to national politics. The Reagan administration responded by attempting to restore the structural arrangements which once contained popular politics. If it succeeds, the arrangements which contributed to the illogical politics and policies of the past will be restored, and conflict will once again be repressed, although fiscal strains will worsen. If the administration fails, the issues of governmental economic and social policy issues which should rightly be the object of national political contention should once again emerge in national politics.

Originally published in 1984.

405

Notes

1. This point of view, which casts state leaders as major historical actors in the shaping of societies, stems from an eminent intellectual tradition that includes Max Weber, in addition to such contemporary analysts as Stein Rokkan, Andrew Schonfeld, Charles Tilly, and Charles Lindblom. The argument made in the present article about urban fiscal strain was alluded to by Joseph Schumpeter when he asserted that in some historical periods the influence of state policies on economy and society "explains practically all the major features of events, in most periods it explains a great deal and there are but a few periods when it explains nothing. Schumpeter, *The Crisis of the Tax State*, 4 Int'l. Econ. Papers 5, 7 (1954). See C. Lindblom, Politics and Markets (1977); S. Rokkan, *Citizens, Elections, Parties* (1970); A. Schonfeld, *Modern Capitalism* (1965), M. Weber, *Economy and Society* (1968); Tilly, "Western State-making and Theories of Political Transformation," in *The Formation of National States in Western Europe* 601 (C. Tilly ed. 1975).

   In focusing on state policies and structures as causes of urban fiscal strain, this article perhaps gives less than adequate attention to the complex processes which shape particular state policies and state structures. Walton, writing of what he calls "the new urban social science," tries to suggest the scope of a complete examination of urban developments when he asserts that the new urban social science "is concerned with the interplay of relations of production, consumption, exchange, and the structure of power manifest in the state." J. Walton, *Economic Crisis and Urban Austerity: Issues of Research and Policy in the 1980's*, at 4 (May 1980) (unpublished manuscript on file with the Yale Law & Policy Review). In other words, a more complete explanation would treat economic and political developments in their complex interactions.

2. Lukes makes this point nicely when he asserts that "[t]o talk of power implies that, if the future facing social actors is not entirely open, it is not entirely closed either." S. Lukes, *Essays in Social Theory* 7 (1977).

3. For earlier discussions of the significance of structural arrangements for politics, see generally F.F. Piven & R. Cloward, *The New Class War* (1982), Friedland, Piven & Alford, "Political Conflict, Urban Structure, and the Fiscal Crisis," in *Int'l. J. of Urb. & Regional Research* 447 (1977); Piven & Friedland, "Public Choice and Private Power," in *Public Service Provision and Urban Development* 390 (A. Kirby, P. Knox & S. Pinch eds. 1984).

4. For a series of well reasoned, scholarly examples of the prevailing perspective, see generally G. Sternlieb & J. Hughes, *Post-Industrial America: Metropolitan Decline and Inter-Regional Job Shifts* (1975). See also President's Comm'n for a Nat'l Agenda for the Eighties, Urban America in the Eighties (1980). For examples of the reiteration of the prevailing view by the press, see Bus. Wk., Oct. 12, 1974. For a critical review of this literature, see Glickman, Urban Impact Analysis, in 2 *Public Policy and Management* 105 (J. Crecire ed. 1981).

5. In the interests of brevity, this article does not delve into the ambiguities attending such phrases as "fiscal strain" or "fiscal crisis," or the appropriate statistical indicators of strain or crisis. By and large, fiscal strain refers to the circumstance when municipal operating budgets exceed current revenues and grants-in-aid, or when municipalities cannot borrow money to finance their capital budgets because they are closed out of the capital markets. However, these circumstances are not unambiguous. As the New York City fiscal crisis made clear, calculations of both revenues and expenditures are subject to manipulation. In addition, the sudden decision by the banks not to lend money to that city could not have been simply a reflection of objective fiscal conditions, which had in fact been worsening for some years. See Alcaly & Bodian, New York's Fiscal Crisis and the Economy, in *The Fiscal Crisis of American Cities* 30 (R. Alcaly & D. Mermelstein eds. 1977).

6. We hesitate to use the term "crisis" to describe these developments. As observers have noted, the calling of a crisis is very much a political act, and should be understood as a political strategy for managing municipal fiscal strain. See Friedland, Piven & Alford, *supra* note 3.

7. Quoted in *N.Y. Times*, June 10, 1982 at 25, col. 6. This argument is similar to that offered by a panel appointed by President Carter, which referred to the "deep-seated and inexorable historical transformation" affecting the cities. President's Commission for a National Agenda for the Eighties, *supra* note 4, at 69.

8. Baer, for example, scolds us for denying that natural death occurs in the urban realm much as it occurs in personal life, a denial he attributes to the American taboo on death and dying generally. See Baer, On the Death of Cities, 45 *Pub. Interest* 3 (1976). Similarly, Starr, writing in the wake of the New York City fiscal crisis, argued that the city ought to plan for its inevitable "shrinkage," rather than wait until "after doomsday has come." Starr, Making New York Smaller, *N.Y. Times*, Nov. 14, 1976, § 6 (Magazine), at 105.

9. The decentralization of corporate investment, and particularly manufacturing investment, into suburban and even rural areas is discussed in R. Schemmer, Making Business Location Decisions 199-210 (1982). Mollenkopf discusses the impact of this movement on the location of employment:

> By 1980, the suburban rings...contained 41.6 percent of all manufacturing employment, while nonmetropolitan areas accounted for another 33.2 percent.... During the 1960s alone, the proportion of the blue collar labor force which worked and lived in central cities...declined from 47.6 percent to 35.6 percent of the total. By contrast, the percentage who lived and worked in the suburbs rose from 30.2 to 36.1 percent, while the total proportion of blue collar workers residing in the suburbs increased from 45.7 to 54.6 percent. J. Mollenkopf, *The Contested City* 38 (1983).

See generally, Kasarda, The Changing Occupational Structure of the American Metropolis, in *The Changing Face of the Suburbs* (B. Schwartz ed. 1976). By the 1970s, even suburban growth in the older metropolitan areas had slowed. The contraction of the central cities accelerated during that decade with the ten largest cities showing population losses ranging from ten percent to more than twenty percent. J. Mollenkopf, *supra*, at 214.

10. See B. Berry, *Inner City Futures*, (paper presented to the Conference on Dynamics of Modern Industrial Cities, Sept. 28, 1978) (on file with the Yale Law & Policy Review) ("Historically, perhaps the most consistent bias in the federal tax code has been the favoritism given to investment in the improvement and repair of existing structures.").

11. Mollenkopf has written of the impact of the new transportation networks on the development of the Boston and San Francisco metropolitan areas. In Boston, the suburban population increased by 50 percent after Route 128 was opened in 1952; the freeway also attracted the growing electronics industry. Sixty-eight new plants with 4.5 million square feet of space were built along the freeway between March 1954 and June 1956 alone. In San Francisco, the federally funded Bay Bridge and Golden Gate Bridge made possible an even stronger spurt of suburban growth, with suburban employment increasing by 38 percent in the 1950's. J. Mollenkopf, *supra* note 9, at 142-144.

12. For an exhaustive examination of the differential impact of federal housing subsidies, including income tax write-offs for private homeowners. see H.J. Aaron, *Shelter and Subsidies* 53-73 (1972).

13. These laws were not limited to the South, of course. See, for example, the discussion by the New Jersey Supreme Court of the effects of exclusionary zoning in Southern Burlington County NAACP v. Mt. Laurel Township, 92 N.J. 158, 210-11 n.5, 456 A.2d 390, 415-16 n.5 (1983):

   ...since World War II, there has been a great movement of commerce, industry, and people out of the inner cities and into the suburbs. At the same time, however, exclusionary zoning made these suburbs largely inaccessible to lower income households. Besides depriving the urban poor of an opportunity to share in the suburban development, this exclusion also increased the relative concentration of poor in the cities and thereby hastened the flight of business and the middle class to the suburbs. The vicious cycle set in as increased business and middle-class flight led to more urban decay, and more urban decay led to more flight, etc.

14. While the United States Supreme Court, at least during Earl Warren's tenure as Chief Justice, was closely identified with the struggle to end legalized discrimination, the Supreme Court in the late 19th and early 20th centuries also accepted southern caste policies. See, e.g., *Cumming v. Richmond County Bd. of Educ.*, 175 U.S. 528 (1899) (states had the right to maintain their school systems as they saw fit, even where a school district did not provide equal facilities for black children); *Williams v. Mississippi*, 170 U.S. 213 (1898) (state codes requiring that voters read and interpret any section of the state constitution to the satisfaction of the voting official were not unconstitutional because they did not on their face discriminate against blacks); *Plessy v. Ferguson*, 163 U.S. 537 (1896) (upholding Louisiana law mandating separate but equal accommodations in

train coaches travelling within the state); *Civil Rights Cases*, 109 U.S. 3 (1883) (Congress may not directly prohibit discrimination in accommodations).

For scholarly discussions of these cases, see Bernstein, Case Law in Plessy v. Ferguson, 47 *J. Negro Hist.* 192 (1962); Bernstein, Plessy v. Ferguson: Conservative Sociological Jurisprudence, 48 *J. Negro Hist.* 196 (1963); Waite, The Negro in the Supreme Court, 30 *Minn. L. Rev.* 219 (1946); Note, Is Racial Segregation Consistent with Equal Protection of the Laws? Plessy v. Ferguson Reexamined, 49 *Colum. L. Rev.* 629 (1949); Note, Segregation in Public Schools—A Violation of "Equal Protection of the Laws", 50 *Yale L.J.* 1059 (1947).

15.

> Nothing in this subchapter shall be construed as authorizing the execution or application of agreements requiring membership in a labor organization as a condition of employment in any state or territory in which such execution or application is prohibited by state or territorial law.

Labor Management Relations (Taft-Hartley) Act, § 101, 29 U.S.C. § 164(b) (1982) (amending National Labor Relations Act, Pub. L. No. 74-198, § 14, 49 Stat. 449, 457 (1935)). See *Lincoln Federal Labor Union v. Northwestern Iron Metal Co.*, 335 U.S. 525 (1949) (upholding the constitutionality of right-to-work laws). See generally, P. Sultan, *Right-to-Work Laws: A Study in Conflict* (1958).

For an example of a current right-to-work provision, see the Arizona Constitution:

> No person shall be denied the opportunity to obtain or retain employment because of non-membership in a labor organization, nor shall the State or any subdivision thereof, or any corporation, individual or association of any kind enter into any agreement, written or oral, which excludes any person from employment or continuation of employment because of non-membership in a labor organization.(Ariz. Const. art. XXV)

16. The percentage of workers who are union members in the nineteen "right-to-work" states is only half the percentage in the remaining states. See F.F. Piven & R. Cloward, *Poor People's Movements* 169-70 (1977). For data illustrating the wage and unionization differentials between older industrial cities in the Northeast and Midwest on the one hand, and growing cities in the Southwest on the other, see J. Mollenkopf, *supra* note 9, at 223.

17. This role of federal programs in stimulating development in the Southwest is not just a recent phenomenon. One commentator has attributed the initial growth of San Diego, Phoenix, San Antonio, and the Santa Clara Valley to federal expenditures on military production in those areas during World War II. J. Mollenkopf, *supra* note 9, at 217-18. For a discussion of the more recent impact of federal contracts on regional shifts in growth, see Watkins and Perry, Regional Change and the Impact of Uneven Urban Development, in *The Rise of the Sunbelt Cities* 19, 46-51 (D. Perry & A. Watkins eds. 1977). The shift in investment was sectoral as well as regional. Investment moved into new prod-

uct lines requiring skills that workers from the old manufacturing industries did not possess. Those workers would therefore have been displaced even if they had been able to follow capital to the new homes of these industries. See Walton, The Internationalization of Capital and Class Structures in the Advanced Countries, in *World Exchange and Domination* (A. Portes & J. Walton eds. 1980). The low skill assembly jobs of the mass production industries largely shifted to the Third World. See Reich, The Next American Frontier, *Atl. Monthly*, April, 1983 at 97-108.

18. For analysis of the impact of federal investments in highways and water and sewer projects on the pattern of regional economic development, see 3 S. Barro, The Urban Impacts of Federal Policies (1978); Watkins, Good Business Climates: The Second War Between the States, *Dissent*, Fall, 1980, at 476.

19. By the 1970s, the South was losing ground to the Caribbean and South Asia in the competition for new investment in labor intensive manufacturing. As Bluestone and Harrison have shown, even this shift can be attributed in part to American tax and tariff provisions. They have concluded that because of the peculiarities of the American tax code, the effective tax on the foreign earnings of U.S. corporations in 1972 was only five percent. Provisions in the U.S. Tariff Code have similar effects. Some federal programs, including the Overseas Private Investment Corporation (see 22 U.S.C. § 2191-94 (1984)), the Commodity Credit Corporation (see 15 U.S.C. § 714 (1982)), and the U.S. Export-Import Bank (see 12 U.S.C. § 632 (1982)), actually subsidize foreign investment. B. Bluestone & B. Harrison, The Deindustrialization of America 129-33 (1982). See also P. Musgrave, *United States Taxation of Foreign Investment Income* 1-162 (1969).

20. Between 1969 and 1976, investment in new plants in the United States created about 3.6 million jobs each year, while plant closings wiped out 3.2 million jobs each year. The pattern varied sharply within and among regions, with the Northeast and Mid-Atlantic showing a net loss of jobs and a parallel loss of population. B. Bluestone & B. Harrison, *supra* note 19, at 27-34, app. Table A.1 (jobs); id. at 99, Table 4.2 (population).

21. This presumption is confirmed by existing records of corporate lobbying activities. See E.E. Schattschneider, *Politics, Pressures and the Tariff* (1935); G. McConnell, *Private Power and American Democracy* (1966) (accounts of business political influence). See also Salamon & Siegfried, Economic Power and Political Influence: The Impact of Industry Structure on Public Policy, 71 *Am. Pol. Sci. Rev.* 1026-43 (1977) (empirical approach to relationship of business to political power). See generally A. Fritschler & B. Ross, *Business Regulation and Government Decision-Making* (1980).

22. See Piven, The Great Society as Political Strategy, in *The Politics of Turmoil* 271-83 (R. Cloward & F.F. Piven eds. 1974) (describing state leaders as actors with distinctive purposes arising from the exigencies of governance). See also C. Lindblom, *supra* note 1, at 122-26.

23. An important line of argument and research attempts to interpret expenditure decisions in terms of quasi-economic models. This public choice literature tries to interpret patterns of municipal expenditure and taxation as the result of the influence of voter-taxpayers who will elect the officials that provide the preferred combination of services and taxes, or move to a locality that more closely matches their preferences. Fiscal strain or crisis in this model is attributed to various imperfections in the market mechanisms that translate the preferences of voter-taxpayers into public policy. See, e.g., R. Musgrave, *The Theory of Public Finance* (1959); P. Peterson, City Limits (1981); Tiebout, A Pure Theory of Local Expenditures, in *The New Urbanization* (S. Greer ed. 1968).

24. Piven & Friedland, *supra* note 3. With these assertions we put ourselves squarely into the camp of what Peterson calls "bargaining models" of local tax and expenditure policies. P. Peterson, *supra* note 23. Peterson develops what he calls a "unitary model" which treats "internal conflicts and competing preferences within a political system" as "theoretically irrelevant." He argues that municipal expenditure decisions can be derived from a series of "environmental" variables which constrain the choices of policy-makers striving to increase the economic prosperity of the local community. One problem with this model is precisely that it is "unitary;" it posits a unity of interest among urban residents in policies that promote economy productivity, even though the effects of particular forms of economic growth on different groups in the urban population are clearly variable. Another problem is that the market calculus he asserts to be the basis of municipal policy would presumably preclude policies that lead to fiscal strain, except as the idiosyncratic result of imperfect information.

25. See *President's National Advisory Commission on Rural Poverty, The People Left Behind* (1967) (summary of the displacement effects of agricultural modernization during this period); T. Dunbar, *Our Land Too* (1969) (detailed study of agricultural displacement in the southern rural economy).

26. See, e.g., Declaration of Policy in the Amendment to the Bankhead-Jones Act of 1935, which states:

    ...the Secretary of Agriculture is authorized and directed to conduct and to stimulate research...relating to the improvement of the quality of, and the development of new and improved methods of the production, marketing, distribution, processing and utilization of plant and animal commodities....

    Amendment to the Bankhead-Jones Act of 1936, Pub. L. No. 733, Ch. 966, 60 Stat. 1082, 1083 (1946).

27. Between 1940 and 1960 the number of farms in the South dropped by half, while the size of the average farm increased from 123 to 217 acres. Bureau of The Census 460-61 (1976). See also President's National Advisory Commission on Rural Poverty, *supra* note 25, at ix-x.

28. See Agriculture Act of 1956, Pub. L. No. 540, Ch. 327, 70 Stat. 188 (1956).

29. The AFDC program, Social Security Act of 1935, Pub. L. No. 87-543, 49 Stat.

60 (1935), as amended, 42 U.S.C. § 601-10 (1981), was a prime example. At the time this was the most important program available to agricultural workers who were not covered by unemployment insurance. The states not only were permitted to set grant levels, but also were able to pass a host of exclusionary rules. F.F. Piven & R. Cloward, *Regulating the Poor*, 205-06 (1971). In the South this license was effectively used to exclude most of the black poor from the program until well into the 1960s. For example, during the 1950s, despite deepening distress among displaced agricultural workers, the AFDC rolls in the South did not grow. To the contrary, this was the period when Southern states were enacting such new exclusions as "suitable home" and "employable mother" laws. See, e.g., 1958 Miss. Gen. Laws 943 (1958) ("suitable homes") ; La. Rev. Stat. Ann. § 233 (West 1963) ("suitable homes" and illegitimacy); Alabama Manual For Administration of Public Assistance, Part I, Ch. 11, § 6 (1964) ("man-in-the-house").

30. White agricultural workers were also displaced during this period, but they were not as likely to migrate to the biggest cities, because smaller cities and towns were not as inhospitable to them as they were to black migrants. Moreover, displaced white agricultural workers were not as likely to be denied welfare supports, in part because the states which relied on a white agricultural labor force tended to have less restrictive welfare practices.

31. In 1940, only half of all blacks lived in urban areas. The proportion reached 62 percent in 1950, 73 percent in 1960, and 80 percent in 1965. Center for Research and Marketing, Inc., The Negro Population: 1965 Estimates and 1970 Projections 8 (1966).

32. More extensive discussions of the bureaucratization of city politics can be found in Lowi, Foreword to H. Gosnell, *Machine Politics: Chicago Model* ix (1968); Piven, The Urban Crisis: Who Got What, and Why? in *The Politics of Turmoil* 314 (R. Cloward & F.F. Piven eds. 1974); Shefter, New York City's Fiscal Crisis, 48 *Pub. Interest* 98 (1977).

33. For a case study of this confrontation, see *Confrontation at Ocean Hill-Brownsville* (M. Beruba & M. Gittell eds. 1969).

34. Housing Act of 1964, Pub. L. No. 88-560, 78 Stat. 769 (codified as amended in scattered sections of 12, 15, 20, 40, and 42 U.S.C.).

35. For discussion of urban renewal as a strategy to promote urban economic growth, see generally Harvey, The Political Economy of Urbanization in Advanced Capitalist Societies, in *The Social Economy of Cities* 119 (G. Gappert and H. Rose eds. 1975); Mollenkopf, The Post-War Politics of Urban Development, 5 *Pol. & Soc'y* 247 (1975). S. Elkins, *Cities Without Power* (paper presented at the Conference on Urban Choice and State Power, Cornell University, June, 1977) (on file with the *Yale Law & Policy Review*).

36. A Gallup Poll taken after the 1956 election concluded that "of all the major groups in the nation's population, the one that shifted most to the Eisenhower-Nixon ticket...was the Negro voter." Moreover, there was a sharp decline in black turnout, particularly in the northern cities. Whereas Stevenson won 80 percent of the black vote in 1952, he won only 60 percent in 1956. Some—but only some—of those voters returned to Democratic columns in 1960, when Kennedy won 68 percent of the black vote, helping him to carry a number of key industrial states by very narrow margins. See F.F. Piven & R. Cloward, *supra* note 16, at 211-229 (1977).

37. See e.g., Community Mental Health Centers Act, 42 U.S.C. § 2681-2687 (amended 1975); Higher Education Facilities Act of 1963, 20 U.S.C. § 701 et. seq. (current version at 20 U.S.C. § 1132a et. seq.) (1976); Juvenile Delinquency and Youth Offenses Control Act of 1961, 42 U.S.C. § 2541-2548 (expired 1967).

38. Brown and Erie present persuasive evidence that the federal programs created during this period triggered a large expansion of black public employment. The expansion occurred mainly at the state and local level, principally in social welfare programs created or expanded in response to federal legislation. They estimate the aggregate employment impact of federal initiatives at two million new jobs, almost all of which were state and local. Moreover, fully 55 percent of the net increase in employment for blacks that occurred between 1960 and 1976 was in the public sector. Much of it was concentrated in state and local programs stimulated by the federal government. See Brown & Erie, Blacks and the Legacy of the Great Society, 29 *Pub. Pol'y 299, 305 (1981).*

39. For a more extensive development of this political analysis of the Great Society Programs, see Piven, *supra* note 22, at 271-83; Piven, The New Urban Programs, in *The Politics of Turmoil* 284-313 (R. Cloward & F.F. Piven eds. 1974).

40. For a more complete discussion of the political pressures underlying rising municipal and state expenditures, see Piven, *supra* note 32. See also Kantor & David, The Political Economy of Change in Urban Budgeting Politics: A Framework for Analysis and a Case Study, 13 *Brit. J. Pol. Sci.* 251, 269 (1983).

41. The fissures that have developed recently in the Chicago machine are bringing some of these relations with business to light. Edward R. Vrdolyak, who is leading the City Council's fight against Mayor Harold Washington, is also head of the Building and Zoning Committee which decides what real estate developers are granted zoning variances and city property leases. Another alderman was recently on trial for 33 counts of selling licenses and jobs in the sheriffs department. In May, 1983, the *New York Times* reported that ten former aldermen were in prison for such practices. As one Council member commented, "[t]here is a lot of money involved in running the City Council...The cable television franchise alone involves millions of dollars." *N.Y. Times*, May 14, 1983, at 7, col. 4

42. The reluctance of local governments to raise taxes and expenditures to offset cuts in federal programs in 1981 and 1982 evidences this pressure, as does the eagerness of some state governments to use the increase in revenues generated by the current economic recovery to justify the proposal of additional tax cuts. See Quint, Economic Scene: Local Fiscal Difficulties, *N.Y. Times*, May 11, 1983, at D2, col. 1-3. See also D. Klingman, The Impact of Changing Intergovernmental Relations on State and Local Expenditures and Revenues (paper presented at the Annual Meeting of the American Political Science Association, Sept. 1982) (on file with the *Yale Law & Policy Review*).

43. From 1960 to 1975, state and local government receipts rose by about 11% annually, while the gross national product increased at an average annual rate of only 7.7%. As a consequence, local government's share of GNP rose from 9% to 14%. Quint, *supra* note 42, at D2. Col. 1-3.

44. The conditional and uncertain impact of economic development on popular political support for local politicians is discussed in Piven & Friedland, *supra* note 3.

45. There has been substantial debate about the net effects of the internationalization of American capital in terms of domestic employment. For an extensive review of the relevant literature, see Walton, The Internationalization of Capital and Class Structures in the Advanced Countries: The Case of the United States, in *World Exchange and Domination: Essays in the Political Economy of Development* (A. Portes & J. Walton eds. 1980). Walton concludes that while internationalization did generate new professional and managerial employment in the United States, the net effect was a reduction in blue collar employment.

46. For example, Daniel Patrick Moynihan, one of the most outspoken critics of the Great Society, charged that the programs were simply inept. Because of the foolish counsel of liberal intellectuals, said Moynihan, "[t]he government did not know what it was doing." D. Moynihan, *Maximum Feasible Misunderstanding* 170 (1969).

47. See F.F. Piven & R. Cloward, *supra* note 3; Piven & Friedland, *supra* note 44; Friedland, Piven & Alford, *supra* note 3.

48. Morgan, The Argument for the States, *New Republic*, April 28, 1982, at 29-34. See also C. Beard, An Economic Interpretation of the Constitution of the United States (1913).

49. G. Kolko, *The Triumph of Conservatism* (1963). See also C. Lindblom, *supra* note 1, at 204-05.

50. For example, when unemployment compensation was established by the Social Security Act of 1935, the states had great latitude in financing and administering the program. Each state continues to have different benefit provisions today. See J. Patterson, *The New Deal and the States* 23, 91 (1969).

51. A number of analysts have argued that the inability of the local polity to control the movement of capital and people across its boundaries inevitably means economic concerns will dictate local political decisions. David and Kantor rely on the observation that local polities cannot control labor and capital flows to assert that only the federal government can afford to pursue meaningful redistributive policies. See David & Kantor, Urban Policy in the Federal System, 16 *Polity* 284 (1983). Lowi reaches a similar conclusion and stresses the need for centrally coordinated redistributive policies. See Lowi, Public Policy and Bureaucracy in the United States and France, in 1 *Comparing Public Policies: Sage Yearbooks in Politics and Public Policy* 177 (1978). Although I do not disagree with these observations, I would place a heavier explanatory emphasis on political rather than on administrative exigencies, and on the variable capacities for mobilizing political influence by different groups at different levels of government.

52. The current fiscal constraints confronted by local governments has spurred the proliferation of these politically insulated agencies, and an even greater proliferation of their spending powers. During the five years preceding August, 1982, the number of special districts and authorities increased by 11%. Their spending increased even more rapidly, from $9 billion in 1977 to almost $25 billion in 1980. The *New York Times* commented, on the basis of interviews with local political leaders, that the growth in spending was a response to new budgetary limits placed on municipalities. *N.Y. Times*, Aug. 6, 1982, at A8, col. 1. The shift of financing of a range of business-oriented public functions into independent authorities removes significant spending decisions from the intense public scrutiny and pressure generated by the budgetary process.

53. For example, in order to obtain certain grants from the Law Enforcement Assistance Administration, created in 1968 by the Johnson administration, the states had to comply with 12 federal regulations. See O. Stolz, *Revenue Sharing: Legal and Policy Analysis* 6-7 (1974); see also American Enterprise Institute for Public Policy Research, Revenue Sharing Bills: *An Analysis of Proposals to Share Federal Revenue with State and Local Governments* 3 (1970).

54. Robert Reich observes that the revival by this administration of the creed of the survival of the fittest, with its "inevitable correlate...that government should do little or nothing to eliminate poverty...has its roots in America's fallen hopes." Reich, The Return of Social Darwinism: Ideologies of Survival, *New Republic*, Sept. 27, 1982, at 34.

55. See Employment Research Associates, *Military Spending* (1984); Employment Research Associates, *The Price of the Pentagon* (1982).

56. Reich estimates that households with the highest annual incomes have been the major beneficiaries of cuts in personal income taxes, while large corporations have been the major beneficiaries of cuts in corporate taxes. See Reich, The Next American Frontier, *Atl. Monthly*, March 1983, at 43; April 1983, at 97. The Congressional Budget Office projected that in 1984 households earning more than $80,000 would gain, on average, $8,390 from the tax cuts. *N.Y.*

Times, April 4, 1984 at A1, col. 1. These reductions contributed to a long-term shift in the sources of federal revenues. The share of federal revenues accounted for by corporate taxation fell from 32% in 1952 to 7% in 1983. In the same period, the share made up by individual income taxes rose from 42% to 47%, while the share accounted for by the relatively regressive social insurance tax had risen from 10% to 36%. See M. Graetz, *Federal Income Taxation: Principles and Policies* ch. 1 (forthcoming 1985).

57. See R. Lekachman, *Greed is Not Enough* 57-79 (1982). Miller and Tomaskovic-Devey argue that corporate tax cuts are unreliable in their effects, since they do not deter speculation. They recommend "targeting" tax benefits to ensure investment in new plant capacity. See S. Miller & D. Tomaskovic-Devey, *Recapitalizing America* 91 (1983). Commerce Department figures show that reductions in the personal income tax have been accompanied by a steady decline in personal savings as a percentage of disposable personal income, from 6.6 percent in 1981 to 4.9 percent in 1983. Hamilton, IRA's: Good for the Taxpayers, but Maybe Not for the Economy, *Wash. Post Nat. Weekly Ed.*, April 16, 1984, at 18.

58. Several analysts have argued that because corporate tax cuts favor the largest and most capital intensive firms, they will encourage acquisitions instead of investment in new plant capacity. See B. Bluestone & B. Harrison, *supra* note 19, at 127-129; R. Lekachman, *supra* note 57, at 68-72. Friedland argues that tax subsidies reward the largest multilocational firms, which have the greatest mobility and therefore are most likely to invest outside metropolitan areas. See R. Friedland, Welfare States and the Geography of Economic Growth (Jan. 1983) (unpublished manuscript on file with the *Yale Law & Policy Review*).

59. Business Week reports that the amount of long-term bonds issued in the municipal market fell precipitously in 1981. Municipalities must now pay rates exceeding 80 percent of the cost of comparable rated but taxable corporate bonds. Borrowing Gets Harder as the Demands Intensify, *Bus. Wk.*, Oct. 26, 1981, at 154-55.

60. There is some evidence of uneven distribution of the benefits of recovery within the older cities. Unemployment rates do not tell the whole story. For example, the number of jobs in New York City rose to a ten-year high in 1983. However, the supply of entry level jobs in blue-collar manufacturing fields has declined. *N.Y. Times*, Feb. 23, 1984, at B6, col. 1. In fact, in July, 1984, at the peak of the recovery, the *New York Times* reported that "[m]ore people than at any time since the Depression are said to be hungry and homeless, and about one of every four New Yorkers is below the federal poverty level." *N.Y. Times*, July 28, 1984, at 1, col. 5.

61. According to an April, 1984 Congressional Budget Office Study, families earning under $10,000 a year lost an average of $410 a year from cuts in cash and "in-kind" benefits, while they gained $20 a year from the tax cuts. *N.Y. Times*, April 4, 1984, at 1, col. 1. Some groups were more sharply affected. For example, a study carried out by the Institute for Research on Poverty and the Wis-

consin Department of Health and Social Services found that AFDC recipients had lost 17% of their income from earnings, AFDC and food stamps one year after the cuts went into effect. Meanwhile, changes in the unemployment insurance program reduced outlays by one third, or $15 billion, from 1975 levels. Institute for Research on Poverty, Poverty in the United States, 7 Focus 4-5 (1984). A 1984 General Accounting Office report concluded that the 1981 legislation had decreased the national AFDC basic monthly caseload by approximately 493,000 cases. General Accounting Office, An Evaluation of the 1981 AFDC Changes: Initial Analysis 3 (1984). The report also found that AFDC families in five cities had experienced "substantial" income losses as a result of the changes brought about by the legislation. Id. at 4. A study released by the Congressional Research Service in July, 1984, indicated that the budget restrictions had caused the number of poor to increase by at least 557,000, while the recession resulted in an increase of 1.6 million, or 7.7 percent, in the number of the poor. *N.Y. Times,* July 26, 1984, at A19, col. 1. None of these studies, however, is designed to grasp fully the social impact of increasing poverty. Some glimmering is suggested by a case study of the impact of cuts in one program, the Maternal and Child Health Block Grant, in five inner-city neighborhood health centers in Boston. The study found significant reductions both in the services offered and in the use of the centers, paralleled by rising infant mortality rates in the census tracts served. P. Feldman & B. Mosher, Preserving Essential Services: Effects of the MCH Block Grant on Five Inner-city Boston Neighborhood Health Centers (paper presented at the Harvard School of Public Health, July 1984) (on file with *Yale Law & Policy Review*). See also Harrington, "The New Gradgrinds," *Dissent,* Spring, 1984, at 171, for a discussion of several dimensions of poverty in the contemporary United States.

62. Relative poverty, defined as income less than 44% of the national median income adjusted for family size, rose to 17.8% in 1982, after falling slightly during the 1965-78 period. Moreover, the numbers of desperately poor were increasing. According to a statement by Rudolph Penner before a House subcommittee, the proportion of those below the official poverty line (set at $9,862 for a family of four in 1982) whose incomes were less than 75 percent of the poverty level had increased from 61% in 1978 to 68% in 1982. The poor were also increasingly concentrated in urban areas. The percentage of the poor living in cities increased from 54 percent in 1969 to 62 percent in 1982, despite the overall decline of the population in the cities. Institute for Research on Poverty, *supra* note 61, at 7.

63. The Reagan Administration eliminated outright the minimum benefits planned for social security recipients and the CETA Jobs Training Program, and succeeded in cutting federal funds and tightening eligibility criteria for a host of federal funds, including Medicare, Medicaid, AFDC, food stamps, unemployment benefit insurance, education, day care, child protective services, services for the elderly and disabled, preventive health services, maternal and child health services, alcohol and drug treatment programs, community health centers, low-income energy assistance subsidies, community development pro-

grams, anti-poverty programs, and subsidized housing. See *N.Y. Times*, Feb. 19, 1981, at B6-7; July 29, 1981, at 18, col. 1; Sept. 21, 1981, at 1, col. 6; Feb. 1, 1983, at 17, col. 1.

64. Economic Opportunity Act of 1964, 42 U.S.C. §§ 2941-48 (1964), repealed by Pub. L. No. 97-35, Title VI, 683(a), August 13, 1981, 95 Stat. 519.

65. The Legal Services Corporation, 42 U.S.C. § 2996, which was also created as part of the Economic Opportunity Act of 1964, has withstood successive attempts by the Reagan Administration in 1981, 1982, and 1983 to eliminate all funds appropriated to it by Congress. *N.Y. Times*, July 29, 1981, at 18, col. 1.; Feb. 1, 1983, at 17, col. 1. After Congress rejected the Administration's effort to abolish the Legal Services Corporation in 1981, President Reagan appointed a president and a majority of directors to the Corporation's board. The new board proceeded to adopt rules enabling the Corporation to "defund" certain programs and to ensure that Legal Aid lawyers assisted only the most destitute clients. *N.Y. Times*, Nov. 13, 1983, at 4, col. 4. As part of Congress' concession to the Administration on the Legal Services Corporation, the Corporation's budget was cut from $321 million in 1981 to $241 million in 1982 and 1983. In order to increase the budget of the Legal Services Corporation to $275 million in 1984, Congress added certain restrictions to the appropriations bill as an inducement for President Reagan to sign, including curbs on lobbying by Legal Aid lawyers and staff, curbs on filing class actions against state and federal governments, limits on assistance to aliens, and procedural changes to make it more difficult for local legal services organizations to renew their grants. *N.Y. Times*, Nov. 15, 1983, at 22, col. 3.; Nov. 29, 1983, at 25, col. 3.

66. The shifts in the distribution of federal largesse associated with the shift from the older federal grant-in-aid formulas to revenue sharing and block grants is examined in National Science Foundation, *The Economic and Political Impact of General Revenue Sharing* (1976); See also David & Kantor, *supra* note 51; M. Levine, *The Reagan Urban Policy: Efficient National Economic Growth and Public Sector Minimization* (paper presented at the Annual Meeting of the American Political Science Association, Sept. 1982) (on file with the Yale Law & Policy Review).

67. See *N.Y. Times*, May 8, 1983, at 18, col. 3, citing R. Nathan & F. Doolittle, Consequences of Cuts (forthcoming 1984). The Nathan and Doolittle study examines the responses of 14 states to the Reagan budget cuts and concludes that the states made their own cuts in the wake of the 1981 upheaval; that when restorations were made, they were often inadequate; and that the character of the restoration was piecemeal rather than inclusive.

68. The major characteristics of the state and local tax system are its regressivity and sluggish response to income growth. Fear of driving out commerce and industry and discouraging the entry of new business restrains the use of most taxes; this is true particularly of the individual income tax, which is the most equitable and most responsive to growth. J. Pechman, *Federal Tax Policy* 247 (1983).

69. See F.F. Piven and R. Cloward, *supra* note 3, at 128-132.

70. Despite President Reagan's pledge to reduce government spending, federal expenditures continued to rise. For example, the federal budget for fiscal 1982, which called for expenditures of $725.3 billion, was increased in 1983 by 4.5% to $757.6 billion. *N.Y. Times*, Feb. 7, 1984, at 30, col. 3. This growth cannot be attributed solely to increased defense spending. For example, in 1983 the Reagan Administration spent a record $19 billion in the farm price support program alone. *Wash. Post*, Feb. 2, 1984, at A16, col. 1.

71. See E. Tufte, *Political Control of the Economy* (1978) for an analysis of the interaction of government policy, the economy and elections.

20

Structural Constraints and Political Development:
The Case of the American Democratic Party

During the electoral realignment of the 1930s, the Democrats gained the overwhelming allegiance of most manual workers and their unions. However, if this signaled the emergence of something like a labor party, it did not last. Working class support for the Democrats dropped precipitously in the presidential contests of the 1950s, recovered briefly in the 1960s, and then plunged again, as the table shows. In other words, working class defections from the American "labor party" began at the very peak of industrialism. Later, postindustrial trends also took their toll, and in the 1970s and 1980s, the ranks of the old working class did indeed begin to shrink. At the same time, however, the numbers of low wage earners were enlarging, not only in the growing service sector but in restructured industrial employment as well. Many of these workers were minorities. Many more were women. And among both low-income people and women, Democratic preferences were increasing, but their voting levels were falling. Not only did the Democrats lose support among older groups of industrial workers, and lose it early, but they failed to mobilize the ranks of this new working class. Clearly, the unraveling of the Democratic party was not a straightforward reflection of postindustrial economic trends—again, as the table illustrates.

421

Percentage of white major party voters who voted Democratic
for president by union membership, class, and nonsouth

	UNION MEMBER	WORKING CLASS	NONSOUTH
1944	67	64	—
1948	79	76	—
1952	53	52	39
1956	50	44	36
1960	64	55	46
1964	80	75	65
1968	50	50	42
1972	40	32	33
1976	60	58	46
1980	48	44	36
1984	50	42	37

SOURCE: Extrapolated from P. R. Abramson, J. H. Aldrich, and D. W. Rohde,
Change and Continuity in the 1980 Elections (Washington, DC: Congressional Quar-
terly Press, 1983), figures 5–2, 5–3, and 5–4. Based on National Opinion Research
Center polls, which are susceptible to substantial over-reporting of voting.

Democratic decomposition—by which we mean both slipping vote totals
and rising levels of split-ticket voting—is better explained by taking
account of distinctive American political structures, including a divided
and decentralized state structure, and unique restrictions on the franchise, which the Democratic party inherited when it reemerged in the
Great Depression as a "labor party." A fragmented and decentralized government meant that the national party was itself fragmented, without an
effective command center to formulate and impose coherent party strategies. Simultaneously, divided and decentralized government and the
restricted franchise nourished the politics of the southern wing, and the
influence of well-organized business groups. Sectional and interest group
influences in turn worked to promote policies which inhibited the growth
of the party's union allies, and stunted the expansion of the welfare state
programs which had earned the party popular support in the 1930s. These
accommodations left the party's infrastructure weak, and its consti-

tuency support fragile, well before the onset of postindustrial changes.

The economic and social transformations of the post-Second World War period aggravated party weaknesses. But these transformations were not exogenous to politics, nor to the inherited structures which mold American politics. A decentered Democratic party collaborated in national policies that shaped the pattern of postwar industrial growth in ways that, from the point of view of the national Democratic party, were entirely perverse. These military, infrastructure, and housing policies, for example, also reflected sectional influence, as well as the heavy hand of investor interest groups. Steadily over a period of three decades, these policies dissipated Democratic support among older constituencies, and aggravated deep-seated constituency conflicts. And this occurred while the party infrastructure fashioned during the New Deal atrophied, inhibiting the party from recruiting new supporters to compensate for the defections generated by disaffection and conflict. By the 1970s, the several sources of weakness of the Democrats were well advanced, paving the way for the ascendance to national power of a revamped Republican party dominated by a temporarily unified business class that had joined in an alliance of convenience with Right-wing populists, many of whose constituents were Democratic defectors.

We need to say a word about the weight we give in this explanation to political structures. Surely, Democratic leaders were not entirely constrained by structural arrangements and the sectional and interest group forces privileged by these arrangements. Or at least there must have been particular junctures when they had at least some latitude so that their choices mattered in shaping the course of events. In principle, we believe that structure and agency together shape political life. But we do not attempt here to sift through the tangled history of the past fifty years to try to identify the specific real options available to Democratic leaders, or why they failed to utilize them. The task we have set for ourselves is more modest; if politics rests on some exercise of agency, it is also the case that structures always restrict agency, and it is that dimension of Democratic Party history that we are trying to illuminate. Moreover, we are struck by the evidence that while the panic years of the early 1930s may have expanded the options of Democratic leaders by stilling opposition, even modest recovery revived opposition and constricted latitude.

It is chastening to note, for example, the failure of Democratic efforts in the late 1930s to overcome the constraints of sectionalism with a concerted campaign to transform the South. In a series of moves that Steve Fraser calls "political strategy at its grandest," the Congress of Industrial Organizations (CIO) tried to organize the southern textile industry; northern liberals in the congress fought for legislation that would raise wages in the South; and Roosevelt worked to purge congressional reactionaries, particularly southerners, from the party in the primary elections of 1938.[1] But within a few months it was over, and it was the South and not the national party that prevailed, suggesting the great weight of the inherited structures to which the south owed its power.

Why No Labor Party in US?

Labor parties everywhere emerged on the crest of industrialization, nourished by the growing numbers of the working class and the expansion of the male franchise which an insurgent working class demanded. In the United States, the Democratic Party became, if not a labor party, at least the party of labor in the 1930s. However, this historic development occurred under conditions quite different from the earlier rise of labor parties in Western Europe. In Europe, the winning of the male franchise and the emergence of labor parties more or less coincided. In the United States, white male workers and farmers had achieved the right to vote much earlier, in a long political process that began with the popular mobilizations of the Revolutionary War and concluded with the elimination of most property, education, and religious qualifications by the third decade of the nineteenth century. This meant that the mass party system which the unions entered in the 1930s was already highly developed, and heavily freighted with a series of structural arrangements developed in response to popular challenges that had welled up in earlier historical periods. Two kinds of structural arrangements inherited by the New Deal Democratic Party were especially important: the constitutionally fragmented and decentralized organization of the United States government; and class-related restrictions on the exercise of the universal franchise.

The American national government was the thoughtful and deliberate construction of elites in the aftermath of the revolutionary war. Half a century ago, Schattschneider commented on the significance of the Constitution they designed:

> Indubitably geography, history, tradition, and national character have had interesting effects on the parties.... But the Constitution has had an influence so important and overwhelming that the peculiarities of the American party system cease to be mysterious once we have begun to look at the Constitution and the parties together.[2]

Schattschneider singles out in particular the elaborate division of powers in the national government, a structure he says was "designed to make parties ineffective...[because they] would lose and exhaust themselves in futile attempts to fight their way through the labyrinthine framework...."[3]

The animus of the Founders toward parties of course reflected their fear of a populace that could be mobilized by parties. There was reason to be fearful. The protection once provided to the propertied by the armies of the British Crown was gone, at a time when radical democratic currents stirred by the revolutionary war were strong, among a still-armed population. If it was unwise to simply ignore democratic aspirations, they could nevertheless be blunted and diffused by a system of "checks and balances" which effectively divided authority for key policies between the Congress, the presidency, and the courts, and also made these decision making centers at least partially independent of each other. As Lipset and Rokkan point out, these safeguards against direct majority power limited party influence over officials in government. They encouraged shifting and flexible alliances, and made it difficult to translate election victories into policy.[4] The long-run effect, in short, was not only to fracture the authority of the central government, but to create lasting impediments to coherent party organization.

At the same time, post-revolutionary elites were themselves leery of the new central authority they were creating, in part because of the sharply diverse economies of the thirteen colonies, as famously signaled by the compromise over slavery embodied in the Constitution. The more general compromise, and it had lasting effects, was to structurally decentralize power. This was done in two ways. First, the authority of the new national government was limited to constitutionally specified policies, thus leaving an enormous reservoir of unspecified power to the state governments and to the local governments chartered by state legislatures. Second, the system of electoral representation was designed to give great weight to regions as opposed to persons, both in representation in the Senate and in the arrangement of the electoral college through which the President was chosen. There are obvious parallels here between sectionalism in American political development and what Bradford and Jenson call the "pluralism" of Canadian politics.[5] As in Canada, the strong sectionalism which has always marked American politics had its roots in regional economic differences, and it was nurtured by a political system which both protected regionalism and lent it weight in national government with, as it turned out, lasting implications for American political parties.

The decentralization of government power also fostered the growth of the local clientelist political organizations for which the United States is renowned, and which marked working class politics particularly during the first decades of industrialization.[6] Decentralization meant that local government did many things with relative autonomy, and could yield enormous patronage resources. At the same time, the wide distribution of the franchise meant that nineteenth-century artisans and laborers in the immigrant wards of the cities attracted the organizing efforts of clientelist parties. These working men had the votes that could produce election victories for the parties, and control over the patronage resources that local or state government yielded. Both clientelist organization and the wide availability of the vote pre-dated industrialization and the experience of proletarianization. Hence, when an industrial working class emerged, powerful local political organizations which appealed to workers on the basis of ethnic, religious, and individual advantage already existed.

Finally, a fragmented and decentralized state also nourished interest group politics, even as it inhibited the party development which might counter interest group influence. In part this was because a government system with multiple points of access was more exposed to well-organized groups with the resources and tenacity to pursue influence.[7] Interest groups could operate in the several branches of government or at different levels of government to promote the policies they favored or to block policies they opposed. Moreover, since the very structural arrangements which exposed the state to well-organized interests also ensured the fragmentation of the national parties, and their consequent lack of a strategic or programmatic center, there was little resistance from party leaders to the demands of well-organized interest groups. This too is a point Schattschneider saw clearly:

> American legislation, the budget, and public administration every-where show the handiwork of the pressure groups which have had their way in American government and imposed their will on Congress, the administrative agencies, the states, and the local government at a multitude of points.[8]

The other set of structural arrangements which had a telling influence on the party-building strategies of the contemporary Democrats evolved a century after the writing of the Constitution, on the eve of industrialization. If the Founding Fathers feared democratic currents, they nevertheless also feared opposing them, and left the issue of enfranchisement to state governments, with the result that the universal male franchise was rather quickly, if somewhat unevenly, established. However, during the closing decades of the nineteenth century, industrialists and Republicans in the North, planters and Democrats in the south, introduced a series of "reforms" into state electoral laws and procedures that effectively disenfranchised many workers and farmers. This effort was especially vigorous in the South, where the disenfranchisement of blacks was linked to the stability of the plantation economy and the serf labor on which it relied. There, new literacy and poll tax requirements, together with onerous personal voter registration requirements, were incorporated into state constitutions, and resulted in the rapid disenfranchisement of the entire black population and of most poorer whites as well. A similar reform effort swept the North, animated less by the race issue and more by elite reactions against insurgent farmer and industrial movements. But the result was similar, if less drastic: in the North, too, literacy tests which had been abandoned half a century earlier were reintroduced, in some states along with a poll tax, and in any case elaborate and obstructive requirements for personal and periodic registration were imposed, at first mainly the big cities where the immigrant working class, and the clientelist local political organizations which depended on immigrant working class support, were concentrated.

At the same time, the local parties, which might otherwise have worked to subvert these restrictions, came under direct attack by reformers who worked to strip the parties of their patronage resources, and to further fragment the local and sometimes state governments they controlled. These reforms unfolded in the context of the 1896 electoral realignment which reduced party competition in much of the country. Together, these several changes took their toll on voter participation. On the one hand, restrictive rules and procedures made voting difficult, and clientelist local parties had fewer resources to help voters through the process; on the other hand, uncompetitive elections lowered the motive of voters to vote or of parties to enlist them. Voter turnout, which had been consistently high for most of the nineteenth century, steadily declined after the turn of the century, falling to barely half the nationwide electorate by the 1920s.[9]

New Deal Party Building Strategies, or the Labor Party Aborted

These structural constraints were ultimately to prevent the emergence of a labor party, which the upheavals of the Great Depression momentarily made seem possible. By 1932, when economic calamity scuttled Republican domination of the national government, blue collar workers constituted about half the workforce. Meanwhile, a series of widespread protest movements—among the unemployed, farmers, the old, and industrial workers—prompted Franklin Delano Roosevelt, as the leader of the ascendant but unsteady Democratic Party, first to inject the language of class into national political rhetoric and then, as panic stilled political opposition, to inaugurate the first federal welfare state programs. Not long afterwards, pressed by an escalating strike movement, Roosevelt threw his support behind legislation to protect unionization efforts. With that development, organized labor broke with its traditional policy of abstaining from national electoral politics[10] to become a full-fledged partner of the Democratic Party.

The sectional party coalition

These developments, however, did not occur on a fresh slate. The Democrats were now the party of northern labor, but they continued to be the sectional party of the rural South. There is a seeming parallel here to the rise to government power of Scandinavian labor parties through alliances with farmer parties. But, in fact, there is no parallel. The alliance with the rural South was not an alliance with family farmers but with a quasi-feudal political formation. That distinctive regional formation in turn was sustained by the structures to which we are directing attention. The decentralization of governmental authority allowed the southern oligarchy to construct a political system that shored up the plantation economy, and to defend that system under the banner of "states rights." At the same time, the disenfranchising arrangements of the late nineteenth century (together with the regular use of state sanctioned violence) protected the southern system from electoral challenges from below, by the simple expedient of purging poor whites and blacks from the electorate. Finally, the decentralization of representation, particularly in the Senate and the electoral college, gave this sectional political system a strong grip on the national government. And a system of divided powers in the national government meant that that grip could become a stranglehold on national policy, especially as powerful southern Democrats in the Congress allied themselves with northern Republicans.

For a time, the alliance with the South shored up the national Democratic Party. No matter their slight totals in the popular vote, the institution of the electoral college gave the southern states a bloc of votes which became the bedrock of Democratic victories. Moreover, the party's dependence on the southern wing was accentuated by persisting weaknesses in its labor base in the north. True, the rhetorical and programmatic initiatives of the New Deal had for the moment sealed the allegiance of working people to the Democrats. And important new federal programs channeled through city governments became a lifeline for the fading big city machines. Together, the appeals of the New Deal and revived local parties helped raise turnout outside of the South, from 66 percent in 1928 to 73 percent in 1940.[11] The unions contributed to this effort, as I will show in a moment. Still, while the increase in turnout was large, it was not as large as it might have been, because recruitment efforts had to hurdle procedural encumbrances on the franchise inherited from the conflicts of the late nineteenth century, as table below shows.

Presidential turnout percentages, 1924–1940

	SOUTH	NONSOUTH	NATIONAL
1924	19	57	49
1928	23	66	57
1932	24	66	57
1936	25	71	61
1940	26	73	62

SOURCE: W. D. Burnham, "The system of 1896: an analysis," in *The Evolution of American Electoral Systems*, ed. P. Kleppner (Westport, CT: Greenwood Press, 1981), p. 100, table 1

A party coalition which embraced the quasi-feudal South and the urban working class north could not last. Indeed, New Deal policies oriented to sectional interests themselves helped to undermine it, by encouraging landowners to take land out of production or to mechanize, while simultaneously allowing the southern states and counties to refuse welfare payments to the millions of sharecroppers, tenants, and laborers who were displaced. Many of them, of course, were black, and they eventually made their way to the cities of the north where already established black communities provided some kind of haven. In the north, blacks gained the vote, and became a factor in Democratic electoral calculations. Their growing voting numbers were concentrated in the heartland of the urban working class, in the industrial states with the largest number of electoral college votes. For over three decades, beginning in 1948, Democratic presidential contenders were forced to choose and lose. They could defer to their white southern coalition partners who were outraged even at rhetorical inroads on the caste system. If they did, they risked losing black support in the North, and with it perhaps some of the industrial states where Democratic majorities were narrow. Or they could defer to black demands, and the black struggle for civil rights which was gaining allies throughout the North, and risk losing the white South. There was, in short, no way to hold this sectional coalition together.

The Democrats lost the South. By the 1980s, the South had in fact become the staunchest Republican region in presidential contests. But southern influence remained large in the decades during which the coalition unraveled. The structural arrangements which gave the southern section so much power also made its loss especially threatening. Democratic presidential contenders exerted themselves to placate the white South and stem the loss of southern electoral votes, and southern Democrats in the Congress continued to wield extraordinary power over legislation. Moreover, the power of the southern section ultimately undermined the possibility of shoring up working class Democratic support in the North.

A crippled union infrastructure

Everywhere, labor parties are allied with unions. Unions are in fact virtually the infrastructure of the parties, functioning to enlist working people in support of the party. In countries where labor parties have fared better during the disturbances of post-industrialism, union membership is high and the unions are relatively centralized. The American rate of unionization is now one of the lowest in the West. Having reached a peak of about one-third of the workforce at the end of the Second World War, union membership stabilized briefly and then began to decline, to 16 percent of the workforce in 1989.[12] To be sure, union density has begun to fall in other industrial countries as well. But in most countries the loss is recent and relatively modest.[13] In the United States, the decline began several decades ago, and was precipitous. This is surely one reason for the troubles of the Democratic Party. But the low level of unionization in the United States itself has to be explained, particularly in light of the scale and vigor of American labor struggles for the right to organize during the New Deal Democratic Party building period.[14] The search for an explanation takes us back to the role of the south in national politics, to the importance of interest groups, and to the structural arrangements that made sectional and interest groups powerful.

Once legal protection for unionism had been won by mass strikes in the mid-1930s, the new industrial unions rapidly allied themselves with the Democratic Party, and shortly thereafter the craft unions did as well. This development seemed to promise the emergence of an entirely new political formation in American electoral politics. As early as 1936, the newly formed CIO began to work for the Democratic ticket, creating a political arm that performed much like a campaign organization, spending money to stage rallies, print leaflets, and recruit voters in the industrial states where the CIO unions were strong. This was only the beginning of the development of a massive and far-flung CIO campaign apparatus, supplemented in 1948 by a comparable AFL effort, that deployed "armies of trade union precinct workers" and often took the place of the local Democratic Party itself.[15] In the late 1940s, the union party formation in the United States did not look very different from that in Western Europe: union density levels were not much lower, and the degree of class polarization in voting was as high as in Western Europe.[16]

However, despite the unions' electoral efforts for the Democrats, the support for unionism by party leaders did not last. Within a few years the legislative protections of the National Labor Relations Act were being whittled away and the once pro-labor National Labor Relations Board was reconstituted, largely as a result of the influence of the fatal alliance that developed between southerners and business-oriented Republicans in the Congress.[17] Meanwhile, decentralization permitted the states to undercut the union protections won from the federal government in 1935, and a good many did just that, especially in the South.

The opposition of the southern section was not the whole of the problem. The other part of the problem was the weakness of the union cause in the north, where labor influence was offset by the continuing power in the Congress of local clientelist politicians, by the persisting low turnout of working class voters,[18] and by the growing susceptibility of the Congress to business lobbyists as the threat wielded by the strike movements of the 1930s and 1940s receded.

Democratic presidents did not much resist the assault on unions either, and in some instances even took the lead, for they too were beholden to business lobbyists and especially to southern congressional powerbrokers. As the Second World War approached, Roosevelt threatened to draft striking workers, and Truman did the same during the strike wave that followed the close of the war. To be sure, facing a third party challenge from the Left in the 1948 election, Truman vetoed the anti-union Taft–Hartley Act of 1947. However, when the Congress overrode his veto, Truman used the powers it granted him twelve times in the first year after its passage. The margin of votes needed to override the veto was consistently provided by southern Democrats in the Congress. And also consistently, for the next two decades, Democratic presidential contenders simply ignored their union allies and made no move to overturn the restrictions of Taft–Hartley.

These reversals marked the end of labor's brief political flowering. The "free speech" rights granted employers under Taft–Hartley were matched by new curbs on strikes, and the outright prohibition of such solidary tactics as sympathy strikes, secondary boycotts, and mass picketing. Noncommunist affidavits required of union officials spurred a long wave of union fratricide. Perhaps most important, the Act explicitly allowed state open-shop laws which were especially prevalent in the South. These several provisions set the stage for the failure of Operation Dixie, the southern organizing drive launched by the CIO in 1946, which ran aground on union infighting and intransigent southern opposition.[19] This meant that as new plants dispersed to the Sunbelt in subsequent decades, the unions did not follow. It was not until the late 1970s, when the bleeding of the unions was well advanced, that a Democratic president threw his weight behind legislation to restore some of the union protections of the 1930s. Business and southern influence again combined to ensure that the initiative was defeated.

These events go far toward explaining the decline of union membership.[20] Like the dissolution of the Democratic party, union decline began too early to be attributed to contracting smokestack industries. Later, of course, the old industries did decline, and new plants and people shifted to the Sunbelt. The failure of union organizing efforts there was not simply a reflection of postindustrialism either, or for that matter of the conservative political culture of the South. The sorry record of union organizing in the South had a good deal to do with the way the ground

433

rules had been changed in the 1940s, by representatives of the southern sectional establishment and northern business interests whose power was lodged in the structural arrangements which the twentieth century inherited from the nineteenth and eighteenth.

Party building and the welfare state

The main American welfare state programs were also inaugurated during the party-building era of the New Deal. But the US programs trailed behind those of Western Europe in benefit levels and scope of coverage and, after the Second World War, a number of the limited programs that had been inaugurated in the 1930s were allowed to languish. Meanwhile, new programs proved impossible to win in the Congress, owing to the vigorous resistance of southern Democrats and business-oriented Republicans on the one hand, and the desultory support of northern Democrats who were also influenced by business interests and by the local clientelists parties to which many congressmen remained beholden.

During the crisis months when Roosevelt first took office, elites everywhere, shaken by the depth of the economic crisis and by mounting protest among the unemployed, supported emergency measures, including emergency relief, and so too did southern congressmen, whose impoverished region had been especially hard hit by the economic calamity. Even so, however, objections from the South to national relief programs that overrode local wage scales or interfered with caste arrangements began early. And when the Social Security Act of 1935 replaced emergency relief, southern representatives who dominated the key committees in the Congress carried great weight.[21] So too did business leaders who organized to oppose the Act because they feared income support programs would interfere with low-wage labor markets. Together with southern representatives, they used the political leverage guaranteed them by divided and decentralized government to ensure that the new national welfare state programs would conform with sectionally and sectorally diversified labor markets.[22]

The intricate provisions of the Social Security Act reflected this confluence of forces. On the one hand, whole categories of low-wage workers were excluded from the old-age and unemployment insurance programs, and in any case eligibility was conditional on a history of steady employment. Moreover, a good deal of authority over the unemployment insurance program, and over the "categorical" or welfare programs, was ceded to the states and even to the counties, where local employers could ensure that conditions of eligibility and benefit levels were calibrated to their requirements.[23]

On the other hand, the inauguration of national welfare state programs under the Social Security Act was primarily a response to the demands of working people who were potential Democratic voters, and it is the bearing of the programs on constituency building that is our primary interest here. Two features of the American welfare state deserve scrutiny in this respect. One is that a complex system of sharply differentiated programs nourished divisions among Democratic constituencies, a feature of the system that became especially pernicious when the programs were enlarged in the 1960s, partly in response to the black movement. White working class taxpayers were especially resentful of categorical programs identified with the minority poor, and perhaps particularly so because they carried the brunt of the steeply regressive state and local taxes which helped fund the categorical programs.

Another feature of the American welfare state was perhaps even more important for its ultimately perverse effects on Democratic party-building efforts. Simply put, there was too little of it. The Social Security Act was not the beginning of a process of welfare state development. For a long time, it was the high point. After the Second World War, the new industrial unions expanded their sights not only to demand higher social security payments, but to demand national health insurance, child care facilities, government housing, and so on. They got none of this from a Congress dominated by southern Democrats and business-oriented Republicans. And so a still-militant and still-strong labor movement used workplace power to bargain with employers for health and old-age protections, and later to bargain for supplementary unemployment benefits as well.[24] The result was that, over time, core working class groups looked less to government for the measures that would guarantee their security, and more to the market place. For example, without a national health program, most Americans relied on employers for health protec-

tions. In turn, a government that did less was less likely to generate confidence or affection. And a party that did less was also less likely to hold
the allegiance of its constituency over time.

Democratic Party Policies and Postindustrialism

All of the rich industrial nations of the West have had to adapt to intensifying international competition, especially in the auto, steel, electronics, and machine tools industries whose workers formed the core base of
labor parties. Inevitably, those adaptations have been troubling for labor
parties built on constituencies and organizations formed in an earlier
industrial era. But labor parties have not only suffered the impact of
those adaptations; they have also helped to shape them.

As is becoming increasingly obvious, strong labor parties, high union
density, and developed welfare states have imposed political limits on
the options of investors responding to the new international economic
order. When the large-scale industrial disinvestment and wage and
social benefit cuts that are the hallmarks of the American adaptation are
politically unfeasible, investors are more likely to turn to competitive
strategies emphasizing increased capitalization, technological and production innovations, and active labor market policies.[25] In the United
States, however, weak unions and a politically compromised and meager
welfare state facilitated rapid and wholesale disinvestment from older
industries and a virtual explosion of speculation on the one hand, and
campaigns to lower wages, break unions, cut welfare state spending,
and roll back government regulatory protections on the other. Partly as
a result, average weekly earnings began to fall in the early 1970s, and
average household income remained more or less stable only because
married women flooded into the labor market to shore up family
income by filling the jobs in the enlarging service sector industries. (In
the 1980s, a more regressive tax system and cuts in social programs
exacerbated these market income trends.) But the conditions which
made these large changes in the economy possible were as much political as economic, as we will explain when we turn to the business mobilization that began in the 1970s.

Politics was in command of postindustrial trends in another sense too. While shifts in international markets encouraged the spatial decentralization of industry, the United States led the way among industrial countries in the extent of decentralization.[26] In any case, international markets did not dictate the specific geography of decentralization or its political consequences. A series of national policies, some dating from the New Deal, others inaugurated later, played a major role in this respect. But rather than using their influence on national policy to moderate the impact of postindustrial change on the party, its infrastructure and its constituencies, Democratic Party leaders happily sold their influence to sectional interests in the South, and to local party bosses and business interest groups in the north. As a consequence, the Democrats supported policies that were perhaps rational from the perspective of particularistic sectional and business interests, but which were entirely irrational from the perspective of the longer run interests of the national Democratic Party, and perhaps from the larger perspective of the national economic well-being as well.

Before we make the case for the large role of sectional and interest group politics in shaping the geography of the contemporary American economy, let us summarize the more usual view. In the United States, the industrial centers of the north and midwest were the mainstays, together with the largely rural South, of the New Deal Democratic Party. These centers were overwhelmed and transformed by the shift of industrial production to low cost areas and the rise of a multifaceted service economy, both at least partly the result of global economic developments. Shifts in investment, in turn, changed the kinds of work people do and the conditions under which they do it, the places where they live, and their political identities and allegiances. Not only did the ranks of industrial workers shrink and a new service sector workforce grow, but as the geography of new investment shifted in response to changes in market advantage, people and enterprises moved from the solidly Democratic central cities to the now Republican suburbs, and from the predominantly Democratic northeast and midwest to the increasingly Republican states of the South and West.[27] Together, these trends both reduced the numerical strength of a core constituency of the New Deal Democratic Party and eroded its political cohesion.

All of this happened, of course, and the impact on the old industrial centers was enormous. The city of Detroit, for example, fabled bastion of the United Auto Workers, lost half of its people and most of its businesses in the years since the Second World War,[28] Chicago lost half of its manufacturing establishments and more than half of its manufacturing employment.[29] But this happened not simply as a result of investor adaptations to new market conditions, but as a result of market conditions that were at least in part the result of government policies promoted by sectional and investor interests. In fact, and as we have already noted, long before the decline of the mass production industries which we associate with post-industrialism, a series of federal policies tilted economic development toward the South. These policies included not only the welfare and labor policies which ratified regional disparities in labor costs, but an array of federal activities which accelerated in the 1960s, including military installations, defense and aerospace contracts directed to the districts of powerful southern congressmen and, to make these and other enterprises possible, an enormously costly federally financed infrastructure, particularly in highways and water projects.[30] In other words, while the shift of mass production industries to low wage areas was a global trend, a pattern of federal—and Democratic—policies created specific additional incentives encouraging the movement of new investment and people away from the urban concentrations of the Northeast and Midwest and into the South and the Southwest.

Much the same point should be made about the shift of economic activity and people to the suburbs which now contain a majority of the nation's voters, and a majority that is turning out to be a major base for the Republican Party.[31] While the prevailing view attributes suburbanization simply to changes in the locational requirements of business investors and to the attractions of home-ownership for the middle class, federal policies were a crucial component of this development as well. Again, federally subsidized highways, and water and sewer grants, enormously enhanced the locational advantages of outlying areas, while federal tax laws created incentives for investment in new facilities rather than the refurbishment of old ones.[32] Meanwhile, federal housing policies which provided low cost mortgages and tax benefits for mainly suburban home-owners vastly overshadowed the modest programs directed to low cost housing in the cities.[33] What the cities did get was urban

438

renewal programs promoted by local "progrowth" coalitions of real estate and downtown business interests and their local political allies, with the result that whole neighborhoods, and often Democratic neighborhoods, were decimated as those who could joined the exodus to the suburbs, those who could not crowded into further impacted slums, and local conflict escalated.[34]

Finally, even the divisive impact of racial conflict on Democratic ranks has something to do with the policies which Democrats themselves promoted. We do not want to overstate this. The race issue is deeply rooted, and in the main the unfortunate Democrats inherited it. White–black conflict was part of the reason the party lost the South, and the Democrats were then torn apart again by racial conflict in the cities. But the several party strategies we have described made race conflict sharper and more telling than would otherwise have been the case. Race conflict was surely worsened by the scale and precipitousness of the displacement of blacks from the South, which in turn had a good deal to do with Democratic agricultural and welfare policies. The failure of the Democrats to shore up unions also mattered, for it deprived the party of an infrastructure that might have worked to moderate racial conflict.[35] And a white working class that felt itself to be getting very little from its party or government was that much more likely to be resentful of programs directed to blacks. Finally, the combination of programs which spurred the great migration to the suburbs of the past three decades may also have worsened race conflict, both by stripping the older cities of employment opportunities and public revenues, and by reifying racial separation in political jurisdictions, so that race polarization came to be seen as a conflict between devastated and pathology-ridden black municipalities and prosperous white suburban jurisdictions.

Not all postindustrial trends necessarily had to work against the Democratic Party. If the ranks of the old working class were reduced and dispersed, new potential constituencies were also being created, among the enlarging numbers of people, many of them young and minorities, who were doing worse, and also among increasingly politicized women. However, the party has done little to recruit either group. Just as this constitutionally fragmented party did not override sectional and interest group influences in order to protect the party's base, neither does it seem capable of strategic action to expand the party's base.

As we noted at the outset, people at the bottom of the income distribution have become increasingly Democratic by preference. Sharply polarizing economic conditions seem to be recreating something of the pattern of political polarization of the New Deal era. Some of the new have-nots are in the industrial sector where the attack on unions and job restructuring had smoothed the way for sharp wage cuts. Many more are in the service sector where the fastest growing occupations—cashiers, nurses, janitors, retail workers—are concentrated.[36] And some are the marginally employed or the never employed who depend on the welfare state. Of course, just how large a Democratic margin this reservoir would actually produce in a given election, and whether it can turn a presidential election, depends on other factors in the contest. For the moment, however, that is beside the point, since the very strata that are turning to the Democrats are also those who are least likely to vote.[37]

The New Deal Democratic majority was made possible by the mobilization of new voters. An unusual concatenation of circumstances and organizations made this possible. On the one hand, economic calamity and rising politicization motivated people to vote; on the other, the new unions, together with big city Democratic organizations temporarily revived by New Deal largesse, helped new voters to hurdle the inherited procedural barriers that had depressed turnout since the turn of the century. In the last two decades, however, this mobilizing infrastructure atrophied, its place taken by media-dominated campaigns associated with particular candidates. But media campaigns do not give people voter registration cards, and the decline of face-to-face recruitment efforts made the procedural barriers inherited from the nineteenth century more telling in their effects. As a result, outside the South where the civil rights revolution had raised registration and turnout, registration levels fell, especially among the low-income strata who were becoming more Democratic in their preferences. Turnout levels fell even faster, from the twentieth century high of 65 percent in 1960 to 51 percent in 1988.[38] As the procedures inherited from the nineteenth century steadily eroded the Democratic base, and the party infrastructure atrophied, a decentered party of loosely connected entrepreneurial politicians exposed to a myriad of special interests remained paralyzed; it could not or would not recruit Democratic voters.

The Democrats have also done little to take advantage of the other large opportunity associated with postindustrial trends, the politicization of women and their shift to the Left. Gender politics is at the core of postindustrial political change. In the Scandinavian countries, as the social democratic parties move vigorously to recruit women, offering them new programs and high levels of representation in the parties, gender is becoming a new axis of party alignment.[39]

That the Democratic Party has taken no comparably large steps is not because women do not constitute a potential target constituency of large importance. To the contrary: women have come to significantly outnumber men in the electorate, both as a result of demographic trends, and because the long-term decline in voter turnout is sharper among men than among women. At the same time as their voting numbers have increased, women have remained more Democratic, while men have veered sharply toward the Republicans. This gap in gender partisanship first became evident in the 1980 election, and since then it has more or less held.[40] Moreover, gender differences in policy preferences are far wider than gender differences in partisan preferences, with women differing from men particularly on issues of war and peace, the environment, and social welfare. These differences in political opinion probably reflect the complex influence of the large-scale entry of women into low-wage and more irregular employment, their increasing involvement with welfare state programs as two-parent family structures weaken and wages fall, and the lingering influence of more traditional "maternal" values.[41] Whatever the reasons, the emergence of a distinct gender politics in the United States has become quite plain. The bungled 1984 nomination of a woman for the vice-presidency aside, the Democrats have not done much to mobilize their gender advantage. They have not championed the issues which incline women toward the Democratic Party, and they have not exerted themselves to represent women prominently in Democratic councils.[42] Perhaps this is why the gender gap broadens between elections, but narrows as each election draws near.

To sum up so far, working class allegiance to the Democratic Party weakened rapidly after the Second World War as a result of the failure of the party to shore up a union infrastructure or to promote welfare state policies oriented to the working class. The economic and demographic trends of the next three decades aggravated the weaknesses that had already developed in the Democratic Party. However, these trends were not simply the result of exogenous market forces. Rather, they were also the result of policies promoted by a centerless Democratic Party. Beholden as it was to sectional and interest group forces, the Democratic Party itself had promoted the dispersal of New Deal Democratic strongholds, and contributed to the growth of the suburban and sunbelt areas that were becoming the base of a revived Republican Party. To be sure, economic transformation was also generating new targets of electoral opportunity for the Democratic Party, both among the enlarging pool of have-nots and among politicized women. But the Democratic Party remained frozen, without a center that could move strategically to mobilize these constituencies in the face of inherited institutional obstacles and the weaknesses in infrastructure that resulted from earlier Democratic Party accommodations to sectional and interest group forces.

Postindustrial Political Strategies:
Republican Countermobilization and Democratic Paralysis

We have so far emphasized the weight of institutional features of the American political system which inhibited Democratic Party building strategies. Those institutional arrangements are a kind of dead politics, the heritage of past political conflicts and the strategies they generated which then come to encumber contemporary actors. But strategic politics continues nevertheless within these constraints, as the Republican–business initiatives of the 1970s and 1980s demonstrate.

The progressive fragmentation of the Democratic Party paved the way for the resurgence of a modernized Republican Party backed by an increasingly politicized and at least temporarily unified business class. There will be disagreements about the turning point. Perhaps it was the election of Richard Nixon in 1968, at the close of a decade of conflict which wracked the Democratic Party. To be sure, the Nixon regime fell in disgrace as a result of the Watergate scandals, but even as it collapsed, business interests and Republican strategists were organizing a new bid for national ascendance.

Indeed, it is not hyperbole to say that, in the 1970s, American business temporarily overcame its usually fractured interest group politics and began to act like a political class. The problems which prompted this transformation were considerable: intensifying competition from Europe and Japan, and later from newly industrializing countries; rising commodity prices demanded by Third World suppliers as dramatized by the oil shocks of the 1970s; and the apparent inability of the administration to stabilize spiralling prices. Prodded by these developments, American business leaders set about developing a political program to shore up profits by slashing taxes and business regulation, lowering wages and welfare state spending, and building up American military power abroad. To that end, they created new organizations to promote the business outlook and revived old ones, poured money into business-oriented think tanks to provide the intellectual foundations for the business program, and set about modernizing and centralizing the Republican Party, using the pooled money of mobilized business contributors to overcome, at least for a time, the usual centrifugal forces of American party politics.

The first results were evident in the toughened stance of employers toward unions in the 1970s. Then, by the end of the decade, business lobbyists succeeded in rolling back regulatory controls, increased military spending, and defeated virtually all of the Carter initiatives on social spending, as well as his modest effort to roll back some of the limits on unions contained in the Taft–Hartley Act. But the real fruits of the business–Republican mobilization were harvested after the election of 1980. The new Republican regime—backed by a now virtually unanimous business community and only weakly resisted by congressional Democrats oriented to sectional and business interests—rapidly slashed taxes on business and the better-off, sharply increased military expenditures, accelerated the deregulation of business, launched a fierce attack on unions with the highly publicized destruction of the air controllers union and a far less publicized series of hostile appointments to the National Labor Relations Board, and, finally, inaugurated a decade-long attack on welfare state programs.

The impact of these several developments was both economic and political, and each reinforced the other. As the decline of the mass production industries proceeded apace, industrial job loss combined with welfare state program cuts to create pervasive economic hardship and insecurity. Under these conditions, new forms of employment spread easily, including "two-tier" hiring arrangements which paid new cohorts of workers sharply less, and increased reliance by business on homework and temporary employees. Of course, these arrangements undercut the unions, already reeling under the impact of employer anti-union campaigns, and union membership continued to drop. Strike levels fell precipitously, reaching their lowest levels in half a century in the 1980s,[43] and average wages continued their downward slide. By the end of the decade, something like a reordering of the class structure had been effected, as the income share of the top 1 percent rose by 87 percent, while the poorest 20 percent lost 5 percent, and most Americans barely stayed even.[44]

These developments did not, however, excite the outrage that might have benefited the Democratic Party. Part of the reason was that while a good many people were doing worse, almost as many were doing better, and these were not only more likely to be voters but were also the more visible participants in a consumer culture. At least as important, however, was the "hegemonic project" which was promulgated along with the new public policies. This was perhaps the most innovative aspect of the Republican–business mobilization, the revival in the 1970s and 1980s of the nineteenth-century doctrine of laissez-faire. The obvious evidence of industrial decline laid the groundwork for a propaganda campaign in which government and business leaders joined with think tank experts to define the policies of the 1980s as the necessary and inevitable response to global economic restructuring. To survive in a competitive international economy, US entrepreneurs had to be stimulated by higher profits and released from government regulation and union constraints. Only then would foreign penetration of the American economy be slowed and domestic economic growth restored, along with the good jobs, high wages, and public programs that economic growth will make possible.

Nineteenth-century laissez-faire naturalized the depredations of nineteenth-century capitalists, defining them as merely the working out of "market laws." Just so does this neo-laissez-faire naturalize the policies that promote US postindustrial strategies, defining these policies as the inevitable adaptation demanded by international markets, no matter that other nations have adopted quite different policies to encourage different postindustrial strategies. Still, this argument is hard to answer. Not only does it resonate with the familiarity of ancient doctrine, but it gains confirmation as people shop for Japanese electronics or Korean clothes, watch foreign investors buy landmarks like Rockefeller Center, and all this while American factories shut their doors.

Still, if some concrete experiences shore up neo-laissez-faire, others contradict it, suggesting that the doctrine is vulnerable. Most important, after a decade with business in command, neo-laissez-faire is not producing its promises of increased prosperity for most people. To the contrary, real wages continue to slide, while public programs become more niggardly, and deficits rage out of control. Meanwhile, the evidence is overwhelming that business-oriented policies have unleashed more greed than entrepreneurialism, with the result that, a long-term boom notwithstanding, American productivity rates have lagged, while income to capital has soared.[45] And, of course, if world capitalist markets collapse, so will the doctrine of neo-laissez-faire.

Our main point, however, is a different one. The exceptional success of neo-laissez-faire and the policies it justifies in the United States itself has to be explained. The explanation obviously has a great deal to do with the political weakness of labor-based political formations, which allowed the business–conservative mobilization of the last two decades to proceed without significant resistance. The historic weakness of American labor, in turn, is traceable to distinctive political structures which allowed sectional and business interests to cripple unionism and the welfare state, and ultimately to prevent the emergence of a labor party.

Conclusion

The political moral of the American story seems clear. The strength or weakness of labor politics matters greatly in humanizing adaptations to the new international economy, and perhaps in rationalizing national

445

adaptations as well. There is a parallel here to the transition to industrial capitalism itself. The imposition of markets disrupted traditional communities, violated ancient rights, and destroyed the subsistence resources of the peasantry. But where traditions were vigorous and older bases of cohesion remained intact, popular resistance to the "new political economy" was also strong. And resistance mattered. The French peasantry won rights to land during the French Revolution, with the result that they could not easily be displaced from the countryside, and industrialization in France was retarded for a century and a half. Similarly, the food riots which spread across Europe in the wake of the introduction of unregulated markets into the countryside significantly moderated the effort to redistribute foodstuffs from the localities to the growing markets of the cities. In these instances, popular resistance moderated some of the cruelties of the transition to capitalism. In just this way, where the labor politics rooted in the mass production industries and the ascendant nation state is still vigorous, its traditions strong; and its bases of cohesion intact, so has it succeeded in moderating the cruelties of the transition to a global economy.

Still, the film cannot be run backwards. If the institutional context of American politics inhibited the political development of labor during the heyday of industrialism and the nation state, the postindustrial context is even less likely to promote labor politics, at least in its familiar union and electoral forms. New popular political struggles will emerge, to be sure, shaped by the new conditions and new understandings generated by postindustrialism. Perhaps in countries where labor politics remains strong, these new political currents will be absorbed into older labor formations, as environmentalists and feminists are being absorbed into some European labor parties. In the United States, however, the Democratic Party remains a bulwark of entrenched interests that is unlikely to yield or adapt unless assaulted by protest movements in the future.

Originally published in 1992.

446

Notes

1. S. Fraser, "The labor question," in *The Rise and Fall of the New Deal Order*, ed. S. Fraser and G. Gerstle (Princeton, NJ: Princeton University Press, 1989), pp. 74–5. See also J. MacGregor Burns, *Roosevelt: The Lion and the Fox* (New York: Harcourt, Brace, 1956), pp. 360–2. Roosevelt campaigned personally and vigorously against what he said was the feudal politics of the south, and tried to defeat Senators Walter George from Georgia, "Cotton Ed" Smith from South Carolina, and Millard Tydings from Maryland. All won easily, strengthening the congressional alliance of southern Democrats and Republicans and weakening Roosevelt. We are grateful to Ronald Shurin for a personal communication reviewing these events.

2. E. E. Schattschneider, Party Government, p. 128. S. M. Lipset develops Schattschneider's argument about the constitutional influences on parties in several places. See for example "Radicalism in North America: a comparative view of the party systems in Canada and the United States," Transactions of Royal Society of Canada, Series IV, 14 (1976), p. 37 *passim*; and "The American party system: concluding observations," pp. 424–6.

3. Schattschneider, Party Government, p. 7.

4. S. M. Lipset and S. Rokkan, "Cleavage structures, party systems, and voter alignments: an introduction," in *Party Systems and Voter Alignments: Cross-National Perspectives*, ed. S. M. Lipset and S. Rokkan (New York: Free Press, 1967), pp. 31–2.

5. See chapter 9 in this volume.

6. On clientelism and working class politics, see A. Bridges, *A City in the Republic: Ante-Bellum New York and the Origins of Machine Politics* (New York: Cambridge University Press, 1984); R. Oestreicher, "Urban working-class political behavior and theories of American electoral politics, 1870–1940," *Journal of American History*, 74, 4 (March 1988), pp. 1257–86; Piven and Cloward, *Why Americans Don't Vote*, ch. 2; M. Shefter, "The electoral foundations of the political machine: New York City, 1884–1897," in *The History of American Electoral Behavior*, ed. J. Sibley, A. Bogue, and W. Flanigan (Princeton, NJ: Princeton University Press, 1978).

7. Ira Katznelson has recently suggested a similar argument, pointing to key features of the American state in explaining the distinctive features of American social policy, including "decentralization and federalism, an institutionally constrained presidency, a porous central bureaucracy, catchall party organizations, a highly autonomous Congress, and the importance of law and the judiciary in policy making and implementation." "Rethinking the silences of social and economic policy," *Political Science Quarterly*, 101 (1986), p. 323.

8. Schattschneider, Party Government, p. 108. The literature on the role of interest groups in American politics is of course vast. See especially T. J. Lowi, *The*

End of Liberalism: Ideology, Policy and the Crisis of Public Authority (New York: Norton, 1969); A. F. Bentley, *The Process of Government* (Cambridge, MA: Belknap, 1967); E. Latham, *The Group Basis of Politics* (Ithaca, NY: Cornell University Press, 1952); and D. Truman, *The Governmental Process* (New York: Alfred A. Knopf, 1951). On the role of interest groups in the Congress, see R. Bauer, I. de Sola Pool and L. A. Dexter, *American Business and Public Policy* (Chicago, IL: Aldine & Atherton, 1963); D. R. Mathews, *US Senators and Their World* (New York: Norton, 1973); A. Denzau and M. C. Munger, "Legislators and interest groups: how unorganized interests get represented," in American Political Science Review, 80 (1986), pp. 89–106; R. H. Salisbury and K. A. Shepsle, "US Congressmen as enterprise," *Legislative Studies Quarterly*, 6 (1981), pp. 559–76; R. L. Hall and F. W. Wayman, "Buying time: moneyed interests and the mobilization of bias in congressional committees," *American Political Science Review*, 84, 3 (1990), pp. 797–820.

9. For an elaboration of this analysis, see Piven and Cloward, *Why Americans Don't Vote*. On early twentieth-century turnout generally, and among immigrant stock urban workers in particular, see P. Kleppner, *Who Voted? The Dynamics of Electoral Turnout* (New York: Praeger, 1982), especially pp. 63–7. See also K. Andersen, *The Creation of a Democratic Majority, 1928–1936* (Chicago, IL: University of Chicago Press, 1982), especially pp. 48–52; and N. H. Nie, S. Verba, and J. H. Petrocik, *The Changing American Voter* (Cambridge, MA: Harvard University Press, 1976), especially pp. 91–2.

10. A resolution adopted at the 1896 AFL convention asserted that "party politics, whether it be Democratic, Republican, Socialistic, Populistic, Prohibition, or any other shall have no place in the convention of the American Federation of Labor." Quoted in Galenson, "The historical role of American trade unionism," p. 49.

11. W. D. Burnham, "The system of 1896: an analysis," in *The Evolution of American Electoral Systems*, ed. P. Kleppner (Westport, CT: Greenwood Press, 1981), p. 100, table 1.

12. See P. Sexton, "Repression of labor," Democratic Left, 18, 5 (September–October, 1990), p. 9. Some estimates indicate that union membership will sink to 13 percent of the workforce by the year 2000. See S. M. Lipset, "Preface," *Unions in Transition* (San Francisco, CA: Institute for Contemporary Studies, 1986), p. xvi.

13. On this point, see L. Troy, "The rise and fall of American trade unions: the labor movement from FDR to RR," in Lipset, *Unions in Transition*, p. 76, table 1.

14. For a provocative treatment which stresses the militancy of American labor in comparative perspective, see G. Arrighi, "Marxism and its history," *New Left Review*, 179 (January–February 1990), pp. 29–63.

15. The phrase is in M. Davis, *Prisoners of the American Dream* (London: Verso, 1986), p. 90. On the impact of unions on the Democratic vote, see E. E. Schattschnei-

der, who estimated that unionism added 10 percentage points to the Democratic inclination of the labor vote, in *The Semisovereign People* (New York: Holt, Rinehart & Winston, 1960), p.50. See also H. Scoble ("Organized labor in the electoral process: some questions," Western Political Science Quarterly, 16 (1963), p. 675) who examined this calculation under different assumptions and concluded that union influence could in fact have an even larger impact on the labor vote.

16. On class voting, see R. Alford, *Party and Society: The Anglo-American Democracies* (Chicago, IL: Rand McNally, 1963).

17. Lipset ("Labor unions in the public mind," in *Unions in Transition*, pp. 287–322), argues vigorously that the decline in union density in the United States is a reflection of declining public support for unions. But the evidence he provides of a correlation between declining public approval of unions and loss of membership does not say anything about the direction of causality.

18. In a 1959 study, Harold Sheppard and Nicholas Masters found that the UAW had registered 90 percent of its members, and 87 percent of them voted ("The political attitudes and preferences of union members: the case of the Detroit Auto Workers," American Political Science Review, 53 (1959), pp. 437–47). However, if this was accurate, it was not typical. Sidney Lens reports that in the late 1950s the director of the AFL–CIO's political arm estimated that, overall, only 40 percent of union members were registered voters. A survey by the Amalgamated Clothing Workers found even fewer registrants. Cited in Davis, *Prisoners of the American Dream*, p. 98.

19. The CIO attempted to penetrate the south early, and had scored some local organizing successes during the war. See N. Lichtenstein, "From corporatism to collective bargaining: organized labor and the eclipse of social democracy in the postwar era," in *The Rise and Fall of the New Deal Order*, pp. 135–7. On the failure of Operation Dixie, see also Davis, *Prisoners of the American Dream*, pp. 92–4.

20. Michael Goldfield attributes the decline of union membership more to employer opposition than to either the contraction of smokestack industries or the shift of industry to the sunbelt. See "Labor in American politics—its current weakness," *Journal of Politics*, 48 (1986), pp. 2–29.

21. Both the House Ways and Means Committee and the Senate Finance Committee were chaired by Southerners. For discussions of the role of the south in the New Deal, see V. O. Key, *Southern Politics in State and Nation* (New York: Alfred A. Knopf, 1984); G. B. Tindall, *The Disruption of the Solid South* (Athens GA: University of Georgia Press, 1965); F. F. Piven and R. A. Cloward, *Poor Peoples' Movements: Why They Succeed, How They Fail* (New York: Pantheon Books 1977), ch. 5; L. J. Alston and J. P. Ferrie, "Resisting the welfare state: southern opposition to the Farm Security Administration," in *The Emergence of the Modern Political Economy*, ed. R. Higgs (Greenwich, CT: JAI Press, 1985).

22. The key group in formulating the main provisions of the Social Security Act is widely agreed to have been the American Association for Labor Legislation (AALL). While the AALL is often defined as a civic reform organization, G. William Domhoff's analysis makes clear that the organization drew its support from business leaders associated with the National Civic Federation. See *The Power Elite and the State: How Policy is Made in America* (New York: Aldine de Gruyter, 1990), pp. 44–64. On the influence of different factions of business on the Social Security Act, see also J. Quadagno, "Welfare capitalism and the Social Security Act of 1935," *American Sociological Review*, 49 (October 1984), pp. 632–47; and J. C. Jenkins and B. G. Brents, "Social protest, hegemonic competition, and social reform," *American Sociological Review*, 54, 6 (December 1989), pp. 891–909.

23. For a fuller discussion, see F. F. Piven and R. A. Cloward, *Regulating the Poor* (New York: Pantheon Books, 1971).

24. For an analysis, see B. Stevens, "Labor unions, employee benefits, and the privatization of the American welfare state," *Journal of Policy History*, 2, 3 (1990) pp. 233–60.

25. For measures of the impact of social democratic corporatist arrangements on economic growth, see A. Hicks and W. D. Patterson, "On the robustness of the left corporatist model of economic growth," *Journal of Politics*, 51 (1989), pp. 662–75.

26. See S. Lash and J. Urry, *The End of Organized Capitalism* (Cambridge: Polity Press), p. 109.

27. Loïc Wacquant describes the impact of de-industrialization on the Democratic bastion of Chicago. In 1954, over 10,200 manufacturing establishments in the city had provided half a million blue collar jobs. By 1982, the number of establishments had been halved, and blue collar employment had fallen to 172,000. See "The ghetto, the state, and the new capitalist economy," *Dissent* (Fall, 1989), pp. 510–11. See Alan DiGaetano, "The Democratic Party and City Politics in the Postindustrial Era," in *Labor Parties in Postindustrial Societies*, ed. Frances Fox Piven (New York: Oxford University Press, 1992).

28. See I. Wilkerson, "Giving up the jewels to salvage the house," *New York Times*, September 10, 1990.

29. See Wacquant. "The ghetto, the state, and the new capitalist economy."

30. On this point, see A. Watkins, "Good business climates: the second war between the states," *Dissent* (Fall, 1980); and P. Ashton, "The political economy of suburban development," in *Marxism and the Metropolis*, ed. W. Tabb and L. Sawers (New York: Oxford University Press, 1978), pp. 64–89.

31. On this point, see T. Edsall, *Chain Reaction* (New York: Norton, 1991), ch. 1.

32. On the impact of highway subsidies, see J. Mollenkopf, *The Contested City* (Princeton, NJ: Princeton University Press 1983), pp. 14–144.

33. There is an obvious parallel here to the promotion of owner-occupied housing by the British Conservatives. See Lash and Urry, *The End of Organized Capitalism*, p. 102

34. The role of real-estate and banking interests in these several housing and redevelopment policies has been very important. A study of business political action committees in 1990 showed that political contributions from these interests were by far the largest of any category. See R. Berke, "Study confirms interest groups' pattern of giving," *New York Times*, September 16, 1990, p. 26

35. While we think a stronger union structure would have worked overall to moderate race conflict, unions were also the focus of conflict, especially in the construction trades. On this point, see J. Quadagno, "How the war on poverty fractured the Democratic Party: organized labor's battle against economic justice for blacks," unpublished paper presented to the Workshop in Political Economy, Florida State University, September 1990.

36. Bennett Harrison and Barry Bluestone cite Bureau of Labor Statistics data showing the ten fastest growing occupations, as well as changes in the distribution of workers by type of employment and wage category. See *The Great U-Turn* (New York: Basic Books, 1990), pp. 70–1, tables A.1 and A.2.

37. According to Harold Meyerson, sales, technical, service, and administrative workers now constitute 28 percent of the voting age population, but only 11 percent of the electorate. Blue collar workers, who are more likely to be unionized, do a little better, constituting 18 percent of the voting age population and 13 percent of the electorate. See "Why the Democrats keep losing," *Dissent* (Summer, 1989), p. 306.

38. On registration and turnout data for this period and a discussion of the biases they contain, see Piven and Cloward, *Why Americans Don't Vote*, appendices A, B and C.

39. On European patterns, see P. Norris, "The gender gap: a cross-national trend?," in *The Politics of the Gender Gap*, ed. C. M. Mueller (Beverly Hills, CA: Sage, 1988), pp. 217–34.

40. Female voting patterns also diverged from male patterns in the 1950s, although then women tilted to the Right. See H. C. Kenski, "The gender factor in a changing electorate," and A. Miller, "Gender and the vote," in *The Politics of the Gender Gap*, pp. 38–60, 258–82.

41. On the institutional changes which underlie gender differences in politics, see F. F. Piven, "Women and the state: ideology, power and the welfare state," in *Gender and the Life Course*, ed. A. Rossi (Hawthorne, NY: Aldine, 1985), pp. 265–87; and S. Erie and M. Rein, "Women and the welfare state," in *The Politics of the Gender Gap*, pp. 173–91.

42. The decentralization of the heated abortion controversy in the United States, however, is prodding some state and local Democratic candidates to headline the right to abortion. In general, women's rights issues appear to have been especially salient as predictors of political preferences among nonvoters, suggesting at least congruence between the potential Democratic constituencies that I am discussing. See J. W. Calvert and J. Gilchrist, "The disappearing American voter," unpublished paper presented at the 1990 Annual Meeting of the American Political Science Association, San Francisco, 1990.

43. In 1978, more than a million workers were involved in stoppages; in 1988, the number of striking workers fell to 118,000. See K. Moody and J. Slaughter, "New directions for labor," *Dollars and Sense*, 158 (July–August 1990), p. 21.

44. The income share of the poorest fifth of the population fell to 4.6 percent, the lowest share since 1954. The next poorest fifth fell to 10.7 percent, and the middle fifth fell to 16.7 percent, both shares the lowest on record. Meanwhile, the share of the top fifth rose to 44 percent, the highest ever. See Center on Budget and Policy Priorities, "Poverty rate and household income stagnate as rich–poor gap hits postwar high," (Washington, DC: Center on Budget and Policy Priorities, October 20, 1989). It is worth noting that a similar polarization of income occurred under Thatcher. See P. Hall, *Governing the Economy* (Cambridge: Polity Press, 1986), pp. 123–6.

45. Again, the parallels with the British pattern are noteworthy. See Hall, *Governing the Economy*, pp. 115, 123.

A Note on the Type

This book is set in the *Transitional* typeface Perpetua, designed by Eric Gill in the late 1920s. Gill said that he drew Perpetua's letterforms "simply as letters—letters as normal as might be according to my experience as a letter-cutter in stone and a painter of signs…. Perpetua is a typographical version of an inscription letter." Gill's biographer, Malcolm Yorke, called the typeface "a balm to the eyes for extended prose."

The typographic scheme and the binding design are by [sic].